# DEMONIC

## ALSO BY ANN COULTER

GUILTY

IF DEMOCRATS HAD ANY BRAINS,
THEY'D BE REPUBLICANS

GODLESS

HOW TO TALK TO A LIBERAL
(IF YOU MUST)

TREASON

SLANDER

HIGH CRIMES AND MISDEMEANORS

ROBESPIERRE

JOSEPH
STALIN
GEORGE
WALLACE
L.A. RIOTS

WEATHERMEN

AL SHARPTON

NANCY
PELOSI

JON STEWART

# DEMONIC

## HOW THE LIBERAL MOB IS ENDANGERING AMERICA

# ANN
# COULTER

CROWN
FORUM
NEW YORK

Copyright © 2011 by Ann Coulter

All rights reserved.
Published in the United States by Crown Forum,
an imprint of the Crown Publishing Group,
a division of Random House, Inc., New York.
www.crownpublishing.com

CROWN FORUM with colophon is a registered
trademark of Random House, Inc.

Library of Congress Cataloging-in-Publication Data
is available upon request.

ISBN 978-0-307-35348-1
eISBN 978-0-307-88536-4

Printed in the United States of America

Jacket design by Jean Traina and David Tran
Jacket photograph by ShonnaValeska.com

10  9  8  7  6  5  4  3  2  1

First Edition

For Peter Thiel

# CONTENTS

## PART I:
## THE PSYCHOLOGY OF THE LIBERAL

ONE. THE LIBERAL MOB                                        3

TWO. AMERICAN IDOLS: THE MOB'S COMPULSION
TO CREATE MESSIAHS                                         16

THREE. CONTRADICTIONS: YOU CAN LEAD A MOB
TO WATER, BUT YOU CAN'T MAKE IT THINK                      35

FOUR. CRACKPOT CONSPIRACY THEORIES—
OR, AS LIBERALS CALL THEM, "THEORIES"                      51

FIVE. I'LL SEE YOUR BIRTH CERTIFICATE CONSPIRACY
THEORY AND RAISE YOU ONE OCTOBER SURPRISE                  79

## PART II:
## THE HISTORICAL CONTEXT OF
## THE LIBERAL

SIX. THE FRENCH REVOLUTION: WHEN LIBERALS ATTACK           99

SEVEN. THE FRENCH REVOLUTION PART DEUX: COME
FOR THE BEHEADINGS, STAY FOR THE RAPES!                   115

EIGHT. THE AMERICAN REVOLUTION: HOW TO THROW A
REVOLUTION WITHOUT LOSING YOUR HEAD                       129

# PART III:
## THE VIOLENT TENDENCIES OF THE LIBERAL

NINE. **THE SIXTIES:** THE MOB GOES TO COLLEGE     157

TEN. **CIVIL RIGHTS AND THE MOB:** GEORGE WALLACE, BULL CONNOR, ORVAL FAUBUS, AND OTHER DEMOCRATS     173

ELEVEN. **TIMOTHY McVEIGH IS NOW A TEA PARTIER**     196

TWELVE. **IMAGINARY VIOLENCE FROM THE RIGHT VS. ACTUAL VIOLENCE FROM THE LEFT**     208

THIRTEEN. **RAPED TWICE:** LIBERALS AND THE CENTRAL PARK RAPE     224

# PART IV:
## WHY WOULD ANYONE BE A LIBERAL?

FOURTEEN. **STATUS ANXIETY:** PLEASE LIKE ME!     249

FIFTEEN. **INHERITORS OF THE FRENCH REVOLUTION:** LIBERALS ♥ MOBS     264

SIXTEEN. **THE TOTALITARIAN INSTINCT AND SEXUAL PERVERSITY OF LIBERALS**     275

SEVENTEEN. **LUCIFER:** THE ULTIMATE MOB BOSS     287

APPENDIX     297

NOTES     305

ACKNOWLEDGMENTS     339

INDEX     341

# PART I:
# THE PSYCHOLOGY OF THE LIBERAL

# ONE

# THE LIBERAL MOB

2  When Jesus got out of the boat, a man with an impure spirit came from the tombs to meet him.

3  This man lived in the tombs, and no one could bind him anymore, not even with a chain.

4  For he had often been chained hand and foot, but he tore the chains apart and broke the irons on his feet. No one was strong enough to subdue him.

5  Night and day among the tombs and in the hills he would cry out and cut himself with stones.

6  When he saw Jesus from a distance, he ran and fell on his knees in front of him.

7  He shouted at the top of his voice, "What do you want with me, Jesus, Son of the Most High God? In God's name don't torture me!"

8  For Jesus had said to him, "Come out of this man, you impure spirit!"

9  Then Jesus asked him, "What is your name?"

"My name is Legion," he replied, "for we are many."

—MARK 5:2–9

The demon is a mob, and the mob is demonic. It is the nihilistic mob of the French Revolution; it is the revolutionaries who seized control of Russia at the beginning of the twentieth century; it is the Maoist gangs looting villages and impaling babies in China; it is the Ku Klux Klan terrorizing Republicans and blacks in the South; it is the 1992 Los Angeles riot that left fifty dead and did $1 billion of damage after the first Rodney King verdict; it is the bloody riots at the 1968 Democratic National Convention; it is the masked hoodlums smashing up Seattle when bankers came to town; it is the 500,000 illegal aliens marching under a foreign flag in Los Angeles; it is throngs of Islamic fanatics attending the Ayatollah Ruhollah Khomeini's funeral, tearing his body out of its coffin; it is left-wing protesters destroying property and attacking delegates at the Republican National Conventions.

Everything else changes, but mobs are always the same. A mob is an irrational, childlike, often violent organism that derives its energy from the group. Intoxicated by messianic goals, the promise of instant gratification, and adrenaline-pumping exhortations, mobs create mayhem, chaos, and destruction, leaving a smoldering heap of wreckage for their leaders to climb to power.

The Democratic Party is the party of the mob, irrespective of what the mob represents. Democrats activate mobs, depend on mobs, coddle mobs, publicize and celebrate mobs—they *are* the mob. Indeed, the very idea of a "community organizer" is to stir up a mob for some political purpose. "As so frequently happens when a crowd goes wild," historian Erik Durschmied says, "there is always one who shouts louder and thereby appoints himself as their leader."[1] Those are the people we call "elected Democrats."

The Democrats' playbook doesn't involve heads on pikes—as yet—but uses a more insidious means to incite the mob. The twisting of truth, stirring of passions, demonizing of opponents, and relying on propagandistic images in lieu of ideas—these are the earmarks of a mob leader.

Over and over again, one finds the Democrats manipulating the mob to gain power. It is official Democratic policy to appeal to the least-informed, weakest minded members of the public. Their base consists of soccer moms, actresses, felons, MSNBC viewers, aging Red-diaper babies, welfare recipients, heads-up-their-asses billionaires, and government workers—who can never be laid off. The entire party gave up on attracting the votes of white men decades ago. It's easier to round up votes by frightening women about "assault weapons" and promising excellent free health care to non–English speakers. Yes, a free health care system that is *so* superior that Democrats exempt themselves and their friends from being in it.

Liberals frighten people about their health care in order to stampede through ObamaCare. They claim the Earth is overheating in order to seize taxpayer money for solar panels and compact fluorescent lightbulbs. They call out union thugs to force politicians to accede to insane benefits packages. They stage campaigns of calumny to get their way on gay marriage. Faddish ideas that would never have occurred to anyone fifty years ago—or even twenty years ago—are suddenly foisted on the rest of us by the liberal mobs.

Although the left in America is widely recognized as hysterical, unreasonable, and clueless, the "root cause" of these traits has generally been neglected. More than a century ago, Gustave Le Bon perfectly captured the liberal psychological profile in his 1896 book, *The Crowd: A Study of the Popular Mind.* Le Bon—a French physician, scientist, and social psychologist—was the first to identify the phenomenon of mass psychology. His groundbreaking book *The Crowd* paints a disturbing picture of the behavior of mobs. Adolf Hitler and Benito Mussolini used his book to learn how to incite a mob. Our liberals could have been Le Bon's study subjects.

Even the left-wing *Guardian* has admitted that Le Bon's study of crowd behavior was "possibly the most influential work of psychology ever written." Presumably recognizing themselves in his psychological profile, liberals have recently tried to undermine Le Bon.

They have complained that he merely "articulated the propertied classes' fear of the mob." Who likes mobs? Renters? Window manufacturers? Rope salesmen? Liberals also objected that Le Bon did not hold the police accountable for a mob's behavior—which is like demanding that we take into account the length of a rape victim's skirt.[2] It is revealing that liberals so fear Le Bon that they try to sully him as "controversial" and "reactionary." (Those particular complaints, incidentally, were lodged by liberal activist George Monbiot, who has called for "citizen's arrests" of former government officials from George W. Bush's UN ambassador John Bolton to former British prime minister Tony Blair. No wonder he doesn't like psychological studies of mob behavior.)[3]

It was all the usual claptrap, but the piercing truth of Le Bon's study speaks for itself. Liberals wouldn't go after him if, even a century later, his theories didn't still ring true. All the characteristics of mob behavior set forth by Le Bon in 1895 are evident in modern liberalism—simplistic, extreme black-and-white thinking, fear of novelty, inability to follow logical arguments, acceptance of contradictory ideas, being transfixed by images, a religious worship of their leaders, and a blind hatred of their opponents.

Many of liberals' peculiarities are understandable only when one realizes that they are a mob. For example, a crowd's ability to grasp only the simplest ideas is reflected in the interminable slogans. Liberals have boatloads of them: Bush Lied, Kids Died! Our Bodies, Our Selves! No Blood for Oil! No Justice, No Peace! Save the Whales; Love Your Mother (Earth); Ban the Bomb; Make Love, Not War; Friends Don't Let Friends Vote Republican; Diversity Is Our Strength! Save the Planet! Pro-Choice, Pro-Child! Support Our Troops, Bring Them Home! Co-Exist! Hey, Hey, LBJ, How Many Kids Did You Kill Today? Dissent Is Patriotic! War Is Not the Answer! Go Green! Health Care Is a Right, Not a Privilege! Imagine Peace; Celebrate Diversity! Beat the Bushes for Peace! No Nukes! Give Peace a Chance; Think Globally/Act Locally; No Tax Cuts for the Rich; Save the Planet! Venceremos! One, Two, Three, Four, We Don't Want Your F—King War! Bush = Hitler; Hell No, We Won't Go! Off the Pig! Eat the Rich! Die Yuppie Scum! Peace Now! We Are the Ones We've Been Waiting For! Solidarity Forever! Bring America Home! You Can't Hug a Child with Nuclear Arms; Meat Is Murder! Books Not Bombs! Fight the Power! Yes We Can!

And those are just the ones on my neighbor's car.

What is the Tea Party's slogan? There is none. Republicans almost never have slogans, certainly none that anyone can remember—except when our presidential candidates are forced to come up with some short-lived catchphrase for their campaigns.

There are only three memorable Republican slogans in the past half century—unless you count what Dick Cheney said to Pat Leahy on the

Senate floor in 2004, in which case there have been four. There was "27 Million Americans Can't Be Wrong," after Goldwater lost in a historic landslide in 1964. There were the YAF buttons made in tribute to William F. Buckley's mayoral campaign platform in 1965: "Don't Let Them Immanentize the Eschaton!" And when there were few other reasons to vote for the reelection of the first President Bush in 1992, there was "Annoy the Media, Vote Bush!" Republicans display crosses and fish, college and sports decals, and a few parodies of liberal slogans ("Imagine an Unborn Child"), but there are no bossy demands on our bumper stickers.

Conservatives don't cotton to slogans. When they finally produce one, it's never the sort of rallying cry capable of sending people to the ramparts, such as "Yes We Can!" or "Bush Lied, Kids Died!" "27 Million Americans Can't Be Wrong" is a wry observation, not an urgent call to battle. "Annoy the Media, Vote Bush!" barely qualifies as a suggestion. Conservatives write books and articles, make arguments, and seek debates, but are perplexed by slogans. (Of course, another reason Republicans may avoid bumper stickers is to prevent their cars from being vandalized, which brings us right back to another mob characteristic of liberals.)

By contrast, liberals thrive on jargon as a substitute for thought. According to Le Bon, the more dramatic and devoid of logic a chant is, the better it works to rile up a mob: "Given to exaggeration in its feelings, a crowd is only impressed by excessive sentiments. An orator wishing to move a crowd must make an abusive use of violent affirmations. To exaggerate, to affirm, to resort to repetitions, and never to attempt to prove anything by reasoning are methods of argument well known to speakers at public meetings."[4]

Liberals love slogans because the "laws of logic have no action on crowds." Mobs, Le Bon says, "are not to be influenced by reasoning, and can only comprehend rough-and-ready associations of ideas."[5] He could be referring to the *New York Times* and other journals of elite opinion when he describes periodicals that "manufacture opinions for their readers and supply them with ready-made phrases which dispense them of the trouble of reasoning."[6]

You will see all the techniques for inspiring mobs in liberal behavior.

There are three main elements to putting an idea in a crowd: affirmation, repetition, and contagion. The effects take time, Le Bon says, but "once produced are very lasting." It's the same reason annoying TV commercials are so effective. "Head On! Apply directly to the forehead. Head On! Apply directly to the forehead. Head On! Apply directly to the forehead."

Affirmation is the creation of a slogan "free of all reasoning and all proof." Indeed, the "conciser an affirmation is, the more destitute of every appearance of proof and demonstration," he says, "the more weight it carries." This is "one of the surest means of making an idea enter the mind of crowds."

Affirmation only works if it is "constantly repeated, and so far as possible in the same terms." The power of repetition "is due to the fact that the repeated statement is embedded in the long run in those profound regions of our unconscious selves in which the motives of our actions are forged. At the end of a certain time we have forgotten who is the author of the repeated assertion, and we finish by believing it."

Short slogans endlessly repeated create a "current of opinion" allowing "the powerful mechanism of contagion" to operate. Ideas spread through the crowd as easily as microbes, Le Bon says, which explains the mass panics common to rock concerts, financial markets, street protests, and Prius dealerships. "A panic that has seized only a few sheep," he observes, "will soon extend to the whole flock."[7]

Liberals have it down to an art: The cacophonous method of yelling until conservatives shut up just because they just want to go home, the purblind assertions—No WMDs in Iraq! Civilian Deaths! Violence at Tea Parties! Head On! Apply directly to the forehead!—and overnight the entire mass of liberals is robotically repeating the same slogans.

It isn't only in their incessant street demonstrations that liberals talk in slogans. This is how liberals discuss serious policy matters with the public. It's as if they're speaking to a vast O.J. Simpson jury, mesmerized by a pair of gloves and a closing argument that rhymes ("If it doesn't fit, you must acquit"). Conservatives talk the same on TV as off TV—unless they are inarticulate politicians using sound bites to avoid saying anything stupid. But regular conservatives talk on TV as if they're having a normal conversation with their friends or neighbors. Liberals don't know how to do this because they don't have normal friends and neighbors—only fellow demonstrators. Their self-image is as little Lenins, rousing the masses at the Finland Station, which is why they always sound as if they've gotten control of the PA system and are broadcasting from Big Brother, Inc.—or if they're Al Gore, addressing a kindergarten class.

Here, for example, is Stephanie Bloomingdale, of the Wisconsin AFL-CIO, being interviewed on MSNBC about the union's beef with Governor Scott Walker: "Well, America, we need all of you to help us with our fight. Because this is a fight to reclaim the values of the middle class. This is the movement of our time. And we need people all across America, working people, to stand up and say, this is the time we need to restore economic justice. And we know that the only—that the union movement is the only thing that stands between unbridled corporate greed and a true economic democracy. And we—what I would like to say is, America, stand with us, stand with us who are fighting for justice and economic justice in our society."[8]

The next night, Katrina vanden Heuvel was engaging in the same sort of "Internationale" hectoring: "People are waking up. And they're in the streets. There are going to be fifty rallies around this country. Maybe a million people in the streets of this country. And what are they saying? Enough! You're giving our people's money away. Invest in our country, invest in jobs, invest in education. Keep cops on the street, keep teachers in the classrooms. Enough with these perks for corporations. There's a movement called U.S. uncut, which is inspired by an article in *The Nation*. If we can recoup from the very richest who brought us this financial crisis and from corporate tax dodgers, we can balance budgets in a fair way. Justice, fairness, concepts that may be coming back to America in this moment."[9]

The advantage of slogans like these—"working families," "economic justice," "unbridled corporate greed," and "invest in our country, invest in jobs, invest in education"—is that liberals never have to talk about the actual issues being discussed. You'd never know in the fog of jargon that the Republican governor of Wisconsin, Scott Walker, was only asking government employees to start paying 6 percent of their pension contributions (up from zero percent) and 12 percent of their health care insurance (up from six percent).[10]

Similarly, the pro-abortion movement depends on never ever using the word "abortion"—only cant, such as "choice," "family planning," and "reproductive freedom."

The Left's robotic speaking style helps explain why liberals have never been able to make a dent in talk radio, despite many tries. Apparently, even the people who get bused in to their rallies can't be paid to listen to liberals hectoring them on talk radio. Being endlessly lectured by deadly earnest liberals is boring. Ask any Cuban.

Based on their public commentary, it appears that not one liberal has the vaguest idea how the economy imploded. The only thing liberals know is—as President Obama explained—"Republicans drove the car into the ditch, made it as difficult as possible for us to pull it back, now they want the keys back. No! You can't drive. We don't want to have to go back into the ditch. We just got the car out."[11] (It was always a "ditch" and not a "pond" because a pond would have been offensive to Teddy Kennedy.)

A liberal would stare at you slack-jawed if you explained that the federal government, via Fannie Mae, Freddie Mac, and the Department of Housing and Urban Development, forced politically correct lending policies on the banks—policies that were attacked by Republicans but ferociously defended by Democrats—and that the banks' suicidal loans were then bundled into mortgage-backed securities and dispersed throughout the entire financial system, which poisoned the economy, bringing down powerful institutions, such as Lehman Brothers, and destroying innumerable families' financial portfolios.

In light of the Democrats' direct role in creating the policies at the heart of the nation's financial collapse, it's not surprising that they prefer metaphors to facts. What's strange is that the image of a car in a ditch is sufficient for the bulk of Democratic voters and commentators to adjudge themselves experts on the economic crisis and refuse to listen to explanations that aren't images of Bush driving a car into a ditch.

Image is all that matters to the mob. Obama can take in the biggest campaign haul from Wall Street in world history, as he did in 2008, but the mob will never believe he is in the pocket of Wall Street bankers. The top-three corporate employers of donors to Barack Obama, Joe Biden, and Rahm Emanuel were Goldman Sachs, Citigroup, and

JPMorgan. Six other financial giants were in the top thirty donors to the White House Dream Team: UBS AG, Lehman Brothers, Morgan Stanley, Bank of America, Merrill Lynch, and Credit Suisse Group.[12] In 2008 alone, Goldman Sachs employees gave more to Obama—nearly $1 million—than any other employer, with the sole exception of the entire University of California, which has 230,000 employees—ten times more than Goldman.[13]

And still Republicans are called the Party of Wall Street. Bush let Lehman Brothers go under—what else do Republicans have to do?

Liberals latched on to the image of Bush, Cheney, and even Representative Tom DeLay as "oilmen" to blame them for everything from Enron's collapse to blackouts and high oil prices.

In 2006, Speaker Nancy Pelosi blamed "oilmen" in public office for high oil prices—and hearing Pelosi try to craft a syllogism is like watching Michael Moore attempt ballet. She said, "We have two oilmen in the White House. The logical follow-up from that is $3-a-gallon gasoline. It is no accident. It is a cause and effect. A cause and effect." That's all liberals needed to know. Two "oilmen" in the White House—cause and effect. Strangely, though, a barrel of oil costs the same on the world market for all those other countries that were not being run by "oilmen."

A few years earlier, she had blamed Bush and DeLay for the blackout throughout the Northeast United States and parts of Canada—presumably because they are both from Texas—saying they had "put the interests of the energy companies before the interests of the American people."[14] In fact, the blackout was due to a failure of humans operating electric power; it had nothing whatsoever to do with oil.

The *New York Times*'s Paul Krugman has written more than a dozen columns making hazy connections between Bush and the corrupt and collapsed Enron—"Some cynics attribute the continuing absence of Enron indictments to the Bush family's loyalty code"[15]—despite Bush's having absolutely nothing to do with the company, other than being from Texas. By contrast, Krugman was on Enron's advisory board while he was writing encomiums to Enron in *Fortune* magazine.[16] Once a year, when I don't feel like writing a column, I think I'll reprint Krugman's column singing Enron's praises—although, again, in fairness, he was being paid by Enron at the time.

Democrats wouldn't make such absurd statements if absurdity didn't seem perfectly logical to their base. This is how Democrats communicate with their constituents: They use mob tactics to rile up the irrational masses. Crowds can't grasp logic, only images. "These imagelike ideas," Le Bon says, "are not connected by any logical bond of analogy or succession, and may take each other's place like the slides of a magic-lantern which the operator withdraws from the groove in which they were placed one above the other."[17]

*Republicans love Wall Street—oh look, Wall Street just made historic campaign contributions to Obama; he must be really cool. . . . Republicans hate the poor because they're trying to block government policies promoting easy mortgages. . . . Oops, I wonder why the economy just tanked. It's because Bush drove it into a ditch! Enron collapsed and Paul Krugman says it's Bush's fault. Krugman was paid by Enron and Bush wasn't? Bush lied, kids died! . . . Oil prices went up under Bush—it's his fault—he's an oilman! Oh but then oil prices went down under Bush. . . . Hey, look over there! A shiny object!*

Despite their perennial enthusiasm for revolution and "change" in almost any form, Le Bon says, crowds are wildly conservative when it comes to scientific progress. Want to scare a liberal? Mention nuclear power plants, genetically modified fruits, new pharmaceuticals, food irradiation, or guns with plastic frames. We could probably get a crowd of liberal protesters to scatter just by coming at them with a modern vacuum cleaner. It certainly works on dogs and cats. The Left's abject terror of technological development is yet another mob attribute.

Le Bon says that the mob's "unconscious horror" of "all novelty capable of changing the essential conditions of their existence is very deeply rooted." While mobs go about changing the names of institutions and demanding radical changes to society, he says, when it comes to scientific progress, crowds have a "fetish-like respect" for tradition.[18]

Thus, according to Le Bon, if "democracies possessed the power they wield today at the time of the invention of mechanical looms or of the introduction of steam-power and of railways, the realization of these inventions would have been impossible." It is lucky "for the progress of civilization that the power of crowds only began to exist when the great discoveries of science and industry had already been effected."[19]

Our liberals are even worse than Le Bon imagined. Democrats don't merely want to block scientific progress, they want to roll it back. Al Gore's global warming fantasy book *Earth in the Balance* called for the worldwide elimination of the internal combustion engine within twenty-five years.[20] (Which, if nothing else, would have ruined Obama's "car in the ditch" catchphrase.)

In 2007, Democrats in Congress banned the incandescent lightbulb, currently scheduled for elimination in 2014. Indeed, banning Thomas Edison's invention was among the very first acts of the new House majority elected in 2006, in a bill cosponsored by 195 Democrats and only 3 Republicans (two of whom are no longer in office). When Democrats came up with the idea of banning the lightbulb, what image appeared in their heads? A lit candle? Only four Democrats voted against the bill in both the House and then Senate, with the vast majority of Republicans voting against it in both chambers.

Consider that the two industries that provoke the most fear and loathing in liberals are two of the most innovative: the oil and pharmaceutical industries. When a majority of the country objected to national health care because, among other things, it would mean the end of innovation in medicine once the government took over, liberals stared in blank incomprehension. (It was almost as if they'd been drugged.) They believe every drug, every diagnosis, every therapy, every cure that will ever be invented has already been invented. Their job is to spread all the existing cures, not to worry about who will discover new ones.

The only traditions liberals are eager to smash are moral and sexual ones, such as monogamy and protecting the unborn. Crowds are too impulsive to be moral, according to Le Bon, which explains why liberals are mad for innovation with respect to thousand-year-old institutions like marriage, but, when it comes to scientific innovation, they are hidebound traditionalists.

Indeed, the only way to get liberals interested in novel scientific research is to propose going after human embryos. When adult stem cell researchers had already produced treatments for eighty different diseases,[21] while embryonic stem cell researchers were stuck in the dark ages, the failed researchers won liberal hearts by pointing out that their method destroyed human fetuses, while adult stem research did not.

As long as Democrats can win elections by demagoguing the mob, they are perfectly happy to turn America into a banana republic. With the country drowning in debt and Medicare and Social Security putting us on a high-speed bullet train to bankruptcy, the entire Democratic Party refuses to deal with entitlements. Instead, they will gin up the mobs to throw out any politician who cuts these increasingly theoretical "benefits." The country will have the economy of Uganda, but Democrats will be in total control.

Rich liberals want chaos for everyone except themselves, confident that they can afford a "green" lifestyle and their children will still attend Sidwell Friends. The rest of us are forced to live in a lawless universe of no energy, gay marriage, girl soldiers, and marauding criminals because liberals can't enjoy their wealth unless other people are living in complete havoc. They promote anarchy, believing the middle class should live in squalor, while liberals will be protected by their wealth from the mob.

The seminal event of the New Testament—Jesus' crucifixion—is a dramatic illustration of the power of the mob.

When the mob was howling for Pontius Pilate to sentence Jesus to death, even Pilate's wife couldn't convince him to spare Jesus. After having a dream about Jesus, Pilate's wife sent her husband a note saying Jesus was innocent—a "just man." Pilate knew it to be true and that the mob hated Jesus out of "envy." But not his wife, not even his own common sense, was enough for him to resist the mob.

Three times Pilate told the "multitude" that Jesus was innocent and should be spared. He pleaded with the mob, proposing to "chastise him, and release him." But the mob was immovable, demanding Jesus' crucifixion. Pilate was required to release one of the prisoners, so he gave the mob the choice of Jesus or Barabbas, a notorious murderer and insurrectionist—in other words, someone who incites mobs. Again, the mob "spoke with one voice," demanding "with loud shouts" that Jesus be crucified.

Capitulating to the mob, Pilate ordered Jesus' death.

Even one of the mob's victims, a thief being crucified alongside Jesus, joined the mob's taunting, saying to Jesus, "If thou be Christ, save thyself and us." The other thief rebuked him, noting that they were guilty, whereas Jesus was not. He said to Jesus, "Lord, remember me when thou comest into thy kingdom." And Jesus said, "Today shalt thou be with me in paradise."[22]

Pilate gave in to the mob out of fear. The thief joined the mob to side with the majority. The mob itself was driven by envy.

Although it all worked out in the end—Jesus died, darkness fell over the Earth, the ground trembled, and the temple veil was ripped in two, and three days later, Jesus rose from the dead, giving all people the promise of everlasting life—here was the stark choice, to be repeated like Nietzsche's eternal recurrence: Jesus or Barabbas?

Liberals say Barabbas: Go with the crowd. C'mon, everybody's doing it—it's cool. Now let's go mock Jesus. (As is so often the case, the mob said, "Kill the Jew.")

Conservatives—sublimely uninterested in the opinion of the mob— say Jesus.

# TWO

# AMERICAN IDOLS:
# THE MOB'S COMPULSION
# TO CREATE MESSIAHS

The mob characteristic most gustily exhibited by liberals is the tendency to idolize their political leaders, while considering "as enemies all by whom [their beliefs] are not accepted."[1]

The creation of an idol is textbook mob behavior. Crowds, Le Bon says, can only grasp the "very simple and very exaggerated."[2] They respond to images that "assume a very absolute, uncompromising, and simple shape."[3] And so, just as Clinton and Obama, for example, represented everything good to the mob, Reagan and Bush represented everything loathsome.

Manifestly, liberals fanatically worship their leaders. FDR, JFK, Clinton, Obama, even Hillary, Liz Holtzman, and John Lindsay—they're all "rock stars" to Democrats. They're the Beatles, Elvis, or Jesus, depending on which cliché liberals are searching for. As Le Bon says, the "primitive" black-and-white emotions of a crowd slip easily into "infatuation for an individual."[4]

Nearly seven decades after FDR was president and five decades after JFK was, we still have to listen to liberals drone on about their stupendousness. It's as if Republicans demanded constant praise for Calvin

Coolidge. Even Republicans are forced to pretend to admire these prof-
ligate Democrats in order to court Democrat voters. Republicans don't
mention Reagan as much and he was a better president.

Liberals worship so many political deities that they're forced to refer
to them by their initials, just to save time—FDR, JFK, RFK, MLK,
LBJ, and O.J. When's the last time you heard a conservative get weepy
about "RWR"?

In a 1986 *Time* magazine cover story on Reagan, reporter Lance
Morrow droned on about the sainted FDR, saying he "explored the
upper limits of what government could do for the individual"—
evidently by putting Japanese in internment camps and fighting a war
against a race-supremacist regime with a segregated military. Reagan,
by contrast, Morrow said, "is testing the lower limits"[5]—one assumes
by ending Soviet totalitarianism and bequeathing America two decades of peace and prosperity.

The most Reagan-besotted conservative would never seriously refer
to his presidency with something as hokey as "Camelot." But in the
bizarro-world of the Democrats' Camelot cult, all we ever hear about is
the youth, the vigor, the glamour, the "Kennedy mystique," and the rest
of the cant. We never hear about the drugs, the prostitutes, a certain mis-
hap at a bridge in Massachusetts, the inept intervention in Vietnam—
including ordering the assassination of our ally—and the complete
calamity at the Bay of Pigs.

Bill Clinton was called a rock star so often, the expression "rock star"
surpassed "perfect storm" as the most irritating cliché of the century. (In
fairness, if "rock star" means someone who sleeps with countless groupies, then Bill Clinton was a rock star.) *Newsweek* reporter Eleanor Clift
described the doughy Clinton-Gore team as "the all-beefcake ticket,"
gasping that she was "struck by the expanse of their chests," and saying
"they could do cameo appearances on 'Studs.' "[6] The *Washington Post's*
Sally Quinn said women identified with Clinton because of "the soft-
ness, the sensitivity, the vulnerability, that kind of thing."[7]

An infatuated Jonathan Alter babbled in *Newsweek* about the Clinton hug: "Bill Clinton hugs other men. It's not a bear hug, usually—
more like a Full Shoulder Squeeze. Women get it, too, but the gesture is
more striking in its generational freshness when applied to the same sex.

He softens the old-fashioned backslap into something more sensitive. These guys are touching each other! It's unselfconscious, gender-neutral, very '90s."[8] Either that or it bolsters my theory that Clinton would have sex with anything that had a pulse.

And it wasn't just Alter and the other ladies swooning! *Newsweek's* Howard Fineman called Clinton the "first sensitive male chief executive,"[9] while Peter Jennings said Clinton "has the kind of hands that people respond to."[10] *Time* magazine's Walter Shapiro said that "for the first time in more than 30 years the nation has elected a President with sex appeal." Shapiro quoted *The Boomer Report* editor Cheryl Russell saying, "Every woman I know is having sex dreams about Bill Clinton."[11] (If you call nightmares about Bill Clinton dropping his pants "sex dreams," I guess I was, too.)

When Obama came along, guess who liberals started having sex dreams about? Yes, the big-eared beanpole. The *New York Times's* Judith Warner reported, "Many women—not too surprisingly—were dreaming about sex with the president." Warner confessed, "The other night I dreamt of Barack Obama. He was taking a shower right when I needed to get into the bathroom to shave my legs." (Judith Warner, Chris Matthews—what is it with liberals and their legs?) The Obamas, Warner wrote, were "a beacon of hope, inspiration and 'demigodlikeness.' "[12]

NBC reporter Lee Cowan—biologically, a man—said he could hardly contain himself when told he was to cover Obama: "When NBC News first assigned me to the Barack Obama campaign, I must confess my knees quaked a bit. . . . I wondered if I was up to the job. I wondered if I could do the campaign justice."[13] (Cowan then spent the rest of the day scribbling in his reporter's notebook, "President and Mr. Barack Obama . . . Barack and Lee Cowan-Obama . . . Lee Obama . . . Mr. and Mr. Obama . . . First Lady, Mrs. Lee Cowan-Obama. . . .")

NBC's Matt Lauer noted that "people" have called Obama " 'The Savior,' 'The Messiah,' 'The Messenger of Change.' "[14] Try to imagine conservatives coming up with such honorifics for Dwight Eisenhower. Being rational individuals, conservatives don't turn their political leaders into religious icons. Liberals, by contrast, having all the primitive behaviors of a mob, idolize politicians.

Obama was also—in the fresh, pioneering words of NBC's Andrea

Mitchell—"a rock star!"[15] To *Newsweek's* Joe Klein, Obama was "the political equivalent of a rainbow—a sudden preternatural event inspiring awe and ecstasy."[16] (If Joe got out of Manhattan more, he'd know rainbows are perfectly natural.)

In one of his more balanced formulations, MSNBC's Chris Matthews babbled, "They're cool people. They are really cool. They are Jack and Jackie Kennedy when you see them together. They are cool. And they're great-looking, and they're cool and they're young, and they're—everything seems to be great." Strangely, he also said, "If you're in [a room] with Obama, you feel the spirit. Moving."[17] What is it about the Obamas that reduces cable news hosts to babbling, pimple-faced losers at a Star Trek convention?

It is impossible to imagine any conservative describing any Republican in such teeny-bopper patois. *Haley Barbour is like totally the dreamiest! And did you see the way he hugs men?* But it's never-ending with the Party of the Mob. Reporting on Senator Teddy Kennedy's endorsement of Obama in 2008, ABC's David Wright said, "Today, the audacity of hope had its rendezvous with destiny. The Kennedy clan anointed Barack Obama a son of Camelot."[18] On ABC's *Good Morning America,* anchor George Stephanopoulos said of Obama's incoming cabinet, "We have not seen this kind of combination of star power and brain power and political muscle this early in a cabinet in our lifetimes."[19] (He left out "affinity for evading taxes.")

It's almost like a "Can You Top This" game with liberals describing their political idols. In a *Time* magazine cover story, reporter Nancy Gibbs compared Obama to Jesus—and not sarcastically, the way the rest of us do. The article began, "Some princes are born in palaces. Some are born in mangers. But a few are born in the imagination, out of scraps of history and hope."[20] Of course, as the leader of twelve apostles, even Jesus had more executive experience than Obama. (But I'm sure the risen Christ appreciated the shout-out.)

Run-of-the-mill Democrats behave the exact same way. *Time* magazine's Walter Shapiro reported that the "swooning and the cooing on the rope lines during the last days of the Clinton campaign were unavoidably reminiscent of Kennedy. In Louisville, Kentucky, the scene seemed out of Beatlemania."[21] Except that when one of the Beatles claimed they were bigger than Jesus, people got upset. *Newsweek*'s Joe Klein talked about the "emotional connection" crowds had for Clinton.[22] The *Washington Post*'s Phil McCombs described the Democratic crowds pouring out to glimpse Bill Clinton: "To watch this President connect with people emotionally is an awesome thing."[23] (And if you think that's awesome, you should see the guy dry-hump a cocktail waitress in an elevator.)

But Clinton was just a hustler from Arkansas compared with Obama. Barack's supporters posted endless YouTube tributes to him, taught schoolchildren to sing paeans to him, wore Obama T-shirts for their mug shots, cried and fainted at his speeches. "You can see it in the crowds," ABC's Terry Moran said on *Nightline* of Senator Barack Obama's supporters. "The thrill, the hope. How they surge toward him. You're looking at an American political phenomenon. . . . He inspires the party faithful and many others, like no one else on the scene today." Except maybe Kanye West, I would have added if anyone had asked me. Moran continued, "Around here, they're even naming babies after him."[24] At that point, Obama hadn't even been in the Senate for two full years.

NBC anchor Brian Williams reported that in Berlin Obama "brought throngs of people" into the center of the city, "surging to get close to him, to hear his message. . . . I heard one American reporter tonight say it's hard to come up with a list of others who could draw such a crowd, but then again it's hard to know what we witnessed here today."[25] Wasn't there another political leader who brought out the crowds like that in Berlin once?

Harold Koplewicz, president of the Child Mind Institute, explained the liberal esteem for Obama by saying, "He was going to end war, end the recession, improve education, improve our image to the world, and provide universal health care. Whether or not he could actually do it wasn't important. It was the belief in him that was."[26] Well, exactly. When a guy's that good at making promises, who cares about actual results? Bush lied, kids died! Go green!

It's remarkable how similar it is for nearly every Democratic president.

Giving President Andrew Jackson the strange new label of "rock star," his biographer Jon Meacham reports that this father of the

Democratic Party drew "staggering" crowds of admirers, with one newspaper describing Jackson as "happy in their affections and loving them with all a parent's love."[27]

A parent's love? What is it with these Democrats? It is nothing more than the mass psychosis of a mob.

In a YouTube video made by actor Ashton Kutcher just after Obama's inauguration, dozens of Hollywood celebrities pledged "to be a servant to our president and all mankind."[28] It was like something out of an Aztec festival of the gods—if what the Aztec gods wanted was for Hollywood actresses like Eva Longoria to use *"less* bottled water."

I don't remember Frank Sinatra and Bob Hope producing a video pledging themselves to be servants of Ronald Reagan. In fact, if anyone had ever made a video with people reading the exact same lines as Demi and Ashton's friends about a Republican president, MSNBC would be running specials on the rise of fascism in America. I mean, even more than it does now. Reagan won the Cold War, rescued the economy, set the country on a decades-long path of peace and prosperity, and was a terrific speaker. And yet Republicans were able to listen to him give a speech without fainting.

In his book *Obama Zombie: How the Liberal Machine Brainwashed My Generation,* Jason Mattera describes liberal blogger Michael Whack's giddy account of his encounter with Obama at a 2008 campaign event. After seeing "the guy" in front of him shake Obama's hand, Whack wrote:

> As the guy drew back his hand I asked him, "You shook his hand didn't you?" Happily the guy said "Yes." I then said, "give me some of that" and the guy shook my hand with the same hand he had just clasped with Barack's. A woman friend of mine who was standing next to me saw me shake hands with the guy. I turned to her and said "He [the guy] just shook hands with Barack," to which she responded . . . "Hey, give it up." We then shook hands. She then turned to the person next to her and shook hands. This chain of handshakes went on for about five or six more persons.[29]

Democrats would drink Obama's bathwater.

Perhaps it is because they don't believe in the real God that liberals are compelled to turn so many humans into living deities. Elena Kagan, liberal Supreme Court justice, said she "sat down and wept" when Liz Holtzman lost the 1980 election for the U.S. Senate.[30] Can you imagine John Roberts crying when G.H.W. Bush lost his reelection bid in 1992? For that matter, can you imagine even Barbara Bush crying over that?

When California Democrats Barbara Boxer and Dianne Feinstein won their 1992 primary elections for the U.S. Senate, *Time* magazine's Margaret Carlson said she felt "a rush, an exultation, that surpassed any political moment I have ever known."[31] Uma Thurman proclaimed Al Gore "adorable" and "sexy," saying that looking at him was like "watching a beautiful racehorse run."[32] (A racehorse who came in second in a two-horse race in 2000.)

Margaret Carlson called Hillary "the icon of American womanhood"—an "amalgam of Betty Crocker, Mother Teresa and Oliver Wendell Holmes."[33] (That last one perhaps explaining why Hillary always wears pants.) The *Washington Post's* Martha Sherrill said Hillary was "replacing Madonna as our leading cult figure."[34] *Time* magazine's Lance Morrow said Hillary was "somewhere between Eleanor and Evita, transcending both," and that her run for the Senate marked the moment "when the civilization pivots, at last, decisively—perhaps for the first time since the advent of Christian patriarchy two millenniums ago—toward Woman."[35]

Conservatives are never disappointed because they never expect much from their leaders. They certainly don't have sex dreams about them, or describe them as "rainbows." Perhaps conservatives aren't looking for a savior on the ballot because they already have one.

Most of the time, conservatives can barely tolerate their leaders. Republican presidents are lucky if their own party doesn't move to impeach them. President Nixon lied once to the country, not under oath, and his own party demanded that he resign immediately. Bill Clinton lied repeatedly under oath in two depositions and a grand jury inquiry, and yet every single sitting Democratic senator voted to keep him in office. (Clinton also lied not under oath, to his friends, to his party, to his wife—we're told—in public and in private.)

Although there may be enthusiasms about a popular Republican leader, the cultlike worship of politicians, common to mobs, is peculiar to Democrats. Republicans didn't even idolize Ronald Reagan, indisputably among the nation's greatest presidents. Forget the warm nostalgia conservatives have for Reagan today, based on his record. There was no hero worship of the man at the time. Contrary to our whitewashed memories, Reagan was criticized early and often by conservatives—or "the New Right," in the parlance of the day.

A year into office, the *Washington Post* ran an article about how Reagan's favorite newspaper, *Human Events,* was devoting a lot of ink to attacking him. "Ronald Reagan's 'favorite newspaper,'" the *Post* said, "is giving him fits lately." Although there weren't "two more committed true-blue-Reaganite-to-the-core conservatives anywhere" than editors Thomas Winter and Allan Ryskind, the *Post* reported, Reagan himself had noticed the attacks, telling them, "I'm still reading you guys, but I'm enjoying it less."[36]

At about the same point in Obama's presidency, Obama singled out his cheerleading squad at MSNBC to praise them for providing "an invaluable service," and keeping "our government honest."[37]

A perusal of the headlines throughout Reagan's presidency makes it clear that conservatives did not view even their most-admired president as a demigod. True, Obama gets the occasional fake denunciations from a few showoff liberal bloggers trying to prove what badass Marxists they are, but it is inconceivable that any Democratic president could produce this many headlines about liberal angst.

Try to imagine a stream of headlines about Obama and his base along the lines of this small sample from the Reagan years:

Conservatives Attack Reagan Appointees
—United Press International, February 25, 1981

"New Right" Disillusionment with Reagan Breaks into the Open
—*Washington Post,* February 25, 1981

The Far Right Splits with Reagan
—United Press International, July 14, 1981

For Reagan and the New Right, the Honeymoon Is Over
—*Washington Post,* July 21, 1981

Conservatives Meeting to Discuss Disappointment with Reagan
—Associated Press, January 21, 1982

President Warned by Conservatives
—*New York Times,* January 22, 1982

Conservatives Disappointed with Administration's First Year Record
—United Press International, January 22, 1982

Is Reagan Betraying the Right?
—*Washington Post,* January 27, 1982

Reagan Hears Thunder from the Right
—*U.S. News & World Report,* February 1, 1982

When Mr. Conservative Is Too Liberal
—*Christian Science Monitor,* February 26, 1982

Rumblings on the Right
—*The National Journal,* March 13, 1982

New Right Meeting Grumbles About Reagan
—*Washington Post,* July 28, 1982

Conservatives Blame White House for GOP Losses
—Associated Press, November 4, 1982

New Right Decides to Part Company with Reagan
—*Miami Herald,* November 26, 1982

Leftward Drift of Reagan Decried; Some Conservatives Shop for a
"New Face"
—*Washington Post,* February 4, 1983

Reagan Bid Reopens Rift with Right
—*New York Times,* February 19, 1983

Conservatives Criticize Reagan
—United Press International, September 4, 1983

New Right Disappointed by Reagan's Reactions
—*Washington Post,* September 6, 1983

Conservatives Divided on Support for Reagan
—Associated Press, September 11, 1983

The Right Is Really Sore at Reagan . . .
—*Washington Post,* September 18, 1983

New Right Poll: Alarm Bells for Reagan
—Associated Press, October 13, 1983

Right Critical of Reagan in Hostage Crisis: Longtime Supporters
Attack Policies
—*Washington Post,* June 29, 1985

Even Conservatives Are Abandoning Ship
—*Los Angeles Times,* December 9, 1986

Trouble on the Right
—*U.S. News & World Report,* December 29, 1986

Baker Helping Reagan Renew Ties to Conservative Leaders
—Associated Press, March 30, 1987

Reagan Seeks to Calm His Right-Wing Critics
—*Los Angeles Times,* September 6, 1987

Reagan's Arms-Control Dream Is Nightmare for Conservatives
—*Washington Post,* November 30, 1987

There would never be such unremitting criticism of Kennedy
or Clinton—to say nothing of the angel Obama—from the Democratic base.

By September of Reagan's first year of office, he was not even the
most popular conservative in the country. According to a poll by the
*Conservative Digest* of more than a thousand of its readers, the Reverend Jerry Falwell was No. 1 and William F. Buckley was No. 2. Then
Reagan.[38]

By contrast, in Obama's first year in office, he was consistently voted
the most popular human on the planet. Even before becoming president,
Obama was showered with awards. He won not one but two "Best Spoken Word Album" Grammy awards for his audiobooks, *Dreams from My*

*Father* (2006) and *The Audacity of Hope* (2008). (He then gave the least profanity-laced acceptance speech of any African-American Grammy winner in history.)

His concession speech after the New Hampshire primary was turned into a music video, which won an Emmy Award. In 2008, the Obama yard sign/bumper sticker became a status symbol accessory like a Prius, solar panels on your house, or an adopted Malawian baby.

Throughout 2009, headlines incessantly announced, "Obama by Far the Most Popular Political Leader in Europe and U.S.; No Other Head of Government Comes Close." Liberals around the globe worshipped Obama, and suddenly America became the most admired country in the world, jumping six places to do so.[39] Obama even won a Nobel Peace Prize based on his first twelve days in office.

Like a first-time bestselling author obsessively checking Amazon rankings, liberals were transfixed by Obama's sky-high popularity, commissioning poll after poll on the subject in February, April, May, and December of 2009. The last such poll taken seems to have come in April 2010, when Obama's worldwide popularity began to sink. At home in the United States, the Dalai Lama beat Obama, who merely tied with Hillary Clinton at 57 percent. And so the poll was taken no more.[40]

Also during his first year in office, Obama was named "the sexiest politician in the world" by OnePoll.com.[41] His wife Michelle was named one of the "100 Sexiest Women on the Planet" by *Maxim* magazine, which called her "the hottest First Lady in the history of these United States." Obama was the runaway winner of Gallup News's Most Admired Man poll in both 2008 and 2009.[42] He came in fifth in *Jockey International*'s "Celebrity Dad Most Women Want to See in Their Undies" list, just behind Brad Pitt, Matthew McConaughey, Hugh Jackman, and Will Smith.[43]

Obama was more popular than Justin Bieber (and for my money, a hundred times dreamier!).

A few years into Obama's failed presidency, liberals were still besotted. *Washington Post* readers got this crucial update in the October 12, 2010, edition: "The moment was vintage Obama—emphasizing his zest for inquiry, his personal involvement, his willingness to make the tough call, his search for middle ground. If an Obama brand exists, it is his image as a probing, cerebral President conducting an exhaustive analysis of the issues so that the best ideas can emerge, and triumph."[44]

Who knows what issue was being probed, what zestful inquiry instigated, or what tough call being made. For all we know, he was deciding which flavor ice cream to order during the next geopolitical crisis. The point was: Obama was a dreamboat.

The Left's passionate adoration of President Obama—and Clinton, FDR, JFK, Hillary, Teddy Kennedy, and on and on—are the primitive emotions of a mob. These are sentiments generally associated with women, children, and savages, according to Le Bon. It's not an accident that when Republicans of all stripes—Arnold Schwarzenegger, Rand Paul, Sharron Angle, and Christine O'Donnell—choose an epithet for Democrats, it's to call them women. Everyone sees it: Democrats are a mob.

The flip side of liberals turning their own leaders into icons is that they also "consider as enemies all by whom [their dogmas] are not accepted."[45]

Being a successful president, Reagan was detested by liberals. There were mob protests throughout Reagan's presidency in all the usual hotspots—Germany, Spain, Italy, London, New York, Los Angeles, Ann Arbor, Berkeley, and Madison. Month after month, filthy wastrels hurled paint and projectiles at police, smashed windows, burned Reagan in effigy, and vandalized military bases—pausing occasionally for a round of "We Are the World."

Forget that liberal mobs are always on the wrong side—protesting, for example, Reagan's bombing of poor, innocent Libya in retaliation for Moammar Khadafy's murdering U.S. servicemen. One does not see conservatives out smashing windows, throwing rocks, or vandalizing buildings even in support of a good cause—such as bombing Khadafy.

Decades later, liberals would force one another to retract the mildest praise of Reagan. During the 2008 presidential campaign, for example, Obama cited Reagan's "clarity" and "optimism," and liberals reacted as if he had praised Hitler. Hillary instantly launched TV and radio ads accusing Obama of actually *liking* Reagan.

Obama was soon forced to deny that he had ever had any warm

thoughts whatsoever about Reagan. "What I said," Obama bleated during a Democrat debate, "is that Ronald Reagan was a transformative political figure because he was able to get Democrats to vote against their economic interests to form a majority to push through their agenda, an agenda that I objected to. . . . I spent a lifetime fighting, a lifetime against Ronald Reagan's policies."

Meanwhile, Republicans issue constant, nauseating praise for FDR and Kennedy.

Depending on who's in the White House, the enemy of the liberal mob is either the president or the people. Americans are either enlightened truth-seekers or racist, paranoid haters. "Dissent is patriotic" only when a Republican is president, and we must have "respect for the office" only when a Democrat is president.

After promising to unite us—following the horror of the Reagan years—President Bill Clinton blamed conservative talk radio for Timothy McVeigh.

When Clinton was caught ejaculating on interns, the First Lady of the United States responded by going on the *Today* show and claiming there was "this vast right-wing conspiracy that has been conspiring against my husband since the day he announced for president." *Newsweek*'s Jonathan Alter called Ken Starr and his assistants "sheet sniffing prosecutors,"[46] and Geraldo Rivera called Starr an "investigative terrorist."[47] Margaret Carlson compared Clinton's impeachment to the legal system in Saudi Arabia.

As the Senate began Clinton's impeachment trial, Ellen Mendel of Manhattan matter-of-factly told the *New York Times* that she felt "the same despair that she did as a girl in Nazi Germany when the efforts of a stubborn group of leaders snowballed, crushing the will of the people." (Clinton never got even 50 percent of the country to vote for him.) It was clear, she said, "that the bulldozing campaign by the Republicans will not end."[48]

But as soon as George W. Bush became president, the only threat to the republic came from the White House itself. Every White House employee was an evil genius, knee-deep in dark conspiracies and cabals. Bush was the target of almost unimaginable calumnies—the sort of invective liberals usually reserve for people who disable detectors on airplanes. Liberals were more sympathetic to Islamic terrorists than they were toward President Bush.

As Le Bon says, "A commencement of antipathy or disapprobation, which in the case of an isolated individual would not gain strength, becomes at once furious hatred in the case of an individual in a crowd."[49] Little did Le Bon know he was the first to discover "Bush Derangement Syndrome"!

Out of a cast of thousands, liberal financier and convicted felon[50] George Soros, former vice president Al Gore, and *Vanity Fair's* James Wolcott compared Bush to a Nazi. In the case of Soros, it was unclear if this was meant as a compliment; Soros had helped the Nazis identify Jewish homes in his native Hungary as a boy.[51] (Hey, we all have to start somewhere. I was on the safety patrol at school when I was a little girl.)

Bookstores overflowed with anti-Bush books. The paper alone destroyed so many trees that Sting's musical career was extended a full decade. A novel released in 2004 advocated the assassination of President Bush "for the good of humankind." A mock documentary depicted President Bush's assassination as a news event—and went on to win the International Critics Prize at the 2006 Toronto Film Festival (not to mention "Best Date Movie of 2006" by *The Nation* magazine).

Bush was heartily disapproved of by the world's most fiendish tyrants—Mahmoud Ahmadinejad, Hugo Chavez, and Air America's Janeane Garofalo.

Bush was called a "miserable failure" by Democratic congressman Dick Gephardt, a guy who ran for president two times without anyone noticing. Journalist Helen Thomas said Bush was "the worst President ever . . . the worst President in all of American history."[52] Forgotten 1950s calypso singer Harry Belafonte—not Louis Farrakhan, I mean the other forgotten 1950s calypso singer who hates America—called Bush "the greatest tyrant in the world, the greatest terrorist in the world."[53] *Time* magazine's Joe Klein said Bush's foreign policy was one of "arrogance" and his domestic policy "cynical, myopic and cruel."[54] *Washington Post* columnist William Raspberry, whose last name means "a rude sound effect made with the mouth to mimic a bodily function, used to express disapproval," called Bush "a devil."[55]

With critics like these, no wonder Bush was elected president of the United States twice.

After the *Washington Post*'s Dana Priest abetted America's enemies by disclosing the government's top-secret rendition program—for which she would win a Pulitzer Prize—NPR's Nina Totenberg said of Bush's rendition program, "It is the first time in my life I have been ashamed of my country."[56] Liberals spent a lot of time being ashamed of their country under George Bush, even when it later turned out the rendition program was started under President Clinton.[57]

CBS's Dan Rather attacked a sitting president on the eve of his re-election with forged documents he used to accuse President Bush of shirking his National Guard duty. When the documents were exposed as phony, Rather attacked the bloggers who exposed the fraud as "powerful and extremely well-financed forces" who decided to "attack" him and destroy his "credibility."[58] Dissent was patriotic, but dissent from CBS News was not.

At a performance on the eve of Obama's inauguration, hip-hop artist Young Jeezy shouted out, to huge cheers, "I wanna thank two people, I wanna thank the mother f**ker overseas that threw two shoes at George Bush and I wanna thank—and listen, listen—and I wanna thank the mother f**kers who helped dem move their sh*t up out of the White House. Keep it moving bitch because my president is mother f**king black, nigga!" Cheers and applause.[59]

And thus Obama ushered in a new era of attacking Americans who opposed the president and concluded the era of dissent being patriotic. Overnight, the soi-disant "adversary press" switched from being the people's watchdogs to the government's guard dogs. (Except at MSNBC, where they became the government's lapdogs.)

Opponents of Obama's health care nationalization were automatically deemed racists, thugs, and lunatics. CNN called them "teabaggers"—a crass sexual reference—as did Democratic senator Dick Durbin (D-IL), who also called Obama's critics "birthers."[60] Senator Chuck Schumer called then–Senate candidate Scott Brown a "far-right teabagger."[61] (Ironically, liberals love actual, sodomitic teabagging, but use the term derisively when talking about ordinary Americans protesting a Democratic president's policies.) Nancy Pelosi called opponents of ObamaCare "Un-American"—and, again, this could have been a compliment. Speaking of "Un-American," Harry Reid called them "evilmongers." Jimmy Carter said an "overwhelming portion" of the people opposed to Obama's health care plan were racists.[62] (And if there's one guy who's got his finger on the pulse of what the American people are thinking and feeling, it's Jimmy Carter.)

The last time I heard this much race-baiting and crass invective I was . . . in my usual front-row pew, as I am every Sunday morning, at Trinity United Church of Christ in Chicago listening to the Reverend Jeremiah Wright.

As a special bonus, mainstream pop culture—timeless classics such as *Law & Order*—portrayed Tea Party people as extremely angry, clearly dangerous, secession-leaning nutters who had the air of the Aryan Nation about them and talked like they were in the old movie *Sergeant York*. ("Ain't that some kind of foreign name? We don't cotton to feriners 'round here!") When Republicans swept Congress in the 2010 midterm congressional elections, MIT professor Noam Chomsky said, "The latest election, a couple of days ago, you could almost interpret it as a kind of death knell for the species."[63]

Why had liberals hated Bush again? A normal person, not under the sway of groupthink, would say U.S. presidents are different in important respects, in ways that can help or harm the nation—but not 180 degrees different. It's not Jesus Christ vs. Josef Stalin. (Except in the case of Martin Van Buren, who may have been Stalin.)

Both Bush and Obama went to Ivy League schools, had traditional families with a wife and two girls, claimed to be Christians, said Islam is a religion of peace, kept Guantánamo open, killed civilians in the war on terrorism, bailed out banks, opposed gay marriage, and sought amnesty for illegal aliens. Their most readily apparent difference is that Obama knows how to pronounce "nuclear" correctly and Bush knows how to pronounce "Pakistan."

Conservatives probably liked Reagan about 70 to 80 percent of the time, Bush 50 to 60 percent of the time, and Obama 5 to 10 percent of the time (admittedly, mostly when he continued the Bush policies he had campaigned against). With liberals it's 100 percent burning hatred for Reagan and Bush and 100 percent adoration for Obama—which briefly fell to 98 percent in 2010 when the Justin Bieber movie *Never Say Never* was released. If you ask the right liberal and he doesn't have time to do the math in his head, he'll tell you that his hatred for Reagan sometimes went up to 120 percent.

Only the mob mentality of the liberal explains such infantile, black-and-white thinking.

Indeed, anyone a liberal doesn't care for will be compared to the worst monsters of history—as Bush was to Hitler. With no explanation whatsoever, the *Washington Post*'s Lonnae O'Neal Parker said award-winning author Shelby Steele, Supreme Court justice Clarence Thomas, activist Ward Connerly, and journalist Armstrong Williams reminded her of the groveling slave, Fiddler, from the movie *Roots*.[64] She provided no quotes or positions from the beastly men to explain the resemblance; indeed, the bulk of the passage is about Parker's sister straightening her hair and watching MTV.

> There is a scene [in *Roots*] where kidnapped African Kunta Kinte won't settle down in his chains. "Want me to give him a stripe or two, boss?" the old slave, Fiddler, asks his Master Reynolds.
>
> "Do as I say, Fiddler," Reynolds answers. "That's all I expect from any of my niggers."
>
> "Oh, I love you, Massa Reynolds," Fiddler tells him. And instantly, my mind draws political parallels. Ward Connerly, I think to myself. Armstrong Williams. Shelby Steele. Hyperbole, some might say. I say dead-on.
>
> "Clarence Thomas," I say to my Cousin Kim. And she just stares at me. She may be a little tender yet for racial metaphors. I see them everywhere.

Parker was so proud of this sparkling gem, she included it in her book, which—like the column—contains not another word about these horrid men, such as, for example, what she didn't like about them.[65] Parker was following Le Bon's playbook for whipping up crowds: Use images, not words.

In the days before Republican Senate candidate Scott Brown won a Massachusetts special election to replace Teddy Kennedy, MSNBC's Keith Olbermann repeatedly raged that Brown was "an irresponsible, homophobic, racist, reactionary, sexist, ex–nude model, teabagging supporter of violence against women and against politicians with whom he disagrees."

Three days earlier, Olbermann had never heard of Scott Brown. With the soul of an actress, Keith borrows other people's opinions, adds the sanctimony and indignation, and delivers speeches in a deep baritone, wearing glasses so morons think he's a genius. (For the huge segment of Keith's audience that watched just to laugh at him, his firing was heartbreaking.)

NPR's Nina Totenberg famously said of Republican senator Jesse Helms, "If there is retributive justice, he'll get AIDS from a transfusion, or one of his grandchildren will get it."[66]

We had important Democratic elected officials, Democratic contributors, and *Vanity Fair* writers calling Bush a Nazi; Pulitzer Prize–winning journalists calling him a devil; network anchors slandering him with dummied documents, and award-winning movies gleefully portraying his assassination. But liberals see a sign at a conservative rally depicting Obama as a monkey and act as if they're staring into the eyes of Lee Harvey Oswald (who happened to be a communist, by the way).

There are other hard comparisons to be made. Conservatives don't threaten to leave the country if a Democrat becomes president. Liberals do every four years. In 1992, Barbra Streisand said she'd leave if the first George Bush were reelected and then, in 2000, with stunning originality, a whole slew of liberals made the same threat if Bush's son were elected—director Robert Altman, Eddie Vedder of Pearl Jam, Alec Baldwin (as quoted by his then-wife), and Kennedy press secretary/ABC News correspondent Pierre Salinger.[67] In 2008, Susan Sarandon said she'd leave if McCain won. The only one to ever leave was Salinger, who was merely moving back to France, though some believe he left out of embarrassment after falling for the Internet hoax that TWA flight 800 had been downed by the U.S. Navy.[68]

True, these are mostly just actors—except Barbra Streisand, who was a key Gore policy adviser. (In 2000, Streisand told *TV Guide* that Gore had "called me from Air Force One" for advice, but "I couldn't take the call. I was in the middle of something."[69] Just as soon as she learns how to spell "Iraq," she'll be getting calls from Obama.)[70] But the Democrats certainly don't dismiss them as mere actors. Hollywood celebrities tour with Democratic candidates, headline their fundraisers, record robocalls, and donate millions of campaign dollars to their campaigns.

The Left's "blind submission" to their leaders and "inability to discuss" their beliefs—consistent with Le Bon's characterization of mobs—leads to one of their most peculiar debate gambits: the appeal to authority. They will cite a prominent conservative's liberal position on the odd issue and brandish it as if that ends the argument. Reagan granted amnesty to illegal aliens! William F. Buckley supported legalizing pot! Goldwater supported abortion! Case closed, QED, let's all go home.

Conservatives are always left dumbfounded at the triumphalism of such nonarguments. We like Republicans, we liked many things about Buckley, Reagan, and Goldwater. They're not God. Not even Reagan.

Only liberals use the sarcastic line "last time I checked" so-and-so is "not a socialist"—as if it matters.

Obama pitched his government takeover of health care by saying Bob Dole and Bill Frist supported it and—"last time I checked they're not socialist."[71] Democratic congressman Gerald Connolly thought he made a devastating point at a hearing on Obama's failed economic policies by saying, "By the way, Ben Bernanke, the Federal Reserve bank chairman here in the United States, announced to us last week at a luncheon that he believes the stimulus here is working—and not a wild-eyed liberal, last time I checked."[72] And Democratic strategist Alicia Menendez thought she had cornered O'Reilly when she responded to his question about government spending to the point of nearly bankrupting states like California by saying, "The last time I checked, California had a Republican governor."[73]

There are, of course, great men who change the course of history and seem to have the spirit of the divine working through them. Most of our founding fathers are among them. Reagan is among them. We honor them. We view their service with reverence. We don't have sex dreams about them. We're not a mob.

# THREE

## CONTRADICTIONS:
# YOU CAN LEAD A MOB TO WATER, BUT YOU CAN'T MAKE IT THINK

L iberals' renowned indisposition to analogies is another classic example of mob thinking. Where normal people see blinding contradictions, liberals see only placid consistency. Le Bon explains that mobs are perfectly capable of holding completely contradictory ideas at the same time because according to circumstances, "a crowd will come under the influence of one of the various ideas stored up in its understanding, and is capable, in consequence, of committing the most dissimilar acts. Its complete lack of critical spirit does not allow of its perceiving these contradictions."[1]

Only the Democratic Party could contain a senator who killed a girl at Chappaquiddick—and then spent the rest of his career digging into other people's pasts.

Only the Democratic Party could lyingly claim credit for the Civil Rights Act—supported by more Republicans than Democrats—while having a former Klansman as their senior senator.

Only the Democratic Party could produce a string of presidential candidates who oppose school choice and vouchers while sending their own children to lily-white private schools.

Only the Democratic Party could hysterically denounce a Supreme Court nominee for allegedly making unwanted sexual advances in the workplace and then applaud a president who was receiving oral sex from a White House intern while discussing deploying American troops with a congressman on the phone. Indeed, only the Democrats could oppose Clarence Thomas, actually block Supreme Court nominee Douglas Ginsburg (for marijuana use), and then run Bill Clinton for president.

Only the Democratic Party could produce a junior senator from New York who denounced George Bush's commutation of Scooter Libby's sentence as "cronyism"—just six years after her husband, Bill, sold a pardon on his way out of office to Marc Rich.[2]

Only liberals could sponsor college speech codes but say that anyone who doesn't want to subsidize *Piss Christ* hates free speech.

Only liberals could love George Soros—convicted of felony insider trading in France[3]—Bill Gates, and Warren Buffett while claiming to detest Wall Street and "the rich."

Only liberals could tolerate a windbag like Al Gore lecturing the rest of us about our carbon footprints while he flies his private jet from energy-guzzling mansion to energy-guzzling mansion—just one of which consumes 20 times the energy of the average American home.[4]

(The alleged myth-busting site Snopes.com claims that that estimate on Gore's house gives only a "mixture" of truth, because Gore's Tennessee mansion actually uses—I quote—"more than 12 times the average for a typical household in that area." Ah! We stand corrected! And how much more compared with the Pentagon? Can't he move? Wouldn't you move if you thought you were murdering the Earth with your insatiable energy demands?)

"Liberal" is the definition of people who can't grasp if/then forms of logic.

Immediately after Jared Loughner's shooting spree in Tucson, Americans were lectured on civility by the likes of Keith "the leading terrorist group in this country right now is the Republican Party"[5] Olbermann.

But the media turned to one man more than any other to discuss how rhetoric can lead to violence: Al Sharpton—someone whose rhetoric actually had inspired violent mobs. In the immediate aftermath of the shooting, Sharpton was interviewed on NBC's *Meet the Press,* on National Public Radio, on CNN, and repeatedly on MSNBC. The *Washington Post* ran an op-ed on the shootings by Sharpton.

It was an in-your-face move for the media to turn to Sharpton for counsel as they were blaming "rhetoric" for the Arizona shootings. *That's right, we're going to have Al Sharpton on to discuss ugly rhetoric that can lead to violence. Do something about it.*

From 1987 to 1988, Sharpton was libeling innocent men in the Tawana Brawley hoax, falsely accusing them of a sickening rape. A long and expensive grand jury investigation determined that the entire case was a hoax. New York attorney general Robert Abrams concluded that Sharpton had engaged in "abominable behavior, deplorable, disgraceful, reprehensible, irresponsible."

A few years later, in 1990, all was calm at the trial of the Central Park jogger's rapists—except, according to the *New York Times,* when Al Sharpton arrived.[6] Saying the proceedings were "just like the old Scottsboro boys case,"[7] he even brought hoax perpetrator Brawley to the trial. He said she was there to "observe how differently a white victim was treated and how the accused in this case have been mishandled a lot differently from the people she [Brawley] accused."[8]

The stunt with Brawley, the London *Guardian* reported, turned the Central Park rape trial into a "racial showdown." Venomous mobs outside the courtroom destroyed television equipment and punched cameramen and reporters. Those who tried to argue with the protesters got their faces smashed. The Sharpton supporters chanted, "The jogger's a whore!" "Slut!" "The jogger's a drug addict!" "The jogger's an actress!" "Lynch the boyfriend!" "Lynch all her boyfriends!"[9] When the frail, off-balance jogger showed up at court one day to testify, the mob chased her van to continue hurling abuse at her.

In the courtroom, Sharpton's supporters jeered and cackled at defense witnesses and screamed "Liar!" at the prosecutor.[10] Only when Sharpton was absent for a few weeks on account of his own trial for fraud and larceny was the courthouse calm, according to the *Times,* with spectators consisting mostly of "young college and law students and four rows of reporters."[11]

The following year, in 1991, Sharpton whipped up angry rock-throwing mobs in Brooklyn's Crown Heights after a car accident killed a black child, Gavin Cato. In the rioting after the accident, a rabbinical student, Yankel Rosenbaum, had been knifed to death.

After days of violent tumult, Sharpton gave a speech at Cato's funeral declaring that his death had not been an accident and, indeed, that a Jewish ambulance had refused to transport the black child to the hospital. "The world will tell us he was killed by accident," Sharpton said. "Yes, it was a social accident. . . . It's an accident to allow an apartheid ambulance service in the middle of Crown Heights." This conspiracy theory arose from the fact that the police had instructed the Jewish-owned Hatzolah ambulance to take only the Hasidim because a city ambulance had already been called for the other victims. (I thought liberals liked government health care!) Sharpton went on to denounce the "diamond merchants right here in Crown Heights" and then led the angry mob on a march through the Hasidic center of Crown Heights.

On account of Sharpton's presence at the funeral, the city was forced to deploy "vastly" more police than there were marchers, as the *Times* put it. The full cavalry was there—double lines of cops on both sides of the street along the march, motorcycle patrols, and even a circling police helicopter.[12] Sharpton would later brag that his march was peaceful.

Then, in 1995, Sharpton famously incited an anti-Semitic pogrom against a Jewish-owned store in Harlem, Freddy's Fashion Mart, telling angry mobs, "We will not stand by and allow them to move this brother so that some white interloper can expand his business." There were weeks of violent protests outside the store, which finally ended in a blaze of bullets and a fire that left several employees dead.

Of course, after all this, Sharpton became a pariah— Oh wait! No, in the opposite of paying a penalty, he became famous and ran for president and Al Gore kissed his ring *after* these spectacles.

In light of Sharpton's history, you'd think that, in the middle of liberals blaming the Arizona shooting on "rhetoric," someone in his organization might have said, *Hey boss, I'd keep a low profile for the next couple of weeks. We just don't want you to be on TV right now because someone is going to say, "Hey, how about Freddy's? What about Gavin Cato's funeral? Weren't you the guy stirring up the violent rabble at the trial of the Central Park jogger's rapists?"*

But liberals, being a mob, are perfectly capable of holding two completely contradictory ideas in their heads at the same time. They can believe that Jared Loughner was inspired by Sarah Palin—even though there's no evidence Loughner liked Palin or even knew who she was. But at the same time, they can resolutely deny Al Sharpton had anything to do with inciting people who were known to have heard Sharpton, and who believed they were following him, when they assaulted, attacked, and murdered those he had denounced as "white interlopers," "diamond merchants," and "racists."

Does the Southern Poverty Law Center have a file on Sharpton? They can feel free to use my notes.

MSNBC'S Ed Schultz turned not only to Sharpton but also to former congressman Alan Grayson to discuss violent right-wing rhetoric after Tucson. Yes, the Alan Grayson who said on the House floor that Republicans' health care plan was: "Die quickly." The Alan Grayson who said he couldn't listen to Vice President Dick Cheney "because of the blood that drips from his teeth while he's talking." And the Alan Grayson who went on radio and called a female official at the Federal Reserve a "K Street whore."[13]

Soon, the media were cheerfully announcing a "center on civil debate" being established at the University of Arizona, despite the overwhelming evidence that the shooting had absolutely nothing to do with public discourse.

Further nailing down its irrelevance, one of the center's honorary co-chairs was that balm of public debate former president Bill Clinton. Clinton had actually hired private detectives to dig up dirt on his "bimbos" and blamed the Oklahoma City bombing on conservative talk-radio hosts. Clinton unleashed adviser James Carville to vilify Independent Counsel Ken Starr as "an out-of-control sex-crazed person," a "spineless, gutless weasel,"[14] engaged in "a slimy and scuzzy investigation." (Which was true, but only because Starr was investigating Clinton.) Carville said, "Ken Starr can go jump in a lake."[15]

Clinton adviser Harold Ickes said the investigation "smacks of Gestapo," and "outstrips McCarthyism," asking, "What is this, a police state?"[16]

Clinton aide Sidney Blumenthal—who looks exactly like that—called Starr "a zealot on a mission . . . waging an assault on American rights [engaging in] anti-constitutional destructiveness, [who acts out] his personal temper tantrums and harasses critics." He called Starr an "inquisitor of unlimited, unchecked power" pursuing an investigation that was "unethical, illegal," and added that he was a "Grand Inquisitor for life" presiding over a "reign of witches" out of "vindictiveness."[17]

And that was in a single breath!

As students of history will recall, the courts found otherwise, holding Clinton in contempt, disbarring him, and accepting his $800,000 settlement with Paula Jones, and then the entire Supreme Court boycotted his next State of the Union address.

But it seems perfectly natural to Democrats that the man who sicced these curs on the public would be made co-chair of the Center for Civil Discourse.

How about making Michael Moore chairman of the President's Council on Physical Fitness? Or naming John Edwards chairman of a commission on tort reform? Why not make Helen Thomas a last-minute fill-in for Alan Dershowitz at a B'nai B'rith awards dinner, allow Senator Patty Murray to operate heavy machinery without adult supervision, or put Barney Frank on the House Banking Committee? (Wait—what? Since when?)

One begins to understand why liberals are constantly misquoting Ralph Waldo Emerson's remark that "a foolish consistency is the hobgoblin of little minds" by surgically removing the word "foolish."

Just in the last half dozen years, this has included Ted Koppel;[18] Charlie Rose (who also incorrectly attributed the line to Churchill);[19] Keith Olbermann, who misquoted Emerson by saying "Consistency is the hobgoblin of small minds, I believe was the original quote";[20] Mark Geragos;[21] the *New Republic*'s Jeffrey Rosen;[22] NPR's Daniel Schorr—explaining—repeatedly[23]—that John Kerry's answer to the flip-flop accusation should be "Consistency is the hobgoblin of small minds";[24] and

Margaret Carlson.[25] Not a single conservative misquoted Emerson on TV to defend inconsistency during that same time period.

The mob's leading TV network, MSNBC, has turned the embrace of inconsistency into a kind of performance art, invariably trotting out the worst possible Democrat to talk about this or that Republican scandal. It's as if they got a grant from the National Endowment for the Arts to act natural while interviewing a pot about the kettle.

Whenever Keith Olbermann needed a Democrat to discuss the sleazy sex scandal of a Republican, he turned to Chris Kofinas, former communications director for . . . *John Edwards*. Yes, *John Edwards*.

Kofinas's star turn in politics was his role covering up the fact that Edwards was carrying on an extramarital affair with New Age groupie Rielle Hunter, who was pregnant with Edwards's child, while he was running for president as a family man with a cancer-stricken wife. Today, Kofinas's specialty is going on MSNBC to blast Republicans for their sex scandals.

Is Kofinas really the best person to be giggling with Keith about Governor Mark Sanford's affair? Surely there are tons of Democrats who were not themselves involved in covering up a major sex scandal of a Democratic presidential candidate. Next up, *Joseph Goebbels joins us to discuss civil rights violations under Abraham Lincoln.*

There's never even an attempted alibi for Kofinas's role in lying about Edwards's affair. Kofinas might say, for example, "I was known to be a nincompoop by the entire Edwards campaign staff, who kept me out of the loop in a terribly humiliating way. Because the campaign treated me like an imbecile, made fun of me behind my back, and turned me into a laughingstock, it's easy to see how I could have been completely unaware of Edwards's affair that even the caterer knew about. There. I have redeemed my reputation!"

Kofinas is such a regular on the Republican scandal beat, it's as if some tiny synapse in Olbermann's brain connected "Kofinas" with "sleazy sex scandal" but wasn't quite sure why.

Anyone not paralyzed by liberal groupthink listening to Kofinas's smirking commentary about Mark Sanford would say, "Hey, you know, I was just thinking, you worked for a Carolina politician, too, and didn't he get his mistress pregnant while running for president? In fact, weren't you the front man for the cover-up?"

*I have no idea what you're talking about. Now let's talk to O.J. Simpson about domestic abuse.*

Similarly, when MSNBC needed an expert to excoriate the wrong-doers on Wall Street and propose needed financial reforms, the anchors turned to . . . Senator Chris Dodd and Representative Barney Frank.

Dodd and Frank are among the top ten individuals most responsible for the nation's economic meltdown. For years, they both ferociously defended the insane practices of Fannie Mae that sent the entire American economy into a near-depression. Even as late as 2008, Dodd was calling Fannie "fundamentally strong" and "in good shape," while Barney Frank assured Americans that Fannie Mae was "just fine."[26]

Naturally, therefore, when the housing market imploded, bringing the entire economy down with it, MSNBC called on Dodd and Frank to explain what had happened. Their response was to denounce Republicans for opposing the Democrats' latest financial reform bill.

On April 16, 2010, Chris Matthews interviewed Chris Dodd; on March 31, 2010,[27] Keith Olbermann interviewed Barney Frank;[28] and on June 25, 2010, Rachel Maddow interviewed Frank. Frank claimed that Republicans were "maintaining that we don't need any financial reform"—with "financial reform" defined as "a bill written by Dodd, Frank, and the Democrats' BFFs on Wall Street."[29] Obama administration financial adviser Elizabeth Warren specifically cited Dodd and Frank on MSNBC's *Rachel Maddow Show* as the two best financial watchdogs in Congress.[30] Because who would be better to regulate large passenger steamships than the captain of the *Titanic*?

This wasn't even the mainstream media's usual obtuse refusal to ask obvious questions when interviewing Democrats. (E.g.: ABC's George Stephanopoulos interviewing John Edwards after a solid year of the *National Enquirer* running stories about Edwards's mistress and neglecting to ask a single question about the alleged affair;[31] CBS's Bob Schieffer failing to ask Attorney General Eric Holder about the Justice Department's refusal to prosecute the New Black Panthers for voter intimidation because he was "on vacation that week [and] . . . didn't know about it.")[32]

MSNBC'S interviews with Dodd and Frank were expressly on financial reforms intended to prevent in the future what Dodd and Frank had caused in the past. Oddly enough, those allegedly being "regulated" were delighted with the Democrats' financial reform bill. In April 2010, both JPMorgan CEO Jamie Dimon and Goldman CEO Lloyd Blankfein said they supported the Democrats' financial reform. What better evidence is there that the Democrats were getting tough with Wall Street than the enthusiastic support of Wall Street?

If liberals can call the main culprits of the financial meltdown "reformers," just imagine what they could do with a word like "torture." Actually, you don't have to imagine. I'll tell you.

Liberals hysterically denounced the CIA's treatment of terrorist detainees at Guantánamo as "torture," but were more understanding when Damian Williams smashed a cinder block on Reginald Denny's head during the L.A. Riots and then did a victory dance around Denny's body. The attack on Denny broke facial bones in 91 places and resulted in permanent brain damage.[33] A jury acquitted Williams of all charges except simple mayhem for dropping the block on Denny's head.[34]

Representative Maxine Waters defended Williams, saying the "anger in my district is a righteous anger" and "I'm just as angry as they are."[35] She even paid a visit to Williams's house after the attack to see if there was anything she could do for him (taking time out from her busy schedule of attending hearings to get more federal support for banks whose boards her husband served on).

But the CIA considers putting a caterpillar in the cell of Osama bin Laden's trusted aide, Abu Zubaydah, and liberals demand war crimes trials.

The Justice Department's top-secret memos on interrogation techniques—released by President Obama in 2009—show that the Bush administration actually rejected the "caterpillar" torture, unless Zubaydah were specifically informed that it was a harmless insect:

> As we understand it, you plan to inform Zubaydah that you are going to place a stinging insect into the box, but you will actually place a harmless insect in the box, such as a caterpillar.
>
> If you do so, to ensure that you are outside the predicate act

requirement, you must inform him that the insects will not have a sting that would produce death or severe pain.[36]

Was this a harrowing account of U.S. brutality or the premise for a children's book? "Zubaydah and the Very Scary Caterpillar." Get Owen Wilson to do the voices and you've got a hit cartoon movie on your hands.

The *New York Times* didn't use the words "brutal," "horror," or "inhumane" in reference to the beating of Reginald Denny but was quick to attach such descriptions to the treatment of terrorists at Guantánamo.

These headlines referred to the detainees in Guantánamo:

- At Human Rights Film Festival, *Horror and Hope*[37] ("graphic depiction . . . stomach-turning experiences of abuse and humiliation . . . devastating indictment . . . inhumane treatment of prisoners")
- Taking a Long, Bumpy Ride to Systematic Brutality[38]
- Justice 5, Brutality 4[39]

These were *Times* headlines referring to the attack on Reginald Denny:

- Trucker Beaten in Riot Is Hospitalized Again[40]
- 5th Man Held in Los Angeles in Beating of a Truck Driver[41]
- 60 Arrested in Disturbance at Site of Los Angeles Riots[42]

Bob Herbert titled a column about the nationwide riots after the Rodney King verdicts "That Weird Day."[43] A column on Guantánamo was titled "Madness and Shame."[44]

Could we run a photo of the cinder block dropping on Reginald Denny's head next to a photo of the caterpillar?

What if we had treated the top leaders of al Qaeda the way a completely innocent bystander was treated in the L.A. riots? Would Maxine Waters defend it?

Other "corrective" techniques used against top-ranking al Qaeda members included facial slaps, abdominal slaps, facial holds, and "attention grasps."[45] If you can't quite picture "the grasp," think back to every department store you have ever been in where you saw a mother trying to get her misbehaving child's attention.

Reginald Denny will never again be able to drive a truck or operate heavy machinery.[46] (Whereas Abu Zubaydah feels uneasy whenever he sees a butterfly.)

But Maxine Waters, who ferociously defended Damian Williams, remains an honored guest at MSNBC, where Rachel Maddow and Keith Olbermann were convinced that once Americans found out the CIA was depriving al Qaeda terrorists of sleep, there would be a revolt.

Contrasting the treatment of Reginald Denny and Abu Zubaydah makes no sense to liberals. They can't see contradictions, so their minds go blank. You might as well be speaking to them in Urdu.

But for breathtaking cognitive dissonance, nothing beats the Left's comparative ranking of Attorneys General Janet Reno and John Ashcroft. Ashcroft was regularly referred to by liberals as the worst attorney general in human history—and that was in his honeymoon phase, before they started saying he was as bad as Osama bin Laden.

The *New York Times*'s Paul Krugman called Ashcroft "the worst attorney general in history"[47]—less charitable than even Anthony Romero of the American Civil Liberties Union, who said Ashcroft "will turn out to be *one of the worst* attorney generals in American history."[48] Rutgers University law professor Frank Askin said Ashcroft was "the worst attorney general in my memory," adding, "There's nothing good I can say about him. I'm glad he's gone."[49]

Ashcroft was repeatedly called a fascist—in the pages of *The Nation* magazine, by elderly protesters at Ashcroft's speeches, and in college faculty lounges. Handgun Control Inc. compared Ashcroft's positions to those of "convicted mass-murderer Timothy McVeigh," and the *Los Angeles Times* ran a cartoon with Ashcroft in the white robe and hood of a Klansman.[50] Presidential candidate Howard Dean proclaimed that Ashcroft was "not a patriot" and, of course, compared him to Joe McCarthy.[51] John Edwards accused him of trying "to take away our rights, our freedoms, and our liberties."[52] Legendary *New York Times* columnist Anthony Lewis compared him to Osama bin Laden.[53]

All in all, it was the worst celebrity roast I've ever attended.

How about we compare Ashcroft to Janet Reno? It's not as if you have to go back to the Garfield administration to find an attorney general who was arguably worse than Ashcroft. Let's look at the attorney general he *succeeded.*

Attorney General Reno's military-style attack on a religious sect in Waco, Texas, led to the greatest number of U.S. civilians ever killed by the government in the history of the United States. The sect's leader, David Koresh, may have run a weird cult, but that falls under "I don't approve," not "This is a threat to the domestic tranquillity of the nation." Reno wanted to target religious fanatics, and the ATF wanted a military confrontation as a demonstration of their manliness, so Americans had to die.

More Americans were killed at Waco than at any of the various markers on the Left's via dolorosa—more than at Kent State (4 killed), more than as a result of the Haymarket Square prosecutions (4 executed), more than at Three Mile Island (0 died).

SCORE......................................................................................................
- American civilians killed by Ashcroft:                    0
- American civilians killed by Reno:                        80

As Dade County (Florida) state attorney, Janet Reno made a name for herself as one of the leading witch-hunters in the notorious "child molestation" cases from the eighties, when convictions of innocent Americans were won on the basis of heavily coached testimony from small children. In 1984, Reno's office charged Grant Snowden with child molestation and convicted him of molesting a child, who was four years old when the abuse allegedly occurred seven years earlier. Snowden, the most decorated police officer in the history of the South Miami Police Department, was sentenced to five life terms—and was imprisoned with people he had put there. He served twelve years before his conviction was finally overturned by a federal court in an opinion that ridiculed the evidence against him and called his trial "fundamentally unfair."

In a massive criminal justice system, mistakes will be made from time to time. But Janet Reno put people like Snowden in prison not only for crimes that they didn't commit—but for crimes that never happened. Such was the soccer-mom-induced hysteria of the eighties, when innocent people were prosecuted for fantastical crimes concocted in therapists' offices.

SCORE.......

- Innocent people put in prison by Ashcroft:      0
- Innocent people put in prison by Reno:    at least 1 that I know of

On August 19, 1991, rabbinical student Yankel Rosenbaum was stabbed to death in Crown Heights by a black racist mob shouting, "Kill the Jew!" as retaliation for another Hasidic man killing a black child in a car accident hours earlier. In a far clearer case of racial jury nullification than the first Rodney King verdict, a jury composed of nine blacks and three Puerto Ricans acquitted Lemrick Nelson Jr. of the murder—despite the fact that the police found the bloody murder weapon in his pocket and Rosenbaum's blood on his clothes, and that Rosenbaum, as he lay dying, had identified Nelson as his assailant.

The Hasidic community immediately appealed to the attorney general for a federal civil rights prosecution of Nelson. Reno responded with utter mystification at the idea that anyone's civil rights had been violated. *Civil rights? Where do you get that?*

Because they were chanting "Kill the Jew," Rosenbaum is a Jew, and they killed him.

*Huh. That's a peculiar interpretation of civil rights. It sounds a little harebrained to me, but I guess I could have someone look into it.*

It took two years of nonstop lobbying from the date of Nelson's acquittal to get Reno to bring a civil rights case against him.

SCORE.......

- Number of obvious civil rights violations ignored
  by Ashcroft:      0
- Number of obvious civil rights violations ignored
  by Reno:      at least 1

Janet Reno presided over the leak of Richard Jewell's name to the media, implicating him in the Atlanta Olympic park bombing in 1996, for which she later apologized.

SCORE......................................................................................................................

- Number of Americans falsely accused of committing
  heinous crimes by Ashcroft:                                                    0
- Number of Americans falsely accused of committing
  heinous crimes by Reno:                                                        1

Reno also seized young Elián González from his Miami relatives to forcibly return him to his sperm-donor, illegitimate father living in Castro's Cuba.

SCORE......................................................................................................................

- Number of six-year-old boys seized at gunpoint and deported
  to communist dictatorships by Ashcroft:                                        0
- Number of six-year-old boys seized at gunpoint and deported
  to communist dictatorships by Reno:                                            1

In what factless, rationality-free universe is Ashcroft a civil liberties nightmare while Janet Reno represents the golden age of attorneys general? From the phony child-abuse cases of the eighties when Reno was a Miami prosecutor to the military assault on Americans at Waco, Janet Reno presided over the most egregious violations of Americans' basic civil liberties in the nation's history. These outrageous deprivations of life and liberty were not the work of fanatical right-wing attorneys in the Bush administration in response to the 9/11 terrorist attack, but of liberal Democrat Janet Reno, serving in peacetime.

The Left's estimation of Ashcroft versus Reno goes well beyond simple partisanship. It would be as if conservatives obsessively denounced President Obama as the worst public speaker ever to sit in the Oval Office, while demanding that everyone acknowledge Bush as a modern-day Demosthenes.

To maintain that sort of contradiction in one's mind is pathological. It is the pathological response of a crowd, as described by Le Bon—the "incapacity to reason," "absence of judgment,"[54] and "complete lack of critical spirit"[55]—that permits such wild contradictions and "does not allow of its perceiving these contradictions."[56]

A liberal is a person who:

- worships President Franklin D. Roosevelt, who carpet-bombed German cities and executed an American-born spy captured on U.S. soil after a secret military trial—but screams that Bush was guilty of war crimes;
- is crazy about Michael Moore—but against child obesity;
- tapes over the sign that said "Too Many Jews at Harvard" with a sign that says, "Ethnic Quotas This Way";
- is enraged with Karl Rove for releasing the name of a CIA paper-pusher (which he didn't do)—but are copacetic with WikiLeaks putting hundreds of thousands of classified national security documents on the Internet;
- categorically opposes the death penalty for convicted murderers—but venerates it as a "constitutional right" for innocent, unborn babies;
- hysterically opposed taking out Saddam Hussein, a mass murderer who gassed his own people and presided over "rape rooms"—but weepily demands that we intervene in Rwanda for humanitarian reasons;
- claims to be pro-children—but supports the public schools;
- champions women's and gay rights—but ignores the brutal treatment of women and gays by Muslims;
- same sentence as above, except take out the words "gay" and replace the word "Muslims" with "Bill Clinton";
- claims it was a vicious slander to be called a communist in the fifties—but didn't see anything wrong with being a communist in the fifties;
- advocates unfettered scientific research and debate—but then, with no evidence, simply declares discussions about evolution and global warming closed;
- says women should be treated like men—but then demands a vast network of speech laws that assume women are hothouse flowers;
- yelps for clean, alternative energy—but violently opposes nuclear power;
- supports sustainable energy sources like offshore wind farms—unless the offshore wind farm obscures his view from Cape Cod;

- decries stereotyping—but when a black conservative comes along denounces that person as "unqualified," "stupid," a "house nigga," "an Uncle Tom," or "window dressing";
- believes Tea Partiers are terrorists—but Islamic jihadists are victims;
- as mayor of New York City, closes off streets to traffic, clogs the remaining streets with bike lanes to be "green"—and then takes off in one of his two Gulfstream jets to London.

This welter of contradictions doesn't even embarrass liberals. Why? Because they are a mob.

# FOUR

# CRACKPOT CONSPIRACY THEORIES— OR, AS LIBERALS CALL THEM, "THEORIES"

**M**obs are particularly susceptible to myths. Le Bon says, "The creation of the legends which so easily obtain circulation in crowds is not solely the consequence of their extreme credulity. It is also the result of the prodigious perversion that events undergo in the imagination of a throng."[1]

Ask any liberal if Sarah Palin boasted of her foreign policy experience by saying, "I can see Russia from my house." In real life, Palin had responded to Charlie Gibson's question about the proximity of Russia to Alaska by remarking that Russia could "actually be seen from Alaska." The "I can see Russia from my house!" line was from a *Saturday Night Live* sketch. But facts are irrelevant to liberal beliefs.

Then in 2010, there were two famous videos, run on TV over and over again, that showed one thing, with liberals demanding that everyone admit the videos showed something else. It was like watching North Korean TV.

The first video was of several black congressmen walking through an anti-ObamaCare protest at the Capitol in March 2010 before the final health care vote. The media neurotically reported that the civil rights hero John Lewis was spat at and called the N-word fifteen times on the video—although the videos of the congressmen walking through the protest showed no such thing. Finally, Andrew Breitbart offered a $100,000 reward for anyone who could produce a video of any black congressman being called the N-word once, much less fifteen times, at a protest crawling with video cameras and reporters hungry for an act of racism. (Also, the charge of using the N-word fifteen times was ridiculous on its face. Have you ever stood in front of someone calling them the N-word fifteen times? Believe me, it's not easy. After a while they start finishing the word for you, and next thing you know they're rolling their fingers and doing that "yada yada N-word yada" thing. It's a nightmare.)

At that point, TV anchors began claiming they had seen it—but, strangely, could never manage to locate the video in order to show it to their viewers. After quoting a guest on *Larry King Live* (me) who had said, "If you can show somebody saying the N-word, well then you can win $100,000 if you can produce that tape, because there is no tape of it." CNN's Don Lemon said that was a lie and he had seen the tape with his very own eyes and would get it up on air so his viewers could see it for themselves:

> *Lemon:* OK. Listen, we have the tape here on CNN. I saw it on CNN's *State of the Union.* . . . So the tape is there and we'll try to get it on CNN so that you can see it and we'll highlight it the same way that Candy Crowley did.

I guess Don's producers couldn't find the tape before the end of his program, or the end of the week, the month, or the year, since it's never been shown on CNN or any other TV network. *Damn it! If only TV stations had some mechanism to show videos to their viewers . . .* To this day, the $100,000 reward remains unclaimed.

After weeks of liberals denouncing ObamaCare protesters for calling Representative Lewis the N-word—which never happened—no one, not one TV anchor, reporter, or commentator, ever apologized for this vicious lie. We just stopped hearing about black congressmen being called the N-word for a while.

But then time passed and most people forgot that when challenged, liberals had backed away from their claim that Tea Partiers had spat at black congressmen and called him a racial epithet. So liberals went right back to citing it as a fact again. After Jared Loughner shot up a Tucson Safeway, former congressman Alan Grayson went on MSNBC and reeled off a list of right-wing violence, including that a black congressman "was spit on."[2]

In October 2010, a crazed liberal woman in a wig charged Rand Paul as he arrived for a Senate debate. The disguised woman, Lauren Valle, was blocked by Paul's supporters, who, not being members of SEIU, did not immediately beat her up. Consequently, Valle was able to break away and make another mad dash for the candidate. When Paul's supporters stopped her a second time, she collapsed to the ground in the famous liberal *"You're hurting me!"* routine. This time, one of Paul's supporters— and my new bodyguard—Tim Proffit, jammed his foot on her shoulder, saying, "Now, stay down."

Inasmuch as the last ten seconds of the woman's performance was replayed one million times on television, it was perfectly obvious that Proffit had stepped on her shoulder, not, as TV anchors kept claiming, "stomped" on her "head." Perhaps there was another video showing the head-stomping, but—as with the N-word video—TV anchors never managed to get that one on air. Maybe Proffit stomped on her head. Maybe he pulled out a gun and shot her. Maybe Lauren Valle stomped on Rand Paul's head. Unfortunately, we don't have any footage indicating that any of that happened.

But type in "rand paul" on Google, and the first two "suggestions" from Google are: "rand paul" and "rand paul head stomp." Such media mistakes are never made in the other direction. No wild misstatement of fact ever gets circulated that makes liberals look worse or conservatives look better. There would never, for example, be a widespread lie that instead of stepping on her shoulder, the Paul supporter had accidentally tapped her shin with his foot.

In 2010, John McCormack of the *Weekly Standard*—an actual reporter with press credentials—was merely trying to ask Democratic Senate candidate Martha Coakley a question when he was assaulted and knocked to the ground by an operative with the Democratic National Committee.[3] If Lauren Valle's "head" was "stomped," then McCormack was knifed. But we didn't hear a peep about that assault.

MSNBC's Keith Olbermann won the prize for best imitation of a North Korean talk-show host, calling Rush Limbaugh a "damned liar" for claiming Valle's shoulder was merely stepped on—as the video ran showing her shoulder being merely stepped on:

> *Olbermann:* The bronze to Tokyo Rose Limbaugh, rationalizing the assault on Lauren Valle by lying about it.
> (BEGIN VIDEO CLIP)
> *Rush Limbaugh:* . . . [N]ow in the video that AP itself posted, the man put his foot down on her shoulder in what looked to me like an effort to help restrain her.
> (END VIDEO CLIP)
> *Olbermann:* You're not only a damned liar, Limbaugh, you're a damned bad liar.[4]

That's ideology trumping the process of your five senses. As Le Bon says, the "simplicity and exaggeration of the sentiments of crowds" result in the crowd's knowing "neither doubt nor uncertainty. Like women, it goes at once to extremes. A suspicion transforms itself as soon as announced into incontrovertible evidence."[5]

MSNBC was also Hoax Central for the claim, during the 2008 campaign, that someone in the crowd had yelled "Kill him!" in reference to Obama at a Palin campaign rally. Olbermann spent most of October 2008 issuing blistering denunciations of John McCain and Sarah Palin based on this absurdity. "There's a fine line between a smear campaign and an incitement to violence," Olbermann lectured. "If Senator McCain and Governor Palin have not previously crossed it, this week, today even, they most certainly did."

Guest-hysteric Richard Wolffe, then of *Newsweek,* said it was "no excuse" that Palin couldn't hear what the crowd was shouting, because "what you're seeing here is a very conscious attempt to paint Obama as un-American, as unpatriotic and, yes, consorting with what they call 'domestic terrorists.'" (Liberals reject the label "domestic terrorists" for former Weathermen, preferring to call them "future Cabinet members.")

After beating the "Kill him!" story to death, Olbermann delivered one of his prissy "Special Comments" about the nonincident, demanding that McCain stop campaigning. He railed, "Suspend your campaign now until you or somebody else gets some control over it. And it ceases to be a clear and present danger to the peace of this nation." *Anything else, Keith? Should I just concede the election now—or would next week be all right? While I'm up, can I get you a sandwich? How about a hot towel?*

As has now been conclusively established, no one ever shouted "Kill him!" at a Palin campaign rally. The Secret Service takes even frivolous threats against a presidential candidate seriously. In 1997, for example, the Secret Service searched the apartment of a student journalist at Berkeley for writing a column about the upcoming football game against Stanford that included the line "Show your spirit on Chelsea's bloodied carcass, because as the *Stanford Daily* lets us know, she is just another student."[6]

Needless to say, the Secret Service undertook a complete investigation of the claim that someone at a Palin rally had shouted "Kill him!" on hearing Obama's name. They listened to tapes of the event, interviewed attendees, and interrogated the boatloads of law enforcement officers who had been spread throughout the crowd. The Secret Service's conclusion was: It never happened. As even an article on the left-wing site Salon noted, "The Secret Service takes this sort of thing very, very seriously. If it says it doesn't think anyone shouted 'kill him,' it's a good bet that it didn't happen."[7]

Because liberals passionately believe their own myths, this wasn't the only time they embarrassed themselves in public. Here are a couple of examples in just one week's time during the 2010 midterms:

After Sarah Palin told a Tea Party crowd to wait for the November election returns before partying "like it's 1773," liberals instantly concluded that Palin meant "1776" but was too stupid to know when the Declaration of Independence was signed. PBS's Gwen Ifill tweeted "Sarah Palin: party like its 1773! ummm," and the Daily Kos's Markos Moulitsas tweeted "Sarah Palin to supporters: 'Don't party like it's 1773 yet.' . . . She's so smart." These ignorant posts were retweeted by dozens of other liberal geniuses, and the Huffington Post reprinted Moulitsas's tweet.

It never dawned on the liberal mob that, when *speaking to a Tea Party group,* Palin might be referring to the year of the Boston Tea Party, which occurred in . . . yes, that would be 1773. Only if you start with the premise that Sarah Palin is an idiot and therefore if she said something, it must be idiotic, would you not even bother to look up the year of the Boston Tea Party before leaping to the conclusion that Palin meant to cite the date of the signing of the Declaration of Independence.

For liberals, Palin's speeches are like one of those puzzles in a children's magazine that say, "Spot the mistakes." Palin was talking, so she must have made a mistake. The problem was, there was no mistake.

The same thing happened when Senate candidate Christine O'Donnell said that the Constitution does not mention a "separation of church and state." Again, liberals believed their own fairy tales rather than the evidence. They've told themselves so many times that "the Constitution clearly provides for a separation of church and state!" no one ever bothered to check.

Whenever liberals talk about "constitutional rights," they are invariably referring to some pronouncement inserted in an opinion by a rogue liberal judge fifteen years ago, which they now demand we treat as if it came from James Madison's pen. *One thing we know is that terrorists who intend to destroy us must be given civilian trials because that's what the founding fathers wanted.*

Really? Can I see the Constitution?

*No, why would you ask?*

Hey! That isn't in the Constitution!

*Yes, it's right here, written in crayon, circa 2006.*

Apparently some conservatives took liberals up on the invitation to read the Constitution and saw that the phrase "separation of church and state" is not there.

What liberals meant by "It's in the Constitution!" was "It was slipped into a Supreme Court opinion around 1950 by Justice Hugo Black, a racist, redneck anti-Papist from Alabama who wanted to make sure no public money would be spent busing students to Catholic schools." But that doesn't sound as impressive as "It's in the Constitution!"

True, the "separation" phrase comes from a letter written by Thomas Jefferson. He also wrote, "The tree of liberty must be refreshed from time to time with the blood of patriots and tyrants," but you don't hear conservatives going around citing the "tree of liberty clause" in the Bill of Rights. Like "the separation of church and state," it's not in the Constitution.

Indeed, a fair-minded person would look at the language of the First Amendment's Establishment Clause—"Congress shall make no law respecting an establishment of religion"—and wonder why it was phrased so clumsily if the idea was to prohibit state involvement in religion. Why not just say, "Neither the federal nor state governments may enact laws favoring religion"?

The answer is: The framers were not only decreeing that Congress could not establish a religion, but also reassuring the states that they *could* establish religions and Congress couldn't stop them. Inasmuch as a number of states had established churches both before and after passage of the First Amendment—decades after in some cases—the Establishment Clause obviously didn't mean the states couldn't establish religions. To the contrary, Congress was being forbidden from passing a law about the entire subject of—or "respecting"—an establishment of religion. That's why they used the word "respecting."

Liberals love to bellow " 'No law' means 'no law'!" but don't want to explain why "Congress" doesn't mean "Congress," "respecting" doesn't mean "respecting," and "establishment" doesn't mean "establishment."

Back to Jefferson's letter: It was written about a decade after the passage of the First Amendment—by a Congress of which Jefferson was not a member, incidentally. He was writing to the Danbury Baptists, who happened to be living in a place where Congregationalism was at that moment *the established state religion of Connecticut.* But neither Jefferson nor the Baptists objected to that. (The Baptists objected to the dancing—but that's another story.) Their dispute was about the *federal* government's involvement in religion. Even Jefferson's "wall of separation between church and state" letter referred only to the federal government and assumed states could have established religions.

The invincibly ignorant eye-rolling from the students and professors at the University of Delaware at the O'Donnell-Coons debate suggests that American history is not really touched on by our educational system. I thought they just took the Bible out of public schools, but apparently the history books have been removed as well.

As with the liberals who agreed with one another that Sarah Palin was a moron for mentioning "1773" to a group of Tea Partiers, liberals cited the audible snickers of morons at the O'Donnell-Coons debate as proof that O'Donnell was wrong.

These people would have snickered at Galileo. They would giggle if you told them the millennium didn't start on January 1, 2000. They would sneer if you told them Albany is the capital of New York. But you'd be right. It doesn't matter if 99.99999 percent of the people listening to O'Donnell think she's wrong. She's right.

But that's not how a mob distinguishes truth from falsehood. They defer to the crowd. *Some students say 2 + 2 = 4, some say it's 5—let's have a vote!*

As Le Bon says, a mob will believe its own myths even though they "most often have only a very distant relation with the observed fact."[8]

The media have reveled in the one myth believed by more Republicans than Democrats: that Obama was not born in Hawaii, despite printed announcements of his birth that ran in Hawaii newspapers at the time, among other evidence. Congratulations, liberals! I've got dozens of myths believed by more Democrats than Republicans.

Which party contained the collection of idiots who believed:

- Sarah Palin's infant child, Trig, was actually the child of her daughter.
- The Rosenbergs were innocent.
- The conviction of spectacularly guilty Mumia Abu Jamal, arrested while literally holding a smoking gun over the body of the cop he had just shot, was a frame-up.
- Alar on apples causes cancer.
- Power lines cause cancer.
- 150,000 women die of anorexia every year.
- Domestic violence against pregnant women is the leading cause of birth defects.

- Global cooling (circa 1976).
- Global warming (circa 2000).
- The Duke lacrosse players gang-raped a stripper.
- There is a "plastic gun"—that shoots bullets—invisible to metal detectors.
- Emergency room admissions for women beaten by their husbands rise 40 percent on Super Bowl Sundays.
- Justice Antonin Scalia threw the 2000 election to Bush so that his son could get a job with the Labor Department.
- Breast implants cause disease.
- O.J. was innocent.
- Dan Rather had documents proving Bush shirked his National Guard duty. (Hint: Rachel Maddow was one!)
- The Diebold Corporation secretly stole 700,000 Kerry votes in 2004.
- Bill Clinton did not have sex with "that woman."
- Al Gore didn't realize he was in a Buddhist temple.
- Heterosexuals are just as likely to contract AIDS as gays.
- Jim Jones was not a sociopathic cult leader but an inspirational visionary in the mold of "Martin King, Angela Davis, Albert Einstein, Chairman Mao" (as put by California Democrat Willie Brown).
- John Edwards didn't have an affair with Rielle Hunter.
- John Edwards's campaign aide Andrew Young fathered Rielle Hunter's child.
- Tawana Brawley was raped by policemen and a prosecutor.
- Someone shouted "Kill him!" at the mention of Obama at a Sarah Palin rally in 2008.
- A census worker found dead in the woods of Kentucky with "Fed" painted on his chest was murdered by a right-wing anti-government nut. (The census employee's death turned out to be a suicide/insurance fraud scheme.)
- Everything that appears in a Michael Moore movie is true.

There you have it: the myth column of the fifth column. What's so striking about liberal myths is not only how many there are, nor even that they're given currency by the *New York Times* and the *CBS Evening News* and in the House and Senate, but that they're so laughably implausible. If 150,000 women died of anorexia every year, the hospitals would be overrun with starving women. That's three times as many people that die in car accidents every year.

Similarly insane was the Left's terror of plastic guns. A gun couldn't fire if it was made of plastic. The explosive force of the bullet would shatter a barrel made of plastic or ceramics. There has never been a gun made without using metal for the barrel. The "plastic gun" that liberals claimed could foil metal detectors was the Austrian Glock—which is 83 percent steel. Only the handle and frame of the so-called plastic gun were constructed of a modern polymer, making the Glock lighter and more comfortable to hold.

And yet, in the eighties, Democrats tried to ban the Glock, despite assurances from both the director of civil aviation security for the Federal Aviation Administration, Billie H. Vincent, and the associate director of the Treasury Department's Bureau of Alcohol, Tobacco, and Firearms, Phillip C. McGuire, that "plastic guns" were easily picked up by the most primitive metal detector.[9]

In response, the Democrats produced some nut in Florida who claimed he had spent seven years drawing . . . a picture of a plastic gun. Yes, a picture. Liberals were terrified! Democratic representative Mario Biaggi said nonexistent plastic guns were a "triple-barrel terrorist threat," and Democratic representative Robert Mrazek warned that the nonexistent gun was going to be "the terrorist's weapon of choice, and certainly we ought to be able to stall it long enough to let technology catch up."[10] I've designed an invisibility potion—only on paper, so far. Imagine what the terrorists could do with that!

Then-representative Chuck Schumer demanded that Glocks be outlawed on the basis of unconfirmed reports that Libyan leader Moammar Khadafy had placed an order for more than a hundred Glocks.[11] Of course, police forces and gun owners across the United States were ordering them, too, because they're very comfortable and reliable guns.

Nonetheless, news articles reported, "The administration declined Wednesday to endorse legislation prohibiting the import or domestic sale of plastic handguns that terrorists could slip through airport metal detectors."[12]

In the end, Congress passed a bill banning guns with less than 3.7 ounces of metal by a 413–4 vote in the House and a voice vote in the Senate. They might as well have outlawed Martian death rays. Even the Glock contains 19 ounces of metal. The National Rifle Association did not object to Congress banning an imaginary gun. With less toleration for fools, Representative Dick Cheney was one of four congressmen to vote against the ban on a nonexistent gun.

Liberals are like the contestants on Monty Python's *Stake Your Claim,* but without the sense to concede the point.

> *Game Show Host:* Good evening and welcome to *Stake Your Claim.* First this evening we have Mr. Norman Vowles of Gravesend, who claims he wrote all Shakespeare's works. Mr. Vowles, I understand you claim that you wrote all those plays normally attributed to Shakespeare?
>
> *Vowles:* (proudly) That is correct. I wrote all his plays and the wife and I wrote his sonnets.
>
> *Host:* Mr. Vowles, these plays are known to have been performed in the early seventeenth century. How old are you, Mr. Vowles?
>
> *Vowles:* Forty-three.
>
> *Host:* Well, how is it possible for you to have written plays performed over three hundred years before you were born?
>
> *Vowles:* Ah well. This is where my claim falls to the ground.
>
> *Host:* Ah!
>
> *Vowles:* There's no possible way of answering that argument, I'm afraid. I was only hoping you would not make that particular point, but I can see you're more than a match for me!

MSNBC manufactures bogus stories and pumps them out a mile a minute, while leaping on the slightest misstatement made on Fox News as proof of malice or lunacy. (Thus uniting the mob's belief in myths and acceptance of contradiction in one dynamite combo platter!)

When the Mississippi River bridge in Minnesota collapsed during rush hour on August 1, 2007, killing thirteen people, Rachel Maddow and Keith Olbermann wildly leapt to the conclusion, on the basis of no evidence, that it was Republicans' fault. They had callously cut taxes and now people had died.

Forty-eight hours after the collapse, Keith cited the remarks of Senator Amy Klobuchar (D-MN)—whom he called "Governor," in the sort of misstatement he deems a firing offense if uttered by a conservative—and Representative Louise Slaughter (D-NY) blaming Republicans for the tragedy. (When something is an actual "tragedy" involving no human will, liberals blame Republicans; when it's an intentional attack, such as the Tucson shooting or the 9/11 terrorist plot, liberals call it a "tragedy.")

Klobuchar blamed the bridge's collapse on "messed-up priorities of spending half a trillion dollars in Iraq while bridges crumble at home." Slaughter also blamed the Iraq War, calling the people who died in the bridge collapse "almost victims of war" because our "perpetual war depletes the funds available to maintain our infrastructure."

Maddow laid the deaths of thirteen people directly at the feet of "Republicans, including Governor [Tim] Pawlenty [and] President Bush," who "have demonized taxes and demonized any Democrat who ever said a tax hike could improve our lives, save our lives at home." Saying, "there aren't Republican bridges or Democratic bridges," Maddow railed: "We're a country that as a whole is paying this incredible deadly price for a brand of American conservatism that hates and demeans government, and that has defined any sort of spending on anything for the common good as something that's soft headed and suspect."

She traced the collapse of the bridge back to Ronald Reagan's "first inaugural, where he defined government as the problem, and to Barry Goldwater before him, and the Republican Party defends itself as uncritical inheritors of the legacy."[13]

All this was two days after the bridge collapsed, before an investigation into the causes had even begun.

A year later, the National Transportation Safety Board concluded that the bridge collapsed because of a design flaw.[14] It had nothing to do with government spending on upkeep of the bridge, it wasn't corrosion or cracks. It was a design flaw. The Democrats' demand for more "infrastructure" spending wouldn't have helped.

After polluting the airwaves with their irresponsible, baseless accusations, liberals never acknowledged that they were wrong, nor did we get an apology from Olbermann, Maddow, Klobuchar, or Slaughter.

In the last year of the Bush administration, terrified that the president would take action against Iran before leaving office, MSNBC and other conscience-of-the-nation types denounced neoconservatives, Zionists, and the right-wing smear machine for insulting the good name of Mahmoud Ahmadinejad. In December 2007 a report was leaked that all sixteen U.S. intelligence agencies had concluded that Iran had ceased nuclear weapons development as of 2003. The leak came after months of warnings from the Bush administration that Iran was pursuing a nuclear weapons program.

In October 2007, for example, President Bush had warned, "If you're interested in avoiding World War III, it seems like you ought to be interested in preventing [Iran] from having knowledge necessary to make a nuclear weapon."

The only people more triumphant than Ahmadinejad about the leaked report were liberals. In *Time* magazine, Joe Klein gloated that the Iran report "appeared to shatter the last shreds of credibility of the White House's bomb-Iran brigade—and especially that of Vice President Dick Cheney."[15]

Liberal columnist Bill Press said, "No matter how badly Bush and Cheney wanted to carpet-bomb Iran, it's clear now that doing so would have been a tragic mistake."[16]

Naturally, the most hysterical response came from MSNBC's Keith Olbermann. After donning his mother's housecoat, undergarments, and fuzzy slippers, Keith brandished the NIE report, night after night, demanding that Bush apologize to the Iranians.

"Having accused Iran of doing something it had stopped doing more than four years ago," Olbermann thundered, "instead of apologizing or giving a diplomatic response of any kind, this president of the United States chuckled."

Olbermann ferociously defended Mahmoud (a fan of the show)

from aspersions cast by the Bush administration, asking if the president could make "any more of a mess" than by chuckling "in response to Iran's anger at being in some respects, at least, either overrated or smeared."[17] Bush had "smeared" Ahmadinejad!

Most sanctimoniously, Keith said, "Given the astonishment with which President Clinton's lie about his personal life was met in the media, in the newspapers, where is that level of interest in this president's lie? That first one was a lie about an intern and maybe some testimony. This is a lie about the threat of nuclear war."[18]

Bush didn't believe the intelligence. Clinton said he wasn't sure if Monica Lewinsky performed oral sex on him.

Keith's Ed McMahon, the ever-obliging Howard Fineman of *Newsweek,* said that the leaked intelligence showed that Bush "has zero credibility."[19] The next night, Keith's even creepier sidekick, androgynous *Newsweek* reporter Richard Wolffe, also agreed, saying American credibility "has suffered another serious blow."[20]

Olbermann's most macho guest, Rachel Maddow, demanded to know—with delightful originality—"what the president knew and when he knew it."[21] Again, this was on account of Bush's having disparaged the good name of a sawed-off, Jew-hating nut-burger, despite the existence of a cheery report on Iran produced by our useless intelligence agencies.

Poor Ahmadinejad!

Keith, who knows everything that's on the Daily Kos and nothing else, called those who doubted the NIE report "liars" and repeatedly demanded an investigation into when Bush knew about it. He was even happier than Ahmadinejad, who proclaimed the NIE report "a declaration of the Iranian people's victory against the great powers."[22]

A lot of Republicans were suspicious of the intelligence, from John Bolton to Dick Cheney. The report's release was precisely timed to embarrass Bush inasmuch as it followed a series of bellicose remarks from the administration about Iran. Moreover, anyone who knows about these things knows that the United States has the worst intelligence-gathering operations in the world. The Czechs, the French, the Italians—even the Iraqis (who were trained by the Soviets)—have better intelligence. Burkina Faso has better intelligence—and their director of intelligence is a witch doctor. The marketing division of Wal-Mart has more reliable intel than the U.S. government does.

After Watergate, the off-the-charts left-wing Congress gleefully set about dismantling this nation's intelligence operations on the theory that Watergate never would have happened if only there had been no CIA. This is a little like dismantling your car because you accidentally hit the mailbox. (Democrats are apparently opposed to intelligence of any sort.)

Ron Dellums, a typical Democrat of the time, who—amazingly— was a member of the House Select Committee on Intelligence and chairman of the House Armed Services Committee, famously declared in 1975, "We should totally dismantle every intelligence agency in this country piece by piece, brick by brick, nail by nail."

And so they did.

So now our spies are prohibited from spying. The only job of a CIA officer these days is to read foreign newspapers and leak classified information to the *New York Times.* It's like a secret society of newspaper readers. The reason no one at the CIA saw 9/11 coming was that there wasn't anything about it in the *Islamabad Post.* (On the plus side, at least we haven't had another break-in at the Watergate!)

CIA agents can't spy because that might require them to break laws in foreign countries. They are perfectly willing to break U.S. laws to leak national security secrets to the media, but not in order to acquire valuable intelligence on other countries. CIA officers spend their days finding reasons to do nothing and then, a month later, say, "Yeah, we heard that request a few weeks ago. Let me tell you why we can't do it." It was constantly being leaked that Dick Cheney was demanding that the CIA do something insane. *You want us to infiltrate al Qaeda? We can't do that!*

But whenever anyone mentioned this about the Iranian nukes leak, Keith accused the "neocons" of choosing "to slander the intelligence community."[23]

Even the *New York Times,* of all places, ran a column by two outside experts on Iran's nuclear programs that ridiculed the NIE's conclusion. Gary Milhollin of the Wisconsin Project on Nuclear Arms Control and Valerie Lincy of Iranwatch.org cited Iran's operation of three thousand gas centrifuges at its plant at Natanz, as well as a heavy-water reactor being built at Arak, neither of which had any peaceful energy purpose. (If only there were something plentiful in Iran that could be used for energy!)

Weirdly, our intelligence agencies missed those nuclear operations.[24] They were too busy reading an article in the *Tehran Tattler,* "Iran Now Loves Israel."

Even if you weren't aware that the United States has the worst intelligence in the world, and even if you didn't notice that the leak was timed perfectly to embarrass Bush, wouldn't any normal person be suspicious of a report concluding Ahmadinejad was behaving like a prince?

Not liberals. Our intelligence agencies concluded Iran had suspended its nuclear program in 2003, so Bush owed Ahmadinejad an apology. Any military response was scuttled. Indeed, then-Senator Joe Biden threatened Bush with impeachment if he bombed Iran.

Then, on February 11, 2010—about a year after Bush left the White House—Ahmadinejad announced that Iran was "a nuclear state." So it would appear that Iran's nuclear program hadn't been *completely* abandoned in 2003. Can we get an apology from liberals? How about after Ahmadinejad drops his first bomb?

Once again, the Left had made triumphal accusations that turned out to be completely wrong—and then we never heard about it again.

In the fall of 2009, the naked body of census worker Bill Sparkman was found hanging from a tree in southwestern Kentucky. Liberals wasted no time in leaping to the conclusion that right-wing extremists had murdered him in a burst of anti-government hate.

A census worker? Lots of Americans—including the liberal ACLU—objected to the detailed personal questions included in the long form of the modern census that go far beyond the "actual enumeration" called for in the Constitution. So did lots of non-Americans worried about their illegal status being revealed to immigration authorities. Presumably, those people didn't answer the personal questions on their census forms. Other than that, a census worker isn't a particularly reviled figure. He's not an IRS agent, who can threaten you with penalties and jail time, an EPA inspector with the power to declare your swamp a federally protected wetland, or an Agriculture inspector, who can arrest you, seize your tractor, and fine you hundreds of thousands of dollars for running over rats. A census worker just asks you to fill out a form but has no power to impose punishment.

Even the *New York Times* wasn't buying the idea of a right-wing militia type murdering a census worker, running only a short, terse AP item about the death. Stranger still, Frank Rich sat this conspiracy theory out.

But the liberal idiocracy was ablaze with fantasies of a violent right-wing uprising sweeping America. After categorically announcing that the census worker's death was "not suicide"—that's "the one thing we know for certain"—the *Atlantic*'s Andrew Sullivan blamed "Southern populist terrorism" for his death, "whipped up by the GOP and its Fox and talk radio cohorts."[25]

*Newsweek*'s story on the census worker's death suggestively quoted a warning in the Census Bureau's manual telling employees not to engage people who say "they hate you and all government employees." The story ominously added, "Perhaps Bill Sparkman wasn't given the time to follow that sage advice."[26]

*New York* magazine ran an article about the dead census worker, asking, "Has Nancy Pelosi's Fear of Political Violence Been Realized?" Somehow blaming Representative Michele Bachmann (R-MN)—whom it called "wide-eyed" and "hysterical"—the magazine said a right-wing vigilante "wouldn't be all that surprising, considering the sheer volume of vitriol directed at the federal government and the Obama administration these days by conservative media personalities, websites, and even members of Congress."[27] Poor besieged liberals! Americans were committing hate crimes against them by asking Congress to cut spending! (Liberals are still trying to figure out how to blame John Hinckley's shooting of Reagan on conservative rhetoric.)

On CNN's *AC360*, Brian Levin, director of the Center for the Study of Hate and Extremism at California State University, said, "At this point, this was such a symbolic and personal anger, that I'm led to lean towards someone who has severe anti-government feelings, perhaps someone who's seeking revenge."[28]

But for truly crazy zealotry, we turn to MSNBC. Asked by Ed Schultz on *The Ed Show* whether political rhetoric was driving people to commit crimes, MSNBC analyst and former FBI profiler Clint Van

Zandt said, "Absolutely. As I say, Ed, there are the fringe of the fringe. There are people sitting there saying, you know, you're going to have to pry the gun out of my cold, dead fingers. . . . They listen to talk radio. They read blogs that are only on one side or the other. They watch programs that only have one side. . . . And for many of us, that just says, well, there, I believe it. For others, that says, by God, I'm not going to take it. I'm going to do something about it. And that fringe of the fringe, one more time, will pick up a gun."[29]

But the one person most hysterically committed to the idea that a right-winger had murdered Bill Sparkman was MSNBC's Rachel Maddow. Rachel's main move is constant eye-rolling at the crazy things conservatives believe—which generally turn out to be true. But then she will transition in an instant to deadly serious earnestness about the possibility of, for example, anti-government right-wingers causing Sparkman's death.

The week the census worker's death first broke, night after night, Maddow devoted large portions of her show to fearmongering over this "troubling story." Letting her feminine side come out, she started to seem more like her MSNBC colleague Keith Olbermann.

Beginning her show with this "very serious breaking news," Rachel reported that the FBI was investigating and that the census chief had called it "an apparent crime." The only reason the FBI would be involved, she said, is that "it is a federal crime to attack a federal worker on the job or because of their job."

And so it went, with Rachel breathlessly reporting this "breaking national news" every night, quoting anonymous sources calling it a homicide and digging up rare video footage of Sparkman to show his human side."[30]

One of Sparkman's friends, retired state trooper Gilbert Acciardo, had been quoted in the *Lexington Herald-Leader* saying he had warned Sparkman to be careful working in that part of the state. Thinking she had found a fellow conspiracy theorist, Rachel invited him on the show. But despite Rachel's portentous, leading questions, Acciardo repeatedly shot down her *Deliverance* fantasies.

*Maddow:* What—what in particular made you worry about him going to that part of the state?

*Acciardo:* Well . . . the road system over there is a little bit—they have smaller roads over there, and I was just afraid for his safety on driving the roads. . . .

*Maddow:* Did he ever express any concern to you about his work with the Census Bureau—any problems he'd ever had on the job?

*Acciardo:* No—just the opposite. He really enjoyed his census work, and he said people were really good to him.

*Maddow:* Are folks in this area familiar with the Census and its purpose? . . . Is there any fear that you're aware of that the Census might be seen as sort of a government intrusion?

*Acciardo:* No. I'm not aware. . . .

The next night, Rachel led with "brand-new details which do not all dampen the worry that Bill Sparkman's death was what we first worried it appeared to be—violence against a federal employee, because he was a federal employee."

The "new disturbing details" were that Sparkman's census ID had been taped to his body. Rachel reminded viewers over and over again that "of course, with the confirmation from the coroner today that the word 'Fed' was written across Mr. Sparkman's chest and then this new information about the ID being taped to his otherwise naked body at the time, this is what's leading us to worry that he was killed in fact because he was a federal employee." Again, she reminded viewers, there's "a strong suspicion of government generally among people who live in that area."[31]

Rachel Maddow owned the Bill-Sparkman-was-murdered-by-right-wingers story.

With law enforcement authorities still refusing to say whether they even believed a crime had been committed, Rachel complained that it was taking them too long to rule out suicide or accident. "We're starting to get to a point," she said, "where it's hard to imagine that this could be anything other than a homicide."[32]

When investigators announced a month later that Sparkman had committed suicide as an insurance scam, Rachel's guest host Howard Dean made the brief announcement, sparing Rachel the humiliation.[33] From that moment on, the story of the census worker was buried in a lead casket and dropped to the bottom of the ocean, as Maddow returned to regaling her viewers with hilarious stories about conspiracy-theorist right-wingers.

Even after having been taken in by the dummied Bush National Guard documents, the collapse of the Mississippi River bridge, the laughably false intelligence report on Iran's nuclear program, and the alleged right-wing murder of the census worker, Rachel didn't pause before issuing the breathless claim, in the middle of Wisconsin's budget crisis in February 2011: "I'm here to report that there is nothing wrong in the state of Wisconsin."

Contrary to what everyone else was reporting, Rachel assured her viewers that "Wisconsin is fine. Wisconsin is great, actually. Despite what you may have heard about Wisconsin's finances, Wisconsin is on track to have a budget surplus this year."

She continued the breaking news: "I am not kidding. I'm quoting their own version of the Congressional Budget Office, the state's own nonpartisan 'assess the state's finances' agency. That agency said the month that the new Republican governor of Wisconsin was sworn in, last month, that the state was on track to have a $120 million budget surplus this year."[34]

Unfortunately, Rachel hadn't bothered to read the entire memo. In that same January 31, 2011, memo, Robert Lang of the Legislative Fiscal Bureau went on to describe an additional $258 million in unpaid state expenses, including a $174 million shortfall in Medicaid services and $58.7 million owed the state of Minnesota in a tax reciprocity deal. Those were just two of the debits that had to be set against the $120 million "surplus."

The result was—as Lang concluded—Wisconsin was facing a $137 million shortfall, which, oddly, was very close to the $137 million shortfall Republican governor Scott Walker had claimed.[35]

Rachel had confused "0" with "$137 million." Next up on *The Rachel Maddow Show*—a story you haven't heard anywhere else: How Big Foot stole government workers' pensions!

A promotion for Rachel's program shows her sitting on the floor surrounded by index cards, with a Magic Marker in her mouth, as she says in a voice-over that news is about "what's true in the world." The promotion ends with Rachel at her anchor desk, opening her show with: "Good evening. We begin today with a story that *no* one is talking about."

Given her record, there's probably a reason no one is talking about it.

MSNBC's celebrated African-American guest, Professor Melissa Harris-Lacewell (now, Harris-Perry), has made a career as an eye-roller about Americans who, in times of economic insecurity, fear "the Other"—immigrants, Muslims, and black presidents. This is the sum total of left-wing social science from the 1960s to the present. And it's manifestly untrue: Some of the most comfortable, cosseted people in America will apparently believe anything.

Unemployed mine workers in West Virginia, clinging to their guns and religion, for example, have shown more skepticism about Obama's alleged Kenyan birth than Melissa Harris-Lacewell showed toward innocent Duke lacrosse players falsely accused of gang-raping a stripper in March 2006.

By May 20, 2006, the liberal legal reporter at the *National Journal,* Stuart Taylor, had written that the available evidence about the case left him 85 percent sure that the rape charge was a lie.[36] Among the evidence that was then publicly known was the fact that not one speck of the DNA taken from the stripper's body, clothes, or fingernails belonged to any of the lacrosse players, who had allegedly raped her anally, orally, and vaginally in a small bathroom.

It was also known that one of the three defendants, Reade Seligman, had an airtight alibi for virtually every minute of the only time period when a rape could have occurred—midnight to 12:31 a.m. on March 13. Phone records proved that Seligman was on his cell phone from 12:05 to 12:14 and that his last call was to a cabdriver. The cabdriver, who happens to be black, said he picked Seligman up at 12:19, drove him to an ATM, where a receipt showed that Seligman used his card at 12:24 a.m., then took Seligman to a fast-food restaurant, and finally drove Seligman back to his dorm, where his key card was swiped at 12:46 a.m.

It was also known that the accuser had a criminal record and had repeatedly changed her story about the alleged rape.[37]

More than a month after all this information had been released to the public, Harris-Lacewell wrote about what she called the "Duke Rape

Case" on her blog and accused Duke athletes of "pervasive misogyny" and "brewing hostility."

> Everything about this story resonates with my experience. . . . The pervasive misogyny that clung to the men's athletics programs and the thinly veiled racism of the university culture were palpable. I distinctly remember a crushing sense of vulnerability and dread when I interacted with some white males on campus. Although many were the model of respectable, genial behavior on the surface, I often sensed a brewing hostility beneath the surface. When I first heard the allegations in this case I wept because it felt like someone had finally revealed that unspoken anxiety I so often felt.[38]

Apparently, she perceives Duke athletes as "the Other."

Contradicting Harris-Lacewell's broad generalizations about white men at Duke were actual facts adduced by a Duke faculty committee two months earlier. Led by liberal law professor James Coleman, who, again, happens to be black, the committee had reviewed the conduct of the entire Duke lacrosse team for the previous five years. The committee found a few alcohol infractions, but concluded that none of the misconduct by the lacrosse players—again, going back *five years*— had "involved fighting, sexual assault or harassment, or racist slurs." The committee also reported that "current as well as former African-American members of the team have been extremely positive about the support the team provided them."[39]

But Harris-Lacewell was too busy inventing a myth about innocent men accused of rape to bother with the facts. In an interview on the Duke lacrosse case, she told BlackAmericaWeb.com that the "sense of entitlement and privilege at Duke is nauseating." She also accused the Duke women's lacrosse team of supporting the accused players because "given the entire history of white men sexually assaulting black women, we always know that white women have been on the side of white men."[40] The actual history of interracial rape—according to FBI crime statistics—is that, since the seventies, approximately 15,000 to 36,000 white women have been raped by black men every year, while, on average, zero black women are raped by white men. (The Department of Justice uses "0" to denote fewer than ten victims.)[41]

As Harris-Lacewell has said (when she's psychoanalyzing Tea Partiers), we know "that there are individuals [who] have sort of a predisposition towards intolerance." When "things start changing very rapidly," people experience "this anxiety, and it creates precisely the kind of intolerance that we're seeing."[42]

Harris-Lacewell was understandably confused and anxious. She was upset that no one asked her to replace Starr Parker on *The View*—as she had proposed on her blog. She was exhausted from carrying that Princeton backdrop around with her for every TV appearance. She couldn't understand why Rachel Maddow was always showering her with sickening praise that was not afforded Rachel's white guests. All this may explain the intolerance we're seeing from Harris-Lacewell.

As she might explain herself—at least when she's talking about conservatives—Harris-Lacewell evinced a "certitude" about her own position and worried that her "way of life" was "under attack." She showed a "capacity to dehumanize" white male athletes because she believes that "they are not as good as" she is. Those were factors 1, 2, and 3 in her explanation to MSNBC's Keith Olbermann of the (nonexistent) "move to violence" among Tea Partiers.[43] (There was never any *actual* violence by Tea Partiers—*but they were moving that way!*)

MSNBC's other black guest, Eugene Robinson, was also a rape truther, long after the evidence suggested otherwise. (I'm going to embarrass Eugene by pointing out that he's won a Pulitzer Prize. Why? Because it's the law.) Invoking classic liberal stereotypes of "preppy privilege" and students who were "downright arrogant in their sense of superiority," Robinson said, "It's impossible to avoid thinking of all the black women who were violated by drunken white men in the American South over the centuries. The master-slave relationship, the tradition of droit du seigneur, the use of sexual possession as an instrument of domination—all this ugliness floods the mind, unbidden, and refuses to leave."[44]

It having been established that the accuser had once stolen a taxi, led the cops on a high-speed car chase, and tried to run down a police officer with the cab, among her other prior crimes, and that none of the lacrosse players' DNA could be found on her person or effects, a rational person would find it quite possible to avoid thinking of drunken white men raping their slaves two hundred years earlier. Me? I thought of Tawana Brawley. But the mob is immune to facts, preferring myths and images.

Liberals are the "some of the people" you can fool all the time. It's easy to implant myths in the minds of mobs because they only grasp ideas in terms of images. As Le Bon explains:

> Crowds being only capable of thinking in images are only to be impressed by images. It is only images that terrify or attract them and become motives of action.
>
> For this reason theatrical representations, in which the image is shown in its most clearly visible shape, always have an enormous influence on crowds. [S]pectacular shows constituted for the plebeians of ancient Rome the idea of happiness, and they asked for nothing more. . . .
>
> Nothing has a greater effect on the imagination of crowds of every category than theatrical representations.[45]

Cut to: Maureen Dowd writing in the *New York Times* that a movie about Valerie Plame and Joe Wilson "makes clear that Plame was not merely 'a secretary' or 'mediocre agent' at the agency, as partisan critics charged at the time, but a respected undercover spy tracking Iraqi W.M.D. efforts."[46]

The movie says so!

Not only that but Dowd noted that *the movie* "reiterates that Plame did not send her husband, who had worked in embassies in Iraq while Saddam and Bush Senior were in charge and was the ambassador in two African countries, on the fact-finding trip to Niger about a possible Iraqi purchase of 500 tons of yellowcake uranium."

Dowd's citation of a movie as proving this or that aspect of the Wilson-Plame fairy tale resembles Le Bon's description of a theater manager who "was obliged to have the actor who took the part of the traitor protected on his leaving the theatre, to defend him against the violence of the spectators, indignant at the crimes, imaginary though they were, which the traitor had committed."[47]

Precisely because of Plame and Wilson's lies, the Senate Intelligence

Committee was forced to hold hearings on these very topics. During those hearings, not only did the CIA's inspector general testify that Plame herself told him she had "made the suggestion" that her husband go on the Niger trip, not only did the CIA reports officer testify that Plame "offered up his name," but the committee actually obtained the memo in which Plame recommended her husband for the job. Indeed, there was no job until Plame came up with the idea of sending someone—perhaps her husband—to Niger.[48]

The movie may tout Wilson's illustrious diplomatic career as reason enough for his being considered for a mission to Niger, but—as the *New York Times* reported back in 1990—Wilson's so-called diplomatic career consisted of his being an administrator, "someone usually more concerned that the embassy heating and plumbing work than with what is going on in the host country."[49] Of course, the *Times* didn't have the benefit of a Hollywood movie before reaching that conclusion.

Apparently, the movie also portrays Karl Rove and Scooter Libby vindictively leaking Plame's name to the press in order to destroy her career as the single most important spy in the nation's history. Dowd says, "The movie is a vivid reminder of one of the most egregious abuses of power in history, and there are deliciously diabolical turns by actors playing Scooter Libby, David Addington, and Rove."

How many times do we have to go through this? As long as one Republican after another is required to go on MSNBC's *Hardball* and stand up to the "birthers," when will Chris Matthews stand up to Maureen Dowd? Can anyone in the Democratic Party stand up to Dowd?

After years of sturm und drang about Karl Rove and Scooter Libby "leaking" Plame's name to the press, it finally emerged in August 2006 that it wasn't anyone in the White House at all, but Richard Armitage, an Iraq War critic, who gave a reporter her name. The *New York Times* story on the shocking revelation began, "Richard L. Armitage, a former deputy secretary of state, has acknowledged that he was the person whose conversation with a columnist in 2003 prompted a long, politically laden criminal investigation in what became known as the C.I.A. leak case."[50]

Have you ever noticed how you have to tell liberals the same thing over and over? Liberals simply cannot learn. They're like children who put their hands over their ears because they don't want to listen to Mother. Most normal people just give up and let liberals enjoy their fantasies. Even when you force an individual liberal to look at evidence and admit the truth, leave him alone for a few days and he'll go right back to spouting the same hokum.

Conservatives heard Obama wasn't born in Hawaii, but then found out there were newspaper announcements of his birth and dropped it—except for the remaining two hundred Americans who still believe Obama was born in Kenya.

Conservatives—like everyone else—believed Saddam was stockpiling weapons of mass destruction. After the invasion, however, no stockpiles were found. The former Iraqi general under Saddam Hussein, Georges Sada, wrote a book claiming Saddam had moved the stockpiles out of the country,[51] but conservatives dropped it, refusing even to mention the nonstockpiled WMD that were found.

Conservatives thought Mohammed Atta met with Iraqi intelligence agents in Prague on April 9, 2001. We thought so because that's what Czech intelligence concluded, and they have a better intelligence service than we do; because an eyewitness claimed to have seen the meeting; because Atta had had clandestine meetings in Prague before; and because the Iraqi intelligence officer wrote in his diary for that day, "Hamburg student," which Atta was, and described himself as in his visa application. But the CIA and 9/11 Commission concluded that Atta was not in Prague on April 9 because, although no eyewitnesses saw him in the United States between April 4 and April 11, someone used his cell phone in Florida on April 6, 9, and 10.[52]

So conservatives dropped it, with Bush and Cheney never mentioning it again—and indeed, being taunted for having ever believed it.

Many conservatives believed Clinton's granting pardons in exchange for donations to his presidential library or payments to his brother-in-law was a crime, but then found out they were wrong: The president has unrestricted power to grant pardons, except in the case of impeachments. So conservatives stopped calling it a crime.

Contrast that with liberals. Even having the *New York Times* acknowledge that: (1) Plame recommended her husband for the Niger trip, (2) Armitage told the press about her involvement, and (3) it was not a crime for Armitage to reveal her name—all that was not enough to get liberals to stop claiming that the leak of "secret agent" Valerie Plame's name was a crime and that someone in the Bush White House had committed it.

Liberals can't learn.

Wasn't welfare reform such a triumphant success that Bill Clinton started claiming credit for it? In 2009, the Democratic "stimulus" bill largely repealed welfare reform. Didn't we already prove that putting criminals behind bars would reduce the crime rate? Liberals are right back releasing criminals again. Haven't concealed carry laws disproved the critics' hysterical predictions and instead been magnificently successful at reducing crime? In 2009, the overwhelmingly Democratic Congress rejected a bill to allow "portability" of state concealed carry permits. (Everything must be national, except laws about guns.)

Ravens can learn to snatch fishermen's untended lines to get fish. Worms learn not to eat harmful bacteria (as opposed to the tasty nutritious bacteria they normally feed on). Fruit fly larvae can learn to detect the scent of predators. But liberals cannot learn that the August 6 Presidential Daily Briefing titled "Bin Laden Determined to Strike in the U.S." had not a speck of what we call "useful information."

I described the August 6 PDB in painstaking detail in my 2006 book *Godless: The Church of Liberalism.* The memo read like a fifth-grader's book report that was left to the last minute and based on quickly cobbled-together information from Google. The only "warnings" of future acts by al Qaeda were completely wrong. Thus, the PDB contained blindingly obvious facts such as "Bin Ladin [*sic*] since 1997 has wanted to conduct terrorist attacks in the U.S.," while warning that bin Laden supporters might be planning an attack in the US "with explosives" and that they might be preparing to attack "federal buildings in New York."

The 9/11 attack did not involve explosives. It did not target a single federal building in New York.

With liberals continuing to cite the August 6 PDB as if it had laid out the 9/11 plot in blinding detail, in frustration I even printed the full memo in the paperback version of *Godless.*

And still liberals cite the August 6 PDB as proof of Bush's incompetence.

On December 3, 2008, MSNBC's Keith Olbermann ominously announced, "The title of the August 6th, 2001, Presidential Daily Briefing, 'Bin Laden Determined to Strike in the U.S': It could have included copies of the terrorist itineraries and the message from the future. If a president did not act on it or perhaps did not even read it, it still wouldn't have made any difference."

In fact, if Bush had directed all members of the executive branch to drop everything and jump on the "warnings" in the August 6 PDB, bomb-sniffing dogs would have been wandering through our major cities and police lookouts would have been stationed at federal buildings in New York City—as planes smashed into the World Trade Center and the Pentagon.

Another plane might have crashed into some bomb-sniffing dogs in Pennsylvania, on its way to an unprotected White House. None of the 9/11 targets would have received special protection as a result of anything in the August 6 PDB. Nor, of course, was the single most important fact—that terrorists would use commercial airplanes as cruise missiles—mentioned as a possibility.

True, the title of the PDB was "Bin Laden Determined to Strike in the U.S." I have a memo titled "Actress Determined to Succeed in Hollywood."

This is textbook mob behavior. As Le Bon writes:

> Evidence, if it be very plain, may be accepted by an educated person, but the convert will quickly be brought back by his unconscious self to his original conceptions. See him again after the lapse of a few days and he will put forward afresh his old argument in exactly the same terms. He is in reality under the influence of anterior ideas, that have become sentiments, and it is such ideas alone that influence the more recondite motives of our acts and utterances. It cannot be otherwise in the case of crowds.[53]

Bush was the enemy, Rove his evil genius, so it didn't matter what the facts were. Hollywood would supply the rewrite.

There's your "reality-based community."

# FIVE

# I'LL SEE YOUR BIRTH CERTIFICATE CONSPIRACY THEORY AND RAISE YOU ONE OCTOBER SURPRISE

**D**emocrats tell fantastic lies, they drag the whole country through their investigations and criminal prosecutions—and then, when the commotion turns out to have been another wild-goose chase, the whole incident drops down the memory hole. Then liberals return to accusing right-wingers of being crazy conspiracy theorists.

The one lonely myth believed by more Republicans than Democrats is that Obama was born in Kenya, not Hawaii, and is therefore ineligible to be president. The "birther" theory was concocted by liberals and shot down by the conservative media. According to John Avlon, the author of *Wingnuts: How the Lunatic Fringe Is Hijacking America*, it was a Hillary Clinton supporter who publicized the claim that Obama wasn't born in the United States during the 2008 presidential campaign.[1]

The allegation was promptly investigated and disproved by every major conservative news outlet—*The American Spectator, Human Events, National Review,* Fox News, and the Sweetness & Light blog, among others. Indeed, it was Sweetness & Light that coined the term "birther." There were small newspaper announcements of his birth at the time in the local press. The "short-form" birth certificate Obama posted on his webpage was determined to be the usual version sent out by the hospital and accepted by the State Department as a "birth certificate."

In October 2008, Hawaii Health Department director Chiyome Fukino put out a statement saying that both she and the state registrar of vital statistics, Alvin Onaka, had personally verified that the health department had Obama's "long-form" birth certificate. She reiterated that state law prohibited anyone without a tangible reason from obtaining a copy of the original. Instead the department would issue the short-form "certificate of live birth," which had already been produced and posted by the Obama campaign on his website.

Then, in 2009, Fukino again put out a statement saying she had personally "seen the original vital records maintained on file by the Hawaii State Department of Health verifying Barack Hussein Obama was born in Hawaii and is a natural-born American citizen."[2]

(Whatever Fukino and Onaka's character and motives, the more people who must be lying for a conspiracy theory to work, the more implausible it is. Only two people—Bill Clinton and Monica Lewinsky—had to keep a secret about what happened in the Oval Office and, yet, within three years, the entire world knew.)

Some people continued to believe the "birther" story anyway. Of course, it might be easier to convince them if every other crazy conspiracy theory about Democrats hadn't been attacked as a vicious lie by the mainstream media before turning out to be true.

Remember when it was a crazy conspiracy theory to imagine Bill Clinton had carried on an affair with Gennifer Flowers? Or that he had flashed Paula Jones? Or that he had molested an intern in the Oval Office? Also remember when the mainstream media believed John Edwards's denial of his affair with Rielle Hunter—and then believed him again when he said her illegitimate child wasn't his? Remember how it took a quarter century to find out what really happened at Chappaquiddick? And remember when conservatives had the nutty idea that global-warming fanatics were cooking the books, but the mainstream media marginalized them by calling them insane? And remember how the entire Democratic Party, Hollywood, and the mainstream media lied about Alger Hiss, Ethel and Julius Rosenberg, I. F. Stone, and dozens of other Soviet agents for nearly half a century until the Venona Papers came out?

Thanks, mainstream media!

Frankly, after all the media's jaw-dropping cover-ups—always in the same direction—it's amazing conservatives aren't bubbling over with conspiracy theories. Instead, the conspiracy theories always come from liberals. Indeed, insane conspiracy theories are often being hatched in the illustrious outposts of the mainstream media, from CBS's Dan Rather to the *New York Times*.

Presumably, if he cared to, Obama could request and release his "long-form" birth certificate. But he doesn't want to. Liberals have intentionally fanned the flames of right-wing conspiracy-mongering in order to make all opposition to Obama seem deranged. Thus, in March 2010, Obama was able to dismiss the entire Tea Party movement as including "some folks who just weren't sure whether I was born in the United States [or] whether I was a socialist."

Those are two very different claims. It's perfectly possible to believe Obama is a socialist—based, for example, on his socializing health care, the auto industry, and much of the banking industry and his statement that he thinks the government should "spread the wealth around"[3]—but not believe he was born in Kenya. Using Obama's sentence structure, the anti-war Democrats included some folks who weren't sure if President Bush should be assassinated or whether he was a right-winger.

It is liberals on TV, not conservatives, who are constantly yammering about Obama's birth certificate. They're not doing this to make conservatives look good. This is the only myth that begins to make conservatives look half as crazy as liberals.

In fact, however, there is not a single Republican in Congress who claims to believe President Obama was not born in this country. Even Salon's major investigative report, titled "Birthers in Congress," produced only a few elected Republicans making utterly innocuous remarks, such as Representative John Campbell (R-CA), who responded to a question about whether Obama was born in Hawaii by saying, "As far as I know, yes." In liberal-land, that's enough to be labeled a "birther."[4]

Salon's leading "birther in Congress" was Representative Bill Posey (R-FL) for simply having said he wouldn't "swear on a stack of Bibles" that Obama was born in Hawaii. I wouldn't swear on a stack of Bibles that Dennis Kucinich was born on Planet Earth, but apparently now Republicans are deemed to believe anything they don't heatedly denounce.

The smoking gun of Posey's alleged "birther" belief is that he introduced a bill that would require presidential candidates to produce their birth certificates. Inasmuch as it is a constitutional requirement that presidents be natural-born citizens, this is hardly an outrageous proposal.

But consider what Posey did not do.

He did not attempt to void a presidential election—as Senator Barbara Boxer and a handful of House Democrats did in voting not to ratify Ohio's votes in the 2004 election based on the Left's conspiracy theory about rigged Diebold voting machines.[5]

Posey did not say, "I believe it" of the birther theory, as DNC head Terry McAuliffe did of Michael Moore's more ludicrous conspiracy theories in his movie *Fahrenheit 911.*[6]

He did not hold mock impeachment hearings covered by CSPAN in the House basement—as Democratic congressman John Conyers did for the impeachment of George Bush.[7]

But liberals demanded that elected Republicans like Posey do more. They were called on to attack birthers and thereby pointlessly alienate people who might vote for them. Before Republicans tell birthers they're wrong, how about the Democrats get around to telling their black constituents that O.J. did it? How about the Democrats issue an official proclamation stating that they believe Tawana Brawley was lying and her advisers were malicious frauds? How about asking the Democratic congressman who represents Durham, North Carolina, to comment on whether he believes the Duke lacrosse players were guilty?

It would be a big step if Democrats would simply stop kissing Al Sharpton's ring. MSNBC's Chris Matthews spends 55 minutes of his every show demanding that elected Republicans vilify the birthers. But then he invites on as an honored guest Al Sharpton—perpetrator of the Tawana Brawley hoax. Maybe Matthews could kick off the conspiracy-squelching extravaganza by denouncing Sharpton's role in that charade.

For years, Al Sharpton, leading actor in the Tawana Brawley hoax, had veto power over all Democratic presidential candidates. If there ever comes a time when Republican presidential candidates have to get the blessing of the head of the birther movement to run, I'll say: I'm wrong—Republicans are as crazy as the Democrats.

It's not just that your average liberal is more likely than a conservative to believe in laughable conspiracies—although that is clearly true. The difference is, the conservative media denounce their nuts. They don't hold hearings on deranged theories or attend the loons' movie premieres. By contrast, the Democratic Party champions its crazies, appearing with them in public and holding congressional hearings to investigate their screwball theories.

The Democratic Party has a hand-in-glove relationship with Michael Moore, crackpot documentarian, whose *Fahrenheit 9/11* is chockablock with demented conspiracy theories, including:

- the 2000 election was stolen
- the Bush family clandestinely spirited the bin Laden family out of the United States after the 9/11 attacks
- Bush went to war in Afghanistan not to avenge the 9/11 terrorist attack but to help the Unocal Corp. obtain a natural gas pipeline in Afghanistan

Again, Terry McAuliffe, then *chairman of the Democratic National Committee,* attended the glittering Washington, D.C., premiere of *Fahrenheit 9/11* and emerged endorsing Moore's wacko Unocal conspiracy theory. "I believe it after seeing that," McAuliffe said. Show me former RNC chairman Michael Steele saying, "I believe the birthers" and I'll give 90 percent of my book profits to the Hugo Chávez reelection campaign.

Other Democrats who attended Moore's movie screening include Senators Tom Daschle, Tom Harkin, Max Baucus, Ernest Hollings, Debbie Stabenow, and Bill Nelson and Representatives Charles Rangel and Jim McDermott. Show me a half dozen Republican senators attending a birther movie premiere and I'll say "both sides" are the Party of the Mob.

In 2004, Democratic presidential candidate Wesley Clark proudly accepted Moore's endorsement. Moore was an honored guest at the

Democratic National Convention that year, sitting with former president Jimmy Carter. What is the likelihood that a birther will be sitting with former President Bush at the 2012 Republican National Convention?

Democratic fundraisers have been headlined by Rosie O'Donnell—a prominent 9/11 "truther," who believes the World Trade Center was blown up with explosives, not taken down by terrorists in airplanes. In 2003, Democratic presidential candidate and future Democratic National Committee chairman Howard Dean approvingly cited the left-wing fantasy that Saudi Arabia had warned Bush in advance about the 9/11 attacks. He promised a caller to National Public Radio that, if elected, he would investigate. Why are Democrats never asked if they really want the support of people who think the Bush family was in on the 9/11 attack?

There's something else Representative Bill Posey didn't do, despite his alleged status as a "birther." He didn't hold congressional hearings costing taxpayers millions of dollars to investigate a kooky conspiracy theory cooked up by Lyndon LaRouche—as Senate and House Democrats did with LaRouche's October Surprise conspiracy theory. LaRouche was a plausible source: You'll recall that he hatched the idea that the Queen of England ran an international drug-smuggling ring. Indeed, LaRouche was the second-most-ridiculous person named "Lyndon" to ever run for president of the United States.

Before it is completely washed down the memory hole, let's review this spectacular Democratic conspiracy theory: The October Surprise.

To set the stage: It was 1980 and Ronald Reagan was running for president against the incumbent Jimmy Carter. Reagan was the sunny, popular right-wing governor of California. Carter was the bumbling, egotistical coward bent on surrendering to the Soviets, who claimed to have been attacked by a giant swimming rabbit.[8] Carter's economic policies had produced a 21 percent interest rate, a 17 percent mortgage rate, and a 15 percent inflation rate in the coveted "hat trick" of presidential incompetence. Not only that, but he had produced skyrocketing unemployment.

Carter's brilliant strategic ploy of abandoning the shah of Iran, an important American ally, soon led to soaring oil prices and, of course,

Islamic lunatics holding fifty-two Americans hostage in Tehran, where they remained for 444 days, until Carter was safely removed from office by the American people. (Carter's abandonment of the shah also gave rise to the global Islamofacist movement we're still dealing with today.) Under Carter, Americans were permitted to put gas in their cars only on alternate days, based on whether the last number on their license plates was an even or odd number. The price of oil had risen 154 percent since the beginning of Carter's presidency. And these, mind you, were Carter's accomplishments. He also gave us Ruth Carter, Billy Carter, and a sweater-based energy policy.

With all that going for them—plus that old Mondale magic—Democrats were dumbstruck that they lost the 1980 election. (Nor could they understand, incidentally, why gas prices, inflation, and interest rates shot down and the nation enjoyed peace and prosperity soon after Reagan became president.) Naturally, liberals asked themselves: What other than a dirty trick could explain Carter's loss?

The Left's theory was that in October, one month before the 1980 presidential election, members of Reagan's campaign clandestinely met with representatives of the Ayatollah Ruhollah Khomeini and offered to sell him weapons in exchange for his promise not to release the hostages before the election. By delaying the release of the hostages, the theory went, Reagan would deprive Carter of a triumphant victory on the eve of the vote. In other words, liberals believed the Islamofascist cutthroats who had been toying with Carter like a cat with a ball of yarn for the past year *wanted Carter replaced by someone stronger, like Reagan.* Even by the standards of conspiracy theorists, this one was crazy.

But it seemed like a perfectly plausible theory to the editorial board of the *New York Times.* After all, the hostages were released immediately after Reagan's inauguration. Surely there was no reason for the Iranians to find Reagan more intimidating than a president who claimed to have been attacked by a giant swimming rabbit. Hadn't the hostage-takers been scared out of their wits by the photos of Carter wilting like a schoolgirl after jogging?

It was as plain as the nose on your face: Reagan had struck a secret deal! As leading conspiracy theorist Craig Unger put it, "One can almost make a prima facie case that surreptitious deals did take place. The hostages, it should be recalled, were released only minutes after Reagan's inauguration." (Even the *Columbia Journalism Review* gently chided Unger for ignoring the investigative journalist's practice of looking for evidence on both sides of a theory.)[9]

A somewhat more obvious motivation for Khomeini's timing in releasing the American hostages was given in a Jeff MacNelly cartoon that showed Khomeini sitting in a circle of Ayatollahs reading a telegram aloud: "It's from Ronald Reagan. It must be about one of the Americans in the Den of Spies, but I don't recognize the name. It says 'Remember Hiroshima.' "

A normal person gets an ice cream headache trying to follow the details of the October Surprise conspiracy theory. It was invented out of whole cloth by LaRouche after the 1980 election and remained in the kook fringe for years, finding brief outlets only in disreputable publications like *The Nation* (Christopher Hitchens, July 1987), the *New York Times* (Flora Lewis, August 1987[10]), and *Playboy* magazine (September 1988).

The lunatics might have spent their days in obscurity, talking to supercomputers of the future—as one October Surprise theorist claimed she did—except that, in April 1991, the *New York Times* began relentlessly flogging the story. Even if the October Surprise theory were plausible—which it wasn't—why the *Times* would suddenly start aggressively promoting a theory about an decade-old event is anybody's guess. Wait—I just remembered why the *New York Times* would so aggressively promote a theory about a decade-old event! They're the *New York Times,* and the theory was an attack on Reagan.

Anyway, in late 1991, the *Times* printed a lengthy op-ed by Gary Sick promoting the October Surprise lunacy.[11] Sick had been President Carter's principal aide for Iran during the Iranian hostage crisis—as impressive a position as being FDR's chief adviser on "sneak attacks" in December 1941. Sick was a professor at Columbia, apparently because the university was unable to hire the aide in charge of gas prices during the Carter administration.

In addition to single-handedly injecting the October Surprise conspiracy theory into the mainstream media, Sick would be responsible for bringing Iranian president Mahmoud Ahmadinejad to speak at

Columbia in 2007. That's a liberal for you: They have undying respect for Holocaust-denying, messianic America-hating dictators, but they denounce Reagan for allegedly being involved in dark conspiracies with Holocaust-denying, messianic America-hating dictators. If "America-bashing" were a category at the Oscars, this guy would be up for a Lifetime Achievement Award. And please: no letters—I know that America-bashing is the principal purpose of the Oscars, but in a technical sense, it's not an actual award category.

More than a decade after LaRouche had dreamed up the idea of a secret deal between the Reagan campaign and the Ayatollah Khomeini, the mainstream media embraced "The Election Story of the Decade," as Sick called it. As we shall see, conspiracy theories are best left in the pages of crackpot rags like *The Nation* magazine. Once they appear in crackpot rags like the *New York Times,* serious people start wasting their time investigating.

After the *Times* turned over two-thirds of its editorial page to Sick's October Surprise theory in 1991, other news outlets, such as PBS's *Frontline* and ABC's *Nightline,* began treating crazies howling at the moon as if they were serious news sources. Soon editorials across the nation were demanding answers. Even Jimmy Carter called for a "blue-ribbon" commission to investigate, saying, "It's almost nauseating to think that this could be true"—which is ironic, because that was my reaction, word for word, upon learning that Jimmy Carter had been elected president. The "evidence is so large," Carter said, "I think there ought to be a more thorough investigation of the allegations."[12]

What is fascinating about the October Surprise theory is that it was pursued notwithstanding the absence of a single person who could credibly claim to have been involved. This was not a Hiss-Chambers case. It was not one of Clinton's "bimbo eruptions." It wasn't even Anita Hill accusing Clarence Thomas. In those scandals, people who unquestionably knew one another disputed the facts of their relationship.

Absolutely no one who could credibly claim to have been involved in a secret deal between the Reagan campaign and the Iranians came forward to attest to the alleged "October Surprise."

According to *Village Voice* reporter Frank Snepp, who was the first to thoroughly discredit the October Surprise hokum,[13] reporters acted as conduits for information, allowing alleged witnesses to conform their stories with one another. "Only by swapping rumors and tacking with the latest ones," Snepp said, "were they able to create an impression that they knew of this event firsthand." Curiously, the Deep Throat conspirators kept changing their stories to fit the available evidence and would wait to hear what other loony tunes were prepared to "confirm" before "confirming" anything themselves.

There were two types of October Surprise conspiracy theorists: international con men and domestic dingbats. The international crooks would suddenly remember being part of the October Surprise conspiracy upon being arrested for some other crime, such as smuggling or fraud.

A classic example was Gunther Russbacher, an Austrian who had pulled off a string of con jobs, including impersonating: an Air Force officer, an Army captain, an Air France pilot, a federal prosecutor, a secret agent, and a stockbroker. During his sentencing for theft while posing as a stockbroker, the *Chicago Tribune* reported that his wife Raye said Russbacher was "actually a deep-cover CIA operative whom the government is trying to suppress because he piloted a flight that carried George Bush to meet with Iranians in 1980 to delay release of the U.S. hostages in Tehran—the so-called October Surprise."[14]

You cannot tell me anyone in the media, even on the *New York Times* editorial page, seriously believed these people. (Frank Rich was still the theater guy for the *Times* back then.)

Then there were the standard nut-bar conspiracy theorists who claimed to have personal knowledge of meetings between representatives of presidential candidate Reagan and the Ayatollah. The two key American "witnesses" to the October Surprise were paranormal expert Barbara Honegger and fake CIA agent Richard Brenneke.

Honegger was a former low-level Reagan staffer, who told reporters she heard voices from the future.[15] She believed in supernatural events and claimed that an intelligence officer told her that satellites were directed to part the clouds during Reagan's inauguration so that the sun would shine only on him.[16] She was briefly famous in 1983 for accusing the Reagan administration of not caring about women, announcing to one of her many fawning media admirers, "I am honored to have been used by the Force, if you will, with a capital F, like in 'Star Wars.' That's how I feel. You know, the Zeitgeist of history."[17] Honegger was Christopher Hitchens's main source for his stories promoting the October Surprise conspiracy in *The Nation* magazine.

In search of an ally, Honegger approached fake CIA agent Brenneke and told him about the October Surprise story. She handed him a list of Reagan associates asking him to put a check by those who were at the Paris meetings. Brenneke's own notes of the meeting show that this was the first he had heard of the October Surprise "thesis," as he called it. He wrote, "Honegger meeting notes: Thesis: Reagan-Bush campaign conspired to delay the hostage release until after the November 1979 election [*sic*] . . . *Howard Hughes was somehow involved. . . .*"

Brenneke was about to be fired from his lucrative job with a left-wing think tank for failing to produce evidence of a different conspiracy theory, so he needed a new gig. Suddenly, it rang a bell. And so, a few weeks later, not only had Brenneke heard of the October Surprise meeting—he had been there! A LaRouchite confirmed that he had seen Brenneke at the meeting, something Brenneke himself had not remembered until that very moment.

According to these three reliable sources—Brenneke, Honegger, and the LaRouchite—in October 1980, George H. W. Bush (later Reagan's vice president), William Casey (later Reagan's CIA director), and presumably Howard Hughes met with the Ayatollah's representatives in Paris to make their nefarious deal. We're still trying to determine if the Freemasons were involved.

Needless to say, Secret Service records established the precise location of vice presidential candidate Bush throughout the 1980 campaign. And he wasn't in Paris. Once that was confirmed, the conspiracy theorists simply dropped Bush from their imaginary meeting but were otherwise undaunted. The dates of the alleged meetings kept changing, depending on what could be proved about William Casey's whereabouts in the fall of 1980. By process of elimination, the wackadoodles finally settled on three days in October for which there appeared to be no evidence of Casey's whereabouts.

With the conspirators having finally decided that October 17–20 were the absolutely, positively definite dates for the alleged October Surprise meetings, it turned out Casey's whereabouts could be proved after all. He was at a conference in London, "The Anglo-American History of World War II." Unfortunately for the conspirators, the conference director kept detailed notes on who attended each session. Not only was Casey present at nearly every talk, including his own, but there were credit card receipts establishing Casey's presence in London even during brief periods when he left the conference. In all, Casey's precise location could be proved for nearly every minute of the three-day period. And he wasn't in Paris, either.

Then it turned out that even fake CIA agent Brenneke was not in Paris during the alleged October Surprise meeting. Having placed himself at the center of the secret meetings in Paris, Brenneke planned to capitalize on it by "writing" a book. So he turned over all his notes and diaries—8,000 pages in all—to his ghostwriter, Peggy Adler Robohm. One can imagine Robohm's surprise when she came across credit card receipts, signed by Brenneke, proving that he had attended—believe it or not—a Star Trek Convention in that week. Okay, it wasn't actually a Star Trek Convention. Brenneke was attending a martial-arts tournament in Seattle on the crucial dates from October 17 to 19.

Robohm promptly contacted Representative Lee Hamilton (D-IN), who was chairman of the congressional committee spending millions of taxpayer dollars to investigate the October Surprise. But Hamilton wasn't interested. So she sent Brenneke's files to Snepp at the *Village Voice*.

At least Brenneke had a good explanation for the credit card receipts placing him at the Seattle martial arts tournament during the crucial meeting in Paris. When Snepp asked him about the receipts, Brenneke said, "No comment." This was the conspiracy that Jimmy Carter demanded a blue-ribbon commission to investigate and on which millions of taxpayer dollars were wasted.[18]

Interestingly, many of the same screwballs pushing the October Surprise nonsense have popped up in more recent conspiracy theories. Brenneke became a star witness in the Mena, Arkansas, cocaine conspiracy by claiming to have flown drugs for the CIA from Mena when Bill Clinton was governor of Arkansas.[19] Honegger is the originator of the peculiar 9/11 conspiracy theory holding that all the clocks stopped at the Pentagon at 9:32 on 9/11, thus proving that the plane could not have hit at 9:37. Oswald LeWinter—another of Gary Sick's critical sources for his book *October Surprise*—attempted to sell forged documents to Mohamed al-Fayed in 1998, allegedly proving that the British intelligence service was involved in the death of Diana, princess of Wales. I'm pretty sure he also started the urban legend about how you can cook an egg with an activated cell phone.

But despite the fact that the October Surprise conspirators made Dan Rather's source on the Bush National Guard story look like Eliot Ness, major mainstream media such as ABC's *Nightline,* PBS's *Frontline,* and the *New York Times* ferociously promoted the October Surprise using these nuts as their sources.

Now here's the most dazzling part of the conspiracy theory: The investigation of the October Surprise was itself an October Surprise.

The Democrats' Show Trials into Sick's cuckoo allegations didn't take place until 1992—a dozen years after the alleged conspiracy but the very year one of the main alleged conspirators, then-president George H. W. Bush, was running for reelection.

Why didn't the *New York Times* start pushing the October Surprise conspiracy theory in 1984, when Reagan was running for reelection? Why not in 1988, the first time alleged conspirator Bush was running for president? The answer is: Walter Mondale and Michael Dukakis. Those elections weren't close. Why waste a mammoth, preposterous lie trying to save the likes of Michael Dukakis?

Rumors about Reagan and the Ayatollah had been buzzing about the dental fillings of nutcakes for more than a decade, but suddenly, just before a presidential election twelve years later, Congress and the media were ravenous to investigate whether the Republican president facing reelection was a traitor. Ironically, Democrats carrying on about how Republicans had engaged in dirty tricks to steal the 1980 election was a dirty trick to steal the 1992 election.

The *New York Times* did not begin hawking the October Surprise theory until the third year of Bush's presidency—and didn't stop until Bill Clinton was elected. Right through the 1992 presidential election, newspapers were crackling with accusations that Bush had been involved in Reagan's fiendish plan to keep American hostages in the hands of Islamic lunatics until Carter lost the election.

ABC's Ted Koppel set the tone on *Nightline,* saying that if the allegations were true, "it would be an act of political treachery bordering on treason."[20] The Associated Press reported—in February of an election year—"Democrats contend that they are not out to get Reagan or Bush but simply want to clear the air of a rumor that, if true, would amount to treason."[21]

Yes, and if it were true that Obama was a secret agent of al Qaeda—think of what that would mean!

Apart from not being true, how was the October Surprise conspiracy different from the late Senator Ted Kennedy engaging in secret negotiations with the Soviet Union in order to undermine Reagan's foreign policy? If the October Surprise was so dastardly that we had to spend millions of dollars investigating it, how about investigating a U.S. senator warning the Russkies that the U.S. president was a belligerent lunatic who was terrifying all "rational people."[22] Unlike the October Surprise, that actually happened. Other people who may still be working in Democratic politics were involved. How about an investigation into that bit of treason?

Even after liberal publications such as the *Village Voice,* the *New Republic,*[23] and *Newsweek*[24] had thoroughly debunked the October Surprise, a Democratic House and Senate were convening lengthy investigations into whether Reagan had struck a secret deal with Iranian monsters holding Americans hostage. Sick, darling of the *New York Times,* denounced the debunkers, claiming Snepp was still connected to the CIA, that *New Republic* reporter Steve Emerson was part of a Zionist conspiracy, and that the Senate report was "another cover-up."[25]

The House investigation of Bush's role in the nonexistent October Surprise began in February 1992 and the Senate inquiry began in the spring of that year—coincidentally, a presidential election year. In the House, not one single Republican voted for the investigation and thirty-four honest Democrats voted against it. Neither congressional inquiry managed to wrap up before the election. So George H. W. Bush ran for reelection while two show trials—er, congressional investigations—were in the process of determining whether or not he had committed treason. That sounds fair.

The Senate completed its inquiry into the October Surprise a few weeks after the 1992 presidential election. The House completed its investigation one week before Bill Clinton's inauguration.

Having served its function, the Senate investigation concluded that "by any standard, the credible evidence now known falls far short of supporting the allegation of an agreement between the Reagan campaign and Iran to delay the release of the hostages."[26]

Amazingly, the *New York Times* refused to accept the Senate committee's findings and expressed hope for "a fuller, fairer understanding" from the House investigating committee. Jimmy Carter was unable to comment because he was in Pyongyang with Habitat for Humanity building Kim Il Sung a new missile silo.

Five million dollars and yet another congressional investigation later, the House report concluded: "There was no October Surprise agreement ever reached" and further that there was "no credible evidence" that the Reagan campaign had attempted to delay the hostages' release.[27] Five million bucks for that. Liberals were hysterical about the famed "30 million dollars" for Independent Counsel Ken Starr's investigation during the Clinton years—and Starr got fifteen criminal convictions and a president's impeachment. The House spent $5 million in an intensive, ten-month investigation to disprove the fantasies of a LaRouchite, a paranormal expert, a fake CIA agent, and the guy who was in charge of Iranian affairs for President Carter.

After foisting this useless investigation on the nation by flacking the crazed conspiracy theories of Gary Sick, instead of apologizing, the *Times* gave Sick equal time on that day's op-ed page to respond. His conclusion: Representative Lee Hamilton, the Democrat who had chaired the House's October Surprise Task Force, was in on the cover-up.

Among other lunacies, Sick wrote:[28]

1. "As a White House official involved in the hostage negotiations, I refused for many years to accept those allegations [about the October Surprise]."

This was preposterous: Sick had been hawking the October

Surprise theory to the media as early as 1988, each time claiming to have resisted believing, but finally being overwhelmed by, the apocryphal evidence.[29]

2. The family of Reagan's CIA director, William Casey, "failed to provide his passport, which had vanished mysteriously."

Wow—that is mysterious! How could a passport simply vanish? This is how: Casey had died in 1987 and the congressional investigation didn't begin until five years later, in 1992. Not being able to readily produce the passport of a man who passed away five years earlier is not especially mysterious.

3. "All this leaves open the possibility that members of the Reagan-Bush campaign may have interfered with the Carter Administration's most delicate foreign negotiation."

This is why you should never argue with homeless people claiming the government is controlling our minds with microwaves, kids! It's easier to just let them write a column for the *New York Times* op-ed page.

It is inconceivable that there would ever be comparable congressional investigations by Republicans. It would be as if Republicans spent millions of dollars investigating Obama's birth certificate—except there is such a thing as a birth certificate. There was no such thing as a secret meeting between the ayatollah's representatives and Reagan's people.

The allegedly serious Democrats aren't just humoring their base. This is what they believe. Years after elected Democrats wasted taxpayer money running down the demented October Surprise conspiracy theory, the Clinton administration's first contact with Tehran was to demand information from the baffled Iranians about the mythical October Surprise.[30]

Hitler falsely blamed the Reichstag fire on a communist to justify the mass arrests of communists and insurrectionists. But at least the Reichstag building really did burn down. Liberals just go about inventing news stories and then demanding the rest of us deal with it. This is the politics of hallucination.

Only a mob could impose their psychoses on the nation like this. Only a mob is illogical and paranoid enough to believe such fantastical stories. And only the liberal mob has professors, *Times* columnists, former presidents, and members of Congress willing to promote liberal delusions. You couldn't get enough conservatives to believe such nonsense to support an Internet chatroom, much less a multimillion-dollar investigation. From beginning to end, the October Surprise lunacy was another project of the liberal mob.

As Le Bon says, the "improbable does not exist for a crowd." Unable to reason, "deprived of all critical faculty," a mob will believe anything.[31]

# PART II:
# THE HISTORICAL CONTEXT OF THE LIBERAL

# SIX

# THE FRENCH REVOLUTION:
## WHEN LIBERALS ATTACK

To understand liberals, one must understand the French Revolution.

It's difficult to track the precise chronology of the French Revolution because there is no logic to it, as there never is with a mob. Basically, the mob would hear a rumor, get ginned up, and then run out and start beheading people. Imagine CodePink with pikes. From beginning to end, the French Revolution was a textbook case of the behavior of mobs. As Le Bon described mobs about a century after the French Revolution: "[A] throng knows neither doubt nor uncertainty. Like women, it goes at once to extremes. A suspicion transforms itself as soon as announced into incontrovertible evidence. A commencement of antipathy or disapprobation which in the case of an isolated individual would not gain strength, become at once furious hatred in the case of an individual in a crowd."[1]

Liberals don't like to talk about the French Revolution because it is the history of them. They lyingly portray the American Revolution as if it too were a revolution of the mob, but merely to list the signposts of each reveals their different character. The American Revolution had the Minutemen, the ride of Paul Revere, the Continental Congress, the Declaration of Independence, and the Liberty Bell.

The markers of the French Revolution were the Great Fear, the storming of the Bastille, the food riots, the march on Versailles, the Day of the Daggers, the de-Christianization campaign, the storming of the Tuileries, the September Massacres, the beheading of Louis XVI, the beheading of Marie Antoinette, the Reign of Terror, and then the guillotining of one revolutionary after another, until finally the mob's leader, Robespierre, got the "national razor." That's not including random insurrections, lynchings, and assassinations that occurred throughout the four-year period known as the "French Revolution."

Here are the highlights of the French Revolution to give you the flavor of the lunacy.

As with most rampages during France's revolution, the storming of the Bastille was initiated by a rumor. The mob began to whisper that the impotent, indecisive Louis XVI was going to attack the National Assembly, which had replaced the Estates General. For some reason, the people were particularly enraged over the king's firing of his inept finance minister, who had nearly bankrupted the country with Fannie Mae–style accounting. The rabble needed weapons to defend themselves from this imaginary attack on their new populist assembly.

Massing in the streets for days after the presentation of the Declaration of the Rights of Man and the Citizen to the Assembly, the people became more and more agitated. By the morning of July 14, 1789, about 60,000 French citizens armed with pikes and axes were running back and forth between the Hotel de Ville (Town Hall), and Les Invalides, a barracks for aging soldiers, demanding weapons and ammunition. Finally, the mob broke through the gate of the Invalides and ransacked the building, seizing 10 cannon and 28,000 muskets, but they could find no ammunition.

Then they rushed off to the Bastille for ammunition—and also because they considered the Bastille an eyesore. Once a fortress, then a jail, the Bastille was in the process of being shut down. It held only six prisoners that day. But the Parisian mob irrationally feared the Bastille based on its menacing appearance and false rumors of torture within its walls.

With legions of Parisians banging on the gates of the Bastille and demanding ammunition, the prison's commander, Marquis de Launay, invited representatives of the mob inside to negotiate over breakfast. They requested that the cannon be removed from the towers because mounted guns frightened the people. De Launay agreed and the cannon were withdrawn.

Meanwhile, the mob outside became more frenzied, believing that their representatives inside, lingering over breakfast, had been taken hostage. The mob interpreted the withdrawal of the cannon to mean that the cannon were being loaded, in preparation for firing into the crowd.

As the mob grew larger and angrier, the Bastille's guards warned them to disperse, shooing them away by waving their caps and threatening to fire. The people interpreted the waving of hats as encouragement to continue the attack.

And so it went, with periodic gunplay interrupted only by De Launay's repeated attempts to surrender. The mob secured its own cannon and began firing at the prison, hacking at the drawbridge, and scaling walls into the courtyard of the Bastille. Facing tens of thousands of angry citizens, De Launay made a final offer to surrender total control of the Bastille to the mob, provided it be accomplished peacefully. He threatened to blow up the entire city block unless his demand for a bloodless transition was agreed to.

His offer was refused amid angry cries of "No capitulation!" and "Down with the bridge!" De Launay surrendered anyway.

The mob poured in and ransacked the entire fortress, throwing papers and records from the windows, killing some guards, and taking others as prisoners. One captured guard who was marched through the street said there were "masses of people shouting at me and cursing me," as "women gnashed their teeth and brandished their fists at me."

De Launay was triumphantly paraded through the streets of Paris with the people cutting him with swords and bayonets until he was finally hacked to death, whereupon the charming Parisians continued to mutilate his dead body. A cook was given the honor of cutting off De Launay's head, which he accomplished with a pocketknife, kneeling on his hands and knees in the gutter to do it. De Launay's head, along with the head of a city official, Jacques de Flesselles, who had failed to assist the mob's search for weapons that day, were stuck on pikes and waltzed through the streets of Paris for more celebratory jeering.[2]

This is the revolutionary event celebrated by the French—the murderous barbarism of a mob.

Or as Parisians called it, "Tuesday." The incident at the Bastille was merely a particularly aggressive version of the rampaging and pillaging they had been doing for weeks, all based on this or that rumor.

Apart from the feral viciousness of the attack on the Bastille, the madness of it was that the Third Estate—peasants and the middle class—had already won themselves a Republic. Under the old system, the French people had had a legitimate grievance: The Third Estate, composed of the great mass of citizens, paid all the taxes but got none of the government jobs. Those were reserved for the nontaxpaying nobility and clergy. (It was much like rich Democrats today—Tim Geithner, who failed to pay Social Security and Medicare taxes but was still confirmed as Obama's treasury secretary; U.S. senator Claire McCaskill [D-Missouri], who failed to pay $287,000 in taxes on a private plane; Tom Daschle, proposed Obama nominee to be Health and Human Services Department secretary, who failed to pay all his taxes; Nancy Killefer, proposed Obama nominee to be White House chief performance officer, who failed to pay all her taxes; Zoë Baird, proposed Clinton nominee as attorney general, who failed to pay all her taxes; and Charlie Rangel, Democratic congressman censured by the House Ethics Committee for failure to pay all his taxes.)

When the Third Estate walked out on the Estates General and formed the new, classless National Assembly, asserting that only it could make laws, and the king recognized this new legislative body, they had won.

Nonetheless, the people decided the utterly pointless attack on the Bastille had been a tremendous success. And so, a few months later, Parisian peasant women decided to storm the Palace of Versailles and murder the queen, Marie Antoinette.

As Alexander Hamilton politely warned American Revolutionary hero the Marquis de Lafayette, after the storming of the Bastille, "I dread the vehement character of your people, whom I fear you may find it more easy to bring on than to keep within Proper bounds, after you have put them in motion."[3]

Initially, the mob had worshipped Maria Antonia, the Austrian princess, christened "Marie Antoinette" upon her arrival in France to marry the future king, Louis-Auguste. Antoinette was young—only fifteen years old—slender, fair, and beautiful. Mobs like that sort of thing, so the people worshipped her. When Antoinette made her first public appearance in Paris, the cheering crowds were so thick, her carriage was frequently stopped for an hour at a time. The besotted Parisians presented the princess with flowers, fruits, salutes, and speeches all along her ride. Most enthusiastic were the common people. As Antoinette stood on a balcony gasping in astonishment at the throng cheering her, a nobleman, Marechal de Brissac, told her, "You have before you two hundred thousand persons who have fallen in love with you."[4]

When Louis-Auguste assumed the throne a few years later, the masses hailed a new era of youth, freedom, hope, and change under their twenty-year-old king and nineteen-year-old queen. Though the new king and queen had done nothing and promised nothing, the masses adored them, putting their portrait up in all the shop windows.[5] They were the French Obamas!

But as so often happens with mobs, the people's passionate love would soon turn into equally passionate hate. As described by Le Bon, mobs "only entertain violent and extreme sentiments," so "sympathy quickly becomes adoration, and antipathy almost as soon as it is aroused is transformed into hatred."[6]

One sees traces of the phenomenon today in liberals' love-to-hate feelings toward Hillary Clinton, John McCain, Tony Blair, Joe Lieberman, Israel, the Supreme Court, wood-burning fireplaces, free speech, cigarettes, and warm weather. Liberals went from love to hate with Christopher Hitchens when he attacked Clinton—but then he won them back with his attack on God. (What a Cinderella story!)

Inflamed by ugly gossip as well as food shortages and fiscal crises, the crowd began to detest the queen. She was called *"l'Autrichienne,"* meaning the Austrian, but with the stress on "chienne," meaning "bitch." In pamphlets and gossip, Antoinette was accused of being a nymphomaniac and a lesbian, of holding sex orgies in the palace, and of engaging in unnatural acts with her dog and infant son.[7]

Antoinette was nearly the exact opposite of the image invented by the mob and passed down in popular mythology. She was genuine, charitable, kind, and good-natured—more like Audrey Hepburn in *Roman Holiday* than Hillary Clinton pocketing the White House silverware. She was not given to excess, avoided ostentation in her decorating style,[8] and was compassionate toward the poor. Antoinette eliminated the class-based segregated seating at the royal palace and often invited children from working-class neighborhoods to dine with her children.

This "lovely woman with the gentle eyes," as Antoinette biographer Stefan Zweig called her,[9] told her mother that what had touched her most about the cheering crowd for her in Paris "was the affection and zeal of the poor people, which, though crushed with taxation, was overflowing with joy at the sight of us." She called such love "infinitely precious."[10] Even years later, when the masses abused her, Marie Antoinette still described them charitably as "persons who declare themselves well-intentioned, but who do and will continue to do us harm."[11]

Marie Antoinette never uttered the words "Let them eat cake." Fittingly, that phrase came from the revolutionaries' philosopher, Jean-Jacques Rousseau, who claimed he overheard it on the lips of some nameless princess. This was written in his *Confessions*, sometime before 1769[12]—back when Marie Antonia was still a preteen making mud strudels in Austria. But the masses were upset by a hailstorm that had damaged the crops and impaired the food supply, so the French seized on this myth and it has lived on forevermore—just as it will live on forevermore that Dan Quayle apologized on a trip to Latin America that he never learned to speak Latin.

The mob was riled up; there was no time for calm reflection or consideration of the evidence.

And so, on October 5, 1789, angry fishmongers and other market women stormed the Versailles Palace intent on offing the queen. Called "8,000 Judiths," the rabble included some men dressed like women.[13] They were armed with pikes, axes, and a few cannon, hollering that they would "cut the Queen's pretty throat" and "tear her skin to bits for ribbons."[14]

Rallying outside the palace all day, by evening the rabble was half-naked, having taken their clothes off on account of the rain, much like the audience at a Rage Against the Machine concert. Early in the morning, around 2 a.m., a gaggle of women broke into the palace, decapitating two guards on the way. They made a wild dash toward Antoinette's bedroom, shouting, "Where is the whore? Death to the Austrian! We'll wring her neck! We'll tear her heart out! I'll fry her liver and that won't be the end of it! I'll have her thighs! I'll have her entrails!"[15]

The dulcet shrieks of the fishmongers call to mind George Washington exhorting his men, "Remember officers and Soldiers, that you are free men, fighting for the blessings of Liberty—that slavery will be your portion, and that of your posterity, if you do not acquit yourselves like men." This was not the American Revolution.

The queen fled her bedroom one step ahead of the howling mob. The crazed women proceeded to smash all the mirrors in the queen's boudoir and slash her bed to bits. After a standoff between the palace and the mob, the king capitulated, and the royal family was marched to the Tuileries Palace in Paris by triumphant hoi polloi. Leading the procession were the heads of the decapitated guards bouncing along on pikes. The king and his family were effectively put under house arrest at the Tuileries, with a guard stationed in Marie Antoinette's room at all times, even when she dressed and slept. The family would never see Versailles again.

The king signed a new constitution, relinquishing most of his power, and the French people lived in liberty and happiness from that moment ever after. No, wait—it didn't happen that way.

The political clubs, once gentlemen's debating societies, suddenly assumed actual political importance during the revolution. The Jacobin Club went from being a prestigious institution of distinguished individuals with little power to a motley collection of left-wing radicals that launched the monstrous revolutionary leader Maximilien Robespierre. Soon, respectable members quit the Jacobin club, leaving only the reprobates behind—much as happened to the American Bar Association in the 1980s.

On the one-year anniversary of the storming of the Bastille, some of the political clubs built model Bastilles, so that they could again be sacked by the people.[16] If there had been a Franklin Mint back then, the "Storming of the Bastille" chess sets would have been a bestseller.

The rabble, often led by the Jacobins, proceeded to smash every trace of the past—religion, law, the social order, eventually even the weights and measuring system and, most absurdly, the calendar.

On November 2, 1789, just a month after the storming of the Tuileries, the Assembly declared everything owned by the Catholic Church to be property of the state. Three months later, the Assembly severed the French Catholic Church's relations with the pope, dismissed about fifty bishops, dissolved all clerical vows, reorganized the church under the civil constitution, with priests to be elected by popular vote, and required all the clergy to swear an oath of loyalty to the state. Convents and monasteries were seized and turned into prisons to house any recalcitrant royals and priests.[17] A few years later, the Assembly would pass a law forbidding priests to be seen in public wearing clerical garb.[18]

Having a general idea where this godless fanaticism was headed, the royal family attempted to flee Paris on June 20, 1791. They got lost and stopped to ask directions from a young boy, whom the king tipped with a gold louis d'or. The boy recognized the king from his visage on the coin and quickly ratted-out the fleeing royals to revolutionary authorities.[19] The royal family was marched back to the Tuileries under a rain of stones, with effigies of the king dangling from trees along their path.[20]

A few months after the royal family's flight, the leftist Jacobins and the comparatively moderate Girondists forced the king to sign yet another new constitution. Louis XVI was reduced to a mere figurehead—and a prisoner.

The mob had no fear of punishment, certainly not from Louis XVI, the David Dinkins of kings. So they exploded in animalistic fury. The bourgeoisie had riled up the masses to storm the Bastille and Versailles. Now they would pay the price. As historian Erik Durschmied says, the king "had been the only constitutional instrument that could stand up to the extremists," but now the moderates had "opened the door to raging madmen willing to use mob brutality."[21]

On August 10, 1792, Parisians were out of sorts over more military setbacks in France's war with Austria and Germany—not to mention the absence of an "exit strategy"—so an armed mob stormed the Tuileries, forcing the royal family to flee to the National Assembly for safety. From there, the weak king, frightened by the sound of cannon fire, ordered the Swiss guards who were defending him to surrender. (This strategy, known as "unilateral surrender," would later become the cornerstone of the Democratic Party's national security policies.)

Refusing to believe such an insane command, the guard's commander went to see the king for himself, telling him, "The rabble is on the run! We must vigorously pursue them!"

Minutes ticked by with Louis XVI unable to make a decision. This was the king, after all, who had written in his diary the day of the storming of the Bastille, "July 14th: nothing." Finally, he repeated his surrender order. The incredulous commander demanded that it be put in writing. The king wrote, "We order Our Swiss to put down their arms immediately and withdraw to their barracks. —Louis."[22]

Ordered by the king to surrender, more than 600 Swiss guards were savagely murdered. The mobs ripped them to shreds and mutilated their corpses. "Women, lost to all sense of shame," said one surviving witness, "were committing the most indecent mutilations on the dead bodies from which they tore pieces of flesh and carried them off in triumph."[23] Children played kickball with the guards' heads. Every living thing in the Tuileries was butchered or thrown from the windows by the hooligans. Women were raped before being hacked to death.

The Jacobin Club, the MSNBC of the French Revolution, demanded that the piles of rotting, defiled corpses surrounding the Tuileries be left to putrefy in the street for days afterward as a warning to the people of the power of the extreme left. (This was easily arranged, as it coincided with a national strike by Paris's garbage collectors.) The next day, foreign ambassadors fled France.[24]

This bestial attack, it was later decreed, would be celebrated every year as "the festival of the unity and indivisibility of the republic."[25] It would be as if families across America delighted in the annual TV special "A Manson Family Christmas."

Back at the National Assembly, the king was arrested and the last flickers of the monarchy extinguished. King Louis XVI would henceforth be known as "Citizen Louis Capet." This time, the royal family was locked up in the filthy Temple prison. Mobs gathered outside, night and day, refining their nuanced political philosophy by chanting, "Death to the king!"

Executive authority was vested in the new National Convention, elected by all the people, including foreigners such as Thomas Paine— but no women, which is the only fact taught about the French Revolution in American schools today.

Maximilien de Robespierre, future president of the Convention, was the first among equals in the Revolution, the engine of the terror, who argued, following Rousseau, that a "Republic of Virtue" could only be achieved by "virtue combined with terror." Alas, the French got mostly terror. He and his fellow Jacobins took the seats high up at the Convention, for which they were nicknamed the Montagnards, or the Mountaineers.

With the royal family rotting in the Temple prison, the mob ran wild. Depressed by the news of their army's defeat at Verdun, the French went on a murderous rampage in the fall of 1792 known as the "September massacres."[26] Propagandists of the revolution warned that traitors to the revolution were planning a comeback from their jail cells and must be given "prompt justice." Revolutionary star Jean-Paul Marat wrote in his newspaper titled *L'ami Du Peuple*—Friend of the People, "Let the blood of the traitors flow! That is the only way to save the country."

On September 2, 1792, a revolutionary mob on the outskirts of Paris surrounded a caravan of twenty-four clergymen being transported to prison and began slashing at the priests through the windows of the carts. One assailant brandished his bloody sword toward onlookers and shouted, "So this frightens you, does it, you cowards? You must get used to the sight of death." At some point, an "ascetic priest" emerged and tried to calm the ruffians, a few of whom were his own parishioners.[27] He was promptly hacked to death.

The rest of the mob joined in the slaughter, until all the carts were dripping with blood. The gruesome caravan, full of mangled carcasses, loped along to the prison, where another crowd was waiting to butcher any priests who had managed to survive the first attack.[28]

About the same time, another mob besieged a Carmelite convent in Paris, where 150 priests were being given revolutionary trials. Armed with guns, clubs, pikes, and axes, the hoodlums shot the first priest to approach them and demanded to see the archbishop. After saying a prayer, the archbishop presented himself and was immediately chopped to death by the crowd, whereupon the assailants began indiscriminately murdering all the priests. Some priests escaped to a nearby church just long enough to give one another last rites before the barbarians burst in and began chopping them up, too.

After the first few batches of clergymen had been killed, the revolutionaries decided to hold mock trials for those who remained. One by one, the priests were called to a makeshift court presided over by a grimy sansculottes ruffian named "Citizen Maillard." Most of the "sansculottes" were lawyers and journalists who dressed like peasants—without the culottes, or knee breeches, worn by gentlemen—but Maillard was the real thing.

He ordered the priests to swear loyalty to the state. Not one would take the heretical oath. And so one after another, the clerics were dragged to the courtyard and sliced to pieces. Their bodies were dumped in fields or down a well, where, seventy years later, 119 skeletons were discovered.[29] This account was provided by the only survivor of the massacre, Abbe Sicard.[30]

One deputy of the Convention, Jean Denis Lanjuinais, estimated that 8,000 Frenchmen were executed on September 2 alone. Another deputy, Jean-Baptiste Louvet de Couvrai, put the number at 28,000.[31]

Rabid bands of men continued the savagery for the next five days, busting into nearly every prison in Paris and carving up the inmates. Not just priests but all prisoners were killed—the poor, the mad, women, old men, and even young girls. Waiting their turns locked in their cells, the prisoners could hear the screams of those who preceded them. The mob spared only two prisons—one for prostitutes and one for debtors, the mob's "base." At one prison, La Conciergerie, 378 of 488 prisoners were murdered in one day.[32]

The killers chopped up humans without pause, except to eat and drink the provisions brought to them by their wives to help the men "in their hard labors."[33] Revolutionary women would sit on the sidelines, enjoying the butchery and cheering the men on. As the bodies piled up, women would poke the corpses and make ribald jokes. Some grabbed severed body parts, such as ears, to wear as decorations. One revolutionary thug carved into a nobleman's chest, pulled out the heart, and asked, "Do you want to see the heart of an aristocrat?" He then squeezed some of the blood from the heart into his wine goblet, drank it, and invited others to drink from it, too. One young girl was forced to drink human blood to save the life of her father.[34]

The "great attraction" of the September massacres, according to French historian G. Lenotre, was the grotesque execution of Marie Gredeler, a prisoner accused of murder. She was bound to a post, her breasts chopped off and her feet nailed spread-eagle on the ground, and a bonfire was lit between her legs.[35]

But for my money, the most chilling murder of the September massacres was that of Princess Lamballe. This wealthy young widow had been Marie Antoinette's best friend and superintendent of the queen's household. For the Jacobins, she was the Karl Rove of the Louis XVI administration. The mob accused the prudish and sensitive princess of all sorts of monstrous depredations, including a lesbian affair with the queen.

After the mob attacked the Tuileries in August 1792, Lamballe had been moved to La Force prison, away from the royal family. A year earlier, the princess had gone to England to appeal to the British to save the French monarchy. She had returned to France out of sheer loyalty to Marie Antoinette. The fact that she wrote her last will and testament while in England suggests she had an inkling of what was to come.

On September 3, 1792, Princess Lamballe was dragged from her prison cell and brought before a revolutionary tribunal presided over by the brute Jacques Hébert. Hébert had nothing but admiration for the "sacrilegious excesses" of the revolution, cheerfully announcing that the universe would soon contain "nothing but a regenerated and enlightened family of atheists and republicans."[36]

He demanded that the princess swear "devotion to liberty and to the nation, and hatred to the king and queen," threatening her with death if she refused. Lamballe replied that she would take the first oath but never the second, because "it is not in my heart. The king and queen I have ever loved and honored."[37]

In the next instant, she was thrown to the howling mob, gang-raped, and sliced to pieces. Her head, breasts, and genitalia were chopped off by the sansculottes multitude and her mutilated corpse was put on public display for the crowd to jeer at and further defile. One beast cut out her heart and ate it "after having roasted it on a cooking-stove in a wine-shop." One of her legs was hacked off and fired from a cannon.[38] Her head was taken to a café and placed on a table for the patrons to laugh at. The princess's head and genitalia were then stuck on pikes and paraded past Marie Antoinette's prison window, with the mob shouting for Antoinette to kiss her lover.[39]

Isn't that what George Washington would have done?

The Convention decreed that France was a Republic on September 21, 1792. One week later, the renowned seventy-three-year-old French author Jacques Cazotte was guillotined for counterrevolutionary writings.[40] According to two contemporaneous accounts, in September 1792, a Jacobin named Philip presented a box to the legislative assembly containing the heads of his mother and father, whom he said he had slayed in a burst of patriotism because they refused to attend a revolutionary church.[41]

This was not a revolution that was likely to end—as the American Revolution did—with the motto *"Annuit cœptis"* (He [God] has favored our undertakings) on its national seal.

Being totalitarians, the French revolutionaries were anxious to inflict their ideas on other perfectly nice countries. In November 1792, the Convention issued the "Edict of Fraternity," calling on the people of other countries to overthrow their rulers.[42]

By the end of 1792, the Jacobins were demanding the king's head. Louis XVI had already tried to flee Paris, but the French wouldn't let him. The entire royal family had been held captive, under constant guard, behind multiple locked doors in the Temple prison for four months, and in the Tuileries before that. But that wasn't enough. Louis XVI was such an object of hatred for the masses that, at some revolutionary clubs, members with the "hideous" name "Louis" were forced to change their names to "Montagnard," as a tribute to the most liberal political faction.[43]

The trial of Louis XVI—or "Citizen Louis Capet"—took place in December 1792, before the entire National Convention. Erstwhile

American patriot Thomas Paine attended as a member of the Convention. Unknown to the hapless Paine, he was watching the original show trial. Citizen Capet was charged with a series of crimes that he knew, "as did his accusers, he had never been party to."[44] Of course, the principal accusation against him was treason for having been king—though it was not a crime to be so until that very moment.

Robespierre was putatively opposed to capital punishment, but like our liberal friends, he was willing to make exceptions on a case-by-case basis depending on the defendant. Fiercely championing death for the king, he argued that even holding a trial was "counterrevolutionary" (the French version of "politically incorrect"). Robespierre said that Citizen Capet was "a criminal toward humanity" and killing him was merely "a measure of public safety." The king "must die," he said, "because the country must live."[45] Johnnie Cochran's summations made more sense.

The Convention debated the king's fate much the way the UCLA faculty debated a resolution to condemn the Iraq War five days after the fall of Baghdad[46] (180 for; 7 against; wild applause). After a unanimous vote of guilt, the Convention then debated whether Louis Capet would be sentenced to detention, deportation, or death. "Give us the head of that fat pig," yelled the Jacobins. "The nation demands his death!"[47]

Thousands of the sansculottes ruffians poured into the streets during the trial, shouting for the king's death,[48] because this is how liberals participate in civic affairs. Some wandered inside to the public seats in the upper balconies to cheer deputies who called for death and heckle those leaning toward imprisonment. Seeing the bloodthirsty mobs in the streets, Madame Roland, a supporter of the Revolution, commented wryly, "What charming freedom we now enjoy in Paris."[49]

The vote inside went back and forth for 72 hours,[50] indicating that even the French revolutionaries were more evenhanded than the typical college faculty. Finally, the king's own cousin, with the promising revolutionary name "Phillipe Egalité," swung the vote by standing and saying, "I vote death."[51]

The Convention ordered the king to be guillotined the following day. So on January 21, 1793, Louis XVI became the only French king ever to be executed. It will not surprise close observers of the Left to learn that the deputies had engaged in vote fraud, with thirteen votes cast illegally, including that of the bloodthirsty "angel of death," Louis-Antoine-Léon de Saint-Just, who was too young to vote.[52]

The night before his execution, the king said good-bye to his family, giving his children religious instruction and telling them to forgive his assassins. The next morning at 5 a.m., he took communion. A few hours after that, the drums began. Hearing the drums, signaling the coming execution, Louis XVI's priest said, his blood ran cold.[53]

Arriving to take the king to the guillotine was a former priest, Jacques Roux, who had renounced his faith and joined the most radical revolutionary sect, the Enrages, or "the Rabid." The king handed him a package containing some personal effects and his last will and testament, asking that it be given to his wife. Roux responded, "I have not come here to do your errands, I am here to take you to the scaffold."[54] The king was taken by cart to the guillotine, trailed by a sneering, cat-calling mob.

After having his hands bound and his hair cut above the nape of his neck, King Louis XVI ascended the platform, motioned for the drummers to pause, and began to address the crowd. He said, "I die innocent of all the crimes imputed to me. I pardon the authors of my death, and pray God that the blood you are about to shed will never fall upon France—"[55]

But like an audience of college liberals, the audience began shouting and the drummers resumed their banging, so the king could no longer be heard. They could hear the king any old time, whereas who knew when they might get to yell and hit drums again?

Once the guillotine blade fully severed the king's thick neck, an attendant yanked the head from a basket and waved it before the crowd while making obscene gestures. The people whooped and cheered, threw their hats in the air, and lined up to dip their handkerchiefs in the king's blood. His carcass was dumped in a pit and the body dissolved with lime.

Within the next year, the king's backstabbing cousin, Mr. Equality, Phillipe Egalité, would himself be guillotined, with the less illustrious final remark: "Merde!"[56] Madame Roland was also executed, after bowing to the statue of Liberty next to the guillotine, saying, "Oh Liberty, what crimes are committed in your name!"[57] Thomas Paine would narrowly escape the guillotine and be imprisoned instead. On the one-year anniversary of the king's execution, the revolutionaries presided over fetes of celebration, including one in Grasse that featured the guillotining of a Louis XVI mannequin.[58]

They had executed a king, but the French had not yet begun the Reign of Terror. The fact that, after all this, the Terror was still to come begins to explain why all the bloody totalitarian dictatorships of the twentieth century have drawn inspiration from Rousseau and the French Revolution.

# SEVEN

# THE FRENCH REVOLUTION PART DEUX: COME FOR THE BEHEADINGS, STAY FOR THE RAPES!

By June of 1793, the radical Jacobins had seized total control of the Convention and begun instituting left-wing government policies, such as price controls and a general draft. Yet another constitution was adopted by the Convention and then immediately suspended by the Convention. Instead, a revolutionary government was decreed "until the peace." Robespierre dominated the tyrannical—and ironically named—Committee of Public Safety. (Similarly, in 2003, Libya was made chairman of the U.N.'s Commission on Human Rights.) Thus began the "Reign of Terror," purging all "enemies of the revolution."

The enforcers, Robespierre and his allies, demanded death to traitors, spies, moderates, and anyone who disagreed with Robespierre. Saint-Just, Robespierre's ally on the Committee of Public Safety, called for "unlimited war," saying the Republic "owes the good citizens its protection. To the bad ones it owes only death."[1]

There were up to fifty executions a day, by a guillotine set up next to the statue of Liberty in the "Place de la Revolution," formerly "Place Louis XV." More than three thousand aristocrats were sent to the guillotine, with huge crowds on hand to cheer the carnage. The victims often had to be dragged up the stairs of the scaffold. Programs called "menus" were distributed, listing the names of the condemned, the better to heckle them. Street jugglers entertained the crowds by staging mock executions with puppets.[2]

With the Jacobins in control, the "de-Christianization" campaign kicked into high gear in 1793. Inspired by Rousseau's idea of the *religion civile,* the revolution sought to completely destroy Christianity and replace it with a religion of the state. To honor "reason" and fulfill the promise of the Declaration of the Rights of Man and the Citizen that "no one may be questioned about his opinions, including his religious views," Catholic priests were forced to stand before revolutionary clubs and take oaths to France's new humanocentric religion, the Cult of Reason (which is French for "People for the American Way").

Only a bare majority of clergy, called "nonjurors," refused to take oaths to the republic. About 20,000 priests did so and another 20,000 left the country. Many ex-priests publicly denounced their religion, swearing they had never believed it, and "vied with each other in ribaldry and blasphemy."[3] Vicar Patin stood in front of a revolutionary club and said the "earmarks" of a priest were: "To bestialize humans in order to better enslave them, to make them believe that two plus one is one and a thousand other absurdities, to enter into a compact with our former tyrants to share with them spoils taken from the people."[4]

Revolutionaries smashed church art and statues.[5] One explained that he had broken the noses off church statues because they were "hideous apes" that deserved to be crushed and used for pavement.[6] At the Cathedral of Notre Dame, hundreds of medieval sculptures of prophets, priests, and kings were yanked from their pedestals and decapitated or hurled in the Seine.[7] The cathedral's priceless thirteenth- and fourteenth-century stained-glass windows were smashed.

Notre Dame fared better than the Third Abbey Church at Cluny, once the most magnificent monastery in the world. Revolutionaries torched the archives and sacked the Romanesque building, leaving behind nothing but a pile of rubble.[8]

The word *"vandalisme"* had to be invented to describe the wanton destruction of the abbey church of Saint Denis.[9] French mobs defaced the prized Gothic architecture, trashing archaeological treasures dating from the seventh century. They ripped open the tombs and threw the skeletons of kings and queens into lime pits.[10]

Deeming any gold and silver held by the churches "an insult to reason," the revolutionaries stole it, either for the "national melting pot" or for their personal use.[11] Churches that were not burned to the ground were turned into headquarters for some of the revolutionary clubs,[12] much as would happen years later to the Cathedral of St. John the Divine in New York City, where they now worship a giant whale. The revolutionaries shredded sacred books, using the paper as wadding for their cartridges, and burned confessional boxes for fuel. The relics of martyrs were ripped from their sacred resting places and thrown in a common pit, with one revolutionary leering about the bones of a male and a female martyr "making out together."[13]

Sacred vessels of the sacristy were thrown to the ground by the French mobs. Church bells, deemed a "relic of fanaticism," were forbidden from being rung, and were sometimes forcibly removed and melted down for armaments.[14] Altars were destroyed or renamed "altars of Reason." The cross, deemed counterrevolutionary, was forbidden from display, with women being required to remove cross necklaces.[15] Street signs, parks, and even cemeteries were stripped of crosses. One revolutionary club proposed outlawing celibacy.[16]

Joseph Fouché had been the headmaster at a Catholic school, but during the Revolution, he switched sides and became a leader of the de-Christianization campaign. Denouncing religion as "superstitious and hypocritical," he proclaimed a new "religion of the republic."[17] He traveled from town to town to snuff out any remnants of Christianity, publicly dressing down priests as "impostors who persist in continuing to perform their religious comedy."[18] In September 1793, Fouché actually did outlaw celibacy and gave priests one month to get married.[19]

In the town of Nevers, Fouché ordered that religious imagery on cemetery gates be replaced with the phrase "Death is an eternal sleep"— a proposal enthusiastically adopted in Paris.[20] In Lyon, the archbishop refused to swear allegiance to the republic and so he was removed, replaced by revolutionary bishop Antoine Lamourette.

The people of Lyon responded to the de-Christianization campaign by clinging to their guns and religion. On account of the resistance,

Convention deputy Bertrand Barere moved that Lyon, the second-largest city in France, be destroyed, and a monument erected on the ashes that would proclaim: "Lyon waged war against liberty; Lyon is no more."[21]

Fouché happily accommodated him, working day and night for months to annihilate the entire city, saying he was doing it "for humanity's sake." Fouché famously proclaimed, "Terror, salutary terror, is now the order of the day here." He arranged for "batch after batch of bankers, scholars, aristocrats, priests, nuns, and wealthy merchants and their wives, mistresses, and children" to be dragged from their homes and killed by firing squad.[22]

Fouché personally stripped even the revolutionary bishop, Lamourette, of his fake vestments and rode him through town on a donkey with a miter on its head and a Bible and crucifix tied to its tail, so the rabble could spit at and kick Lamourette. When Fouché was done, he proudly wrote to the Convention that Christianity in the provinces had "been struck down once and for all."[23]

Just a year earlier, at the beginning of the new Republic, Lamourette's idea had been to fuse revolutionary principles with Catholicism, much like today's pro-life Democrats. Even in the earliest days of the revolution, church property had been confiscated by the state, priests expelled from their posts, and the priesthood put up to popular vote.

But Lamourette thought they could all still get along. And so, prattling about "men of goodwill," in July 1792 Lamourette had asked members of the Assembly to embrace one another. There was hugging and kissing all around . . . and, one year later, Lamourette was being ridden through town, like a clown, on the back of an ass. So in addition to "counterrevolutionary" and "vandalisme," the French Revolution gave us the expression for a false truce: "the kiss of Lamourette."

Fouché's siege of Lyon became the revolution's standard operating procedure in the rest of France.

In October 1793, the powerful Paris Commune decreed that ministers were not allowed to perform religious services or wear religious garb in public, forbade the sale or display of rosaries and other "objects of superstition," and overturned the blue laws.[24] That same month, the Committee of Public Instruction banned priests from being teachers[25]— nearly two hundred years before our own Supreme Court did.

In lieu of religious holidays—which were banned—the revolutionaries put on "Fetes of Reason" with parades, dances, and public burnings of the symbols of nobility "on a scale as never before."[26] The first and most spectacular of these pagan rituals was held in November 1793, in the Notre Dame Cathedral or, as it was renamed, "The Temple of Reason." The words "To Philosophy" were carved into the façade of the magnificent Gothic cathedral. Stripped of crucifixes and other religious insignia, its altar was renamed the "Altar of Reason," decorated with broken crowns and a shredded Bible. It was an ACLU fantasy come true!

As a special highlight, Madame Momoro, a nun turned prostitute, portrayed the "Goddess of Reason" at the pagan festival of reason and paraded through the cathedral for all to worship.[27] Four months later, the Goddess of Reason was guillotined.[28] Fouché, Saint-Just, Barrere— the very revolutionaries who had propelled Momoro's ascent as a "goddess" to celebrate an end to religion—were on hand to applaud her beheading.[29]

At the fetes of reason being held throughout France, mannequins of priests were tied backwards on donkeys and ridden through the street. There were also obscene parodies of the clergy, with performers dressed as priests delivering mock sermons and dispensing scatological communions. "Come receive your God," they taunted, wiping their behinds with paper "hosts" and throwing the host in a chamber pot. "Here is your divinity. Come adore him for nothing. Here is a present of him."[30]

Religious marriages and funerals were discouraged and in some places banned entirely, replaced with civic versions of the same. The already-married were encouraged to remarry in revolutionary ceremonies. One club proposed that eulogies at the civic funerals include attacks on the recently departed, to distinguish them from religious funerals.[31]

This was not the American Revolution. This was the revolution of a mob.

France's new leaders—fishmongers, cobblers, and butchers, and lots of lawyers and journalists—also set out to invent a new, nonreligious calendar. Created by the Committee of Public Instruction, the "revolutionary calendar" is exactly what one would expect from a government commission.

It began with "Year 1," which, for simplicity, was the previous year, 1792. Based on "reason" and "nature," the revolutionary calendar had twelve 30-day months, divided into three 10-day weeks. Inasmuch as this didn't account for all the days in a year, the leftovers were tacked on as complimentary days: Virtue Day, Genius Day, Labor Day, Reason Day, Rewards Day, and, on leap years, Revolution Day. George Orwell had it easy in some ways.

The years were further divided into four-year spans called "Franciades."

Each month was given a crackpot name that was supposed to sound like a Greek or Latin word for seasonal attributes: Vendémiaire (harvest); Brumaire (mist); Frimaire (cold); Nivôse (snow); Pluviôse (rain); Ventôse (wind); Germinal (seeding); Floréal (flowering); Prairial (meadow); Messidor (summer harvest); Thermidor (heat); and Fructidor (fruit). (The new calendar also included an observance known as "Kwanzaa," which to this day no one has ever been able to explain.)

The British recast the new French months as "Slippy, Nippy, Drippy; Freezy, Wheezy, Sneezy; Showery, Flowery, Bowery; Heaty, Wheaty, and Sweety."

Napoleon mercifully abolished the French Revolutionary Calendar on January 1, 1806, twelve years after its creation. Only the strong arm of a military dictatorship could save the French from themselves.

Even clocks and personal names weren't spared this out-with-the-old insanity. Clocks were redesigned in decimal time, with a second being equal to 0.864 normal seconds, 100 seconds making one minute (which was now 86.4 seconds), and 100 minutes making an hour (144 minutes to the rest of the world). This is why freedom lovers everywhere detest the metric system.

Citizens were forced to drop their Christian names, which were deemed tyrannical and superstitious. One revolutionary proposed that the Convention issue a decree abolishing all Christian names at once.[32] The clubs urged people to adopt "civic" names, such as Brutus—the Roman who assisted in the knifing of his friend Caesar, prompting the dying Caesar to ask (in Shakespeare's words), "Et tu, Brute?" But then in another instant the adopted Roman names fell out of fashion, were duly renounced, and were replaced with names from the preposterous French calendar, leading to such names as "Fig-Pumpkin Ligeret."[33] *You know Figgy? He's my cousin! I'm Brie Surrender-Vomit.*

Yes, the French Revolution was just like the American Revolution.

The mob's consuming hatred of Marie Antoinette would finally be satiated with her public execution during the Reign of Terror. The revolutionaries had already come for the queen's eight-year-old son, Louis XVII, in July 1793. (In other important business that summer, the Convention decreed that William Pitt, prime minister of the United Kingdom, was "the enemy of the human race.")[34] Antoinette put up a fight, refusing to relinquish her son, but young Louis was literally torn from her arms. Six months earlier, the morning after the king had been guillotined, Antoinette had wiped away her son's tears, instructing him that a king should not cry. She then set him down, stood, and saluted him as the new king.

What awaited her young son was worse than the guillotine. He was turned over to an illiterate cobbler, Simone, who was instructed to re-educate the boy into hating his parents and loving the revolution. Young Louis was dressed in revolutionary clothes and made to curse his mother and sing revolutionary songs. Under the influence of the extreme left-wing journalist Jacques Hébert, Simone beat and brainwashed the boy into saying his mother had committed incest with him.[35]

By the fall, Marie Antoinette was ill, hemorrhaging constantly, and possibly dying from tuberculosis. She was only thirty-seven, but her hair had turned nearly white and she appeared a much older woman. On August 1, 1793, she had been moved to a filthy prison called the Conciergerie, where she was "prisoner 280." The former queen was put on display like an animal for "inhuman wretches" to stand outside her cell "continually vomiting forth" insults against her.[36]

Antoinette had found out her husband had been guillotined when a guard mockingly called her "the widow Capet." She found out her best friend, the Princess Lamballe, had been executed when the princess's head was bounced on a pike outside her prison window. Her son had been torn away from her. Now she sat trapped in a prison cell with riff-raff hurling invective at her, in the liberal style.

But the mob still saw Marie Antoinette as a threat to their "liberty." This is how liberals would treat Sarah Palin.

On October 13, Antoinette was informed that her trial before the Revolutionary Tribunal would begin the next day. Her written request for time to prepare was ignored. And so the trial of Marie Antoinette commenced on October 14, 1793, before a jury of eleven men, chosen from the lowest classes.

To the delight of the spectators, Antoinette was accused of presiding over plots, conspiracies, and "midnight orgies," and of being the "scourge and the blood-sucker of the French."[37] In the words of Scottish historian Thomas Carlyle, the witnesses against her were "Patriot Washerwomen," with "much to say of Plots [and] Treasons."[38]

Antoinette answered each accusation with politeness, calmly revealing the emptiness of the charges against her. As Carlyle reports, "Her answers are prompt, clear, often of laconic brevity; resolution, which has grown contemptuous without ceasing to be dignified, veils itself in calm words. 'You persist then in denial?'—'My plan is not denial: it is the truth I have said, and I persist in that.' "[39] Among the charges was the accusation by Hébert that she kept a religious book containing a "counterrevolutionary" image of Jesus inscribed with the words "Heart of Jesus! Have pity on us!"[40]

Then came Hébert's monstrous allegation that Antoinette's son had accused his mother and aunt of having sex with him—an idea Hébert had himself implanted in the boy through his vile underling, Simone. Hébert testified:

> Simone said to me, "I am surprised at young Capet committing so many indecencies"—(too gross to mention). Astonished at seeing this child so initiated in wickedness, I asked him who were his instructors. He replied, with all the ingenuousness and candour of his age, that he had learnt all these abominations of his mother and aunt. I shall not offend your ears with recounting the impurities which this child related; I shall content myself with saying, that he has had an incestuous intercourse with his mother and his aunt and that young Capet has been ill of a disorder which was brought on by these debaucheries.[41]

Antoinette ignored the vile accusation, until a juror demanded that she answer it. Antoinette famously replied, "I remain silent on that subject because nature holds all such crimes an abhorrence. I appeal to all mothers who are present in this Auditory—is such a crime possible?"[42]

According to Carlyle, at that moment, Robespierre cursed the stupidity of Hébert for making such a despicable charge and risking a sympathetic response from the jurors.[43] Robespierre underestimated the inhumanity of a mob. For having passionately denied the charge, one spectator complained of Antoinette's arrogance, another of her pride, while one of the jurors sneered, "A mother like you . . ."[44]

When Antoinette said nothing, the jury was enraged by her silence and demanded an answer. When she answered, denying the grotesque accusation, the jury denounced her as arrogant. It's almost as if the mob would accept no answer she gave. As Le Bon says, a crowd "accepts as real the images evoked in its mind, though they most often have only a very distant relation with the observed fact."[45]

The proceedings against Antoinette were irrelevant in any event. The verdict was preordained. After two days of the mock trial, Antoinette was declared guilty of treason and given a sentence of death scheduled for the next day. Asked if she had anything to say, Antoinette simply shook her head.

Hours before her execution, the former queen wrote a letter to her sister-in-law, Princess Elisabeth, stained with her tears. An excerpt gives the lie to portrayals of Antoinette as a frivolous airhead. She begins:

16TH OCTOBER, 4.30 A.M.
*It is to you, my sister, that I write for the last time. I have just been condemned, not to a shameful death, for such is only for criminals, but to go and rejoin your brother. Innocent like him, I hope to show the same firmness in my last moments. I am calm, as one is when one's conscience reproaches one with nothing.*

Antoinette raises the incest charge at her trial, asking Elisabeth to forgive her son:

*I have to speak to you of one thing which is very painful to my heart, I know how much pain the child must have caused you. Forgive him, my dear sister; think of his age, and how easy it is to make a child say whatever one wishes, especially when he does not understand it. It will come to pass one day, I hope, that he will better feel the value of your kindness and of your tender affection for both of [my children].*

She concludes by reaffirming her faith and forgiving her enemies:

*I die in the Catholic Apostolic and Roman religion, that of my fathers, that in which I was brought up, and which I have always professed. Having no spiritual consolation to look for, not even knowing whether there are still in this place any priests of that religion (and indeed the place where I am would expose them to too much danger if they were to enter it but once), I sincerely implore pardon of God for all the faults which I may have committed during my life. I trust that, in His goodness, He will mercifully accept my last prayers, as well as those which I have for a long time addressed to Him, to receive my soul into His mercy. I beg pardon of all whom I know, and especially of you, my sister, for all the vexations which, without intending it, I may have caused you. I pardon all my enemies the evils that they have done me. I bid farewell to my aunts and to all my brothers and sisters. I had friends. The idea of being forever separated from them and from all their troubles is one of the greatest sorrows that I suffer in dying. Let them at least know that to my latest moment I thought of them.*

*Farewell, my good and tender sister. May this letter reach you. Think always of me; I embrace you with all my heart, as I do my poor dear children. My God, how heart-rending it is to leave them forever! Farewell! farewell![46]*

The mob had intended to extinguish the idea of the divine right of kings and queens, but Marie Antoinette's preternatural grace in the face of their barbarism might have caused some Frenchmen to reconsider whether God had a role in choosing their queen.

The humiliations heaped on Antoinette continued to her last breath. To suppress sympathy from the crowd, she was stripped of her mourning clothes and ordered to wear a white smock. Bleeding badly,

Antoinette needed to change her undergarments before leaving for the guillotine, but the gendarme guarding her refused to let her out of his sight even for this.

To protect France against a beaten, half-starved, prematurely gray, tuberculosis-ridden, hemorrhaging widow, the full cavalry was called out and the streets and bridges throughout Paris were lined with cannon and bayonet-toting soldiers. Shackled to a rope held by the executioner and surrounded by armed guards, Antoinette rode to the guillotine on a rough cart used to transport hardened criminals. The drive was long and slow, the better to allow the mob to taunt her. Her face was placid, as she continued to pray quietly, showing neither fear nor defiance. On the scaffold, Marie Antoinette uttered her last words after accidentally stepping on the executioner's foot: "Monsieur, I beg your pardon."[47]

After the guillotine fell, the executioner lifted Antoinette's head from the basket and the crowd cheered, "Vive la Republique!"

Hébert, the revolutionary who had accused her of incest, said, "The whore, for the rest, was bold and impudent to the very end."[48] It's impossible to win with a mob. The queen was accused of frivolity, stupidity, licentiousness—every possible base quality. For exhibiting serenity in the face of a ravenous mob, she was deemed "impudent."

Hébert would later be executed himself, as was Antoinette's prosecutor, Antoine-Quentin Fouquier de Tinville. Both showed far less dignity in their final moments than Antoinette. Hébert fainted repeatedly on the way to the guillotine, and Fouquier-Tinville cried out, "I'm the axe, you don't kill the axe!"[49]

The killings went on, mercilessly, day after day, without reason. Saint-Just demanded that people be guillotined not just for being traitors but for being "indifferent as well."[50] (This roving indictment was unknowingly adopted by key Obama advisers William Ayers and Bernardine Dohrn in the SDS's anti-war pamphlet titled *The Opposite of Moral Is Indifferent.*)[51]

Politicians, unsuccessful generals, writers, nuns, the old, the young, the poor, and the well-to-do alike were sent to the national razor. Great scientists and mathematicians were sent to the guillotine, too, on the grounds that the republic "does not need scientists."[52]

Before the end of the year, the mayor of Paris was guillotined; 90 priests were drowned; and, in Dunkirk, 150 citizens guillotined. Entire families were guillotined. Girls overheard remarking that the killing was going overboard were sent to the guillotine.[53] When one of the accused explained to the Revolutionary Tribunal that they had confused him with his brother, he was ordered executed because "we've got him—we haven't got his brother." A woman proved to the court that she had been arrested in a case of mistaken identity, but was executed because "since she's already here we might as well execute her too."[54] In the first few months of 1794, more than 5,000 citizens of Lyon were executed.[55]

The revolutionaries began executing one another to avoid execution themselves. Consider the cases of Jacques Pierre Brissot, Camille Desmoulins, and Robespierre.

Brissot was a leading philosopher of the revolution—he had even been imprisoned by the king for his revolutionary writings. Although renowned for his incendiary speeches to the Jacobin Club, he belonged to the more moderate faction in the Convention, the Girondists—the Blue Dog Democrats of the day. He had opposed, for example, executing the king, voting to keep him under house arrest instead. For that counter-revolutionary vote, the Montagnards—the Nancy Pelosi Democrats—issued a warrant for his arrest on June 2, 1793. Brissot was promptly guillotined, at the age of thirty-nine.[56]

Brissot's principal accuser had been Desmoulins, a fellow writer and habitué of the Jacobin Club. Although Brissot had repeatedly leapt to the defense of Desmoulins and his crazed and often libelous writings, in 1793, Desmoulins turned his acid pen on his former mentor and friend. In a pamphlet titled *Jacques Pierre Brissot Unmasked,* Desmoulins accused Brissot of being a spy and enemy of the revolution, resulting in Brissot's beheading.[57]

Desmoulins's next tract, *Fragment of the Secret History of the Revolution,* had helped incite the Reign of Terror, but when he proposed a clemency committee for some of the accused, his high school classmate, Robespierre, denounced Desmoulins. Robespierre referred to Desmoulins and his associates as *"les indulgents"* and demanded that Desmoulins's newspaper be burned. Desmoulins was sentenced to death on April 5, 1794, and executed the very same day. He was thirty-four years old. A few days later, Desmoulins's wife was guillotined.

Robespierre was godfather to the Desmoulinses' son. Both Robespierre and Brissot had been witnesses at their wedding.[58]

To speed things along, on June 10, 1794, the Committee on Public Safety issued its infamous "22 Prairial" decree, which dispensed with even the pretense of a trial before execution. No longer would the accused be entitled to lawyers or be asked any questions—unless it was for the purpose of uncovering co-conspirators. Juries were instructed to decide cases on "moral proof," not "positive proof." Basically, an accusation was proof of guilt. And there was only one penalty: death.[59]

The prosecutor, Fouquier-Tinville, was delighted with these legal reforms, cheerfully reporting that heads were falling "like tiles."[60] (Soon, one of those heads would be his own.) Within the first two months after 22 Prairial, 1,500 people were guillotined. Having already run through the clergy and nobility, by now, most of the executed were peasants.[61]

Robespierre's own execution was prompted by a rumor planted by Joseph Fouché. Fouché knew Robespierre was about to condemn him as an enemy to the revolution, so he told all the other members of the Convention that they were on Robespierre's list. When Robespierre began to give his speech, denouncing traitors and calling for the arrest of "all conspirators," the entire Convention rose up to demand Robespierre's execution before he could mention any names. And that is how the worm Fouché survived to serve Napoleon.[62]

Robespierre had counted on the mob to save him. His allies at the Jacobin Club were so devoted to him, they vowed to drink hemlock should he be condemned to die.[63] But when the time for action came and Robespierre needed the mob to rally and prevent his arrest, it rained. The rabble ran indoors and drank spirits instead of hemlock, inspiring Tallyrand's remark "Rain is counterrevolutionary."[64]

Robespierre, Saint-Just, and the rest of the leaders of the Reign of Terror were cornered and captured at City Hall. By virtue of the speedy procedures of 22 Prairial, they were sent to the guillotine the next day, July 28, 1794. At Robespierre's execution, the mob was cursing him as if he were an Austrian queen. That was the end of the Reign of Terror, the Jacobin Club, and the French "Republic."

But it wasn't the end of the French Revolution, whose influence would spread around the globe, inspiring catastrophes from Russia and Germany to China and Venezuela. Though it was the inverse of the American Revolution, the ideas of the French Revolution would even take hold in some quarters of America.

# EIGHT

# THE AMERICAN REVOLUTION:
# HOW TO THROW A REVOLUTION WITHOUT LOSING YOUR HEAD

**O**ur history is the exact opposite of the French Revolution and their wretched masses guillotining the aristocracy and clergy. It has become fashionable to equate the two revolutions, but they share absolutely nothing beyond the word "revolution." The American Revolution was a movement based on ideas, painstakingly argued by serious men in the process of creating what would become the freest, most prosperous nation in world history.

The French Revolution was a revolt of the mob. It was the primogenitor of the horrors of the Bolshevik Revolution, Hitler's Nazi Party, Mao's Cultural Revolution, Pol Pot's slaughter, and America's periodic mob uprisings, from Shays' Rebellion to today's dirty waifs smashing Starbucks windows whenever bankers come to town. The French Revolution is the godless antithesis to the founding of America.

And yet the *New York Times* has written, "In this millennium, documents like the Magna Carta of 1215, the English Bill of Rights of 1689, the French Declaration of the Rights of Man and of the Citizen of 1789, and the American Constitution of 1787 and the Bill of Rights of 1791 advanced the universality of human rights."[1] This is on the order of saying, "In this millennium, things like mosquitoes, moths, and DDT advanced the universality of bugs." Why not throw in the Soviet constitution or Mao's *Little Red Book*?

One small difference is that the Americans and the English did win freedom and greater individual rights with their documents. France's Declaration of the Rights of Man and of the Citizen led to bestial savagery, followed by Napoleon's dictatorship, followed by another monarchy, and then finally something resembling an actual republic eighty years later.

In another editorial, the *Times* claimed that France had "helped launch the worldwide democracy movement with its 1789 Revolution against monarchy and feudal privilege," claiming the Declaration of the Rights of Man and of the Citizen "inspired democrats throughout the late-18th-century world and reinforced the ideas of America's own, earlier revolution."[2] The only movements inspired by the French Revolution were those of other dictators who discovered they could slaughter without mercy, provided they claimed to be acting in the name of the people.

Both revolutions are said to have come from the ideas of Enlightenment thinkers, the French Revolution informed by the writings of Jean-Jacques Rousseau and the American Revolution influenced by the writings of John Locke. This is like saying Presidents Reagan and Obama both drew on the ideas of twentieth-century economists—Reagan on the writings of Milton Friedman and Obama on the writings of Paul Krugman.

Locke was concerned with private property rights. His idea was that the government should allow men to protect their property in courts of law—as Supreme Court Justice Thurgood Marshall realized—rather than have each man be his own judge. Rousseau saw the government as the vessel to implement the "general will" and thereby create men who were more moral. Through the limitless power of the state, the government would "force men to be free."

The theories of the French revolutionaries, as summarized by historian Roger Hancock, were founded on "respect for no humanity except that which they proposed to create. In order to liberate mankind from tradition, the revolutionaries were ready to make him altogether the creature of a new society, to reconstruct his very humanity to meet the demands of the general will."[3]

Contrary to the purblind assertions of liberals, who dearly wish our founding fathers were more like the godless French peasants, skipping around with human heads on pikes, our founding fathers were God-fearing descendants of Puritans and other colonial Christians. As Stephen Waldman writes in his definitive book on the subject, *Founding Faith*, the American Revolution was "powerfully shaped by the Great Awakening," an evangelical revival in the colonies in the early 1700s, led by the famous Puritan theologian Jonathan Edwards, among others. Aaron Burr, the third vice president of the United States, was Edwards's grandson. The churches were so integral to the philosophy behind the revolution that there are books of Christian sermons on the American Revolution. In fact, it was the very irreligiousness of the French Revolution that appalled the Americans and British alike, even before the bloodletting began.

Americans celebrate the Fourth of July, the date our written demand for independence from Britain based on "Nature's God" was released to the world. The French celebrate Bastille Day, a day when thousands of armed Parisians stormed a nearly empty prison, savagely murdered a half-dozen guards, defaced their corpses, and stuck heads on pikes, all in order to seize arms and gunpowder for more such tumults. It would be as if this country had a national holiday to celebrate the L.A. riots.

Among the most famous quotes from the American Revolution is Patrick Henry's "Give me liberty or give me death!"

Among the most famous slogans of the French Revolution is that of the Jacobin Club, "Fraternity or death," recast by Nicolas-Sébastien de Chamfort, a Jacobin who turned against the revolution, as "Be my brother or I'll kill you."

Our revolutionary symbol is the Liberty Bell, first rung to herald the opening of the new Continental Congress in the wake of the Battle of Lexington and Concord, and rung again to summon the citizens of Philadelphia to a public reading of the just-adopted Declaration of Independence.

The symbol of the French Revolution is the "national razor"—the guillotine.

Of the fifty-six signers of the Declaration of Independence, all died of natural causes in old age, with the exception of Button Gwinnett of Georgia, who was shot in a duel with a fellow officer during the Revolutionary War, though unrelated to the revolution.

Exactly fifty years after the Declaration of Independence was signed, on July 4, 1826, both Thomas Jefferson and John Adams died in their homes at age eighty-three and ninety, respectively. Apart from Gwinnett, only one of our founding fathers died of unnatural causes—Alexander Hamilton. He died in a duel with Aaron Burr because as a Christian, Hamilton deemed it a greater sin to kill another man than to be killed and, before the duel, in writing, vowed not to shoot Burr. President after president of the new American republic died peacefully at home for seventy-five years, right up until Abraham Lincoln was assassinated in 1865.

Meanwhile, the leaders of the French Revolution all died violently a few years after the revolution began, guillotine by guillotine.

The most moblike incident associated with the American Revolution was the Boston Tea Party. With no beheadings, disembowelings, or defilement of corpses—or any corpses at all—the Tea Party wouldn't even merit a passing mention in a history of the French Revolution. It was debated for hours, was carefully planned to avoid damaging any property other than the tea, and was specifically defended for not being the act of a mob. The only event less violent than the original Boston Tea Party is a modern-day Tea Party rally.

Moreover, unlike the French before the storming of the Bastille or Americans today, the rebels had no other ability to influence British policies. In that sense, they were in the position of pro-lifers in modern America with no options for affecting the law except violence.

Forget the cheerful retelling of the Boston Tea Party in children's books: That event had little to do with the success of the American Revolution. Coming three long years before the Declaration of Independence, the Boston Tea Party instigated nothing, other than repressive measures by the British Parliament in closing the Boston port and putting the entire town under martial law.

The Boston Tea Party was considered an embarrassment by many of our founding fathers and was not celebrated at all for another half century. Benjamin Franklin insisted that the tea be paid for, and a collection was taken up and offered to the India Tea Company. George Washington disapproved of the Boston Tea Party, making a point of saying "not that we approve their conduct in destroying the Tea" even when complaining of Britain's retaliatory actions in response to the Tea Party.[4]

America's friends in the British Parliament, such as Edmund Burke, were appalled by the Tea Party, unable to keep defending the Americans after this destruction of private property. Only when the Americans promised to repay the tea company for the ruined tea were America's British partisans able to take up the rebels' cause again.

The reason most of our founding fathers opposed the Boston Tea Party was that it seemed to be the act of a rabble. Interestingly, even Samuel Adams, who is believed to be an instigator of the Tea Party, immediately defended the raid by arguing that it was not the action of a mob but a reasoned protest when all other avenues of redress had failed. Paul Revere, who participated in the Tea Party, made sure to replace a broken lock on one of the ships and severely punished a participant who stole some of the tea for his private use.[5] Though they destroyed the tea, the rebels fervently believed in otherwise following the law, much like the overwhelmingly law-abiding abortion clinic protesters today.

John Adams, Samuel's second cousin, privately approved of the Tea Party, exalting in a letter, "The die is cast! The people have passed the river and cut away the bridge!" But even he stressed how calm and orderly the town of Boston was immediately following the Tea Party.[6]

Just a few years earlier, in 1770, John Adams had famously defended the British soldiers who shot and killed Americans in what came to be called the Boston Massacre, and Paul Revere testified for the defense.[7] Five Americans died in the incident, but Adams argued to the jury that the Redcoats were justified in firing because they had been attacked by a mob.

Although Adams blamed Britain's policy of quartering soldiers for provoking the citizens of Boston, he blamed the mob for instigating the violent altercation.

In his closing argument, Adams portrayed the crowd as a howling "rabble" that shouted, "Kill them! Kill them!" and threw "every species of rubbish" at the soldiers: "We have entertained a great variety of phrases to avoid calling this sort of people a mob. Some call them shavers, some call them geniuses. The plain English is, gentlemen, [it was] most probably a motley rabble of saucy boys, Negroes and mulattoes, Irish teagues and outlandish jacktars. And why should we scruple to call such a people a mob, I can't conceive, unless the name is too respectable for them."

The American jury acquitted the British officer involved, as well as six of his eight soldiers. After the verdict, there was no rioting or looting; all was calm. Respect for Adams increased, and he would later say that his defense of the British soldiers for firing on the mob was "one of the best pieces of service I ever rendered my country."[8]

This country's founders were strongly against the mob—as are today's Tea Party patriots. Noticeably, modern Tea Partiers haven't engaged in one iota of property destruction, in contradistinction to nearly any gathering of liberals. Violence and property destruction are specialties of the Left. As the *New Yorker* reported, a twenty-six-year-old Tea Partier from the Massachusetts Institute of Technology thought about printing out a copy of the entire 2,000-page 2010 health care bill and throwing it in Boston harbor, but changed his mind when he found out it would be against the law.[9]

That's why—until recently—it has been liberals pushing the Boston Tea Party as a crucial event in the American Revolution, while conservatives have preferred to celebrate the signing of the Declaration of Independence and the bicentennial of the Constitution. Liberals hate the idea of a revolution by gentlemen, which is why they celebrate hairy, foul-smelling revolutionaries like Che Guevara, Fidel Castro, and Susan Sarandon. They want to elevate the rabble and place the spectacularly unique American Revolution in the tradition of France's mob revolt.

Thus, for example, Russell Bourne, a regular guest on NPR and PBS, has written a sad little book titled *Cradle of Violence: How the Boston Waterfront Mobs Ignited the American Revolution*. More accurately, the waterfront mobs nearly derailed the revolution.

Fear of mobs was a primary rationale of the Loyalists. Even those wishing independence from Britain worried that without British protection, the hoodlums might run wild. As the left-wing historian Howard

Zinn admits, the "well-to-do merchants" of the Sons of Liberty "worried about maintaining control over the crowds at home."[10]

Consider the case of Lord Hugh Percy. He had been a fervent supporter of the Americans, taking their side repeatedly in the British Parliament, including voting against the hated Stamp Act. When he arrived in Boston as a brigadier general of the British army in 1774, Percy was a strong advocate of American independence. But he took one look at the Boston waterfront and changed his mind, so "shocked" was he "by the mobbings he witnessed."[11]

This is why, today, we know Patrick Henry's name. We know Paul Revere's name. We know the names of John Hancock, Thomas Jefferson, and of all the other signatories to the Declaration of Independence. We know the names of the authors of *The Federalist*. We know the name of pamphleteer Thomas Paine. We don't know the names of the lowborn workers at the Boston Harbor engaging in tumult and property destruction. (Other than by the general catchall term "Celtics fans.")

The men behind the American Revolution—the militias, the Minutemen, and the signers of the Declaration of Independence, as well as the framers of the Constitution—were the very opposite of a mob. Today we would call them "Republicans." They were educated, aristocratic property holders, doctors, lawyers, ministers, and other respectable tradesmen with everything to lose should the revolution fail.

The Minutemen were called that because they could be ready for battle in a minute, having been preparing for years to launch a disciplined military response. They were not a rabid mob, full of festering hatreds, ready to dash out and impale their fellow citizens. (And virtually none of these brave men under arms, I might add, were dating one another.) They were a citizen army with ranks, subordination, coordination, drills, and supplies.

The spark that ignited the first battles of the Revolution was the news that British troops—who were under constant surveillance by Paul Revere and others—were on the move, planning to arrest Sam Adams and John Hancock that night in Lexington.

Luckily, the Minutemen had planned ahead and were not lunatics running around in a burst of manic energy guillotining people, like the

French. Because the Minutemen had been watching and waiting, they knew exactly what the British were up to. Indeed, Paul Revere knew more about the Redcoats' plans that night than the British soldiers themselves did.

Although most Whig leaders had fled Boston to avoid arrest, a few remained, including Doctor Joseph Warren. Through his confidential source—probably the American wife of British general Thomas Gage—Warren confirmed the British plans to arrest the two revolutionary leaders. By prearrangement, Warren contacted Paul Revere.[12]

Warren had already sent two other messengers to warn Adams and Hancock. One was William Dawes; the other is unknown to history. All three men took different routes to Lexington in order to increase the odds that at least one of them would make it. (Why? Yes, that is correct: because they had planned ahead.)

Fearing that none of them would make it past the British across the Charles River out of Boston, Revere had arranged with the sexton of a Boston church to signal the countryside with lanterns in the steeple window. The British were going by sea, so the sexton sneaked past the British regulars in Boston, climbed the 154 steps of the Anglican Christ Church—whose minister was a Loyalist—and held two lanterns outside the steeple window. The Charlestown Whigs, waiting and watching, saw the brief flicker of two lights in the distance and knew the British were leaving by boat. They sprang to action, preparing to receive Revere and provide him with a horse.[13]

It is precisely this advance preparation that is celebrated in Henry Wadsworth Longfellow's poem: "One if by land, and two if by sea."[14] By contrast, the French Revolutionary ditty "It Shall Be" includes the line "Take the aristocrats to the lantern and hang them."

Every detail of Paul Revere's ride had been meticulously arranged with scores of other American patriots. Even the horse Revere rode, Brown Beauty, had been carefully chosen by the Whigs as the best horse for the job. And indeed, Brown Beauty was so sure-footed, she allowed Revere to escape his first British ambush that night.

Revere alerted Whig leaders in towns all along his ride, setting off a chain of communication to the Minutemen throughout the countryside. The town leaders—doctors, lawyers, and ministers—spread the alarm with bells, drums, cannon, and musket fire. "The astonishing speed of this communication," historian David Hackett Fischer writes, "did not occur by accident. It was the result of careful preparation."[15]

At around midnight, Revere arrived at the house where Adams and Hancock were staying and was promptly rebuffed by the Lexington militiaman standing guard, who told Revere to stop making so much noise or he'd wake up everyone. "Noise?" Revere replied. "You'll have noise enough before long! The Regulars are coming!"[16]

With Adams and Hancock awake, and Dawes arriving half an hour later, the men went to a tavern to talk things over with the Lexington militia. (The third man, whoever he was, never arrived.) Wondering why the British were mobilizing so many troops for a simple arrest, they soon realized the British were planning to seize the Americans' artillery in Concord that night, too.

Once again, Revere and Dawes mounted their horses and took off for Concord, planning to wake up the surrounding towns. They immediately ran into a young, wealthy doctor from Concord, Samuel Prescott. A "high son of liberty," Prescott offered to ride with them, since he knew the terrain and he knew the people.[17]

Halfway to Concord, they ran into some Redcoats. Outnumbered, they insanely tried to bolt past the Regulars. The British didn't shoot, but didn't let Revere's group pass either, shouting, "God damn you! Stop! If you go an inch further, you are a dead man!"[18]

They were taken prisoner and brought to join other American prisoners captured that night. While being led off the path, Prescott and Revere spurred their horses, taking off in different directions. Revere's route took him straight into a group of Redcoats, but by distracting their captors, he allowed Prescott to escape—across a wall and into the backwoods he knew so well. As Revere had done before him, Prescott would set off a chain of warnings to the militias in the towns all around Concord.

As the Redcoats surrounded Revere, Dawes escaped, pretending to be one of the Regulars in pursuit of a fleeing rebel—"Halloo, my boys I've got two of 'em!"[19] He got away, but his horse soon threw him and his journey was over.

Both the Redcoats and their famous prisoner were remarkably polite to each other, with Revere later recalling that the British officer in command was "much of a gentleman." Surprised to have captured the well-known rebel leader Paul Revere, the British began interrogating him and were stunned by his candor.

Revere openly told them about British plans that night—of which they were unaware. Hoping to keep them away from Hancock and Adams, he warned the British soldiers that they would be killed if they went anywhere near Lexington Green, where up to five hundred militiamen were mobilizing. The other prisoners listening to Revere were astonished at how boldly he spoke to his captors. When one captain put a gun to Revere's head and demanded that he tell the truth, an indignant Revere said he didn't need to be threatened. "I call myself a man of truth," he said, "and you have stopped me on the highway, and made me a prisoner I knew not by what right. I will tell the truth for I am not afraid."[20]

The rattled Redcoats began to ride their prisoners toward Lexington, but when they heard gunfire on the outskirts of town, seeming to confirm Revere's warnings of an armed militia, they released their prisoners and hurried back to Boston.[21] They weren't going to start a war without clearer orders.

Hancock and Adams were safe, the rebels' military supplies hidden, and the British about to be amazed.[22]

The face-off in Lexington would not have given Americans much hope that day. British troops blew past the disorganized and outnumbered militia without much difficulty.

But Concord was a different story. By the time the British reached Concord, militias from dozens of towns had received the call and were ready for battle. The Americans punched back so hard that the British retreated all the way back to Boston. The British fought bravely, but the Americans overwhelmed them.

Shell-shocked and bleeding, Redcoats began surrendering on the trek back to Boston. An old American woman picking weeds accepted the surrender of six British soldiers that day, telling them, "If you ever live to get back, you tell King George that an old woman took six of his grenadiers prisoner."[23] (That woman, of course, was TV's Betty White.) About a hundred British were killed in the Battle of Concord, many of them officers, and another hundred were wounded. Only fifty Americans were killed and thirty-nine wounded.

Having seen the Minutemen fight, even Lord Percy, who had been disgusted by the Boston mobs, had a new view of the rebels. He said they had attacked "with perseverance and resolution," adding "Whoever looks upon them as an irregular mob, will find himself very much mistaken."[24]

If the American rebels had not planned every detail in advance—practicing, training, mapping strategies, gathering information, preparing a vast network of patriots to spread the warning, and employing endless contingency plans—the British might have crushed the incipient rebel forces on April 19, 1775. Instead, victory belonged to the Americans in the first battle of the Revolutionary War. Paul Revere's ride is the seminal event of our Revolutionary War. It bears no resemblance to screeching washerwomen beheading guards at the Bastille.

The American Revolution was unique not only for the strategy and planning involved, but also for the explosion of literature explaining the reasons for the Revolution. Perhaps foremost among the pamphlets defending the war was Thomas Paine's *Common Sense,* in which Paine methodically addressed each of the arguments against rebellion, point by point, for all to see and critique.

In addition to Paine's *Common Sense,* there are virtual encyclopedias of erudite, Christian sermons given on behalf of the American Revolution. Christian ministers were a crucial part of the war effort, inspiring the local militias. Before the battle of Concord, the town's minister, William Emerson, urged on the outnumbered rebels as the Redcoats approached, saying, "Let us stand our ground. If we die, let us die here!" He slapped one terrified young soldier on the back and said, "Stand your ground, Harry! Your cause is just and God will bless you!" Harry fought bravely for the rest of the day.[25]

This was a revolution waged by thinkers and debaters constantly prattling about the reasons for the war. Although they were "rebels," the Americans were very chatty about their revolution. By contrast, mob uprisings like the French Revolution are sparked by tumult, pandemonium, and violence, not thoughtful sermons and pamphlets.

There wasn't much literature explaining the French Revolution—apart from Paine's hapless attempts (which would nearly lead to his beheading). The revolutionaries were too busy rushing out to desecrate Notre Dame, murder a priest, or do some other new wild thing to have the time to read or think. Bernardine Dohrn and the rest of the SDS would have fit right in with the filthy Jacobins, without even having to change clothes.

In contrast to the French, who celebrate the spontaneous emotion of their revolution—the storming of the Bastille, the storming of Versailles, the storming of the Tuileries—Americans celebrate the Minutemen's preparedness, Paul Revere's methodically planned ride, and the vast literature arguing America's case, especially the specific demand for separation from the British in the Declaration of Independence.

The reason our revolution was the opposite of a directionless, violent mob running wild in the streets is that the dominant American culture was Anglo-Saxon and Christian. Even while fighting "the British," as we now call them, Americans considered themselves British with the rights of Englishmen, who bore the tradition of the Magna Carta. In fact, one rebel explained that he was fighting the Redcoats to protect his house by saying, "An Englishman's home is his castle."[26]

They just wanted to be free of meddling from the Crown. Having been born and raised in the distant and expansive American colonies, Americans objected to the high-handed way King George was dealing with them. They didn't hate the king—to the contrary, John Adams and Alexander Hamilton dispassionately acknowledged that the English political system was better than most others in the world.

Our revolutionary document, the Declaration of Independence, is a religious document through and through, with the colonies demanding rights entitled to them by "the Laws of Nature and of Nature's God." As founding father James Wilson put it, the "will of God" was the supreme law of nations.[27]

Consequently, the Declaration cites "certain unalienable rights" given to men "by their Creator." For the "rectitude" of their intentions, the drafters appealed to "the Supreme Judge of the world." The Declaration reads like a legal brief, with causes of action and prior attempts at resolution enumerated, and a specific demand for relief: *We'd like to go our own way please, Supreme Judge of the World.* One can read the Declaration of Independence centuries later and understand the whole point.

Admitting that "Governments long established should not be changed for light and transient causes," our Declaration sets forth "a long train of abuses and usurpations" by the Crown. The purpose of the document was to explain America's case to the world, because "a decent respect to the opinions of mankind requires that they should declare the causes which impel them to the separation." Manifestly, the French couldn't care less that the rest of the world was appalled by them.

Stating that facts "submitted to a candid world" would prove that the king was attempting to create "an absolute Tyranny over these States," the Declaration concisely listed abuse after abuse, including the Crown's quartering soldiers, protecting the king's soldiers from charges of murder, and depriving Americans "in many cases" of trial by jury. These were rights well familiar to the British, inasmuch as they came from English common law and were enjoyed by British citizens.

Significantly, among the Declaration's enumerated grievances was that the king had encouraged mobs. As the document puts it, the king had "excited domestic insurrections amongst us," including uprisings by "merciless Indian Savages" whose idea of warfare was "an undistinguished destruction of all ages, sexes and conditions."

The Americans' complaints were clear, as was their objective: separation from the British Crown in order to establish their own government. This was not a rash decision. As the authors explained, they had tried other approaches: "In every stage of these Oppressions We have Petitioned for Redress in the most humble terms," but those requests were "answered only by repeated injury."

Fifty-two of the fifty-six signers of the American Declaration were orthodox Christians who believed in the Father, Son, and Holy Ghost, or as they would be known today, "an extremist Fundamentalist hate group."[28]

The Declaration was written on behalf of the thirteen colonies unanimously and signed by each member of the Continental Congress, name by name, beginning with the famously supersized signature of John Hancock. These weren't anonymous brutes chopping off the breasts of princesses in pursuit of "fraternity" or some other amorphous concept.

Our revolutionary document was inspired by God—as put by John Adams, a signatory and second president of the United States. He said,

"The general principles on which the fathers achieved independence were the general principles of Christianity. I will avow that I then believed, and now believe, that those general principles of Christianity are as eternal and immutable as the existence and attributes of God."[29]

The French Declaration of the Rights of Man and of the Citizen was inspired by a paranoid hypochondriac who denied divine revelation and original sin: Jean-Jacques Rousseau.

The very logic and clarity of the Declaration of Independence were qualities specifically rejected by Rousseau. "One of the errors of our age," Rousseau said, "is to use reason in bare form, as if men were only mind." Yes, much better to fire up a crowd with emotional appeals. Thus, Rousseau recommended using "signs that speak to the imagination," complaining that words make too weak an impression. "[O]ne speaks to the heart far better," he said, "through the eyes than through the ears."[30]

This is the essence of how one riles up a mob—by using images, not words. (Republicans drove the car into a ditch.) Rousseau perfectly describes the governing strategy of all mob leaders, from Robespierre to Fidel Castro to today's Democratic Party.

The mob's revolutionary document, France's Declaration of the Rights of Man and of the Citizen, is precisely what one would expect from people who prefer images to logic. The document enumerates lots of abstract principles without ever coming to what used to be known as "a point." It doesn't assert any God-given rights, but merely announces that the Declaration is being issued "in the presence and under the auspices of the Supreme Being."

Not surprisingly, Thomas Jefferson is said to have had a hand in it, but this time, without the sobering influence of John Adams and the rest of the Continental Congress's drafting committee. (The committee deleted nearly 500 of Jefferson's words, made dozens of other changes, and added numerous references to God.)[31]

The coming bloodshed in France should have been obvious from the title, Declaration of the Rights of Man *and of the Citizen*. In other words, the document addressed your natural rights as an individual . . . *and your duties to the government*.

From the very first sentence, the Declaration of the Rights of Man swerves off the rails from the ideas of the Declaration of Independence by stating that "the sole causes of public miseries and the corruption of governments" are "ignorance, forgetfulness, or contempt of the rights of man."

You could ask every signatory to the Declaration of Independence—indeed, you could probably poll every colonial American—and not one would have said the problem with King George was that the rights of man had slipped his mind. Rather, our founding fathers believed—as Madison wrote in *Federalist 10*—that men are more likely to oppress another than to "co-operate for their common good." In particular, he said the power to tax created the greatest temptation to "trample on the rules of justice," because increasing someone else's taxes "is a shilling saved to their own pockets."[32]

According to the French, King George was disregarding the rights of man. But according to Madison, he was merely following "the nature of man."

That's why, in our Declaration, the founding fathers cited the only authority even higher than a king. The French reeled off a series of airy "rights" that could as easily have been any other random collection of rights. A sensible reader of the French Declaration might ask, Says who?

The only demand in the Declaration of the Rights of Man and of the Citizen, which is really more of a suggestion, is that "members of the social body" compare executive and legislative acts to the principles stated in the Declaration. Or not. Whatever.

The National Assembly that drafted the French Declaration never says what it wants changed exactly, except by implication. There are, for example, assertions that all citizens should be treated equally, suggesting that they were not already being treated equally, and the demand that no one "be accused, arrested, nor detained but in the cases determined by the law," suggesting that some men had been accused, arrested, or detained outside of the law. But who, when, or how—or what the Assembly had done about it—is left to conjecture.

The Declaration of the Rights of Man and of the Citizen announces a slew of abstract "rights" of the sort we have come to associate with all bloodthirsty dictatorships. For example, the Declaration proclaims:

"Liberty consists of doing anything which does not harm others."

"Law can only prohibit such actions as are hurtful to society."

"No one may be questioned about his opinions, including his religious views, provided that their manifestation does not trouble the public order established by the law."

"[A] common contribution is indispensable; it must be equally distributed between all the citizens, by reason of their ability to pay."

This mishmash of English natural rights doctrine and Rousseauian argle-bargle was ignored ten minutes later, when the Assembly voted to confiscate church lands, decreed that the pope's authority was null and void throughout France, and demanded that all priests take an oath to the state-controlled civil constitution of the clergy.

As a tribute to its success, just three days after the completion of the Declaration of the Rights of Man and of the Citizen, the mob stormed the Bastille.

Practically overnight, the greatest nation in continental Europe became a human abattoir. That is why the French Revolution remains an inspiration to liberals everywhere. France's revolution-by-mob would be imitated in Germany, Russia, China, Vietnam, Cambodia, North Korea, Cuba, Venezuela, and elsewhere, always with the same bloody consequences. With less success—so far—mob action is the governing strategy of our own Democratic Party.

This is why the British philosopher Edmund Burke—who had been a staunch supporter of the American Revolution—denounced the French Revolution even before the guillotining began. Presciently, Burke wrote in 1789 that the "old Parisian ferocity has broken out in a shocking manner. It is true this may be no more than a sudden explosion. . . . But if it should be character rather than accident, then that people are not fit for Liberty, and must have a Strong hand like that of their former masters to coerce them."[33]

Similarly, Americans didn't recognize the French Revolution as bearing any relationship to their own revolution against a king.

Consider the fate of the French hero of the American Revolution, the Marquis de Lafayette. The wealthy and titled Lafayette came to

America to fight for independence, serving with distinction under General George Washington. Lafayette was so important to the American cause that dozens of U.S. cities, towns, parks, and streets across the nation are named after him. When he was buried in Paris, dirt carried from Bunker Hill was sprinkled on his coffin, and an American flag has flown at his grave ever since.

Lafayette began as a supporter of the French Revolution, foolishly imagining that it would proceed along the lines of the American Revolution. In the summer of 1789, he joined the National Assembly, the populist outgrowth from the class-based Estates General. It was Lafayette, the National Assembly's vice president, who presented the soon-to-be-ignored Declaration on the Rights of Man and of the Citizen to the Assembly.

But for the next three years, Lafayette commanded the French National Guard in a losing battle against the lunatic Jacobin mobs. In the summer of 1792, he was declared a "traitor," subject to immediate execution, whereupon he fled France just ahead of the guillotine.

Apart from Lafayette, the only prominent supporter of the American Revolution to sign on with the mob revolt of the French was Thomas Paine, who was not born in America and perhaps never fully understood its philosophical underpinnings. (Even the French revolutionaries grasped this, refusing the request of an American delegation to release Paine from prison on the grounds that Paine was not an American but an Englishman.)[34] Paine hit his peak with the American Revolution, but got bored after the war was won, crossed the ocean to France, and leapt into the middle of a much less noble endeavor. He was a historical one-hit wonder, desperately trying to find that follow-up single that would put him back on top.

Paine justified the insanity of the French Revolution with the argument that all royalty was bad and therefore any alternative was better. When the French revolutionaries threw him in prison, Paine found out there were some political systems worse than a monarchy.

In so little esteem did Americans hold mob action, particularly the atheistic French mob, that when Thomas Paine returned from participating in the French Revolution, he was universally reviled, his name written on the bottom of people's shoes to indicate their disdain. Paine's only American defender was, of course, Thomas Jefferson, mob sympathizer and father of the Democratic Party.

The French Revolution was spontaneous, impulsive, passionate, emotional, romantic, utopian, resentful, angry, dreamy—anything but rule-bound and reasoned. No one knew, from one year to the next, where the Revolution was heading. That's why, at the end of it all, they enthusiastically threw themselves into the arms of the dictator Napoleon.

By contrast, Americans concluded their revolution with a Constitution, meaning we have agreed rules, baselines, and standards, as well as continuity, stability, and legal reasoning.

Indeed, it was a mob uprising after the Revolution, Shays' Rebellion, that propelled Americans to abandon the Articles of Confederation and create a strong national government capable of suppressing mobs. Shays' Rebellion was instigated by Daniel Shays and other poor farmers and debtors in Massachusetts, who couldn't pay the taxes being levied to pay for the war. They were a motley rabble, attacking debtors' courts and armories.

Not only aristocrats but "lowly farmers" as well were terrified by Shays' Rebellion and driven to support a national government that would have the power to protect their rights against the mob. In his introduction to the *Federalist Papers,* Isaac Kramnick cites an "obscure farmer," Jonathan Smith, arguing in favor of the Constitution purely as a response to Shays' Rebellion:

> People I say took up arms, and then, if you went to speak to them, you had the musket of death presented to your breast. They would rob you of your property; Threaten to burn your houses; oblige you to be on your guard day and night . . . poor persons were set in the front, to be killed by their own friends. How dreadful. How distressing was this. Our distress was so great that we should have been glad to snatch at anything that looked like a government. Had any person that was able to protect us, come up and set up his standard, we should all have flocked to it, even if it had been a monarch, and that monarch might have proved a tyrant. So that you see that anarchy leads to tyranny, and better have one tyrant than so many at once. But the new Constitution is our cure.[35]

The *Federalist Papers,* written by Alexander Hamilton, James Madison, and John Jay to make the case for a national Constitution, are brimming with warnings against mobs. In *Federalist 9,* Alexander Hamilton cites with contempt the "tempestuous waves of sedition and party rage" that periodically swept through Greece and Italy. Even in peaceful times, he said, one feels regret over the certainty that "the pleasing scenes before us are soon to be overwhelmed" with angry mobs.[36]

Hamilton assured Americans that their new Constitution would incorporate "wholly new discoveries" in the science of government able "to suppress faction and to guard the internal tranquility of States." He denounced the flimsy Articles of Confederacy precisely because they created "tumultuous commonwealths, the wretched nurseries of unceasing discord."[37] By creating "an assemblage of societies," the Constitution would calm the unruly crowds. Under the Constitution, should "a popular insurrection happen in one of the confederate states," Hamilton said, "the others are able to quell it."[38]

Clearly, the framers recognized how bad mobs were and created a government designed to squelch them. James Madison dedicated *Federalist 10* to explaining how the Constitution would cure the "dangerous vice" of factions, or what we might call "special interests." Democracies were threatened, he said, by groups of people "united and actuated by some common impulse of passion," opposed "to the rights of other citizens" or the "interests of the community." Madison complained of the propensity of democracies to become "spectacles of turbulence and contention," unable to safeguard either property rights or personal security.

Because democracies were generally unable to control mobs—or factions, as Madison called them—they have been "as short in their lives as they have been violent in their deaths." Pure democracy, even in the hands of "enlightened statesmen," was no good because, as Madison said in *Federalist 55,* even if every Athenian had been a Socrates, "the Athenian assembly would still have been a mob."[39]

According to Madison, there were only two methods "of curing the mischiefs of faction": Eliminate the causes or eliminate the effects. The principal advantage of a "well constructed union," he said, would be to control the effects of violent mobs by diffusing them and supplying "opposite and rival interests" to counteract one another.[40]

The French chose the other path: They resolved to remove the cause of faction by always exercising the "general will." There would be no disagreement because everyone would always agree. But as Madison said, to eliminate the cause of faction, one either had to extinguish liberty or require all citizens to have "the same opinions, the same passions, and the same interests." That, he said, was a cure "worse than the disease."[41]

Two years after Madison wrote those words, the French would embark on their program of eliminating factions by killing people. To fashion a republic of "virtue," they simply exterminated anyone who did not agree with "the general will." The only way to ensure unanimity of opinion was to kill those who disagreed. Then—just as Rousseau foresaw—obeying the general will was completely free, because people were simply obeying themselves. All it took was a few years of murder and terror to make man free!

The whole history of liberal thought, back to Marx and ultimately back to Rousseau, is that political authority rests on force—until the revolution gives us true and perfect freedom at the sharp edge of a guillotine. Our founders realized there is no "general will," and therefore were never required to slaughter citizens in order to create it.

If our revolution had been won by a mob, why would *The Federalist* keep saying how scary mobs are? Why would they jabber on and on about how the new Constitution would prevent mobs from arising? Wouldn't they celebrate mobs? Why didn't Americans cheer Shays' Rebellion, rather than using it as an argument to create an all-new form of government? Both during the Revolution and for the next two centuries, mobs in America were dealt with swiftly and without remorse.

We have had plenty of violence in America. But until fairly recently, mobs didn't drive events. One of the goriest episodes was the Civil War Draft Riots in New York City in 1863—perpetrated, of course, by Democrats. There was enough burning, pillaging, murdering, and corpse desecrating there to earn professional courtesy from a French mob.

In an explosion of animalistic violence, Irish Democrats, enraged by the Emancipation Proclamation, which they believed would force them to compete for jobs with blacks coming up from the South, ran through the city, lynching blacks and burning black establishments to the ground. As described in the book by Leslie M. Harris, *In the Shadow of Slavery: African Americans in New York City, 1626–1863*:

> On the waterfront, they hanged William Jones and then burned his body. White dock workers also beat and nearly drowned Charles Jackson, and they beat Jeremiah Robinson to death and threw his body in the river. Rioters also made a sport of mutilating the black men's bodies, sometimes sexually. A group of white men and boys mortally attacked black sailor William Williams—jumping on his chest, plunging a knife into him, smashing his body with stones—while a crowd of men, women, and children watched. None intervened, and when the mob was done with Williams, they cheered, pledging "vengeance on every nigger in New York." A white laborer, George Glass, rousted black coachman Abraham Franklin from his apartment and dragged him through the streets. A crowd gathered and hanged Franklin from a lamppost as they cheered for Jefferson Davis, the Confederate president. After the mob pulled Franklin's body from the lamppost, a sixteen-year-old Irish man, Patrick Butler, dragged the body through the streets by its genitals. Black men who tried to defend themselves fared no better. The crowds were pitiless. After James Costello shot at and fled from a white attacker, six white men beat, stomped, kicked, and stoned him before hanging him from a lamppost.[42]

So America has always had people capable of behaving horribly. We call them "Democrats." But the one-week riot had no effect on events.

President Lincoln sent the army from Gettysburg and restored order. The war continued. Even the draft continued. Even Irish service in the army continued.

One year after the Draft Riots, blacks and Republicans in New York City celebrated their alliance with an all-black regiment raised for the war. As the regiment marched through the streets, joined by members of the Union League Club and a hundred policemen, it was remarked upon how much more orderly and sharp the black regiment was, compared to some of the ragtag white regiments.

And then the South was finally crushed, slavery abolished, and

America marched on. The Draft Riots didn't even prevent Lincoln from carrying New York State in the next year's elections.

The first exception to Americans' abhorrence of mob action came in the sixties. The civil rights movement gave mobs a halo. Disgust with the Jim Crow laws overcame Americans' natural aversion to disorder. At the outset, the civil rights movement consisted of peaceful citizens battling mobs that were oppressing blacks—mobs that were, as always, led by Democrats. Orval Faubus, Bull Connor, George Wallace, and the Grand Wizard of the Ku Klux Klan—Democrats all.

But as soon as blacks started to vote in large enough numbers to matter, the whole Democratic Party switched sides. Unable to win elections by appealing to the racist mob, the anti–civil rights wing of the Democratic Party disappeared virtually overnight. In the blink of an eye, the Democrats went from being the Party of Bull Connor to being the Party of Al Sharpton. The Democrats simply traded one mob constituency for a new one. You might say they traded their white robes for a track suit and a giant medallion.

This is the history of the Democratic Party: Find out what the mob believes, then leap in front of the mob in order to lead it.

One man who didn't like mob action even on behalf of civil rights was Thurgood Marshall. A skilled lawyer, he was redeeming civil rights for blacks the American way—by bringing lawsuits, making arguments, and winning in court. Marshall was the anti-Rousseau, using words, not pictures, to get justice.

Martin Luther King Jr. was the heir to Rousseau. He used images in order to win publicity and goodwill for his cause, deploying children in the streets for a pointless, violent confrontation with a lame-duck lunatic: Theophilus Eugene "Bull" Connor.

Connor was a machine-politics, pro-union Democrat who had been elected to the Democratic National Committee from Alabama. He was also a vile racist, endorsed by Alabama's Democratic, segregationist governor, George Wallace. After witnessing Connor's brutal tactics to enforce segregation, the good citizens of Birmingham stepped in to remove him from his position as Commissioner of Public Safety. Birmingham's middle class, business leaders, and Jewish community weren't interested

in having beery KKK nightriders in their town. First, they voted to eliminate Connor's office; then—to be extra clear—they decisively voted
against Connor when he ran for mayor.

It was over—responsible citizens and civil rights advocates had won.
But Martin Luther King planned one last protest before Connor's term
expired. City merchants, including the black millionaire A. G. Gaston,
opposed King's protest on the grounds that Connor had already been
beaten at the ballot box. On the day of Connor's electoral defeat, Burke
Marshall, a champion of civil rights in Kennedy's Justice Department,
called King and asked him to call off the Birmingham protests.[43]

But King decided to deliberately provoke Connor, who was insane.
This was a way to extend the movement, just as, years later, King would
branch out from racial justice into "social justice."

With television crews crawling all over Birmingham, King arranged
for hundreds of black children to march on the city. As expected, this
led to a total conflagration when Connor turned fire hoses and police
dogs on little children, some as young as six years old. The explosive
images from this confrontation were instantly broadcast around the
world.

King had stoked this incredible fire to ignite his dying movement—
dying because civil rights had won in the courts, at the ballot box, and in
the hearts and minds of Americans. But King and the Southern Christian
Leadership Conference's Wyatt Walker were "overjoyed" at the mayhem
they had caused. Walker gloated, "There never was any more skillful ma-
nipulation of the news media than there was in Birmingham."[44] Connor
was delighted, too—the protests helped him rally his dwindling racist
following.

The only people who weren't happy were the decent citizens of Birmingham, pro-integrationists in the Kennedy administration, and civil
rights lawyers. As businessman Gaston put it, King was "messing things
up just when we were getting a new start."[45]

Thurgood Marshall had always disdained King's methods, calling
him an "opportunist" and "first-rate rabble-rouser."[46] Indeed, when
asked about King's suggestion that street protests could help advance desegregation, Marshall replied that school desegregation was men's work

and should not be entrusted to children. King, he said, was "a boy on a man's errand."[47]

But it was too late. Americans had capitulated to the idea of the "good mob," and that opened the door to near-constant riots and protests for every group of citizens upset about a hangnail. The civil rights movement had made mobs respectable, to the great misfortune of the nation. In no time, liberals began engaging in what I believe Gandhi called "active resistance" every time they didn't get their way through legitimate legal processes.

Democrats have made out like bandits—this is their moment! They are skilled manipulators of the mob. It was Democrats who kowtowed to Southern racists, blocking the schoolhouse door and campaigning on "segregation forever!" It was Democrats who responded to the Black Power movement by demanding racial quotas and Kwanzaa celebrations in the public schools. (The Democratic Party has consistently favored racial discrimination, it just switched which race should be discriminated against.) It is Democrats who have adopted every crackpot "share the wealth" program from Huey Long to Jesse Jackson and Barack Obama. It was Democrats who instantly transformed themselves into the antiwar party in response to protests during the Vietnam War. It was Democrats who embraced the wacko Marxist cult leader Jim Jones, who got nine hundred of his followers to commit "revolutionary suicide" by drinking cyanide-laced grape Flavor Aid at the cult's "Jonestown" settlement in Guyana. It was the Democratic Party that welcomed former leaders of the SDS and the Weather Underground into their party. It was Democrats who turned themselves into the abortion-on-demand party to grab the feminist vote—with the Reverend Jesse Jackson going to sleep one night against abortion and waking up the next morning in favor of abortion and a viable Democratic Party candidate. It was Democrats who co-opted the labor union movement and then invented the absurdity of government "unions" providing them with a new guaranteed voting bloc.

By now, mob action has become so integral to the Left that it permeates every aspect of their political behavior. Don't like Bush? Burn him in effigy. Upset the Kyoto treaty wasn't signed by the United States? Throw rocks at cops. Don't like the international monetary system?

Smash a Starbucks window. A stripper claims she's been raped by rich frat boys? Bang pots and pans outside the athletes' home.

Republicans are baffled by mobs, opposed to disorder, but paralyzed with indecision about what to do. Meanwhile, Democrats are hurling bricks from the barricades. If Democrats knew who he was, they would admire Robespierrre. Liberals' history is not this country's history—theirs is the history of the mob.

# PART III:
# THE VIOLENT TENDENCIES OF THE LIBERAL

# NINE

# THE SIXTIES:
# THE MOB GOES TO
# COLLEGE

The closest this country has been to the violent mobs of the French Revolution was the upheaval of the anti-war protests and race riots of the late sixties—all led by liberals.

The beginning of the student insanity of the sixties is commonly marked by the June 1962 Port Huron Statement issued by the Students for a Democratic Society at the University of Michigan. Among the vaporous idiocies of this proclamation was the demand that work "should be educative, not stultifying; creative, not mechanical; self-directed, not manipulated, encouraging independence; a respect for others, a sense of dignity and a willingness to accept social responsibility."

So it was either the manifesto of the New Left or a cheap imitation of *Jonathan Livingston Seagull*. Written mostly by Tom Hayden, the manifesto pompously drones on about "the emptiness of life." This from a man who married Jane Fonda, whose most important career move was getting breast implants. But Hayden's nails-on-a-blackboard, Valley Girl gibberish was hailed as the voice of the new "Youth Culture."

In no time, a series of student riots erupted on college campuses based on rumors and hyperbole, following the French pattern. Students would create chaos and tumult, and then the college administrations would promptly capitulate to the student mobs and their incomprehensible causes. Nathan Glazer said that the student protests all came down to the argument that "any mob is right as against any administrator, legislature or policeman."[1]

The Berkeley "Free Speech" movement kicked off the campus riots in 1964. There were protests, sit-ins, even Joan Baez singing folk songs to demand "free speech." (Liberals supported free speech until they realized, years later, how bad speech is for them and began demanding hate crimes legislation, speech codes, and sexual harassment laws restricting speech.) After days of protests, the Berkeley faculty responded forcefully by passing a resolution calling for no discipline for the students.

Shockingly, this did not bring the protests to a screeching halt. Vagrants and professional protesters joined the party. Putting their love of speech on hold, the thugs firebombed buildings and hurled rocks at the police. Soon the free speech protests turned into rallies for cop-killer Huey Newton, even though murder wasn't exactly speech either.

Seeing how well total capitulation had worked in the past, college administrators tried it over and over again. A few years later, student and nonstudent protesters objected to a new dormitory building at Berkeley. They wanted a "People's Park" so they would have a nice place for more demonstrations. Students, homeless people, and recently paroled criminals occupied the university-owned property and violently attacked the police with rocks, bricks, and pipes. Protesters painted graffiti saying "Yanqui go home"—to demonstrate their solidarity with the Third World against "Amerikkka."

During one of the brick-throwing melees, a twenty-five-year-old nonstudent, James Rector, who had heard about the riots and come to join the fun, was on a roof above the clash heaving debris on the police. Rector was hit with police buckshot, from which he later died.

Governor Ronald Reagan ordered the National Guard to shut down the violent student protests throughout the state. He blamed Rector's death on "the first college administrator who said it was all right to break laws in the name of dissent."[2] Appalled by their first-ever glimpse of manly force, the Berkeley faculty and administration were soon demanding that Reagan call off the Guard. Hirsute counterculture girls gave the guardsmen LSD-laced juice and brownies, requiring some to be taken off duty. These were the "idealists" the faculty was protecting.

Eventually, the protesters prevailed when the college administrators refused the protection of the National Guard and surrendered to the students—as they had always planned to do. The "People's Park" was established and to this day remains a picturesque quadrant where criminals, drug dealers, and homeless people congregate.

This was the basic set piece for all the university protests of the sixties. The students would cook up some synthetic "cause" that seemed to link them to Third World people, and law enforcement would move in and restore order. Then college administrators would demand an immediate surrender to the drug-fueled protesters while heaping praise on them as the most idealistic and brilliant generation in all of human history. It was the perfect incubator for creating the Worst Generation.

Would the herd of individualists on college campuses in the sixties have been so brave without the approval of college administrators and the mainstream media? Why so violent at home but afraid to go to war?

Student radicals behaved like feral beasts not only because of the group dynamic of a crowd, but because they had no criticism. They never had a reason to pause, reflect, or repent because, between acts of violence, they were busy reading the press reports describing them as "idealists"—indeed, "the best informed, the most intelligent and the most idealistic this country has ever known," as the Cox Report on the student riots at Columbia University put it.[3] In a self-reinforcing circle, the mobs took their cues from the elites and the elites praised the "idealistic" mobs.

Far from rebelling, student radicals were perfectly in tune with authority figures in their lives, both at home and on campus. As political sociologist Seymour Martin Lipset pointed out, because of the "enormous growth in the number of liberal Jewish faculty" in the post–World War II years, American universities went from being mostly apolitical to places with strong liberal views.[4] The alleged radicalism of the students, Lipset says, was "approved by the community within which they operate."

The alleged radicals weren't even rebelling against their parents. Numerous studies at the time showed that left-wing students were

"largely the children of left-wing or liberal parents."[5] Weatherman Eleanor Raskin attended protests at Columbia University and the Pentagon with her mother, who was "as militant as protesters one-third her
age" and whose antics "seemed excessive, even unseemly."[6] The left-wing
congressman from Boulder, Colorado, Jared Schutz Polis, elected in
2008, has childhood memories of being brought to anti-war rallies by
his parents.[7]

To be sure, the conservative students tended to reflect the views of
their parents as much as the liberal students did. Also like the liberal
activists, politically involved conservatives had higher IQs than apolitical students.[8] The main difference between the conservative and
liberal activists, based on a comparison of SDS and YAF conventions,
was that the conservatives came from less wealthy families than the
liberals.[9]

In 1970, a violent student mob rampaged for three days at Kent
State University, smashing store windows, breaking into a jewelry store,
and starting street bonfires. The ROTC building at the university was
burned to the ground, as hundreds of students stood around cheering.
When the fire trucks arrived, the mob threw rocks at the firemen and
slashed the fire hose. The riot had been instigated by Terry Robbins, the
Weatherman leader who had sex with Bill Ayers and later blew himself
up while assembling a bomb intended for soldiers at Fort Dix.

Day after day, thousands of protesters ran wild, throwing beer bot-
tles, bricks, rocks, and smoke grenades at the police. Wielding baseball
bats, golf clubs, and foot-long pieces of steel wire, they screamed "Bring
the war home!" and "Death to pigs!" Even after the National Guard had
been called in, for days law enforcement responded with nothing more
than tear gas.

On May 4, National Guard officers were trying to disperse thousands of violent protesters in the middle of the campus. According to
the recent reporting of James Rosen,[10] the guardsmen were fired upon
first, leading twenty-nine guardsmen to shoot back at the protesters,
killing four students in thirteen seconds—Allison Krause, Jeffrey Miller,
Sandra Scheuer, and William Knox Schroeder.[11]

If Louis XVI had been that decisive, 600,000 Frenchmen might
not have had to die. As his grandfather, Louis XIV, had said: When

war is necessary, it is a "grave error to think that one can reach the same aims by weaker means." Though decried thoughout the land—and in a Neil Young song!—the shooting at Kent State soon put an end to the student riots.

Student radicals had never imagined anyone would fail to praise them, much less shoot at them. Taken in by the establishment, they were instantly commercialized, hailed as "idealists"—and then most of them headed off to law school and university jobs.

Consider the complete absorption of Weathermen member Kathy Boudin into the liberal elite of this country.

Truly psychotic radical behavior was the only thing Kathy Boudin had left to impress her father when she couldn't get into a top-notch law school. As described by Susan Braudy in her book *Family Circle: The Boudins and the Aristocracy of the Left,* poor Kathy had terrible board scores. First, she couldn't get into Oberlin, then she couldn't get into Yale Law.[12] She was terrified of "losing her place as [her father] Leonard's most cherished offspring."[13]

Her brother Michael, the Republican, had nearly perfect board scores and would go on to graduate magna cum laude from Harvard, attend Harvard Law School—where he was president of the *Law Review* back when it meant something—and work for the Reagan administration. Today, he is a federal appeals court judge, appointed by the first President Bush.

The only path Kathy had to impress her radical lawyer father was to be more insane than he. It wouldn't be easy. Boudin père was a member of a communist front group, the National Lawyers Guild, and had represented Fidel Castro and Soviet spies Judith Coplon and Alger Hiss, as well as Pentagon Papers leaker Daniel Ellsberg, among other left-wing celebrities. When passing through customs at Logan Airport after arriving from London, Boudin grandly announced to the nonplussed Customs official, "I am the lawyer for the revolutionary government of Cuba. My destination is my office at Harvard Law School."[14]

Leonard and his wife Jean relished inviting celebrities to their home for dinner, where they showily displayed tchotchkes from their radical fame, such as Kathy's motorcycle helmet from her participation in the Days of Rage in Chicago. Jean Boudin's "pride in her aristocratic position on the left," Braudy writes, made her "the match of any Palm Beach hostess."[15]

Kathy called her branch of the Weathermen "the Fork" in honor of the Manson family's murder of Leno and Rosemary LaBianca. Manson's followers had defiled the bodies, most famously by leaving a two-tined carving fork protruding from Mr. LaBianca's gut. This charming scene was first commemorated by Boudin's fellow Weatherman Bernardine Dohrn, who gave the "fork" salute at a rally, saying, "Dig it. First they killed those pigs, then they ate dinner in the same room with them. They even shoved a fork into a victim's stomach! Wild!"

These are the people who became respected advisers to a Democratic president.

The Weathermen predicted that 20,000 students would show up at their Days of Rage protest of the Chicago 7 trial in October 1969, an imitation of the riots at the Democratic National Convention in Chicago the year before. Planning for war in the streets, they did push-ups and practiced street fighting in public parks to prove they weren't "hippie faggots associated with SDS."[16]

The Weathermen were too psychotic even for the Black Panthers, who denounced the Days of Rage in a beautiful statement from Fred Hampton saying, "We oppose the anarchistic, adventuristic, chauvinistic, individualistic, masochistic, Custeristic Weathermen."[17] The Black Panthers may not have been the Girl Scouts, but they were not insane. While liberal elites enjoyed the constant tumult, most blacks did not; they just wanted the crime to stop. In 1968, the NAACP's Harlem branch was calling for mandatory five-year sentences against muggers, minimum ten-year sentences for drug pushers, and thirty-year sentences for first-degree murderers.[18]

In the event, no more than a few hundred wastrels showed up, prepared for battle with the police by wearing helmets and fatigues and carrying poles and baseball bats. Flying the Vietcong flag, they called themselves the "Americong." They started a bonfire with park benches and blew up a statue of a policeman by placing a bomb between its legs. The explosion was so huge it blew out nearly a hundred windows in surrounding buildings. Then the Weathermen ran into the streets, smashing cars and storefront windows, throwing rocks, and swinging their bats at cops. Approximately ten minutes later, they were all in police custody with lots of broken eyeglasses.[19]

In a way, what the Weathermen did was even more serious than Sarah Palin's putting crosshairs on congressional districts.

After a Chicago Democratic official, Richard Elrod, became paralyzed for life while fighting with a privileged looter during the Weathermen's Days of Rage, Obama adviser Bernardine Dohrn led the Weathermen in a song sung to the tune of Bob Dylan's "Lay Lady, Lay":

> *Lay, Elrod, Lay,*
> *Lay in the street for a while*
> *Stay, Elrod, stay*
> *Stay in your bed for a while*
> *You thought you could stop the Weatherman*
> *But up-front people put you on your can,*
> *Stay, Elrod, stay*
> *Stay in your iron lung,*
> *Play, Elrod, play*
> *Play with your toes for a while*

The author of that ditty, Ted Gold, was later blown up in an elegant Greenwich Village townhouse while assembling the bomb intended for a new-recruits dance at Fort Dix.

Kathy was part of the brain trust that blew up the townhouse, but fled before the police could talk to her. Kathy's parents were delighted with the townhouse bombing. Her mother had always envied the home's owners for their wealth anyway,[20] and her father thought seeing his daughter on FBI "Wanted" posters was "good for his legend."[21]

Usually the aging radicals cite their ineptitude at setting bombs to brag about how few humans they murdered. But these bombs were made with nails, and nails don't destroy property, they maim and kill people. The three Weathermen who accidentally dynamited themselves were completely dismembered, their body parts splattered all over the walls and ceiling.[22]

Fortuitously, going underground after the townhouse explosion finally gave Kathy an excuse to get a nose job. She also dyed her hair bright red—the better to hide—mimicking Bernardine Dohrn, born Bernardine Ohrnstein.[23] These revolutionaries would engage in sex orgies to "smash monogamy," but one convention the gritty radicals adhered to was the WASP ideal of beauty and gentrified names.

Being "underground" gave them all celebrity status. The only thing that terrified Kathy, Braudy says, was that "if stripped of her glamorous and dramatic revolutionary attachments and subterfuges, she would be the dullest person in Leonard's circle of admirers. . . . She would be a woman, no longer young, whose work was waiting tables and cleaning houses."[24]

In 1974, Kathy, Dohrn, and Bill Ayers were thrilled when a documentary filmmaker, Emile De Antonio, offered to make a movie about the Weather Underground. De Antonio was solidly in the liberal firmament, having made the movie *Point of Order,* attacking Senator Joseph McCarthy. In a letter to the Weathermen, he gushed over them, praising their "masterstroke of political theater" and the "tender loving care" they took making bombs. He signed his letter "Bang. Bang. Bang."[25] He also offered to give them final approval over content, location, cinematographer, and film editor.[26] (I wonder if McCarthy got that for *Point of Order.*)

Some would argue that setting bombs, rioting in the streets, and trying to blow up American servicemen was even worse than identifying a communist as a communist. But that wasn't the view of American liberals.

After the Weathermen led De Antonio on a two-hour game of hide-and-seek before their first meeting, the steeplechase ended at a restaurant, open to the public. But they couldn't have said, "Let's meet at Appleby's" because, you see, they were "underground." Their subsequent meetings with the filmmaker were in restaurants, on street corners, and in public parks, including Central Park.

They apparently relished playing cops-and-robbers—but it turns out the FBI wasn't even looking for them anymore. Kent State had put an end to the student riots, and in any event, the Vietnam War was over. No one cared about the Weather Underground. Around the time of the filming, a newspaper in Wisconsin printed David Gilbert's whereabouts and—nothing happened. "No one arrested him," Braudy writes, the "authorities weren't interested in him."[27] But De Antonio asked them if he should bring a gun to the filming.[28]

After five more years of playing underground, in 1981, Kathy conspired with addled, drug-addicted members of the Black Liberation Army to rob a Brinks armored truck in Rockland County, New York. They wanted drug money and she wanted something exciting to do. Her six BLA co-conspirators murdered Brinks guard Peter Paige and wounded two others at the Nanuet Mall, then hopped in the back of the getaway truck, with Kathy and her partner, David Gilbert, in the truck's cab.

When the truck was stopped by the police minutes later, thirty-eight-year-old Kathy played the innocent housewife, frightened by firearms. She emerged from the cab, begging the police to put down their guns. The perplexed cops, who had been told to look for a U-Haul truck full of black gunmen, did so. No sooner were their weapons holstered than six black men leapt out of the back of the vehicle, guns blazing. Firing wildly at the cops, they instantly killed the force's only black officer, Waverly Brown. Sergeant Edward O'Grady died a few hours later on the operating table.[29]

Decades later, Kathy continued to deny she intentionally disarmed the cops by pretending to be a middle-class suburbanite afraid of guns. And yet her partner, David Gilbert, tried the exact same ruse about an hour later. Stopped by a policeman, Gilbert calmly walked toward the cop, innocently asking for help, as his co-conspirators in the car loaded their weapons. It didn't work a second time. The cop yelled for Gilbert to get down and soon another cop arrived with a shotgun. Gilbert and his posse were taken into custody.[30]

A mob's behavior, Le Bon says, is an "atavistic residuum of the instincts of the primitive man." It is the fear of punishment, he says, that "obliges the isolated and responsible individual to curb" his barbarism.[31] But the Weathermen never faced punishment. To the contrary, they were showered with praise and admiration.

Even in 2000, the *New York Times* was still describing Kathy Boudin as "deeply committed to civil protest against what [she] saw as injustices." Leonard—Castro's lawyer—was said to have been "on the front line fighting for civil liberties and human rights." And Kathy's uncle,

I. F. Stone—a paid Soviet agent, as established in the Venona papers in 1995—is simply identified as a "liberal journalist." After reeling off these insane encomiums, *Times* critic Mel Gussow concluded, "Kathy grew up surrounded by activists and artists. Her social consciousness came naturally."[32]

If the Weathermen had succeeded in transporting their bombs to the Fort Dix dance, instead of blowing themselves up, they would have murdered lots of U.S. servicemen and their dates. For liberals, that's "social consciousness."

Dustin Hoffman, who lived next door to the Greenwich Village townhouse destroyed by the inept revolutionaries, reminisced in 2000 about the explosion that blew out his living room wall. He told the *Times,* "Since then, we've seen killings of abortion doctors, killings by Christian fundamentalists."[33] (In the four decades since *Roe v. Wade* took away Americans' right to vote on abortion, eight people working at abortion clinics have been killed—versus 53 million babies.)

Even when a liberal's own house is blown up by left-wingers, he still somehow manages to blame right-wingers.

At her trial, Kathy was represented by a string of dazzling attorneys, many of them working free, and received celebrities in her jail cell as if she were a visiting dignitary. Meanwhile, one of her pro bono attorneys, Dan Pochoda, grandly announced to reporters, "The test of a civilization is how it treats the people it dislikes."[34] Dislikes? Boudin was bigger than Sean Penn, with slightly less moustache.

Her father Leonard, a great advocate of the communist redistribution of wealth, felt differently when it came to his own money. After ponying up $1.5 million in legal costs for Kathy's defense, he heatedly argued to his tax accountant that he should be able to deduct it as a "business expense."[35]

In prison, Kathy wrote poems about her incarceration and her crime, mostly focusing on herself as the victim and what it was like to be stopped at gunpoint by the police. Luckily for Kathy, her boundless self-love was shared by the elites. She won first prize for her prison poetry at the PEN awards in 1997.[36]

Actor Danny Glover read one of Kathy's poems at a PEN ceremony, dedicated to political prisoners. Her poetry was also read at a Lincoln

Center benefit in the late nineties. (Perhaps they can rustle up a poem from Jared Loughner for next year's benefit!) In 2001, the *New Yorker* ran an admiring feature story about Kathy—a "model prisoner"— endorsing her utterly tendentious version of the Brinks robbery. Alas, the piece laments, "friends and families of the victims are not interested in what Boudin is really like." [37]

After decades of recounting her sufferings since the robbery that left Waverly Brown dead, Kathy was told that Brown's son still attended the memorial service held for his father and Sergeant O'Grady every year. Hundreds of uniformed policemen from all over the state attend the ceremony, replete with bagpipes and a color guard, held at 4 p.m. every October 20.

"Really?" Kathy said. "I never knew the guy had a son." [38] There's the mob's idealist.

But according to the *New Yorker* article, it was "one of the crime's crueller ironies" that the "revolutionaries" had killed the first and only black member of the Nyack police force. [39] Ironic, one surmises, because the Weathermen had done so much to enrich the lives of black people in America. Kathy would surely agree—if only she could remember who Waverly Brown was. The $1.6 million stolen from the Brinks armored car wasn't going to build charter schools in the South Bronx. It was to buy cocaine.

And yet Kathy portrayed her participation in a robbery that left nine children fatherless as a charitable act, saying, "Had I been Roman Catholic, perhaps I would have been a nun." [40]

When the police searched Kathy's Morningside Drive apartment after the Brinks robbery, amid the food stamps and welfare forms they found Kathy's application to New York University Law School. [41] That's what it was always about.

Not anyone could go to a good law school, but anyone could become part of a violent America-hating rabble—and be a superstar. Kathy couldn't get into a good law school, so she had to declare war on the country. If only this pathetic creature had been accepted by a decent school, she would never have had to become a radical. But the academic establishment spurned her. So she did the only thing she could to make the fashionable set revere her, make movies about her, and publish admiring profiles in the *New Yorker* about her. Had student radicals received a fraction of the contempt heaped on Sarah Palin daily, it might not have been so much fun.

They were showered with fawning press coverage and numerous admiring documentaries and sought out by Hollywood celebrities. They have won tributes in endless magazine profiles, awards ceremonies, Hollywood documentaries, and sympathetic portrayals on television shows like *Law & Order.* Before fleeing from the townhouse explosion, Kathy had to cancel an appointment with a Random House editor.[42] Weatherman Bernardine Dohrn was photographed in a leather miniskirt by celebrity photographer Richard Avedon.

Compare the bien-pensants' treatment of women who participated in bombings and cop-killings to their treatment of Carrie Prejean. Dohrn and Boudin enthusiastically endorsed the Manson murders; pageant contestant Prejean only endorsed marriage. Guess which one was relentlessly mocked? Christianity is never trendy, which is one reason Christians can never be a mob.

Where are Prejean's celebrity photographs hanging in chichi New York museums? To the contrary, Prejean—the actually attractive one—has been called ugly, stupid, hateful, and bigoted and has had her plastic surgery broadcast around the globe, while the genetic misfit Weathermen are hailed for their glamour and style. To applause and laughter, Obama adviser David Axelrod went on NPR and said the president was naming the White House dog Miss California after Prejean.[43] If only Prejean had praised Manson instead of marriage, liberals would finally have a female "idealist" who doesn't look like the Wicked Witch of the West.

Dohrn and her husband Ayers have dined out for half a century on the glory of their days as Weathermen. They're the domestic terrorist version of *Whatever Happened to Baby Jane?* They give dramatic renderings of their days "underground" as if it took wily stratagems to hide in a country where 12 million illegal aliens stroll about Los Angeles undetected.

The aging lothario, five-foot-four Ayers particularly enjoys recounting his sexual exploits. Here's a selection from his 2001 book on—guess what?—his days as a Weatherman: "She felt warm and moist" . . . "Her mouth opening slightly, our tongues touching secretly" . . . "Another night Diana and Rachel and Terry and I bedded down together" . . . "You were supposed to f—k no matter what." . . .[44]

In 2002, there was yet another movie made about these narcissistic sociopaths, *The Weather Underground*. Naturally, it was nominated for an Oscar.

The moment Yale-reject mediocrities became "radicals," throwing rocks at cops and setting bombs, they entered a lifetime of praise—and insta-rehabilitation. When it was time for them to make money, they were hired for cushy teaching jobs at the nation's universities.

To name just a few:

• Ron Karenga, aka Dr. Maulana Karenga, was a founder of United Slaves, a violent nationalist rival to the Black Panthers and a dupe of the FBI. In 1971, Karenga was convicted of torturing two members of United Slaves. The *Los Angeles Times* reported on the trial testimony of one of Karenga's victims:

> Deborah Jones, who once was given the Swahili title of an African queen, said she and Gail Davis were whipped with an electrical cord and beaten with a karate baton after being ordered to remove their clothes. She testified that a hot soldering iron was placed in Miss Davis' mouth and placed against Miss Davis' face and that one of her own big toes was tightened in a vise. Karenga, head of US, also put detergent and running hoses in their mouths, she said.[45]

Karenga is a professor of black studies at California State University, Long Beach.[46]

• William Ayers put a bomb in the Pentagon and now teaches childhood education at the University of Illinois at Chicago.

• Ayers's wife, Ohrnstein/Dohrn, called for revolutionary war in the United States, praised the Manson family, laughed about a paralyzed DA, said "Bring the Revolution home, kill your parents—that's where it's at," and participated in the bombing of the Pentagon. She is a professor at Northwestern University's Children and Justice Center.

• Mark Rudd, also a Weatherman leader, who led the student strike at Columbia University, taught at a community college in New Mexico until retiring in 2007.

• Angela Davis, former Black Panther, was the legal owner of the guns the Panthers used to blow off the head of Marin County judge Harold Haley in an attempt to free Davis's boyfriend, George Jackson. Today she is a professor at the University of California at Santa Cruz.

• Eleanor Raskin was involved in all the Weathermen's lunacy, from the Days of Rage to the Greenwich Village townhouse bombing. She now teaches at Albany Law School.

• Mike Klonsky was National Chairman of SDS in 1968, during the violent riots at the Democratic National Convention, and founded the Maoist October League, which later adopted the catchy name "The Communist Party (Marxist Leninist)." In 1977, he was an honored guest of the Communist Chinese government, where he comically vowed to "topple the U.S. imperialist ruling class" and told the Chinese "we are determined as well to make a contribution to the worldwide struggle against the two superpowers." The Chinese enjoyed his presentation because they don't speak English.

Today, Klonsky is a professor of education at the University of Illinois at Chicago. When Barack Obama was doling out various foundation grants, he funneled nearly $2 million to Klonsky and Bill Ayers. Klonsky was also on President Clinton's Advisory Council of the National Campaign Against Youth Violence.

• David Hilliard, the Black Panthers' "Field Marshal," did not do anything as threatening as ask to see a president's birth certificate, but he did stand in front of a quarter million people and scream, "Later for Richard Milhous Nixon, the motherfucker! . . . Because Richard Nixon is an evil man! . . . Fuck that motherfucking man! We will kill Richard Nixon!"[47]

Hilliard has taught at Merritt College, Laney College, New College, and the University of New Mexico.[48]

• Susan Rosenberg was a member of the Weather Underground, the Black Liberation Army, *and* The Family. She conspired to kill cops, blow up buildings, and stage an armed robbery of the Brinks truck in Nanuet, New York. Sentenced to fifty-eight years in prison for felony murder and possession of more than 700 pounds of explosives, Rosenberg was released from prison by President Clinton on his last day in office.

Just a few years later, Rosenberg was offered a teaching position at Hamilton College, despite having absolutely no qualifications to teach—with only a master's degree in writing she got through a correspondence course in prison.

In addition to springing various Weathermen from prison, President Clinton also pardoned sixteen Puerto Rican terrorists who had set off more than a hundred bombs in New York and Chicago in the seventies and eighties, killing a half dozen people and injuring more than seventy. They hadn't even asked for pardons.

If Charles Manson's followers hadn't killed Roman Polanski's wife, Sharon Tate, Clinton would have pardoned him, too, and he'd probably be teaching at Northwestern University.

And yet we still have to hear it asked: Why did this group of privileged kids declare war on their own government? Perhaps the next batch of glowing articles, books, and movies will get to the bottom of that brainteaser. If only liberal elites had treated these social climbers a little bit less like Jennifer Aniston and a little bit more like Mel Gibson, nine children in Nyack, New York, might have grown up with their fathers.

With embarrassing bravado, Bill Ayers told his fellow Weathermen, "It's not a comfortable life, it's not just a dollar move, it's standing up in the face of the enemy, and risking your life and risking everything for that struggle."[49]

Of course it was a dollar move. Like no-name rock bands and comedians staging "benefits" ostensibly for left-wing causes, but actually to benefit themselves, student radicals declaring "war" on Amerikkka had found a surefire path to celebrity. Ted Gold was making note for his memoir before blowing himself up in the townhouse. For some people, nothing is more important than fame. The Weather Underground was the sixties version of *The Jersey Shore*—except Obama doesn't know Snooki. Let's see these brave dissidents, allegedly willing to risk "everything," try to get through one day in the life of non-elite-approved Sarah Palin, Scooter Libby, Mark Fuhrman, Linda Tripp, Clarence Thomas, Dan Quayle, Ken Starr, Karl Rove, Carrie Prejean, Michele Bachmann, or Katherine Harris, to name a few people liberals would run over with their cars and laugh about it.

A century earlier, Fyodor Dostoyevsky captured the identical sickness in 1860s Russia in his novel *The Demons,* depicting the corrosive effect of the French Revolution's ideas on Russian society. After so many years of peace and calm, the older generation couldn't imagine that anything could possibly go wrong with the conscienceless children they had raised. Exhibiting the mad narcissism of the liberal intellectual set, the fashionable people in *The Demons* are constantly entertaining deranged revolutionaries at the town's most desirable social events. One character, a failed Russian novelist, toys with nihilistic anarchists to feed his own ego, flattering them as the only generation to speak truth boldly, while boasting about his own atheism.

*The Demons* was as prescient a warning regarding the disaster about to befall Russia as Edmund Burke's *Reflections on the Revolution in France* was about that cataclysm. On the eve of the French Revolution, Burke cautioned that "criminal means, once tolerated, are soon preferred." He said the moment one capitulates to the idea that mayhem and murder are justified for the greater good, the greater good is forgotten and mayhem and murder become ends in themselves, until only violence can "satiate their insatiable appetites."[50]

Beginning in the 1960s, American liberals were unable to stop flirting with mob violence. Like Dostoyevsky's unsuccessful author, they embraced sociopathic malcontents because it made them feel hip and young. Today, the angry rabble is simply another faction of the Democratic mainstream. As Harvard professor Harvey Mansfield has said, the sixties bequeathed us radicals who are "neither so outrageous nor so violent as at first. The poison has worked its way into our soul, the effects becoming less visible to us as they become more ordinary."[51]

# TEN

# CIVIL RIGHTS AND THE MOB: GEORGE WALLACE, BULL CONNOR, ORVAL FAUBUS, AND OTHER DEMOCRATS

t was the Democratic Party that ginned up the racist mob against blacks and it is the Democratic Party ginning every new mob today—ironically, all portraying themselves as the equivalent of the Freedom Riders. With real civil rights secure—try to find a restaurant that won't serve a black person—modern civil rights laws benefit only the mob, not the victims of the mob, as American blacks had been. Just as fire seeks oxygen, Democrats seek power, which is why they will always be found championing the mob whether the mob consists of Democrats lynching blacks or Democrats slandering the critics of ObamaCare as racists.

Democrats have gone from demagoguing white (trash) voters with claims that Republicans are the party of blacks, to demagoguing black voters telling them Republicans are the party of racists. Any mob in a storm.

The liberal fairy tale that Southern bigots simply switched parties, from Democrat to Republican, is exactly wrong. What happened is: The Democrats switched mobs. Democrats will champion any group of hooligans in order to attain power. As Michael Barone said of the vicious segregationist (and Democrat) George Wallace, he was "a man who really didn't believe in anything—a political opportunist who used opposition to integration to try and get himself ahead."[1]

This is why the Democrats are able to transition so seamlessly from defending Bull Connor racists to defending Black Panthers, hippies, yippies, Weathermen, feminists, Bush derangement syndrome liberals, Moveon.org, and every other indignant, angry mob.

Every segregationist who ever served in the Senate was a Democrat and remained a Democrat except one. Even Strom Thurmond—the only one who later became a Republican—remained a Democrat for eighteen years after running for president as a Dixiecrat. There's a reason they were not called the "Dixiecans."

Democratic senators Ernest Hollings, Richard Russell, and Sam Ervin all voted against the 1964 Civil Rights Act and all remained Democrats for the rest of their lives.[2] Al Gore's father, Albert Gore, voted against the 1964 Civil Rights Act; both he and his son remained lifelong Democrats. J. William Fulbright voted against the 1964 Civil Rights Act; he remained a Democrat and became the political mentor to Bill Clinton. Senator Robert "Sheets" Byrd voted against the 1964 Civil Rights Act; he remained a senior statesman in the Democratic Party until his dying day.

A curious sleight of hand is required to hide from the children the fact that all the segregationists in the Senate were Democrats. In history books, such as Robert A. Caro's biography of Lyndon Johnson, the segregationists are not called "Democrats." They're called "Southerners."[3]

Except it wasn't just "Southerners" voting against civil rights. Not every senator who opposed black civil rights was a Southerner, but every one was a Democrat. In addition to the Southern Democrats who voted against putting the 1957 civil rights bill on the Senate calendar, for example, there were five Democrats from nowhere near the South: Democratic senator Wayne Morse of Oregon—a favorite target of Senator Joe McCarthy—Democratic senator Warren Magnuson of Washington, Democratic senator James Murray of Montana, Democratic senator Mike Mansfield of Montana, and Democratic senator Joseph O'Mahoney of Wyoming.[4]

According to Caro, the Western Democrats traded their votes on civil rights for a dam authorization on the Idaho-Oregon border.[5] That's how dear black civil rights were to liberals—they traded them away for a dam.

While Democrats are the party of the mob, Republicans are the party of calm order, willing to breach the peace only when it comes to great transgressions against humanity—slavery, abortion, and terrorism.

Republican president Abraham Lincoln fought a Civil War and sacrificed 600,000 American lives to preserve the union, rallying the union with the principle that all men are created equal. The Democrats favored allowing slavery in the territories, and the Whigs were pro-choice on slavery—rejecting extremist rhetoric on both sides. The Republican Party was founded for the express purpose of opposing slavery.

After the Civil War, it was Republicans who passed the Thirteenth Amendment, granting slaves their freedom; the Fourteenth Amendment, granting them citizenship; and Fifteenth Amendment, giving them the right to vote. It was Republicans who sent federal troops to the Democratic South to enforce the hard-won rights of the freed slaves.

Then, as now, the Democrats favored the hooligans. The Ku Klux Klan was originally formed as a terrorist group to attack Republicans who had come to the Democratic South after the Civil War to help enforce legal equality for freed slaves.

It was—again—Republicans who passed the Civil Rights Act of 1866 and the Reconstruction Act of 1867, both signed into law by Republican president Ulysses S. Grant. Under the "living Constitution," the Supreme Court upheld fraudulent "separate but equal" accommodations for blacks in the 1896 case *Plessy v. Ferguson.*

Republicans kept introducing federal civil rights bills and Democrats kept blocking them—a bill to protect black voters in the South in 1890; antilynching bills in 1922, 1935, and 1938; and anti–poll tax bills in 1942, 1944, and 1946.

With a lock on the racist mob vote, Democratic politicians won elections and promptly resegregated the entire South with Jim Crow laws. In 1913, Progressive Democrat president Woodrow Wilson even instituted segregation in Washington, D.C., bringing Jim Crow to the federal workforce. Wilson summarily dismissed black officials from their federal jobs in the South and in D.C. "Segregation is not a humiliation," Wilson explained to a black delegation that came to the White House to complain, "but a benefit, and ought to be so regarded by you gentlemen." During Wilson's first term, Booker T. Washington went to Washington, D.C., and reported, "I have never seen the colored people so discouraged and bitter as they are at the present time."[6]

President Wilson's racist policies were fully supported by Democrats in Congress, and angrily denounced by Republicans.

Much as elected Democrats promote deranged documentarian Michael Moore today, Wilson hailed the virulently racist, pro-KKK movie *Birth of a Nation* as "writing history with lightning," saying his only regret was that "it is all so terribly true." Wilson even held a special showing of *Birth of a Nation* at the White House for cabinet members and members of Congress. (By contrast, President Reagan showed Dr. Bernard Nathanson's anti-abortion documentary, *Silent Scream,* in his White House.)

A friend of Wilson said that with him running the country, "Negroes should expect to be treated as a servile race."[7] There's your post-racial Democratic Party.

A crucial part of the Democrats' victim folklore is that they have been losing the South to Republicans over the past half century because the Democrats stood on principle to oppose race discrimination, while the Republican Party pandered to racists in the South—a region of the country liberals believe is composed primarily of Klan members. (That might be your first clue as to why Southerners don't like liberals.) The Republican Party's allegedly racist appeal to Southerners is darkly referred to seventeen times a day in the mainstream media as the "Southern Strategy."

In 1996, R. W. Apple, then–*New York Times* Washington bureau chief, casually referred to "the Republican Party's recent record as the vehicle of white supremacy in the South beginning with the Goldwater campaign and reaching its apex in Richard M. Nixon's 'Southern Strategy' in 1968 and 1972."[8]

Apple continued, "Republicans appealed to Nixon Democrats (later Reagan Democrats) in the northern suburbs, many of them ethnic voters who had left the cities to escape from blacks, with promises to crack down on welfare cheats and to impose law and order, and they fought against affirmative action."[9]

It never dawns on liberals that people might actually want to crack down on welfare cheats, impose law and order, and abolish racially discriminatory "affirmative action" plans. In any event, Nixon wasn't one of them: He invented affirmative action. Apple's statement was the opposite of the truth.

In 2002, Jack White, which I believe is a pen name for Keith Olbermann, wrote an article for *Time* magazine online accusing the Republican Party of having a "four-decade-long addiction to race-baiting." White said Reagan "set a standard for exploiting white anger and resentment rarely seen since George Wallace stood in the schoolhouse door."[10] To insult Republicans, liberals compare them to Democrats.

In 2008, *Newsweek* matter-of-factly reported, "In 1968, Richard Nixon used code words like 'law and order' to exploit racial fears as part of his 'Southern Strategy.' "[11]

In fact, it was Eisenhower who broke the Democrats' hold on the South in 1952, and if anyone was appealing to bigots that year, it wasn't Eisenhower. Democrat Adlai Stevenson, known to experience "personal discomfort in the presence of Negroes,"[12] chose as his running mate John Sparkman of Alabama, a Democrat segregationist.

And yet the Old South—which according to mainstream media accounts voted Republican solely out of racial resentment—suddenly started voting Republican in 1952. Ike carried Tennessee, Virginia, and Florida outright, and nearly stole Kentucky, North Carolina, and West Virginia from Stevenson. (Eisenhower lost Kentucky by a microscopic .07 percent and lost West Virginia and South Carolina by fewer than 4 percentage points.) This was just four years after Democrat-turned-Dixiecrat Strom Thurmond won four Southern states. But running with a segregationist didn't help Stevenson in the South a few years later.

Then, in 1956, the Republican Party platform endorsed the Supreme Court's 1954 decision in *Brown v. Board of Education* that desegregated public schools; the Democratic platform did not, and would not, as long as Democrats were winning elections by appealing to the racist mob. This led the black congressman Adam Clayton Powell Jr. to break with his party and endorse Eisenhower for president.

Governor Orval Faubus, progressive New Deal Democrat, blocked the schoolhouse door to the Little Rock Central High School with the state's National Guard rather than allow nine black students to attend. In response, President Eisenhower federalized the Arkansas National Guard to take it out of Faubus's hands. Then he sent the 101st Airborne Division to walk the black children to school and stay with them throughout the day.

Eisenhower implemented the 1948 executive order President Truman had issued—but then ignored—desegregating the military. Also unlike Truman, Eisenhower hired blacks for prominent positions in his administration, such as assistant secretary of Labor (J. Ernest Wilkens), chairman of the U.S. Board of Parole (Scovel Richardson), UN delegate from the United States (Charles Mahoney), administrative officer on White House staff (Fredrick Morrow), minister to Romania (Clifton R. Wharton), and members of the U.S. Commission on Civil Rights (George M. Johnson and J. Ernest Wilkens).[13]

It was Republicans who overwhelmingly introduced, promoted, and passed every civil rights act from the end of the Civil War right up to and including the 1964 Civil Rights Act. President Eisenhower pushed the Civil Rights Act of 1957, written by Attorney General Herbert Brownell, guaranteeing black voting rights, to be enforced by the U.S. Department of Justice.

During the endless deliberation on Eisenhower's civil rights bill, Senator Lyndon Johnson warned his fellow segregationist Democrats, "Be ready to take up the goddamned nigra bill again." Senator Sam Ervin, another liberal luminary—instrumental in the destruction of anti-communist Republicans Joe McCarthy and Richard Nixon—told his fellow segregationists, "I'm on your side, not theirs," and advised them to face up to the fact that "we've got to give the goddamned niggers something."[14]

As president of the Senate, Vice President Richard Nixon "came down strongly on the side of civil rights," as even Robert Caro admits, by issuing an advisory opinion that the filibuster could be stopped with a simple majority vote changing Senate rules.[15] Meanwhile, Democrat Lyndon Johnson gutted the enforcement provisions of the 1957 bill to nothing: Anyone accused of violating a person's voting rights was guaranteed a jury trial—and, consequently, jury nullification by Democratic juries.

Republican senator Charles Potter stood on crutches in the well of the Senate, having lost both legs in World War II, to denounce LBJ's killer amendments, saying, "I fought beside Negroes in the war. I saw them die for us. For the Senate of the United States to repay these valiant men . . . by a watered-down version of this legislation would make a mockery of the democratic concept we hold so dear."[16] Even in its watered-down form—thanks, Democrats!—all eighteen "nay" votes came from the Democrats.

The following year, President Eisenhower introduced a bill to create the U.S. Civil Rights Commission and to fix the enforcement provisions of the 1957 civil rights bill that had been gutted by the Democrats. In response, Democrats staged the longest filibuster in history—more than 125 hours. But in the end, the bill passed and was signed into law by Eisenhower on May 6, 1960.

The Senate vote on the 1960 Civil Rights Act was 71–18. Once again, every single vote against a civil rights bill came from a Democrat, including legendary liberal, hero of Watergate, Sam Ervin.[17] Representative George McGovern voted "present." He would also be the Democrats' candidate for president in 1972.[18] The vote of the Tennessee delegation in the House was typical: The two Republicans from Tennessee voted for the 1960 civil rights bill, the six Democrats from the state voted against.[19]

Until 1964, every civil rights act had presented no possible constitutional problems—those federal laws were fully within Congress's enumerated powers to enact because they were directed at government officials (Democrats) who were violating the Constitution by denying black citizens the right to vote.

Federal laws aimed at discrimination by government actors are expressly within Congress's authority under the Fourteenth Amendment. The Democrats opposed these civil rights laws not because of any questions about Congress's authority to enact them—they couldn't care less about the Constitution—but because they wanted to keep discriminating.

The 1964 Civil Rights Act was again supported overwhelmingly by

Republicans and less so by Democrats. As with the 1957 and 1960 civil rights acts, it was Republicans who passed the 1964 Civil Rights Act by huge majorities, with a distinctly smaller majority of Democrats supporting it. In the Senate, for example, 82 percent of Republicans voted for the 1964 Civil Rights Act, compared with only 66 percent of Democrats. In the House, 80 percent of Republicans supported the '64 bill, compared with only 63 percent of Democrats.

The only reason Democratic majorities were beginning to support civil rights for blacks was that by 1964—thanks to Republican voting rights acts—more blacks were voting. Democrats couldn't keep winning elections in some parts of the country by appealing to the racist mob. As Democratic senator Carter Glass of Virginia had explained years earlier, "Discrimination! Why that is exactly what we propose," saying the Democrats sought to "remove every negro voter who can be gotten rid of, legally, *without materially impairing the numerical strength of the white electorate.*"[20] The Democrats' position on civil rights depended on where the votes were.

Of course, there were some serious civil rights champions among Democrats in the twentieth century—we've been hearing endless panegyrics to them our entire lives. This is the history you've never read.

Although Democrats act as if the 1964 act was the only civil rights act that ever mattered, it is a curious fact that, as Thomas Sowell says, "the rise of blacks into the professional and other high-level occupations was greater in the years preceding passage of the Civil Rights Act of 1964 than in all the years following passage of that act."[21]

Once the Democrats got involved, civil rights became just another racket with another mob. Unlike previous civil rights laws, the 1964 Civil Rights Act included provisions aimed at purely private actors, raising the hackles of some constitutional purists, notably Barry Goldwater, the Republicans' 1964 presidential nominee. Goldwater, like the rest of his party, had supported every single civil rights bill until the 1964 act. But he broke with the vast majority of his fellow Republicans to oppose the 1964 Civil Rights Act.

Like many other conservatives opposed to a living, growing, breathing Constitution, Goldwater actually opposed only two of the seven major provisions of the bill—those regulating privately owned housing and public accommodations. But there were other provisions he would have made tougher. For example, Goldwater wanted to make it mandatory that federal funds be withheld from programs practicing discrimination, rather than discretionary, as President Kennedy had requested.[22]

Goldwater was a vehement foe of segregation. He was a founder of the NAACP in Arizona, donating the equivalent of several thousand dollars to the organization's efforts to integrate the public schools. When he was head of the Arizona National Guard, he had integrated the state Guard before Harry Truman announced he was integrating the U.S. military. As the *Washington Post* said, Goldwater "ended racial segregation in his family department stores, and he was instrumental in ending it in Phoenix schools and restaurants and in the Arizona National Guard."[23]

But he was also a believer in limited government. It was, after all, racist Democratic politicians in the South using the force of the government to violate private property rights by enforcing the Jim Crow laws in the first place. As Sowell points out, it wasn't the private bus companies demanding that blacks sit in the back of the bus, it was the government.[24]

Goldwater not only had personally promoted desegregation, he belonged to a party that had been fighting for civil rights for the previous century against Democratic obstructionism. Lyndon Johnson voted against every civil rights bill during his tenure in the Senate. But by the time he became president, he had flipped 180 degrees. Appealing to regional mobs wouldn't work with a national electorate.

Unlike mob-appeasing Democrats, Goldwater based his objections to certain parts of the 1964 Civil Rights Act on purely constitutional principles. Along with other constitutional purists in the Republican Party, Goldwater opposed federal initiatives in a lot of areas, not just those involving race. By contrast, segregationist Democrats routinely criticized the exercise of federal power and expenditure of federal funds when it involved ending discrimination against blacks—but gladly accepted federal pork projects for their states.

It would be as if, after fighting the Democrats for a hundred years over the issue of abortion, Republicans finally got *Roe v. Wade* overturned, and then, out of pure political calculation, Democrats jumped on the bandwagon and demanded a federal law outlawing abortion. Some pro-life Republicans would probably object that federal law outlawing abortion is not one of Congress's enumerated powers. On the basis of Republicans' constitutional objections, Democrats would then reverse the entire history of the pro-life movement and start claiming the Democratic Party alone fought to end abortion in America. That is exactly what they have done with the history of civil rights.

This is why idiots like Bill Maher can make jokes like this (about the 2010 Republican sweep of Congress)—"I haven't seen Republicans so happy about taking seats since they made Rosa Parks stand up."[25] When Rosa Parks refused to give up her seat, the mayor of Montgomery enforcing segregation on the buses was—of course—a segregationist Democrat, William A. "Tacky" Gayle.[26]

Even after a federal district court struck down segregation on Montgomery's buses, Gayle appealed the decision to the Supreme Court, which also ruled against Gayle. That's when the Montgomery buses were finally desegregated. But try searching Gayle on Google—try searching his name in the history books—and see if you can find his political party. Who's the "dumb twat" now? (As Maher called Sarah Palin on his HBO show.)[27]

In fact, it was only when there was an electoral risk to their political careers that the entire Democratic Party made a big show of supporting civil rights. Even then, both Eisenhower and Nixon did a better job enforcing the Court's color-blind rulings than Kennedy or Johnson did. The Democrat presidents were always dragging their feet, trying not to upset the segregationist Democrats, the same way today's Democrats refuse to upset abortion-mad feminists. In a hundred years, liberals will rewrite the history of abortion to make pro-life Democrat Robert Casey Sr. the country's sole defender of the unborn.

Nixon indeed had something called the "Southern Strategy," but it had nothing to do with appealing to racial resentment. His idea was to force nice patriotic, churchgoing Southerners to recognize what a rotten, treasonous bunch the Democrats had become. It was a regional version of his appeal to the Silent Majority.

Nixon had worked to pass the Civil Rights Act of 1957, for which he was personally thanked by Martin Luther King. He was a card-carrying member of the NAACP in 1960. His Democratic opponent, John F. Kennedy, was not.

After losing his race for governor of California in 1962, Nixon began his political comeback with a 1966 column proclaiming that the Republican Party stood for small government and a strong national defense and would leave it to the Democrats "to squeeze the last ounces of political juice out of the rotting fruit of racial injustice." Nixon referred contemptuously to the Democrats as the "party of Maddox, Mahoney and Wallace"—all segregationists.

Not surprisingly, with an opening gambit like that, in the 1968 presidential election the segregationist votes went to Democratic candidate Hubert Humphrey, not Nixon. As Michael Barone notes, Nixon's "status as a longtime supporter of civil rights in the Eisenhower administration and at the 1960 national convention, made it difficult for him to steal away Wallace's votes."[28]

Provably, Humphrey got the Wallace vote. At the outset of the campaign, Nixon was polling at 42 percent compared with Humphrey's 29 percent. Meanwhile, segregationist George Wallace was polling at 22 percent. On Election Day, Nixon's percentage remained virtually unchanged at 43.4 percent. Wallace's had dropped to 13.5 percent. Where had the rest of the Wallace vote gone? It didn't go to Nixon. Humphrey's vote surged by about 12 percentage points—nearly as much as Wallace lost—giving him 42.7 percent of the votes cast on Election Day.[29] Even if those Wallace voters stayed home, Nixon's and Humphrey's vote percentages ought to have increased by exactly the same factor. But Nixon's percentage remained steady, while Humphrey's skyrocketed.

And yet—just as with the Tea Partiers today—when Americans opposed Lyndon Johnson's Great Society programs, liberals accused them of racism—of *really* opposing LBJ over civil rights. Here's a thought: Maybe they were angry about the massive, wasteful government spending on expensive federal programs wrecking society. Or maybe they were upset about intrusive rulings out of the Warren Court having nothing to do with race but discovering new rights for pornographers, atheists, and criminals. Or maybe they were alarmed by the Democratic Party transforming itself into the party of acid, amnesty, and abortion—as an anonymous Democratic senator told journalist Bob Novak in 1972.

But as Johnson's popularity nosedived, liberals just kept patting themselves on the back and saying it was because he was pushing desegregation. Except he wasn't. It took the Nixon White House to get the schools desegregated.

In Nixon's first inaugural address, in January 1969, he said, "No man can be fully free while his neighbor is not. To go forward at all is to go forward together. This means black and white together, as one nation, not two. The laws have caught up with our conscience. What remains is to give life to what is in the law: to ensure at last that as all are born equal in dignity before God, all are born equal in dignity before man."

And then he started feverishly desegregating the schools, something his Democratic predecessors had refused to do. On a statistical basis, there was more desegregation of Southern schools in Nixon's first term than in any historical period, before or after. Practically overnight, Southern schools went from being effectively segregated to being effectively integrated. To highlight the Democrats' double-talk, Nixon's attorney general, John Mitchell, famously said, "Watch what we do, not what we say."

While presiding over massive, voluntary desegregation of the schools, Nixon forbade his cabinet members to boast about it. But between his election in 1968 to the end of his second year in office in 1970, black students attending all-black schools in the South declined from 68 percent to 18.4 percent and the percentage of black students attending majority white schools went from 18.4 percent to 38.1 percent.[30]

Despite all this, when black agitator Julian Bond was asked about Nixon's civil rights record, he said, "If you could call Adolf Hitler a friend of the Jews, you could call President Nixon a friend of the blacks."[31]

If Nixon had planned to appeal to white racists, speeding up desegregation was not an effective strategy. But he turned around and won an even bigger landslide in 1972, running against George McGovern and the party of acid, abortion, and amnesty. Yes, racism must explain the Republicans' sweep of the South.

Not only did Nixon desegregate the schools, but he broke the back of the discriminatory building trades in 1968 with his "Philadelphia Plan," the first government affirmative action program. In response to aggressive racial discrimination by construction unions to keep wages high, Nixon imposed formal racial quotas and timelines in hiring on the building trades. Under Secretary George P. Shultz, Nixon's Labor Department rode federal contractors hard, demanding results. Even back when he was Eisenhower's vice president, Nixon had been recommending "a positive policy of nondiscrimination" for government contractors. When running for president in 1967—the zenith of his alleged "Southern Strategy"—he had said, "People in the ghetto have to have more than an equal chance. They should be given a dividend."

Most histories drone on and on about LBJ's beneficence in having proposed a similar Philadelphia Plan, but LBJ completely abandoned it the instant his comptroller general vetoed the idea. Nixon, by contrast, overruled the comptroller and staged a full-throttle campaign to get congressional approval for his affirmative action plan. As he said, the Democrats "are token-oriented. We are job-oriented."

Imposing racial quotas has generally not been seen as one of Nixon's greatest moments by modern conservatives, who oppose all race discrimination. However, it has to be understood as a reaction to a century of Democratic obstructionism on civil rights. Democrats only came around on civil rights when blacks were voting in high enough numbers to make a difference at the ballot box—and then they claimed credit for everything their party had ferociously blocked since the Civil War.

Black civil rights groups gave Nixon little credit for the plan, and white construction workers hated it. He knew the Philadelphia plan hurt him politically, but he did it anyway.[32]

Being a Republican, Nixon was not a demagogue. He had no interest in demonizing the South—as if that were the sole locus of discrimination in America. As Mitchell said, "Watch what we do." Democrats were the exact opposite, demanding hallelujahs for every kind word they ever spoke to a black person, while doing very little to actually end racial discrimination.

In the 1960 campaign, for example, an exceedingly reluctant JFK was pressured by adviser Harris Wofford into placing a quick call to Coretta Scott King when her husband was in the Reidsville jail in Georgia—and then allowed that two-minute phone call to be wildly publicized in the black community.[33] His opponent Nixon—who would go on to preside over the most massive desegregation drive the nation had ever seen as well as the country's first affirmative action program—made no comment on King's jailing.

But the Kennedy campaign played up that phone call for all it was worth. Pamphlets were printed up titled *"No Comment" Nixon Versus a Candidate with a Heart, Senator Kennedy.*[34] The phone call even persuaded longtime Republican and Nixon supporter Martin Luther King Sr. to switch his support to Kennedy, saying, "I had expected to vote against Senator Kennedy because of his religion." But now, he said, Kennedy "can be my President, Catholic or whatever he is. It took courage to call my daughter-in-law at a time like this."[35] MLK Jr. stayed neutral, while all the other leading black Baptist ministers "firmly" reendorsed Richard Nixon.

Democrats spent a hundred years enforcing legal discrimination against blacks, or—at best—dragging their heels on enforcing black civil rights, but then turned around and crowed for fifty years about a friendly phone call to Mrs. King. With a few symbolic gestures, the Democrats grabbed the civil rights mantle in 1960 and never let it go.

In fact, it was the Democrats' obstructionism that created the environment for nonviolent—and then violent—civil rights protests in the first place. Thurgood Marshall was bringing lawsuits and winning case after case before the Supreme Court, including the 1954 case of *Brown v. Board of Education.* Redeeming blacks' civil rights could have been accomplished without riots, marches, church burnings, police dogs, and murders. Except the problem was, Democrats were in the White House from January 1961 to January 1969 and only Republican presidents would aggressively enforce the law. If Nixon had been elected in 1960, instead of Kennedy, we could have skipped the bloodshed of the civil rights marches and today we'd be celebrating Thurgood Marshall Day, rather than Martin Luther King Day.

Consider that *Brown v. Board of Education,* eliminating "separate but equal" in the public schools, was decided in 1954. President Eisenhower sent federal troops to enforce the decision. And then, from the end of his presidency until Nixon's election in 1968, nothing much changed. Nixon came in and wiped out segregated schools in one year.

In 1976, the entire South—all eleven states of the Old Confederacy, except the great Commonwealth of Virginia—flipped right back again and voted for Democrat Jimmy Carter. Was that because Carter was appealing to bigots? Or is it only a secret "Southern Strategy" of pandering to racists when Republicans win the South?

By 1980, Southerners as well as the rest of the country realized Carter was a complete nincompoop and voted overwhelmingly for Ronald Reagan. Carter and his vice presidential candidate, Walter Mondale, won only their own respective states of Georgia and Minnesota, plus Hawaii and West Virginia.

In 1984, Reagan won every state in the union, except Democratic candidate Mondale's home state of Minnesota, which Reagan lost by only 3,761 votes out of more than 2 million votes cast—the closest presidential race in Minnesota history since 1916. Reagan's margin in the popular vote was nearly 16.8 million votes, second only to Nixon's 18 million popular-vote margin in 1972. It was the largest electoral vote total in history. (No one at the *New York Times* could bear to write the story on Reagan's historic victory, so the article giving these figures is bylined "Associated Press.")[36]

A party that attributes Nixon's and Reagan's landslide victories to a secret Republican plan to appeal to racists has gone stark raving mad. Democrats disdain Americans, so unlike the Europeans they fetishize *(Why can't we be more like the Netherlands?)*. So they dismiss these "flyover" people as racists. The entire basis of liberals' "Southern Strategy" myth is the sophisticated belief that anyone who votes Republican must be a racist.

According to liberals' theory, racists like Orval Faubus should have become card-carrying members of the Republican Party once Nixon came along—or at least by Reagan's time—and that's how Republicans swept the South. In fact, however, Faubus never became a Republican. He was finally defeated for governor in 1966 by Republican Winthrop Rockefeller in a state with only 11 percent registered Republicans. Rockefeller's "Southern Strategy" against Faubus involved running as a strong integrationist, and he immediately desegregated Arkansas schools and rapidly integrated the draft boards.

In addition to being a ferocious segregationist, Faubus was, naturally, a liberal, and an admirer of Socialist presidential candidates Norman Thomas and Eugene Debs, from whom he got his middle name, "Eugene."[37]

Years later, Bill Clinton invited Faubus to his gubernatorial inauguration, where he warmly embraced Faubus, to the disgust of Southern Republicans. *Arkansas Democrat-Gazette*'s Paul Greenberg, who had won a Pulitzer Prize for editorials advocating racial integration and opposing George Wallace's presidential candidacy, called it a shocking moment for those Arkansans "who had fought—not just for years but for decades—against all that Orval Faubus had stood for, this willingness to exploit racial hatred."[38]

So what else might explain the South gradually voting more and more Republican, starting with Eisenhower in 1952? What else was going on in the last half century?

In the mid-sixties, the Worst Generation burst onto the scene and took over the Democratic Party.

That was the decade that launched legalized obscenity, the birth control pill, student riots, the Weather Underground, the Symbionese Liberation Army, and the Black Panthers. The crime rate skyrocketed as the courts granted ever more elaborate rights to criminals. Prayer and Bible-reading were banned from the public schools. The most privileged, cosseted generation in history began tearing apart the universities. One of every ten universities would be hit. The Aquarius generation turned into a drugged-out hippie cult of Manson family murderers.

In other words, the South began to go Republican about the same time as the Democratic Party went insane.

Another minor issue, even in the fifties, was the Cold War. Throughout the second half of the twentieth century, there was growing admiration in the South for the Republicans' belligerent approach to national security. Southerners are hawks: Sooner or later they were going to join the patriotic party. How long were Southerners going to tolerate a party that ran a peacenik like George McGovern for president in the middle of a war? Name a Southern university that's ever banned ROTC before answering that question. (Even Duke has an ROTC program.)

Moreover, if it was hostility to civil rights that drove Southern Democrats into the Republican Party, that shift should have come to a screeching halt by the mid-seventies, when segregation was no longer an issue—thanks to Richard Nixon. But in fact, the South only gradually became Republican over the course of several decades, even flipping back to the Democrats to vote for fellow Southerners Jimmy Carter and Bill Clinton. The South's move to the Republican Party was as gradual as the Democrats' shift from the party of Harry Truman to the party of Rosie O'Donnell.

Even the Wallace vote wasn't exclusively a segregationist vote. Not everything was about the blacks. Cold War hawks thought Nixon would be soft on communism—correctly—and the Democrats were complete pansies. The great World War II general Curtis LeMay—"Old Iron Pants"—was Wallace's running mate. LeMay supported integration 100 percent, but he didn't trust Nixon to be tough enough with the Russkies, so he turned down Nixon's offer to join his ticket and ran with Wallace instead. LeMay was a Reaganesque Cold Warrior. With the slogan "Bombs Away!," he was as bellicose toward communism as Goldwater had been in 1964—which explains Wallace's winning a lot of the same states Goldwater won.

Southerners were not the only demographic that shifted party registration in reaction to the turmoil created by the Worst Generation. In 1972, the whole country became the South. Nixon's "Southern Strategy" was, in reality, a "landslide strategy." If you look at the facts, Republicans have been so clearly right about everything, it's frightening.

Now that the battle for civil rights has been won—the Southern Poverty Law Center is going to have to start placing monitors in people's homes to ferret out an incident of racism—liberals have suddenly become mighty pugnacious on the matter of of racial equality. (The really great thing about yammering on and on and on, endlessly, day after day, year after year ad infinitum about race is that it pays such big dividends in easing tension between the races.) All these pretend-heroes of the civil rights movement self-righteously claim that any suggestion that size of government be cut is de facto racist. False, indeed preposterous, accusations of racism are just another way for liberals to whip up the mob.

Obama is hysterically defended from every little criticism as if liberals are at war with the Klan. You know, we could have really used them when Republicans actually were at war with the Klan. But back then, Democratic politicians were pandering to the segregationist mob. On the basis of—let's see—nothing . . . liberals labeled the loose-knit group of Tea Partiers "racist." They broadcast to America: You are not allowed to associate with Tea Partiers. We'll let you off with a warning this time, but the next time you are caught agreeing with Tea Party people, you're going to be called a racist, too.

MSNBC's Chris Matthews, whose life history betrays little association with black people, fancies himself a hitherto unheralded hero of the civil rights movement. He is a scrupulous bean counter when it comes to the number of blacks at Tea Parties—as if some central Tea Party bureaucracy controls who shows up at their rallies. Inasmuch as blacks vote overwhelmingly Democratic, you wouldn't expect to see a lot of them at Tea Parties. Still, the Tea Parties are not as white as Chris Matthews's staff. They're not as white as a Jon Stewart audience. They are not as white as Janeane Garofalo's fans.

But night after night, Matthews accuses conservatives of harboring secret racist views, asking, "What are the Tea Partiers really angry about? Health care reform or the fact that it was an African-American president and a woman speaker of the House who pushed through major change?"[39] When Governor Bill Richardson of New Mexico endorsed Obama, Matthews called it a "stunning picture" to have a very white but technically Latino governor endorsing the half-black Obama.[40] In a special tribute to his own post-racial attitude, after Obama's first State of the Union address, Matthews announced, "You know, I forgot [Obama] was black tonight for an hour."[41]

So we know Matthews is down with the brothers. Needless to say, he sends his own kids to white-as-snow private schools. Washington, D.C., is majority black, whereas St. Albans is probably about 3 percent black. Matthews had to go to a lot of trouble to get his kids into a school like that. It's not Eeny, meeny, miny, moe. So Matthews may not be the best person to be hectoring Tea Partiers, "How dare you not have black people at your rallies!"

The placid acceptance of glaring contradictions is the essence of mob behavior, according to Le Bon. Neither Matthews nor the rest of the herd grasp any inconsistency between Matthews's personal behavior and his blustery public accusations against others. He is "in reality under the influence of anterior ideas, that have become sentiments, and it is such ideas alone that influence the more recondite motives of our acts and utterances. It cannot be otherwise in the case of crowds."[42]

Also on the Republican racism beat is MSNBC's Rachel Maddow. (Because if a Jewish lesbian doesn't speak for the black man, then I don't know who does.) On September 21, 2009, Rachel Maddow introduced a video as if she were presenting a snuff film, saying, "Behold, a Missouri congressman, candidate for U.S. Senate, . . . telling what seems to be a really long, meandering, gut-churning racist joke."

(BEGIN VIDEO CLIP)

*Representative Roy Blunt (R, Missouri):* Supposedly it's the turn of the 19th century, the end of the 19th century, beginning of the 20th century, there was a group of British occupiers in a very lush, very quiet, very peaceful, very uneventful part of India. And this group of British soldiers who were occupying that part of India decided they'd carve a golf course out of the jungle of India. And there was really not much else to do. So, for over a year, this was the biggest event going on getting this golf course created.

And they got the golf course done and almost from the day the first ball was hit on this golf course, something happened they didn't anticipate. Monkeys would come running out of the jungle and they would grab the golf balls. And if it was in the fairway, they might throw it in the rough. If it was in the rough, they might throw—they might throw it back at you.

And I can go into great and long detail about how many things they did to try to eliminate the monkey problem, but they never got it done. So finally, for this golf course and this golf course only, they passed a rule, and the rule was you have to play the ball where the monkey throws it. And that is the rule in Washington all the time.[43]

(LAUGHTER)

(END VIDEO CLIP)

You could play that tape for the NAACP, and they would say, "I'm sorry, why are you showing us this?" Obviously, Blount was saying, This is how things work in Washington. It could be senators, representatives, government bureaucrats—or other Republicans—who are grabbing the balls. It actually tells you something about liberals that they instantly assume any mention of monkeys must be a reference to Obama.

Longtime *New York Times* blubberbutt Tom Wicker wrote endlessly about civil rights and racial reconciliation. Naturally, Wicker was another educational chicken hawk, sending his own children to elite, very white private schools and then retiring to Vermont, literally the whitest state in the nation.[44] When asked about the glaring inconsistency of his kids' white private schools, he said, "It gives me a lot of intellectual discomfort, but I am not going to disadvantage my children to win more support for my views."[45]

The point wasn't whether Wicker was required to "win more support" for his views, but that he didn't actually hold those views in the first place. Manifestly, liberals who don't send their own children to public schools believe those schools are inferior, but don't mind dumping poor kids into them—provided they can send their own children to sanitary, private schools. It tells you a lot when the actual behavior of people is at variance with their public position.

Liberals who send their own kids to fancy private schools while wailing about the racism of other people are like stockbrokers pushing stocks they got out of a long time ago. All these friend-to-the-blacks liberals adamantly refuse to give other people the same opportunity they have to escape the public schools through things like school vouchers and parochial schools.

In 2002, when marbles-in-his-mouth Trent Lott stepped down from a leadership position with the Senate Republicans for praising Strom Thurmond (who had a better record on civil rights than Bill Clinton's pal Orval Faubus), Hillary Clinton said, "If anyone thinks that one person stepping down from a leadership position cleanses the Republican Party of their constant exploitation of race, then I think you're naive."

Where did Chelsea go to school again? (Fancy private school, Sidwell Friends.)

In fact, could we get a list of all the sanctimonious white liberals constantly accusing other people of racism who sent their kids to private schools? We'll start with Al Gore, Bill Clinton, and Barack Obama—all of whom sent their kids to lily-white private schools. What other pompous liberals who rank themselves with Martin Luther King won't let their kids go to school with blacks?

It's always the people with the most secure, taxicab, doorman-protected lives lecturing those who live on the front lines of integration about their racial attitudes. Howell Raines was editorial page editor of the *New York Times* from 1993 to 2001. During that time, more than one-third of his signed editorials somehow brought up "racism" (11 out of 29). Raines's main interaction with actual black people was apparently limited to the family maid, about whom he wrote a book, *Grady's Gift*. Like Wicker's "intellectual discomfort" with sending his kids to elite private schools, Raines felt bad about leaving the maid outside in the car when his family ate at "Whites Only" restaurants.

Raines's only other famous interaction with a black person consisted of his utter humiliation of Jayson Blair, whom Raines hired, retained, and promoted, despite Blair's manifest inability to do the job, culminating in an indelible scandal at the *Times* and both of their firings. When Raines "retired," he chose the Poconos as his home,[46] a famous white-flight destination that lawyer Ron Kuby calls "outer whitelandia."[47]

Contrast these hairy-chested civil rights champions with Republican-appointed judge Charles Pickering. He took on the Ku Klux Klan as a prosecutor in the sixties—you know, before it was safe. As a consequence, Pickering required full-time FBI protection for his family. In the seventies, he sent his children to public schools in Mississippi, the state with the highest percentage of blacks in the nation. *60 Minutes* found a picture of Pickering's daughter sitting happily in a classroom with nearly all black faces.

But when George W. Bush nominated Pickering to the Fifth Circuit

Court of Appeals, Democrats said Pickering was bad on . . . civil rights! Yes—civil rights. Of course, by "civil rights" liberals meant abortion on demand. These days, "civil rights" is nothing but a cat's-paw for the mob's left-wing social policies, such as abortion. Back when civil rights meant rights for blacks, Democrats were standing in the schoolhouse door.

The fact that Pickering's nomination to the Fifth Circuit Court of Appeals under Bush was blocked by Senate Democrats tells you all you need to know about the mob. Pickering was supported by the Mississippi NAACP, which knew him and knew his history. His nomination was fiercely promoted by Charles Evers, brother of slain civil rights leader Medgar Evers. But Pickering was opposed by an oddball collection of pro-abortion left-wingers. So in the name of "civil rights," the Democrats filibustered a man who risked his life to take on the Klan.

The inferior reasoning of crowds described by Le Bon allows liberals to puff themselves up and act as if they are Freedom Riders by waiting a safe fifty years after the racist mobs have been defeated and then running around denouncing everyone else for "racism." A mob's logic, Le Bon says, resembles that of "the savage, who imagines that by eating the heart of a courageous foe he acquires his bravery."[48]

Republicans are always the party of the law-abiding and the productive; Democrats are always the party of the resentful mob. Now that Hispanics are gaining demographic ground, watch for the Democrats to drop blacks as their special friends and move on to illegal aliens.

Angry violent mobs are always Democratic: Code Pink, SDS, The Weathermen, Earth First!, anti-war protesters, and union protesters in Wisconsin. Like them, the Ku Klux Klan was, of course, another Democratic undertaking, originally formed to terrorize Republicans, but later switching to terrorize blacks. It was Democratic juries that acquitted Klansman after Klansman. It was Democratic politicians who supported segregation, Democratic governors who called out the National Guard to stop desegregation, Democratic commissioners of public safety who turned police dogs and water hoses on civil rights protesters.

As the historian Paul Johnson explains, "Christianity was content with a solitary hate-figure to explain evil: Satan. But modern secular faiths needed human devils, and whole categories of them. The enemy, to be plausible, had to be an entire class or race."[49]

Once, Democrats used blacks as the mythical enemy to rally their troops. Today, it's conservatives, Tea Partiers, and Fox News. To increase their own power, Democrats are perfectly happy to gin up violent ruffians—from the Klan to Moveon.org—to battle this or that human devil. Democrats are always the party of the mob. The only thing that changes is which mob they're supporting.

# ELEVEN

# TIMOTHY McVEIGH IS NOW A TEA PARTIER

**W**henever a Democrat is elected president, the media's standard response is to start looking for armed rebellion in the red states. With mob savagery woven into the history of the Left, they use their media mobs to broadcast stories about the omnipresent threat of right-wing violence, hoping that no one will notice that the actual violence—as opposed to the supposed threat of violence—has always come from the Left.

Consider that liberals have been citing Timothy McVeigh, Oklahoma City bomber, as a right-wing terrorist for fifteen years. Liberals simply assumed that McVeigh was a conservative because he was a white male who knew how to use a gun. After a century of violence from the Ku Klux Klan, the labor unions, the communists, the anarchists, the anti-war protesters, the Weathermen, the SDS, the Black Panthers, Jim Jones's People's Temple, Squeaky Fromme, and Earth First!, liberals were desperate for any hooligan who looked like a Republican.

But McVeigh was neither conservative nor Christian. This alleged right-winger was a drug-taking self-proclaimed agnostic, who was thrown out of the Michigan militia and who declared, "Science is my religion," sounding more like Janeane Garofalo than Wayne LaPierre.

Liberals were undeterred. McVeigh was white and he was male: he *had* to be a Republican. (To liberals, we all look alike.) In *Harper's Magazine,* Lewis Lapham said McVeigh's views were "not unlike those expressed by the members of the nation's better country clubs." *Time* senior writer Richard Lacayo called talk radio "an unindicted co-conspirator in the blast." *Today* show host Bryant Gumbel said, "The bombing in Oklahoma City has focused renewed attention on the rhetoric that's been coming from the right and those who cater to angry white men." Then-representative (now senator) Chuck Schumer blamed the bombing on the National Rifle Association.

(Luckily, McVeigh was captured before the Unabomber, so liberals didn't have to explain how the Green movement wasn't responsible for Ted Kaczynski's bombing spree.)

Even the president of the United States, Bill Clinton, blamed the Oklahoma City bombing on talk-radio hosts, accusing them of "fostering hatred, division and encouraging violence." He said some rhetoric "pushes fragile people over the edge," adding, "their bitter words have consequences. . . . They leave the impression, by their words, that violence is acceptable."

In response, Brent Bozell, Media Research Center chairman, offered $100,000 to Clinton's favorite charity if he named a single credible radio talk-show host who had called for violence against the American people or the government. The reward remains uncollected.[1]

Again, in January 2011, when twenty-two-year-old, left-wing pothead Jared Loughner shot up a Gabrielle Giffords political event at a Tucson Safeway, killing six people, liberals immediately blamed the Tea Party, Sarah Palin, and all conservatives for inspiring the shooter.

To make their case, they needed to prove:

a. Right-wingers had called for violence against anyone, especially moderate Democratic congresswomen
b. Loughner was listening to them
c. Loughner was influenced by them

But as more information came out, the truth was nearly the opposite. Loughner's attack would have gone down in history as another act of terroristic violence by a right-winger, just like McVeigh, except this time conservatives had the Internet and other media outlets to publicize the truth.

No conservative had called for violence against anyone. Nor had any conservative engaged in any "rhetoric" that was likely to lead to violence. Every putative example of "violent rhetoric" these squeamish liberals produced kept being matched by an identical example from the Democrats.

Sarah Palin, for example, was accused of complicity in murder for having produced a map with crosshairs over the congressional districts being targeted by Republicans. So did the Democratic Leadership Committee. Indeed, Democratic consultant Bob Beckel went on Fox News and said he invented the bull's-eye maps.

Similarly, every time liberals produced an example of military lingo from a Republican—"we're going to target this district"—Republicans produced five more from the Democrats. President "whose asses to kick" Obama had warned of "hand-to-hand combat" with his political opponents and said, "If they bring a knife to the fight, we bring a gun"—making Obama the first American president to advocate gunfights since Andrew Jackson.

These are figures of speech known as "metaphors." (Do liberals know where we got the word "campaign"?) It's not that both sides did something wrong, neither side did anything wrong. But the drama queens ran riot for weeks after the Tucson shooting. MSNBC's Chris Matthews recalled Palin's statement "We're not retreating, we're reloading" and then he said—I quote—"That's not a metaphor." If it wasn't a metaphor, whom did she shoot?

By blaming a mass killing on figures of speech, liberals sounded as crazy as Loughner with his complaints about people's grammar. After insisting that we drop metaphors, liberals were on the verge of demanding a ban on metonymies—until they realized no one was buying it. (Wait until they find out about gerund phrases!)

As for Loughner being influenced by Tea Partiers, Fox News, and talk radio— oops, another dead end. According to all available evidence, Loughner was a liberal. Every friend of Loughner who characterized his politics described him as liberal. Not one called him a conservative. One friend said Loughner never listened to talk radio or watched the TV news. Throw in "never read books" and you have the dictionary definition of a liberal. Being completely uninformed is precisely how most liberals stay liberal.

According to voluminous Twitter postings the day of the shooting by Caitie Parker, one of Loughner's friends since high school, he was "left wing," "a political radical," "quite liberal," and "a pot head."[2] If any public figure influenced this guy, my money's on Bill Maher.

But liberals were so determined to exploit the massacre to get conservatives to stop talking, they told calculated lies about Loughner's politics. In a shocking example, the *New York Times* implied—against all evidence—that Loughner was a pro-life zealot. Only because numerous other news outlets, including ABC News and the AP, reported the exact same incident in much greater detail—with eyewitness quotes—do we know that the *Times* rendition was complete bunk.

ABC News reported:

One Pima Community College student, who had a poetry class with Loughner later in his college career, said he would often act "wildly inappropriate." "One day [Loughner] started making comments about terrorism and laughing about killing the baby," classmate Don Coorough told ABC News, referring to a discussion about abortions. "The rest of us were looking at him in shock. . . . I thought this young man was troubled."

Another classmate, Lydian Ali, recalled the incident as well. "A girl had written a poem about an abortion. It was very emotional and she was teary eyed and he said something about strapping a bomb to the fetus and making a baby bomber," Ali said.

Here's the *Times* version: "After another student read a poem about getting an abortion, Mr. Loughner compared the young woman to a 'terrorist for killing the baby.'" That's how the *Times* transformed Loughner from a sicko laughing about a dead fetus to a deadly earnest pro-life fanatic. (Never believe a news story written by Eric Lipton, Charlie Savage, or Scott Shane of the *New York Times*—or, for simplicity, anything in the *Times*.)

Loughner's liberal worldview might have passed unnoticed, as it has with other random nuts committing violence. But liberals opened the door by blaming what they hoped would be Loughner's right-wing politics.

The *New York Times*'s Paul Krugman got the ball rolling two days after the shooting spree in a column titled "Climate of Hate," announcing that the cause of the shooting was "toxic rhetoric" coming "overwhelmingly, from the right."[3] This was followed by the usual torrent of exactly zero examples.

Rather, Krugman cited the McVeigh canard, as well as this crucial evidence: Other liberals saying right-wing rhetoric is dangerous! This would be like one birther citing another birther as proof that Obama was born in Kenya.

Thus, Krugman said the Obama administration had issued reports claiming "right-wing extremism was on the rise, with a growing potential for violence." Liberals spend a lot of time worrying about the "potential" of violence from the right, whereas conservatives have to worry about actual violence from liberals.

But according to Krugman: "[T]here's a huge contrast in the media. Listen to Rachel Maddow or Keith Olbermann, and you'll hear a lot of caustic remarks and mockery aimed at Republicans. But you won't hear jokes about shooting government officials or beheading a journalist at the *Washington Post*. Listen to Glenn Beck or Bill O'Reilly, and you will."

Only a complete zealot like Krugman could say black is white and white is black—not even gray!

Krugman was referring to a remark Bill O'Reilly made about *Washington Post* reporter Dana Milbank that had roiled the mainstream media for weeks in 2010.

To be fair to O'Reilly, which he wouldn't be to me, he was joking. We know that because he specifically said so. Milbank had flat-out lied in a column, claiming that Fox News's election night coverage included only one Democrat. There were, in fact, at least six. O'Reilly called him out on it, then switched to a story about Sharia law in Oklahoma and asked his guest: "Does Sharia law say we can behead Dana Milbank? That was a joke for you 'Media Matters' people out there, because you know—'O'Reilly says we want to behead Dana!'"[4]

In response, Milbank wrote what has already been recorded as the gayest column in world history that didn't include a picture of the cast of *Glee:*

> Bill O'Reilly wants my head—literally. On Thursday night, the Fox News host asked, as part of a show that would be seen by 5.5 million people: 'Does Sharia law say we can behead Dana Milbank?' He then added, 'That was a joke.' Hilarious! Decapitation jokes just slay me, and this one had all the more hilarity because the topic of journalist beheadings brings to mind my late friend and colleague Danny Pearl, who replaced me in the *Wall Street Journal's* London bureau and later was murdered in Pakistan by people who thought Sharia justified it. . . . But what was he trying to say? That America would be better if it were more like Iran?[5]

The liberal blogs soon lit up with red-hot indignation over O'Reilly's direct threat to personally behead Milbank. It was even discussed on CNN's *Reliable Sources,* with Milbank again bleating, "I think it's a serious issue when people are suggesting violent imagery . . . as Bill O'Reilly did."

When host Howard Kurtz pointed out that Milbank was, in fact, wrong about how many Democrats had appeared on Fox News election night, Milbank said, "That's a fair argument. Maybe I should have written it differently, but let's not talk about cutting off heads."[6] Yes, he should have "written it differently" by not lying.

Now, here's some of that lighthearted "mockery aimed at Republicans" Krugman sees from Keith Olbermann. After Fox News's Brian Kilmeade chastised the media for refusing to identify Muslim terrorists as Muslims, Keith commented: "There is 'stupid' and there is 'bigoted' and there is 'paranoid' and there is 'Islamophobic'—though it takes a big man to combine all four of them. . . . Not every un-American bastard is Brian Kilmeade, but all Brian Kilmeades are un-American bastards and tonight's 'Worst Person in the World.' "[7]

The mind reels at such dazzling, frothy wordplay. If you close your eyes, it's almost like you're listening to Oscar Wilde!

A few years earlier, Keith accused Bush of inspiring the anthrax attacks (in his wry, Noel Coward–like way).

Rachel Maddow's caustic repartee includes her making up stories about right-wingers killing a census-taker and a Republican congressman being warned in advance about the Oklahoma City bombing—both stories requiring subsequent corrections.[8]

Maddow has also tied Republican Senate candidates to the killing of late-term abortionist George Tiller by describing her documentary on the shooting as important because "there are five Senate candidates running right now who have a position on abortion that has never really been seen in mainstream politics before."[9] Apart from "for" or "against," one wonders what the other positions on abortion might be. (Pro, but feel really bad about it? Against, except in cases where Charlie Sheen might be the father?)

Claims of "toxic rhetoric" invariably mean a conservative is talking. *We just passed this wonderful health care bill and it really debases the tone to hear all this criticism.* Liberals are blind with rage that conservatives get to talk now, too. They would prefer to return to a kinder world when there were just three TV networks and no Internet, back when Walter Cronkite told everyone what to believe and liberals didn't have to win arguments.

Krugman is not exactly a sardonic bon mot–dropping wit himself. He's more of an angry, red-faced ranter. His 2008 election-night party included effigy burnings of conservative politicians, according to an admiring profile in the *New Yorker* magazine.[10] Evidently, it's mocking, rakish wit when liberals burn political figures in effigy, but an incitement to murder when conservatives do it.

Democratic ex-congressman Paul Kanjorski of Pennsylvania wrote a column for the *New York Times* calling for "an atmosphere of civility and respect in which political discourse can flow freely, without fear of violent confrontation." Just months earlier Kanjorski had called for a Republican candidate to be shot: "That [Rick] Scott down there that's running for governor of Florida. Instead of running for governor of Florida, they ought to have him and shoot him. Put him against the wall and shoot him."[11] I'm not from around here, but that sounds like toxic rhetoric to me.

As much as the media stacked the deck with lies, they still couldn't win a hand.

In our next Portrait of Scumbag,* two days after the shooting, former congressman Alan Grayson was all over the networks blaming conservatives for inciting violence.

Grayson was most famous for the "Taliban Dan" video about his congressional opponent, Daniel Webster, in which Grayson edited Webster's remarks to precisely reverse their meaning. Webster had told a men's church group to pick a verse from the Bible that required something of them, such as "Love your wife even as Christ loved the church," adding "Don't pick the ones that say, 'She should submit to me.'" Grayson's campaign ad showed Webster saying only, "She should submit to me," playing "submit to me" over and over again, and helpfully adding, "Religious fanatics try to take away our freedom in Afghanistan, in Iraq and right here in central Florida."[12]

Appearing on MSNBC two days after Jared Loughner's shooting spree, Grayson claimed there had been attacks or "threats of attacks" against Democrats "for two years now." Apparently, it was all gentlemanly disagreement until Obama became president.

Note how many lies Grayson packs in to prove his point:

1. "[Democratic Rep.] Tom Perriello is burned in effigy."

Big deal—but also, by the way, a lie. One guy thought it would be a fun part of the bonfire, other Tea Partiers objected, so it never happened.[13]

2. "Frank Kratovil was hung in effigy."

Again: big deal—but it was done by one guy, who was promptly denounced for doing it by the official Tea Party group.[14]

3. "Debbie Wasserman Schultz had her initials used for target practice by one of her Republican opponents."

Yes, and the opponent who shot at the letters "DWS" went on to lose the primary. The organizer of the event where it happened immediately sent a handwritten apology to the congresswoman and resigned from his position with the local Republicans.[15]

---

*By "scumbag," I do not mean that Grayson is literally a used condom, I mean he is a piece of garbage wrapped in skin, who lies whenever he talks.

4. "[Black congressman] Emanuel Cleaver was spat on."

To be fair, that was not a distortion or half-truth. It was a complete lie.

5. "When you show a picture of someone, use her name, or represent her district and use it with the rifle sight the way Sarah Palin did, that is inexcusable. That is inviting people to commit violence on another human being."

Here we have a despicable, sneaky lie. Sarah Palin did not put crosshairs over Giffords's face. She did not put crosshairs on Giffords's name. She put crosshairs on a map of Giffords's district—just like the Democratic Leadership Committee and a million others have done with their political opponents. But notice how Grayson sleazily throws in three alternative claims—crosshairs were put on Giffords's face, name, or district—just to release the two false allegations into the atmosphere. This is on the order of saying, "Alan Grayson has engaged in child rape, murder, or bad taste."

6. "[Michele Bachmann's comment, she wants her constituents armed and dangerous] that's over the line."

The rest of the sentence was "I want people in Minnesota armed and dangerous *on this issue of the energy tax.*" Her full quote was: "But you can get all the latest information on this event, this . . . a must-go-to event with this Chris Horner. People will learn . . . it will be fascinating. We met with Chris Horner last week, twenty members of Congress. It takes a lot to wow members of Congress after a while. This wowed them. And I am going to have materials for people when they leave. I want people in Minnesota armed and dangerous on this issue of the energy tax because we need to fight back."

She was telling people to arm themselves with information, nothing more.

7. "So is [Sarah Palin's statement] 'don't retreat but reload.'"

That, also, is a metaphor, you complete moron. But anticipating princess-and-the-pea liberals like Grayson, Milbank, Matthews, and Krugman, nearly a year earlier, Palin had told a political rally,

"When we take up our arms, we're talking about our vote. We're talking about being involved in a contested primary like this and picking the right candidate, too."[16]

8. "Dan Gainor (ph), a Republican operative, telling people that he paid them $100 to punch me in the nose—that's all over the line."[17]

That, frankly, is shocking. I would have paid them at least $1,000.

Well done, Alan! That's more lies per second than anyone in the history of television!

And finally, to top off a week of conservatives getting blamed for a left-wing pothead's shooting spree, a liberal made a death threat to a conservative . . . at a televised town-hall meeting to discuss the shootings. Liberal J. Eric Fuller, who had been shot in the leg by Loughner the week before, was apparently enraged at a suggestion by Arizona Tea Party leader Trent Humphries that people not politicize the shooting. Fuller screamed at Humphries "You're dead!" and was arrested on the spot. As he was being dragged from the room by the police, Fuller kept yelling at the crowd, "What's the matter with you—whores!" according to the *New York Times*.[18]

A month later, during the government union strikes in Wisconsin, Democratic assemblyman and prostitute frequenter Gordon Hintz yelled at Republican assemblywoman Michelle Litjens, "You are F**king dead!"[19]

Liberals possess in abundance all the characteristics of mobs identified by Le Bon: "impulsiveness, irritability, incapacity to reason, the absence of judgment and of the critical spirit, the exaggeration of the sentiments, and others besides—which are almost always observed in beings belonging to inferior forms of evolution—in women, savages, and children, for instance."[20] I would add that liberal mobs are composed of individuals with an unresolved infantile disorder, resulting in humorlessness and rage.

So it's particularly irresponsible for the mainstream media and elected Democrats to be ginning up these impulsive, prone-to-violence liberals by accusing conservatives of complicity in murder. We'd prefer it if you'd just make crosshair maps of our contested congressional districts, please. The false imputation of violence to conservatives is far more dangerous than anything Palin has ever done, particularly when processed by the primitive, mob-susceptible liberal brain. If Sarah Palin is inciting people to commit murder, wouldn't it be an act of public service to kill her?

And when the violence comes, liberals will ignore it, defend it as harmless fun or "free speech," or hoot with laughter about it. Then they will blame it on conservatives. A few years later, the perpetrators will be pardoned by a Democratic president and hired as university professors.

Liberals cite the killing of abortionists as an example of right-wing violence. For those of you keeping score at home, in the past four decades, abortion foes have killed eight abortion clinic workers, and abortion supporters have killed 53 million unborn babies. That score again, with we're not sure how much time left to play, is 53 million to eight.

Besides the numbers, another difference is that fans of unborn babies don't praise the murders of abortionists or call such attacks a "constitutional right." To the contrary, every person affiliated in any way with the pro-life movement has roundly condemned all abortion clinic violence, even when the target is a mass murderer like George Tiller.

But more important, abortion clinic violence should not be filed under "Political Violence" at all. It should be filed under "Things Liberals Won't Let Americans Vote On." As upset as liberals were by the Vietnam War, when JFK started that war, he was a president, duly elected by constitutional means—plus a little Daley machine magic. So was LBJ when he escalated the war, as was Nixon when he ended it.

Liberals invented a constitutional right to abortion out of thin air and, in one fell swoop, withdrew abortion policy from all democratic processes. Wishing very hard for something to be a constitutional right does not make it so. When there is no legal process for pro-lifers to pursue to outlaw abortion—unlike every policy liberals violently protest—some pro-lifers will inevitably respond to lawlessness with lawlessness.

Noticeably, the first abortion doctor was killed not after *Roe,* but twenty years later, immediately after the 1993 decision upholding Roe, *Planned Parenthood v. Casey.* In the first few years after Casey, about six more people were killed in attacks on abortion clinics. Most of the abortionists were shot or, depending upon your point of view, had a procedure performed on them with a rifle.

Americans opposed to abortion had spent two decades fighting within the law against a constitutionally groundless decision. They elected two Republican presidents, patiently waited for Supreme Court justices to retire, and fought bruising nomination battles to get conservative nominees on the Court. Then they passed an abortion law in Pennsylvania, which was immediately appealed to the Supreme Court. But the Court upheld the utterly fraudulent "constitutional right" to abortion announced in *Roe*. There were no more constitutional options left to fight judicial tyranny on the little matter of mass murder.

Thus, abortion clinic violence is more akin to the Tiananmen Square protests in Communist China than any liberal riot in America. Want to stop violence at abortion clinics? Repeal *Roe* and let Americans vote.

Conservatives constitute about 40 percent of the population— compared with only 20 percent who are liberals.[21] If "both sides" were equally guilty of committing political violence, there would be twice as much political violence coming from conservatives as liberals. Instead, there is none. All the political violence comes from either random lunatics or liberals—to the extent that those categories can be disaggregated.

# TWELVE

# IMAGINARY VIOLENCE FROM THE RIGHT VS. ACTUAL VIOLENCE FROM THE LEFT

Somewhat astoundingly, in the entire nation's history, there's never been a presidential assassination attempt by a right-winger. There have been more than a dozen by left-wingers. I wouldn't mention it—I assume we're all against political assassinations—except liberals keep warning us about the burgeoning violence on the verge of exploding from the right wing.

It could still happen, but in the first 222 years of this nation's history, every single shooting of a national politician has been committed by either a liberal or someone even more deranged than the average liberal.

Some would-be assassins were simply delusional nuts. Richard Lawrence, a painter who thought he was King Richard II of England, tried to shoot Andrew Jackson because he believed the United States owed him money. John Schrank, inspired by the ghost of William McKinley, tried to kill President Teddy Roosevelt because he was angry about Roosevelt running for a third term. Francisco Martin Duran, a paranoid schizophrenic who believed he was going to become Jesus Christ, shot at some men on the White House lawn during Clinton's presidency.[1]

The rest were political activists, who may have been crazy enough to be left-wingers but were not so crazy as to believe they were King Richard II.

Actor/peace activist John Wilkes Booth—not to be confused with actor/peace activist Sean Penn—shot President Abraham Lincoln on April 14, 1865, because, as he explained in a letter to his family, he was furious with Republicans for foisting the war on the South. He said he loved "peace more than life." (But he really wanted to direct.)

Charles J. Guiteau, who shot President James Garfield in 1881, had a long relationship with a utopian commune called the Oneida Community, where free love and communal child-rearing were practiced, kind of like Berkeley.

Leon Czolgosz, who killed President William McKinley in 1901, was a socialist and anarchist inspired by a radical speech given by socialist Emma Goldman that same year.

Giuseppe Zangara, who plotted to kill both Republican president Herbert Hoover and President-elect Franklin Roosevelt, just missed shooting Roosevelt, killing Chicago mayor Anton Cermak instead. Zangara was motivated by his all-consuming envy of the rich and intended to assassinate "all capitalist presidents and kings." This would have made him an ideal pick for Obama's cabinet, apart from his habit of shooting elected officials.

Lee Harvey Oswald, who shot President John F. Kennedy on November 22, 1963, was a stone-cold communist ever since he read a communist pamphlet about Julius and Ethel Rosenberg as a teenager. Oswald studied Russian and moved to the USSR in his late teens. When his application for Soviet citizenship was declined, he slit his wrists. Oswald married a Russian woman, brought her and their child back to the United States, and planned to escape to Cuba, whiling away his days passing out *Fair Play for Cuba* leaflets. In other words, Lee Harvey Oswald was Michael Moore, if Moore didn't hate guns and wasn't a fat, disgusting pig.

Ginned up by publications of the Communist Party and the Socialist Workers Party, Oswald first tried to kill Major General Edwin A. Walker, a John Bircher. Oswald next plotted to kill former vice president Richard Nixon, but was waylaid the day Nixon was in Dallas.

So he shot President Kennedy. Upon his arrest, Oswald immediately called John Abt, lawyer for the American Communist Party, planning to ask Abt to defend him so he could use the trial to showcase his Marxist beliefs. (And who hasn't used his one phone call after being arrested for murder to make arrangements to share Marxism with the world?)

Lynette "Squeaky" Fromme, who shot at President Gerald Ford in 1975, was part of Charles Manson's countercultural hippie cult. She pulled the gun on Ford because she was incensed about the plight of the California redwood.

Seventeen days later, Sara Jane Moore tried to kill Ford because, she said, "the government had declared war on the Left." (Would that it were so!)

In the entire history of the nation, only two senators and two congressmen have been assassinated.[2] Both the first and the last were killed by Democrats for political reasons, and the other two were killed for nonpolitical reasons.

The first member of Congress to be assassinated was Republican James M. Hinds of Arkansas. He was killed in 1868 by secretary of the Democratic Committee of Monroe County and Ku Klux Klan member George A. Clark. (This was contrary to initial reports on the *Rachel Maddow Show* that he had been killed by a right-wing anti-government Tea Partier.

Senator Huey Long was shot and killed in 1935 by Carl Weiss for no political reason, but apparently because Long had targeted Weiss's father-in-law, a judge, for removal from the bench.

Senator Robert Kennedy was killed on June 5, 1968, by Sirhan Sirhan, a Palestinian extremist angry with Kennedy for his support of Israel. Sirhan keeps coming up for parole these days and is hoping to be released in time to get his own prime-time show on MSNBC. (It was a strange name for an assassin, unless you think about it.)

The last assassination of a member of Congress was in 1978, when Representative Leo Ryan was killed by members of Jim Jones's left-wing cult in Guyana.

Conservatives, we're endlessly told, create "an atmosphere of hatred and fear." This is as opposed to liberals who just go around shooting elected officials.

Among recent examples of political violence on a massive scale in this country—not rhetorical violence, but real violence—was that committed by the Weathermen and their ilk just a few decades ago. Not only were those people embraced by the establishment, they would be welcome today at any Democratic gathering. America's current president launched his political career in the home of two such radicals who incited violence, set bombs, praised Charles Manson—and only through their own ineptitude avoided murdering anyone.

Guess which political group both the Southern Poverty Law Center and the FBI consider the most dangerous in America? Moveon.org? Tea Partiers? The Kennedy family?

The answer is: environmentalists.

Citing the $43 million in damage done in the past two decades only by the Animal Liberation Front and the Earth Liberation Front, the Southern Poverty Law Center concludes, "Extremists within the environmental and animal rights movements have committed literally thousands of violent criminal acts in recent decades—arguably more than those from any other radical sector, left or right."[3] In 2002, the FBI described the Earth Liberation Front as America's most dangerous domestic terrorist group.[4]

There are other hard comparisons to be made. No conservative has ever charged at a liberal testifying before Congress, waving bloody hands in the witness's face—as was done to Secretary of State Condoleezza Rice at a hearing of the House Foreign Affairs Committee. (Or as liberals would put it if she were a Democrat: the *first black female* secretary of state, Condoleezza Rice.)

No conservative has ever sneaked into a Democratic National Convention and heckled the speakers.

No Democratic politician has ever been rushed by a conservative and hit in the face with a stupid sign, as was done to Republican Senate candidate Rand Paul in 2010. Indeed, no conservative has rushed anyone, other than maybe a laggard waiter.

No conservative has ever thrown food at a prominent liberal. This is done all the time to conservative public figures. Limiting this review of liberal food-throwing to the baked dessert section—and liberals throw all sorts of food at conservatives—liberals have thrown pies at

William F. Buckley, Phyllis Schlafly, Anita Bryant, Milton Friedman, Bill Kristol, David Horowitz, and G. Gordon Liddy, among others.

No conservative has ever demonstrated outside a private citizen's home. This is done repeatedly by liberals—to the Duke lacrosse players;[5] to AIG officials;[6] to Republican House speaker John Boehner;[7] to a Wal-Mart developer;[8] to a Bank of America executive (who was a Democrat, but SEIU didn't care);[9] to Wisconsin governor Scott Walker; and to Wisconsin State Senate leader Scott Fitzgerald.[10] (And that was despite a union rule prohibiting work on Tuesdays!)

When the Bank of America officer's young son was trapped, alone and terrified, inside his home with fourteen busloads of Service Employees International Union thugs pouring out onto his front yard to protest, the police refused to arrest the trespassers so as not to "incite them."[11] His parents had both worked in the Clinton administration. Even liberals know that they are in danger of a physical assault only from their fellow liberals. But they still playact terror of anti-ObamaCare protesters.

It is possible that, somewhere, at some time, an audience of conservatives has shouted down an invited liberal speaker—though no such incidents come to mind. But it is not possible that conservatives would defend or embrace the hooligans. Conservatives think civil society needs to be, you know, civil.

We are not counting the voices in Maureen Dowd's head that heard Representative Joe Wilson shout, "You lie, *boy!*" rather than "You lie!" during Obama's 2010 State of the Union address. First of all, we're in trouble if people can be found guilty for what Maureen Dowd knows they really meant in their hearts—especially since Maureen seems to base her experience of the world on having recently read *Uncle Tom's Cabin.* Second, if Democrats are going to be interrupting the president's speech every three minutes with raucous standing ovations, that makes it a participatory speech. A rule condemning Wilson's two-syllable shout-out "You lie!" would mean that only one side is allowed to participate. Third, and by the way, Wilson was roundly condemned by everyone but me and quickly apologized.

Liberals, by contrast, defend and even celebrate outrageous behavior on their side. By now, it has become so expected for liberals to aggressively disrupt and shut down conservative speakers that people hardly notice it anymore. They shout down conservatives with alarming frequency on college campuses—those crucibles of enlightenment—and are invariably protected by college administrators.

No conservative has ever tried to stage a "citizen's arrest" of a political opponent. Republican presidents and their staff are constantly being threatened with "citizen's arrests." In 1984, liberal nut and third-party presidential candidate Sonia Johnson stood in front of the White House announcing that she planned to make a citizen's arrest of President Reagan for "war crimes." This was based on Reagan's invasion of Marxist Grenada to rescue American medical personnel trapped there. Many considered this the high point of Sonia's presidential campaign.

A few years later, Greenpeace employee Terry Fernsler showed up at the Westin Hotel in Seattle, where President Reagan was speaking, and tried to make a citizen's arrest for his "war crimes" against the communist regime in Nicaragua in violation of "international law."[12] In 1987, the liberal group Pledge of Resistance plotted to kidnap a federal official in a "citizen's arrest" if President Reagan invaded Nicaragua or El Salvador.[13] Then, again, in 1988, liberal protesters at the G-7 meeting in Toronto tried to make citizen's arrests of both Reagan and Margaret Thatcher, presumably for preventing the worldwide triumph of communism.

The incidence of citizen's arrests came to a suspicious halt throughout the Clinton presidency—rape and perjury being deemed "personal matters" rather than "crimes"—but, strangely enough, the trend came roaring back for the second President Bush.

Liberals tried to make a citizen's arrest of President Bush in Britain in 2001 for crimes against the planet;[14] at the European-American Summit in June 2004;[15] again in 2004 in Ottawa;[16] and back here in the good old U.S. of A. at the 2004 Republican National Convention in New York (on the grounds that he was "responsible for the misfortune of everyone who's disabled").[17]

Anti-war protesters issued warrants for the citizen's arrest of Bush in the United States,[18] in Britain (for having caused "grievous harm to thousands of people in Iraq"),[19] and in Paris, where a mock arrest was made of a Bush impersonator in lieu of the real thing.[20]

Even after Bush left office and happiness reigned throughout the world, liberals stormed a luncheon where Bush was speaking in Alberta, Canada,[21] and so many protesters threatened to derail a scheduled January 2011 Bush speech in Geneva that the event had to be canceled.

Even Bush's advisers have been—and continue to be—threatened with citizen's arrests, including Bush's UN ambassador John Bolton at the Hay Festival in Wales in May 2008—years after the end of his employment with Bush.[22] Bush adviser Karl Rove has been repeatedly threatened with citizen's arrests—by the Des Moines Catholic Workers Party when he was giving a speech in Iowa,[23] by a college student when he was giving a speech at Oberlin College,[24] and by liberals throughout the country who show up to disrupt his book events, which are often canceled because of the liberal hordes.

Conservatives make documentaries of people talking, explaining things, arguing points. Michael Moore makes documentaries showing him trying to make citizen's arrests or otherwise ambushing private citizens.

These aren't just a few random nuts that might turn up on either side of the political spectrum. Otherwise, conservatives would be staging citizen's arrests of Bill Clinton for allegedly raping Juanita Broaddrick, of Al Gore for committing fraud when he babbles about global warming in the middle of a blizzard, and of Joe Biden for "Recovery Summer." Conservatives wouldn't do it.

If someday, someplace in America, a conservative mob ever shuts down a liberal speaker, tries to make a citizen's arrest, throws food at a liberal public figure, or assaults a congressional witness, it won't be defended by other conservatives. You won't find conservatives writing letters to the editor praising nitwits trying to make a citizen's arrest, saying they "deserved a laurel," as was said in the *Toronto Star* about the violent Reagan and Thatcher protesters.[25] You won't find a Republican U.S. attorney general refusing to prosecute Republicans captured on tape standing outside a polling precinct, making armed threats on election day. You won't find a Republican member of Congress defending a criminal for dropping a cement block on a trucker's head.

Liberals constantly engage in mob violence—and allegedly respectable liberals encourage the ruffians. The *Guardian,* billing itself as "the world's leading liberal voice," ran a column by the nut who tried to arrest Bolton, in which he encouraged others to make a citizen's arrest of Tony Blair.[26]

It is simply taken as a given that Michael Moore and James Carville can stroll undisturbed through the most conservative parts of the country—even through the Republican National Convention!—while conservative public figures need bodyguards anywhere liberals might be.

Indeed, it's nonstop physical confrontation for conservatives. To take an example at random: Former New York mayor Rudy Giuliani was strolling out of the Bridgehampton arts fair in May 2009 when a "slim, well-dressed man," identified as sixty-nine-year-old John McCluskey of East Hampton, came charging at him, screaming "I'm gonna punch your lights out," and poking Giuliani in the chest.[27] Nothing like this has ever happened to a liberal, and if it did, right-wing publications wouldn't turn the nut into a hero. Meanwhile, the deranged McCluskey was hailed by the liberal Gawker website—in a brave, untitled piece—as "a true New York hero," while Giuliani, who was merely attending a local art show, was called a "perpetual asshole."[28]

But Keith Olbermann stormed out of the 2008 Republican National Convention early because MSNBC wouldn't double his security in the presence of scary Republican delegates.

No matter how much liberals wail about the threat of right-wing violence, all the nontheoretical violence keeps coming from the Left.

This is why it was laughable, even to themselves, when liberals began trying to portray Tea Partiers as potentially violent. These endlessly violent liberals never pass up an opportunity for indignation. Whenever it suits their purposes, they will transform themselves from supporters of violent anarchists into fainting Victorian virgins—"I can't believe my opponent would stoop so low!" Liberals believe anything ever said by a Republican is an incitement to violence. But when no violence ensues, we never hear, "Oh, okay, I overreacted." As soon as liberals think they can get away with it, they reintroduce their hoax charges. *It didn't get much press that our accusation was a lie—let's run with it.*

The Democratic National Committee called the Tea Party movement "rabid right-wing extremists" and "angry mobs."[29] ABC called them a "mob." CNN anchor Suzanne Malveaux introduced a segment on the Townhalls asking, "What is all this shouting about?"[30] CNN called them "rabble-rousing critics" of the president. Representative Brian Baird (D-WA) said citizens opposed to ObamaCare had a "lynch mob mentality" and were using "close to Brown-shirt tactics."[31] (Meaning what? Light brown shirt tactics? Beige, maybe? Taupe? Ecru?) The AFL-CIO—yes, the AFL-CIO—said the anti-ObamaCare citizens were "using mob rule."[32]

In an unexpected twist, Democrats also attacked the Tea Partiers for being too well dressed. (You're always arguing from a real position of strength when you attack your opponent's clothes.) White House spokesman Robert Gibbs said they looked like the "Brooks Brothers brigade." Senator Barbara Boxer complained that the ObamaCare protesters were suspiciously "well dressed." Chris Matthews repeated Gibbs's "Brooks Brothers brigade" line, demanding to know who these "well-dressed, middle-class people in pinks and limes" were.[33] Liberals don't consider protesters believable unless they're homeless people hired to protest by SEIU with a free T-shirt and a box lunch. They would find out in the next election just how real those protests were.

With the "too well dressed" attack not making much of an impact, liberals reverted to calling the anti-ObamaCare protesters a dangerous mob.

Senator Harry Reid called them "evil-mongers"—twice, to be sure he was understood.[34] Nancy Pelosi and Steny Hoyer wrote an article in USA Today calling them "un-American" for allegedly shouting down speakers. Pelosi and Hoyer should come to one of my college speeches.

Liberals acted as if they had encountered the Night Riders every time they saw a sign that said "T(axed) E(nough) A(lready)." It seemed perfectly plausible to liberals that a bunch of out-of-control, badass headbangers would call their rallies "Tea Parties." But while we kept hearing about the violent, racist rednecks at conservative rallies, the only violence at the Tea Parties and Townhalls kept being committed by liberals.

At a Townhall meeting on ObamaCare in St. Louis on August 6, 2009, Kenneth Gladney, a conservative black handing out pens and buttons, was punched in the face by union thugs yelling racial slurs—*"What kind of nigger are you?"* According to the police report, Gladney's assailants, Elston McCowan and Perry Molens, are both members of the SEIU. In all, six union thugs were arrested that day.[35]

About a month later, on September 3, 2009, sixty-five-year-old ObamaCare opponent Bill Rice had his finger bitten off at a health care rally in Thousand Oaks, California, by an ObamaCare supporter.[36] To repeat: A man had his finger bitten clear off by another human being at a political rally. Oh and by the way, the *New York Times* never mentioned it. Only two news outlets carried the story, according to Nexis: the *Washington Times* and Neil Cavuto, who interviewed the victim on Fox News. Ironically, having your finger bitten off by a left-wing crackpot while protesting ObamaCare is not covered by ObamaCare, but erectile dysfunction therapy for federal inmates is.

In January 2011, radio host Michael Smerconish was babbling to Chris Matthews about his terror of some angry birthers he had seen *eighteen months earlier* at a Mike Castle Townhall meeting in Delaware. He said, "I looked at that video and I was frightened. These are people who are on the edge and if somebody pushes them over, God help us all."[37]

Perhaps the good Lord stepped in—or perhaps the excitable attendees at the Castle meeting were never especially dangerous. Even the nutty birthers at the Mike Castle Townhall seemed to have managed not to attack anyone in the eighteen months since Smerconish had been "frightened" by what he saw there. If these wacky right-wingers are constantly on the verge of violence, why isn't there ever any violence?

You could throw a glass of cold water on a liberal in the middle of the night and he'd wake up denouncing "right-wing rhetoric."

Liberals keep warning us about right-wing violence—the Tea Partiers, the gun nuts, the militias, the abortion protesters, the Republicans in Hush Puppies terrorizing Jesse Jackson during the 2000 Florida recount. But they can never produce any examples. And when they do, it turns out to be a liberal.

In June 2009, liberals thought they finally had an act of violence they could pin on a right-winger—besides the old McVeigh chestnut— when there was a shooting at the Holocaust Museum in Washington, killing a black security guard.

The night of the shooting, Keith Olbermann hysterically warned,

"Five months—less than five months actually, into this presidency of this Democratic president, half-white, half-African-American, and a shooter opens fire in the National Holocaust Museum. Eleven days after an OB-GYN in Kansas is assassinated and his women's health clinic closes its doors apparently for good. Is this a coincidence of timing that these attacks are happening now?"[38]

The next night, Rachel Maddow noted that the Holocaust museum shooter was a birther, adding that such thinking was common among conservatives: "At the conservative tea parties that were held across the country in April, you couldn't get away from it."[39]

That day on the Ed Schultz show, Ed raised the prescience of the Department of Homeland Security report warning of an upsurge in violence among conservatives, sneering that "it was mocked by a lot of conservatives . . . but this guy that committed this crime yesterday, we knew what he was all about."[40]

In fact, however, the shooter, James Von Brunn, was every bit as angry about Bush's election as Obama's. On his webpage—about to be sold to AOL for $315 million—he raged against Bush, McCain, and all "neoconservatives." In addition to apparently being a birther, he was a 9/11 truther and—naturally—detested Christianity.[41]

Not every liberal will commit political violence, but all political violence keeps being committed by liberals.

Liberal hearts again leapt with anticipation on February 18, 2010, when a nut flew his plane into the IRS building in Austin, Texas. Those of you who are familiar with my previous work can probably guess what's about to happen.

The pilot, Joseph Stack, turned out to be a Marxist. Stack was upset not only about his IRS audit but also about the fact that America didn't have national health care. In what could have been a script from MSNBC's *Countdown with Keith Olbermann*, Stack's suicide note complained that "the joke we call the American medical system, including the drug and insurance companies, are murdering tens of thousands of people a year." He concluded his suicide note—Stack, not Olbermann—by denouncing capitalism and praising communism: "The communist creed: From each according to his ability, to each according to his need. The capitalist creed: From each according to his gullibility, to each according to his greed."

And just like that, what could have been a brilliant career as an MSNBC prime-time host came to a fiery end.

Just a week before Stack flew his plane into the IRS building, on February 12, 2010, University of Alabama professor Amy Bishop shot up a room full of professors, hitting six and leaving three of her colleagues dead. We didn't hear much about Bishop's massacre of her colleagues, probably because, according to the *Boston Herald,* Bishop "was a far-left political extremist who was 'obsessed' with President Obama to the point of being off-putting." That fact was never acknowledged by the *New York Times* or other major media, except inadvertently by the mainstream media's instantaneous dropping of all mention of the rather spectacular crime.

It was the same with the satanic cult the "Westboro church," which protests outside soldiers' funerals with charming signs saying things like "God hates fags." The patriarch of the cult, Fred Phelps, has run for office five times—as a Democrat. The *New York Times* submitted an amicus brief on his behalf in a lawsuit brought by the father of a soldier whose funeral Phelps's crew had disrupted.

Then, in late March 2010, there was exultation throughout the media when federal law enforcement officials arrested nine members of an alleged "Christian militia group" based in Michigan. The group, calling themselves the "Hutaree," was charged on weapons and drug offenses, and also with plotting to kill law enforcement officers. Inasmuch as they had not actually committed any violence yet, if the Hutaree had been Muslims, liberals would have been wailing about their civil rights.

The case, apparently just another white-trash bust, was featured on every MSNBC prime-time program that night. You'd think Michael Steele had been arrested. On *The Ed Show,* guest Bill Press said, "Ed, I have to tell you, I don't see any difference between what [conservative blogger] Erick Erickson said and what that militia did, the Hutaree."

Just making some back-of-the-envelope notes here: One difference is that Erickson wasn't accused of plotting to murder police officers.

Erickson, editor of the conservative Red State blog, had said on radio that he was perfectly happy to fill out the census form, but got worked up complaining about the detailed personal questions on the long form, saying, "This is crazy. What gives the Commerce Department the right to ask me how often I flush my toilet? Or about going to work? I'm not filling out this form. I dare them to try and come throw me in jail. I dare them to. Pull out my wife's shotgun and see how that little ACS twerp likes being scared at the door. They're not going on my property. They can't do that. They don't have the legal right, and yet they're trying."[42]

Life with liberals is a constant game of *Sesame Street*'s "One of These Things Is Not Like the Other."

Liberals are allowed to call us curs, dogs, and fascists, but conservatives must make precious measured statements, so that, in the end, perhaps, the truth may emerge. To take one example at random, just a few weeks before Erickson's word crime, HBO's Bill Maher commented on his TV show about the death of a deranged pothead who tried to shoot his way into the Pentagon, saying, "When we see crazy, senseless deaths like this, we can only ask why, why, why couldn't it have been Glenn Beck?"[43]

Two weeks after the Hutaree bust in Michigan, another group of anti-government extremists were arrested in New York City. New York police arrested more than a hundred violent extremists who had been caught on phone taps engaging in anti-government rhetoric, including a plot to shoot law enforcement officers. They had also already committed at least two murders, eleven shootings, and one home-invasion robbery, as well as some assorted drug crimes. But unlike the Hutaree, the New York group did not inspire media speculation about conservative rhetoric encouraging violence. The New York group was the Bloods and the Crips.[44]

The liberal rule is: Any criminal act committed by white men with guns is a right-wing conspiracy, whereas any criminal act committed by nonwhites with guns is the government violating someone's civil liberties. (If a black man ever shot an abortionist, liberal brains would explode.)

Despite liberals designating all white male criminals "right wing," right-wingers weren't leaping to defend the Hutaree. *They were planning on killing cops? Fine, lock 'em up.*

Incidentally, it isn't a crime to own guns or to dislike the government. In fact, each one gets a shout-out in the Constitution or the Declaration of Independence. As I recall, liberals were rather hopped-up about allegedly intrusive governmental powers during the Bush years. Indeed, the very people who would have been screaming about fascism in America if the Hutaree had been Muslim completely forget their "civil liberties" concerns with any criminal conspiracy involving white men.

Thus, for example, liberals portrayed the Lackawanna Six—six Yemenis who had attended an al Qaeda training camp with a Muslim terrorist involved in the bombing of the USS *Cole*—as high-spirited young lads in the wrong place at the wrong time. Evan Thomas sniffed in *Newsweek* that the evidence against them was "underwhelming."[45]

Reprising the McVeigh refrain, *Washington Post* columnist (and MSNBC's genuine black person) Eugene Robinson said of the Hutaree arrest, "The danger of political violence in this country comes overwhelmingly from one direction—the right, not the left. The vitriolic, anti-government hate speech that is spewed on talk radio every day—and, quite regularly, at Tea Party rallies—is calibrated not to inform but to incite." Meanwhile, back here on Planet Truth, not only weren't the Hutaree "right wing," but the Michigan militia, which *is* right wing, was working with law enforcement to build the case against the Hutaree.

For the bow on top, it turned out . . . that the only member of the Hutaree who was registered with any party, Jacob J. Ward, was registered as a Democrat.[46]

A review of the endless political violence from liberals in this country solves a sick puzzle from American history. In Juan Williams's book *Eyes on the Prize,* he describes an ugly confrontation during the integration of the Little Rock high school after Democrat governor Orval Faubus—and friend of Bill—sent troops to prevent black students from entering. As Elizabeth Eckford was being blocked from entering the school, she said, "I tried to see a friendly face somewhere in the mob. . . . I looked into the face of an old woman, and it seemed a kind face, but when I looked at her again, she spat on me."[47]

A normal person winces at that story and wonders how any American could treat a fellow citizen with such hatred. Who are these people?

And then you remember Cindy Sheehan, also an innocent-looking older woman howling about "this lying bastard, George Bush" . . . "that filth-spewer and warmonger, George Bush" . . . "They're a bunch of f**king hypocrites!" . . . "Is there yet any sane adult in this country whose skin does not crawl when this murderous liar [Paul Wolfowitz] opens his mouth and speaks?" . . . "The biggest terrorist is George W. Bush."[48]

And you remember the sixty-two-year-old woman delivering Bush-Cheney stickers to a friend on the Upper West Side of Manhattan before the 2004 election who was attacked in the lobby of her friend's building by an eighty-two-year-old resident, who shouted, "Get out of here with that trash," ripped up one of the stickers, and hit the woman with her cane.[49]

You remember Weatherman Eleanor Raskin's mother, whose behavior at Weatherman protests was described by a fellow liberal as "excessive," "unseemly," and "militant."[50]

You remember Vietnam veterans being spat upon, incidents that were called an "urban myth" by liberals, until *Chicago Tribune* columnist Bob Greene asked in his newspaper column if any Vietnam veterans were personally spat upon when they returned to the United States. He received more than a thousand replies, sixty of which are included in his book *Homecoming*.[51]

And you remember Tom Hayden, former SDS leader and current Occidental College professor, hoping in 2004 that liberal protesters would force New York City police into "defending the GOP convention as if it is the Green Zone in Baghdad," so that voters would see that the reelection of Bush could "plunge the country into strife not seen since the '60s."[52]

And you remember how, in 2006, the Columbia University students violently drove conservative speakers Jim Gilchrist and Marvin Stewart from the stage, turning over tables and chairs to seize control of the event.[53]

Indeed, you remember hateful attacks on any conservative who shows up to give a speech on a college campus—or shows up in public merely to dine at a restaurant or go to an art show.

You also remember delegates and cops at the 2004 and 2008 Republican National Conventions being beaten and sprayed with foul substances by liberal protesters.[54]

Is it becoming clearer now who that old woman who spat at Elizabeth Eckford was? What kind of person would engage in an ugly physical confrontation with a stranger? It's always a liberal.

What's confusing is that liberal historians keep telling us that those angry, contorted faces screaming at black people are "Southerners"— probably someone like Phyllis Schlafly. Only when you realize they are all Democrats—usually liberal, "progressive" Democrats, in the mold of Wilson, Faubus, and Ervin—do the pictures make sense.

It's always liberals: Like Robespierre, they commit violence for the greater good.

# THIRTEEN

## RAPED TWICE: LIBERALS AND THE CENTRAL PARK RAPE

I n 2006, when the Duke lacrosse players were accused of gang-raping a stripper—falsely, it turned out—mobs of students appeared outside the players' homes to bang pots and pans. One of these blithering idiots, Manju Rajendran, explained on MSNBC that the "symbolic" banging of pots and pans was borrowed from Latin American protesters:

> Women in Lima, Peru, initiated this as a way of surrounding the houses of women who were being assaulted by their husbands or by their partners. And it was a very confrontational way of saying, "We demonstrate solidarity with the women who are being attacked in this way or by anyone who's being persecuted in this fashion." We challenge the racism and the sexism and the classism implicit in these actions. We want to shame the attackers, and we want to invite the witnesses to step forward and come clean.[1]

In America—unlike Peru, evidently—we have a system of justice based on rules, a presumption of innocence, and a fair hearing. The fact

that the Duke lacrosse players later turned out to be completely innocent of the charges illustrates one of the benefits of that system compared with mob lynchings. But as Le Bon says, Latin people are easily
whipped into a frenzy on the basis of the most tenuous facts. Crowds,
he says, "are everywhere distinguished by feminine characteristics, but
Latin crowds are the most feminine of all."[2]

Liberals despise the rule of law because courts interfere with their
ability to rule by mob. They love to portray themselves as the weak taking on the powerful, but it is the least powerful who suffer the most
once the rule of law is gone. The only purpose of government—as opposed to the state of nature—is to replace "might makes right" with a
system of justice. The Left's relentless attack on the judicial system is yet
another example of their Jacobin lunacy in opposition to calm order.

One of the main differences in the political systems to emerge from
the French and American revolutions is the prominence of the judiciary in America. While this has had malignant effects, such as John Edwards, the idea was that the courts would be a bulwark against tyranny
by protecting individuals from the popular passions of the majority. Our
Constitution not only places strict limits on Congress's powers, but also
elevates the judiciary to nearly equal standing with the legislature, allowing the courts to review laws as an additional protection for individual
rights.[3]

Of course, those who benefit from mobs have never cared for the
American form of government. From their contempt for the Constitution to their "Europeans Need Not Apply" immigration policies, liberals
apparently would prefer to live in a country more like Zimbabwe. Their
fondness for powerful governments is premised on the assumption that
they would get to be Mugabe. It never occurs to them that they might
be Mugabe's dinner. Robespierre and his cohorts had the same idea.

The two main impulses of the Legal Left in America appear totally
contradictory to a normal person. On one hand, they act as if judges are
all-seeing visionaries capable of expressing the "general will" in accordance with Rousseau. But at the same time, liberals don't trust judges to
do their jobs, which is to hold trials.

While Justice William Douglas's crayon scribblings on the Constitution are treated like Moses' stone tablets, liberals believe no judge can

possibly preside over a fair criminal proceeding, unless the defendant is (1) a white male, and (2) accused of rape, blowing up a building in Oklahoma City, or shooting an abortionist.

In all other cases, liberals automatically denounce criminal trials as unfair. This is why the record for the fastest trial-to-execution in the second half of the twentieth century is held by Timothy McVeigh. If only he had claimed he blew up the Alfred P. Murrah Federal Building to protest U.S. imperialism, courts would still be hearing his appeals.

This is not only because liberals admire marauding violent criminals—which they do—but also because they want to create widespread distrust of the justice system. Liberals would prefer it if courts limited themselves to abortion policy and war strategy and steered clear of actual trials.

Both hallucinatory constitutional rulings and attacks on the criminal justice system have the same goal: undermining the rule of law in order to establish mob rule and anarchy. Trust only the media; liberals will tell you who's guilty. In the world of the liberal, as in the world of Robespierre, there are no crimes, only criminals. And the criminal is usually Sarah Palin.

The crown jewel for the Left in destroying people's faith in the courts was the Central Park jogger case, one of the most shocking, brutal crimes in the nation's history.

On April 19, 1989, a twenty-eight-year-old investment banker working at Salomon Brothers went for a run through Central Park around 9 p.m. During her run she was attacked, dragged into the woods, savagely beaten, raped, and left for dead. It wasn't until 1:30 a.m. that night that police found a bloody, disfigured creature moaning in a puddle of mud. The jogger had been dragged 200 feet down a muddy ravine. She was barely alive, still thrashing four hours after the attack.

By the time the police found her, she was semiconscious, still gagged, bound, and bleeding. She had lost three-quarters of her blood. The police couldn't tell at first if she was male or female, a homeless person or an investment banker. The homicide unit of the Manhattan DA's office initially took the case because not one of her doctors believed she would be alive in the morning.

The New York City Police Department, the best in the world, gathered evidence; cases were assembled and brought to trial. About a year later, three teenagers—Antron McCray (fifteen), Yusef Salaam (fifteen), and Raymond Santana (fourteen)—were convicted in one trial and two more, Kevin Richardson (fourteen) and Kharey Wise (sixteen), were convicted in a second trial of various crimes against the jogger.

Those convictions were based almost entirely on the defendants' detailed, videotaped confessions. When they confessed, they were subjecting themselves to criminal prosecution and lengthy prison terms. They didn't know what the evidence would show, what the other suspects would say, or even if the jogger would emerge from her coma and identify them. (She did not identify them, having blocked all memory of the attack.)

Those confessions were obtained in accordance with due process, admitted by the judge after a six-week hearing, played for the jurors, and attacked by defense counsel.

In the trials, evidence was ruled on by the judge and tested in court. Witnesses were presented for both sides, subjected to cross-examination and argument. The defendants were given the right to testify in their own defense. Two unanimous, multiethnic juries found the defendants guilty of some crimes and acquitted them of others. Their convictions were later upheld on appeal by other judges.

The only way liberals could get those convictions thrown out was to change venues from a courtroom to a newsroom.

And so, thirteen years later, the convictions were vacated based not on a new trial or on new evidence, but solely on the confession of Matias Reyes, a career criminal, serial rapist, and murderer who had nothing to lose by confessing to the rapes—and much to gain by claiming he acted alone.

As in the French tribunals, the Show Trials were based on a lie—to wit, that Reyes's confession constituted "new evidence" that might have led to a different verdict at trial.

In fact, Reyes's admission that he had raped the jogger changed nothing about the evidence presented in the actual trials. It was always known that others had participated in the attack on the jogger, which is why prosecutor Elizabeth Lederer said in her summation to the jury, "Others who were not caught raped her and got away." It was known at the time that semen from the the jogger's sock and cervix did not match any of the defendants'. The only new information Reyes provided was that he was one of those who "got away."

Reyes might have been part of the wolf pack attacking the jogger, he could have joined the wolf pack in progress, or he might have come along afterward and raped the beaten, semiconscious jogger. No barbarity was out of the question with Reyes—this is a man who had sexually assaulted his own mother and raped and killed a pregnant woman in front of her children.

Although Reyes made the shocking claim that he had acted alone, there was no new evidence suggesting that this was true—apart from his own word. Unlike the detailed, videotaped confessions given in the days after the rape from all five convicted of rape in the real trials, Reyes's confession was never subjected to cross-examination. He faced no penalty for his confession.

Reyes's confession not only cost him nothing, it helped him. When he confessed, he happened to be imprisoned with one of the convicted Central Park rapists, Kharey Wise, who was a leader of the prison Muslim community and a member of the Bloods gang. Before Reyes made his confession, he requested a transfer to one of the most desirable prisons in New York on the grounds that he feared retaliation from Wise's gang.

Inasmuch as the statute of limitations for rape in New York was five years[4] and the Central Park jogger's rape occurred in 1989, Reyes could have confessed in 1994, 1995, 1996, 1997, 1998, 1999, 2000, or 2001 and risked nothing. But it was not until Reyes was incarcerated with Wise that he decided to announce that he had raped the jogger all by himself and win a favorable prison transfer.

It's remarkable how many "confessions" purporting to exonerate others come from people who will face no penalty for the confession, either because the statute of limitations has run out or because they are already serving thirty-three years to life in prison or both—as in Reyes's case. Confessions that clear the convicted dramatically improve an inmate's standing in the prison pecking order by sticking it to the authorities, even without an advantageous transfer.

But liberals put enormous pressure on the doddering district attorney, Robert Morgenthau, to vacate the convictions. The entire left-wing apparatus, from the media to the defense bar, was fixated on getting those convictions overturned—and overjoyed when they were. Another victory for the Innocence Project!

For the Central Park rape convictions to be vacated was almost as much a blow to civilization at the attack itself. If those juries, under those circumstances, could convict wholly innocent young lads, then the whole legal system was a scam and a fraud.

Here's the truth about the Central Park rape.

It is undisputed that a mob of about forty African-American and Hispanic teenagers were running wild in Central Park the night of April 18, 1989, assaulting anyone in their path. At least a dozen of them had been arrested leaving the park before the jogger's body was even discovered. They implicated others, who were rounded up over the next few days, until the police had questioned thirty-seven boys who had been in the park that night.[5]

Only ten of the thirty-seven interviewed were charged with any crimes. Of those, only five were tried for the rape of the jogger—the five who confessed. Manifestly, the police were capable of interviewing suspects without coercing them to confess. But five confessed anyway, four on videotape with adult relatives present and one with a parent present but not on videotape. All five gave vivid, largely consistent accounts of the attack, implicating themselves and the others.

Other members of the Central Park mob provided various corroborating details to the police, such as one who said Kevin Richardson told him, "We just raped somebody," and another who heard Raymond Santana and another boy laughing about how "we made a woman bleed." Various other witnesses said they saw the defendants walking from the 102nd Street transverse area where the jogger was raped.[6]

As one of the lead detectives on the case, Mike Sheehan, told *New York* magazine: "*They* are telling *us*—the sequence may be off, but they're essentially telling us the same stuff. They remember a guy they beat and took his food, they remember hitting this guy running around the reservoir. They went through all of these things, each kid. And they also tell you about the jogger. And they place people, so you have a mental picture of where they were around this woman's body. And their parents are with them, not only in the interviews but in the videotape, for the record. That's enough for me. I'm satisfied."[7]

Although the suspects accused others of attacking the jogger, too, no one was tried for that crime unless he confessed. Steven Lopez, for example, was implicated by two of the defendants, including Kharey Wise, who matter-of-factly told the police that while Lopez was raping the jogger, he "got sick of looking at her face," so he picked up a brick to smash it.[8] Also, a hair was found on Lopez's jacket "consistent" with the jogger's hair but not sufficient to be used at trial.

Lopez did not confess to assaulting the jogger, so he was never tried for any crime against her and only pleaded guilty to the robbery of another man in the park that night. That's how important the confessions were—and how unimportant the "forensic evidence" was back in 1989.

Yusef Salaam started talking immediately after Detective Thomas McKenna told him, "I don't care what you say to me. We have fingerprints on the jogger's pants." At that point, Salaam said, "I was there, but I didn't rape her."[9] A juror later told 60 Minutes, "We never doubted the veracity of Detective McKenna for a minute."[10]

If the police had manufactured the confessions, how did the defendants know facts about the crime that the police couldn't have known? On April 21, 1989, Kharey Wise told a detective that someone he thought was named "Rudy" stole the jogger's Walkman and belt pouch.[11] The jogger was still in a coma and the police had no way of knowing that a Walkman had been stolen from her.

Indeed, that was one of the DA's main reasons for buying the entirety of Reyes's jailhouse confession in the Show Trial: the false claim that Reyes was the only one who knew about the jogger's Walkman. Kharey Wise told the police at the time about the Walkman, and it was Wise who was in the same prison with Reyes when, thirteen years later, Reyes had his sudden attack of conscience.

Two of the defendants, Santana and Richardson, independently brought investigators to the precise location of the attack on the jogger.[12]

Moreover, their videotaped confessions were not vague, five-minute statements that anyone could have given. They were multiple, lengthy statements that included damning minutiae. In separate interrogations taken by various investigators, all five of the defendants independently identified where the jogger was when they first saw her. All five said they charged her, dragged her into the woods, beat, molested, and raped her before leaving her lying on the ground, semiconscious and half naked. None of them admitted to raping her themselves, instead pinning the rapes on others. But all of them admitted to assisting in her rape, which is all that was required for a rape conviction for all of them.

McCray confessed to participating in the attack on the jogger only after his mother said to him, "Tell the truth. We brought you up better than this." He proceeded to give a vivid account of a wolf pack attack in the presence of both his parents. This was before law enforcement, much less the media, knew exactly what had happened that night.

Here is a small part of McCray's confession given the day after the attack (the full excerpt from New York *Newsday* is printed in the Appendix):

*Prosecutor Elizabeth Lederer (Q):* What happened as she came closer?
*A:* That's when we all charged her.
*Q:* Did you charge her?
*A:* Yes.
*Q:* What happened when you charged her?
*A:* We charged her, we got her on the ground, everybody started hitting her and stuff, she was on the ground, everybody stompin' and everything. Then we got each, I grabbed one arm, some other kid grabbed one arm and we grabbed her legs and stuff. Then we all took turns getting on her, getting on top of her.
*Q:* Did you hit her?
*A:* Yes, kicked her.
*Q:* Where did you kick her?
*A:* I don't know, just kicked her, I felt it, just kicked her, it was like a whole bunch of us.
*Q:* Who else kicked her?
*A:* Um, um, Kevin [Richardson, another defendant], um, all of us.
*Q:* That tall thin black guy I was asking you about, did you see him hit her in the ribs?
*A:* I heard it. I heard it.

*Q:* What did you hear?

*A:* It sounded like when you get hit in your chest. Sounded like that.

*Q:* Was she screaming, is that how you could tell she was being hit?

*A:* She wasn't screaming. She was hurt, though. She wasn't screaming.

*Q:* How could you tell she was hurt?

*A:* 'Cause she was lying there.

. . .

*Q:* Did you see her get hit in the head?

*A:* I heard it, not only, I seen it.

*Q:* Who did it?

*A:* The tall, black kid.

. . .

*Q:* What was she wearing?

*A:* I think a white T-shirt, something like that.

*Q:* Who took off her shirt?

*A:* The tall black kid.

*Q:* Who took off her pants?

*A:* I think it was him.

*Q:* Did somebody have sex with her?

*A:* Yeah.

*Q:* Did a lot of people have sex with her?

*A:* Yeah.

*Q:* Who was the first person to get on top of her?

*A:* The tall black guy.

. . .

*Q:* Did somebody else get on top of her then?

*A:* He grabbed one of her arms, this other kid got on top of her.

*Q:* Who was that?

*A:* This Puerto Rican guy.

*Q:* Did you have your fly open?

*A:* Yeah, but my penis wasn't in her.

. . .

*Q:* How long did you do that for?

*A:* I don't know, a couple of minutes.

*Q:* What happened after Kevin was done?

*A:* Then we left her then, then this guy hit her in the head. Then we left.

*Q:* Who hit her?

*A:* I don't know. I just, the pipe, I think the tall skinny kid.[13]

As an article in the *New York Times* said at the time, the case was won not in the courtroom "but in three grubby New York City police station houses, where detectives smoothly convinced the three young men to confess."[14]

In addition to the videotaped confessions and written statements, the defendants also made incriminating statements to the police and to their friends. When Santana was picked up by the police, he blurted out, "I had nothing to do with the rape. All I did was feel the woman's tits." Which is a little like saying, "I didn't shoot him, Officer, I just tied up the victim, bought the gun, and loaded the bullets. Someone else pulled the trigger. Can I go now?"

Melody Jackson, the sister of a friend of Kharey Wise, testified that she talked to Wise by phone when he was in jail after the arrests and he told her that he didn't rape the jogger, he "only held her legs down while Kevin [Richardson] f—ked her."[15] (In the district attorney's argument for vacating the convictions, this admission was watered down to: "Wise replied that he had not had sex with her, but had only held and fondled the victim's leg.")[16]

The Central Park jogger's assailants were not making deals when they gave detailed, corroborated, videotaped confessions. Their stories never unraveled, but rather were corroborated by other evidence. Both juries were well aware that the semen in the jogger's cervix and on her sock did not match any of the defendants' DNA.[17]

Although it's difficult to imagine these days, in 1989, DNA was not a big part of criminal investigations. Back then, DNA testing was being called a "novel," "high-tech," "sophisticated" test. The month the jogger was attacked, newspapers were excitedly reporting "a powerful and still unfolding laboratory discovery, a genetic 'fingerprint' created from the body's deoxyribonucleic acid, or DNA," as the *Chicago Tribune* put it. This "still unfolding" discovery was said to be "a breakthrough weapon in the war against violent crime."[18] In state and federal courts across the nation, DNA had been used in only about eighty court cases.[19]

DNA identifications were first invented by Alec Jeffreys in 1984—five years before the Central Park rape. The first time DNA was ever used to help solve a crime was in Leichester, England, in 1986. The first time DNA evidence was ever given as evidence in a U.S. trial was in November 1987, in a rape case in Florida. DNA evidence was not even *permitted* in New York courts until November 1988[20]—just six months before the Central Park jogger was attacked.

Needless to say, DNA evidence was immediately, virulently attacked by defense lawyers. One month *after* the Central Park wilding, a New York court refused to admit DNA, which the judge termed "novel scientific evidence"—based on the arguments of future Innocence Project attorney Peter Neufeld.[21]

The *New York Times*—the same newspaper that would be howling about the lack of DNA evidence against the Central Park rape defendants thirteen years later—ran an article on the unreliability of DNA testing one month after that attack. The National Association of Criminal Defense Lawyers had set up a committee headed by Peter Neufeld along with his future Innocence Project colleague and Axis of Evil cohort, Barry C. Scheck, to reopen all convictions involving DNA testing done by a major genetics testing laboratory.[22]

In the next few years, obviously, DNA became the gold standard for criminal evidence (except to Scheck, who argued against the DNA in the 1995 O.J. case). But in April 1989, no sane detective would plan on winning a conviction based on forensic evidence: It wasn't clear that the "novel scientific evidence" of a DNA test would even be admissible, and all other forensic evidence generally narrowed the suspect pool down to about 40 percent of the population.

Complaining about the lack of forensic evidence in a 1989 case would be like complaining that the cops didn't use Google maps on their iPhones to locate the jogger.

As even defense attorneys told the *New York Law Journal* at the time, there were lots of reasons the defendants' DNA might not be found at the crime scene: The police might have failed to retrieve all of the semen, the defendants might not have ejaculated (as several of the defendants stated in their confessions), or the sample could have been contaminated.[23]

The evidence in the Central Park wilding trial was out of Perry Mason, not *CSI–New York*. Collecting physical evidence was not important to saving the jogger's life; nor, in 1989, was it particularly relevant to making a criminal case.

DNA is like fingerprint evidence. Your DNA at the crime scene proves you were there, but the absence of your DNA doesn't prove you weren't. That's why two juries, fully aware that the defendants' DNA was not at the crime scene, convicted them anyway.

What the prosecution had was better than DNA: detailed, videotaped confessions from four of the five defendants and an unvideotaped confession from the fifth. Even the O.J. jury might have convicted had they seen the defendant in a thirty-minute video, giving a detailed description of how he killed his wife and Ron Goldman.

Perhaps liberals could tell us in advance what evidence of guilt they intend to consider probative, instead of waiting to see what the evidence is and then saying they were really looking for something else. Whatever the evidence is, they react like Diogenes in the *New Yorker* cartoon, staring at an honest man and saying, "Actually I was looking for a *taller* honest man."

The judge in the real trials, Justice Thomas B. Galligan, held a six-week hearing on the admissibility of evidence, primarily the confessions, taking testimony from twenty-nine witnesses, including four defendants and their parents and relatives, who were contesting the confessions. Galligan found all the confessions were given voluntarily, with Miranda warnings and following proper procedure.

Despite attempts to discount the videotaped confessions with claims that they were preceded by hours of brutal police grilling, every defendant but one was questioned only in the presence of his parents or other adult relatives. The exception was Yusef Salaam, who lied to the police and told them he was sixteen, even showing them his adult transit pass. His questioning ended abruptly as soon as his mother showed up and told the police he was only fifteen. Yusef was the only defendant who did not make his confession on videotape.

Although each of the defendants had denied penetrating the jogger, they all admitted to fondling or restraining her as others raped her. If the defendants assisted in the jogger's rape, they were guilty of rape even if they didn't deposit their semen anywhere in Central Park that night.

In Antron McCray's thirty-four-minute videotaped statement, for example, he said, smirkingly, "Everybody started hitting her and stuff. She was on the ground, everybody stompin' and everything. . . . I grabbed one arm, some other kid grabbed one arm and we grabbed her legs and stuff. Then we all took turns getting on her, getting on top of her. . . . I just like, my penis wasn't in her. I didn't do nothing to her . . . I was just doing it so everybody . . . Everybody would just like, would know I did it."[24]

If the jury believed this, they had to find him guilty of rape as an accomplice.

In the opposite of a rush to judgment, the two juries deliberated for ten days and eleven days, respectively. At the first trial, all three defendants were acquitted of the most serious charge, attempted murder, but convicted of assault and rape on the "acting in concert" theory. The first three defendants were also convicted of riot and of assaults on other park-goers that night.

Defense counsel attacked the confessions as coerced, and evidently the jurors took these arguments seriously: The second jury concluded that Kharey Wise's videotaped confession resulted from "subtle forms of coercion" and acquitted him of rape and attempted murder, convicting him only of assault and sexual abuse.

Kevin Richardson was convicted of rape and attempted murder—the only defendant convicted of the latter charge. The evidence against Richardson included his leading prosecutors to the exact location of the crime; his vivid description of the attack given on videotape in the presence of his father; and a deep scratch wound on his cheek that he told police was from the jogger. Also, the crotch of the underwear he was wearing the night of the attack was suspiciously stained with semen, grass stains, dirt, and debris. Someone else's semen on the jogger's sock couldn't explain that away. Richardson's own half-sister, who signed his confession as a witness, took the stand to attack his statement as involuntary, but ended up admitting under oath that those were her brother's own words.[25]

For being found guilty of a savage attack on a female jogger that only by the grace of God didn't kill her, the defendants were each sentenced to five to ten years in prison, except Richardson, who got five to fifteen years. Former congressman Tom DeLay was sentenced to three years in prison for putting campaign money in the wrong account.

All but one, Raymond Santana, appealed their convictions. All convictions were upheld.

But thirteen years later, the media told astonishing lies about both the original trials and the alleged "new evidence." New York *Newsday,* for example, breathlessly reported that it had gotten its hands on "a confidential police report" concluding that "all forensic evidence used at trial . . . has now been determined to be useless." Congratulations, *Newsday!* You could have run a Nexis search for that "confidential" information. It was known to be perfectly useless at the trials, too.

According to AP reports at the time, for example, the most powerful "forensic" evidence came from retired detective Nicholas Petraco, who testified that hairs found on Richardson's clothes "could have" or "might have" come from the jogger. On cross-examination, he admitted that "he could not determine that a hair definitely came from a specific individual." He also said "that hair could end up on someone's clothing by casual contact or from being airborne."[26]

Forensic evidence didn't convict the defendants. Their confessions did. Reyes's jailhouse confession changed nothing about those cases: He had merely revealed himself as one of the rapists who "got away."

But when a case is tried in the media, rather than a courtroom, new rules of evidence apply. In a courtroom, juries are able to see videotaped confessions, note inconsistencies or corroborating evidence, evaluate the credibility of witnesses, and consider alternative theories of the crime. They get to hear both sides of the argument.

Under the media's Show Trial rules, only one side is heard, much like political debates on MSNBC. Any evidence tending to implicate the defendant is suppressed or denied, while any evidence tending to exonerate the defendant is treated as ironclad.

Thus, Innocence Project–style defense lawyers dismiss eyewitness testimony as notoriously unreliable—unless it's an eyewitness providing an alibi. If a defendant's DNA is found at the crime scene, it is mocked as merely circumstantial evidence and probably contaminated.

But if the defendant's DNA is *not* found at the crime scene, it's deemed bulletproof evidence of innocence.

Voluntary confessions that carry a penalty are said to prove nothing—they were coerced, given under duress, extracted in exchange for leniency. But jailhouse "confessions" are apparently never questionable—even if the primary beneficiary is a gang member in the same cellblock and the confession leads to a desirable prison transfer.

Confessions outside of court are not subject to cross-examination or evaluated by a jury. But if they exonerate the guilty, the media believe those confessions with all their hearts!

We know Reyes raped the jogger based on his DNA at the scene. The only question was whether he acted alone, as he claimed, or there were many attackers, as the five defendants said in their confessions and two juries believed.

But the only question for Robert Morgenthau, the Manhattan district attorney, was how to get a good write-up in the *New York Times*. So while newspapers repeated nonsense fed to them by the Innocence Project, Morgenthau's office wrote a brief for the defense. His office began with the assumption that Reyes was telling the truth about acting alone and then scoured the record for evidence to support that theory. Unfortunately, there was no evidence to support Reyes's single-rapist claim. So all the DA's office was able to supply was sophistry.

Curiously, Reyes remembered raping the jogger with Technicolor clarity. But he couldn't remember another brutal rape he committed a mere two days before the attack on the jogger.

Regarding the earlier attack, he said he vaguely recalled accosting a woman in Central Park, but he wasn't sure if he had actually raped her. The DA investigated and determined that on April 17, 1989—two days before the attack on the jogger—Reyes had "in fact attacked, beaten, raped, and robbed a twenty-six-year-old white woman who had been exercising in the park. . . . The victim was badly beaten about the head. She had a large hematoma on her forehead, abrasions to both knees, bite marks on her left upper arm and neck, scratches over her neck, face, knees and back, and multiple bruises. In addition her right eye was bruised and shows subconjunctival hemorrhages."[27]

Reyes couldn't remember that. But he remembered amazing details about his alleged solo rape of the jogger, occurring just two days later. Reyes knew, for example, the exact point on the trail where the jogger was first assaulted, which side of the jogger's head had been bashed, where the blood was on her shirt, and what she was wearing. You know, the sort of details that only someone with access to a newspaper would know.

If Reyes had been facing a criminal penalty for being the sole rapist, liberals would have been denouncing his confession as obvious hokum. But the DA's report cited Reyes's freakish accuracy about details of the jogger's attack as proof of his credibility, rather than as what it was: evidence that he had been coached.

Indeed, the DA's report even made excuses for Reyes's failure to remember raping the first woman, claiming that it "may be explained by the fact that, according to the victim, he apparently did not ejaculate."[28] Not ejaculating explains why the five defendants did not leave semen on the jogger—a possibility ignored by the Show Trial tribunal. There is no scientific study suggesting that a failure to ejaculate affects memory of a rape, but this was the scientific theory invented on the spot by Morgenthau's office.

By contrast, the DA was suddenly shocked to discover minor discrepancies in the confessions of the five who had been convicted of the attack. The alleged discrepancies consisted of things like the defendants' inability to uniformly agree about who hit the jogger first. This was a mob attack in a dark wooded area, after 9 p.m. at night in April. After everything we've heard about the unreliability of eyewitness testimony, it defies reason that predators in a gang attack would give identically worded, play-by-play accounts of a wilding.

Maybe next time, the wolf pack should assign one member to take detailed meeting minutes of the rape, so they can get the order right. *"Yusef, could you read that back to me please? I want to make sure there's no confusion about who grabbed her breasts and who hit her with the pipe."*

Honest eyewitness accounts are never perfectly consistent in all respects. That's why Matthew, Mark, Luke, and John give slightly different versions of the same story. It's identical statements that ring false—such as liberals all claiming at the exact same moment that Clinton's impeachment was a "rush to judgment." An eyewitness who happens to remember that the victim was wearing colored contacts and Fruit of the

Loom underwear and was humming a Backstreet Boys song at the time of the attack seems to be drawing on something other than his memory.

But the DA's report complains that, "on the issue of who actually knocked the jogger to the ground, Kevin Richardson said Antron, Raymond and Steve did it; Antron McCray said everyone charged her; Raymond Santana said Kevin did it; Yusef Salaam said he did it; Kharey Wise first named Raymond, and then named Steve."[29]

Again, it would be more suspicious if all the suspects named the exact same person.

In the very next breath, the DA's report cited the defendants' *consistency* as proof that they were lying: All the defendants except Kevin Richardson said Kevin raped the jogger. To explain the wacky consistency of all the defendants naming Richardson, the DA hypothesizes "a possible motive for others to accuse him."[30]

So when the five defendants' confessions are inconsistent, the DA said it proved they're lying. And when they were consistent, the DA said it proved they had an ulterior motive to lie. *They must be out to get Richardson!* Heads, I win; tails, you lose.

The DA's report exonerating the five defendants was a conclusion in search of evidence, not an honest examination of evidence in search of the truth.

Another alleged "discrepancy" in the defendants' description of the attack concerned who hit the jogger. The general theme of their confessions was that they all hit and stomped her. But they did not give carbon-copy descriptions of who hit her, in which order, and with what object. The DA's office found that highly suspicious.

Antron McCray and Raymond Santana said Steve Lopez—who was never charged with a crime relating to the jogger—hit her in the face with a brick. Kharey Wise also said Lopez hit her in the face with a "hand-rock." Yusef Salaam said someone he couldn't name hit her in the face with a brick. Richardson said Michael Briscoe—also never charged—hit her in the face. Separately, both McCray and Yusef Salaam said that at some point Salaam hit her with a pipe.[31]

I doubt a football color commentator could be more accurate describing a pileup.

The DA's report was looking for excuses to exonerate, not answers. The fact that five defendants could not provide the names of the other assailants was said to cast doubt on their confessions—as opposed to indicating that not all members of the wolf pack knew one another. We're talking about a mob, not a bowling league. But the fact that Matias Reyes was among the assailants they couldn't identify was supposed to prove they couldn't possibly have all attacked the same woman.[32] Wouldn't it be more suspicious if the defendants *had* been able to name everyone else in the gang, but not Reyes?

The DA also claimed a multiple offender rape was not part of Reyes's "pattern" and that he was a "loner" in his criminal behavior. This was apparently meant to demonstrate that Reyes, whose entire life was a welter of criminal violence and sexual depravity, was such a creature of habit that he would not have deigned to join a gang rape he stumbled into by accident.

Like horoscope readers, the DA picked out anything in the Central Park rape that matched Reyes's other rapes, and ignored anything that didn't fit, to prove a "pattern" in Reyes's rapes. Thus, the DA's report said:

- Reyes picked women who were Caucasian or "appeared to be Caucasian."

  In addition to being almost Caucasian, some of his victims were pregnant and some were not. One was his own mother and the others were not. One had her children with her during the rape and others did not. One was raped in her apartment, one in a church, one in a foyer, one while exercising in broad daylight in the park. Some he killed, some he let live. Some were attacked at night, some during the day, some indoors, some outdoors.

  You see the pattern? Yes, gang rape is definitely outside Reyes's pattern—why, it's as different from his usual crimes as insider trading.

  As for Reyes's "pattern" of choosing white-ish women, that criterion would restrict his potential target list to a majority of the female population of Manhattan.

  Reyes's alleged "pattern" wasn't even limited to rape and murder.

He also shoplifted and committed robberies, usually by himself but sometimes with acquaintances. So he was capable of participating in multiple-offender crimes.

• All his rapes involved conversations with women as initial contact.

He didn't have a "conversation" with the jogger, so the DA's report quickly dismissed this as a deviation from his "pattern," stating that it is "explained by the circumstances in which he targeted his victim." If circumstances might propel him to vary his pattern to skip the formalities of his usual rapes, what if the "circumstances" were that Reyes stumbled upon a woman being gang-raped? Mightn't he diverge from his pattern if that opportunity struck? No, the DA's position is Reyes would stride boldly past a gang rape, refusing to deviate from his alleged "pattern."

• All his rapes involved violence and robbery—in particular, stolen Walkmans.

This is like saying Reyes's rapes involved violence and robbery—in particular, stolen money. Walkmans were very common in the eighties and, thus, common items of theft. Can we get the Innocence Project on the record agreeing that robbery of small electronics during a rape constitutes a unique criminal pattern, admissible against a defendant in court as a prior bad act?

• He asked his victims for their pin numbers and he claims he asked the Central Park jogger for her address.

An address isn't a pin number, which raises another dissimilarity ignored by the DA's whitewash. Reyes usually raped women who would have their wallets on them in order to carry out the "robbery" part of his pattern. But we know he raped the jogger, so evidently he was capable of varying this part of his "pattern," too.

In the end—as had been planned from the beginning—the DA's report concluded that had the jury known about Reyes's raping the jogger, they might have found the five defendants innocent—*even though the juries knew there were other rapists who got away.* On the DA's theory of "new evidence," no gang rape can ever be prosecuted unless every single perpetrator is caught right away. Otherwise, any rapists who escaped can always materialize five years later and the original convictions will have to be tossed.

What new information did Reyes's confession add to what the juries knew? "Others who were not caught raped her and got away"—as the prosecutor told them—pretty clearly captures the idea that others raped her and got away.

While the DA's office was formulating preposterous excuses to find the five convicted rapists innocent, the New York Police Department was also reexamining evidence. Among the people they reinterviewed was Ronald Williams, who had told police back in 1989 that when he bumped into Kharey Wise the day after the attack, Wise had said, "You heard about that woman that was beat up and raped in the park last night. That was us!" When Matias Reyes unveiled his stunning single-perpetrator theory in 2002, the police reinterviewed Williams. He recalled Wise's admission precisely and stood by his account.[33]

If only we had some way of sorting out these facts that relied on uniform rules of evidence. What we need is a group of unbiased decision-makers drawn from all walks of life—we could call them "jurors"!

But that's not how the Central Park rape case was finally resolved. It was decided not by multicultural juries hearing both sides and carefully weighing the evidence, but in law offices and pressrooms by a remarkably undiverse group of mostly Irish and Jewish college-educated New Yorkers, who lied about the evidence in order to vindicate a mob and destroy trust in the judicial system.

This was a bigger victory for the Left than forcing Nixon to resign in 1974.

After the convictions were vacated, the five who had been convicted promptly brought a $250 million lawsuit against the city, and Ken Burns announced he was making a documentary about the "Central Park Five," as liberals dubbed the jury-convicted rapists.

Even the fairest judicial system is not infallible. There will always be human error and human malice. This is why the criminal justice system is carefully designed to err on the side of innocence at every step of a criminal prosecution. The guilty are constantly being set free. Incriminating evidence is thrown out at the drop of a hat. Not so, evidence of innocence. The criminal justice system is a one-way, pro-defendant ratchet. So is the media, the difference being that in court, evidence of guilt is not actually prohibited.

Still, some truly innocent people have been falsely accused and sent to prison. But liberals don't care about the truly innocent: They want to spring the guilty. The child-hysteria prosecutions in the 1980s were mostly brought by liberals. Notably, while Gerald Amirault was serving eighteen years in a Massachusetts prison for crimes that had never happened, the Innocence Project did not ever lift a finger to help him. He was finally released in 2004 under Republican governor Mitt Romney, and then hired by a conservative group, Citizens for Limited Taxation.

When the Duke lacrosse players were falsely accused of gang rape in 2006, once again we didn't hear a peep out of Barry Scheck and the Innocence Project—even when none of the defendants' DNA was found on the accuser, her underwear, or her fingernails—and this was using 2006 testing techniques. Only after their convictions were thrown out were the lacrosse players invited to an Innocence Project gala, to create the false impression that people released from prison on legal technicalities were as innocent as they.

Freeing the innocent is merely an accidental—and rare—by-product of the Left's campaign to discredit legitimate criminal convictions. Liberals' real goal is to foment disorder, release marauding criminals on society, and destroy the citizenry's faith in institutions that protect their rights. The liberal intellectual mob creates anarchy in the courts in order to foist literal mobs on society. Don't trust the courts; trust only the Show Trials.

Recall that Antron McCray's mother said to him, "Tell the truth. We brought you up better than that." With those parents, he probably was brought up better than that. But mobs allow people to "pass the moral buck," as the psychiatrist M. Scott Peck says, so the moral conscience of the group becomes "so fragmented and diluted as to be nonexistent."[34]

That's more comprehensible than what motivates liberals. Why do they want to turn criminals loose on us?

Liberals defend criminal mobs to boost their own power and prestige. In a world of courts and rules, everyone is equal before the law. That's no good. Liberals need to be above the rest of society in order to impose the Rousseauian "general will" on us. And so the same judiciary they trust to express the general will, when it is proclaiming rights for abortionists, pornographers, and Guantánamo detainees, is deemed utterly incompetent when involved in a simple criminal trial.

This is why liberals prefer to go straight to the Show Trials, where they can proclaim violent criminals innocent, while applying 22 Prairial—the accusation is proof of guilt—to politically incorrect defendants. Our all-seeing mob leaders will tell us who's guilty on the TV networks and in the pages of the *New York Times*. In the world of the liberal, as in the world of Robespierre, there are no crimes, only criminals.

# PART IV:

# WHY WOULD ANYONE BE A LIBERAL?

# FOURTEEN

## STATUS ANXIETY: PLEASE LIKE ME!

The same mob mentality that leads teenaged girls to bully another teenager to the point of suicide compels people in all walks of life to engage in all sorts of appallingly bad behavior. Usually, the fragmented conscience of a mob means violence. But there's also a species of intellectual mob, relying on praise and ridicule to enforce its views. Many people, especially in New York, Washington, D.C., and Los Angeles, would rather be punched in the face than be sneered at by the elites. We call them liberals.

The mob mentality is irresistible to people with a desperate need to be popular, those who are perennially afraid of getting a bloody nose in the playground of life. This is why conservatives can never be a mob. By definition, it's not a mob if it's called a mob, denounced by the chattering class—the media, politicians, college professors, and celebrities. Anyone who doesn't mind being sneered at by *The Daily Show* and other temples of the status anxious is not susceptible to groupthink.

Recent studies on high school bullies found that bullying behavior is driven by status anxiety. People with some status, but not the highest status, bully others because of their need to climb the social hierarchy.[1]

As the *New York Times* summarized the studies, bullying behavior is correlated with "how much the student cares about being popular."[2]

People who think of themselves as sophisticated professionals who would never hiss "slut" at a girl for dating her friend's boyfriend are driven by the same desperate need for social acceptance. They're just appealing to a different in-group. As Eugene Lyons said of communist-sympathizing liberals in the 1930s, "Under the guise of a nobly selfless dedication they were, in fact, identifying themselves with Power."[3]

What most people care about is their standing in their own worlds—not what people they will never meet might think of them. The Dixie Chicks insult President Bush in London, not in Lubbock, Texas. The liberal mob operates not only by terrifying nice, law-abiding Americans with bottle-throwing lunatics, but also by imposing a powerful group-think on public discourse. Le Bon says it is the human instinct to imitate that makes fashion so powerful. "Whether in the matter of opinions, ideas, literary manifestations, or merely of dress, how many persons are bold enough to run counter to the fashion?"[4]

Self-styled intellectuals—virtually all residents of New York City—appeal to the imaginary *New York Times* editor they fantasize is listening to their every hoary declamation; lawyers take positions that will make them superstars at the next ABA convention; actors strike poses that they think will make them seem intelligent and passionate.

Who cares what people in Missouri think of them? Without a flicker of self-examination, craven suck-ups fancy themselves Thomas More standing up to King Henry VIII, when, in fact, they are Richard Rich, who testified falsely against More, resulting in More's decapitation and Rich's promotion.

Singer Lady Gaga has bragged that she is "mastering the art of fame," which consists of an adolescent's imitation of the in-crowd. The mob demands total chaos in sexual traditions, morals, and decorum—but fascistic uniformity when it comes to opinions. As Le Bon says, "It is by examples not by arguments that crowds are guided."[5]

Gaga has made a name for herself beyond her music for supporting gay marriage and denouncing the Clinton-era policy of "Don't Ask, Don't Tell" in the military. For this, she has been hailed as a visionary in the *Washington Post,* which called her "smarter than the average pop star. Better read. More extensively traveled. Deeper. And she wants you to know it."[6] She was ranked No. 1 on dosomething.org's "Top 20 Celebs Gone Good,"[7] and praised on CNN as the "most socially conscious celeb of 2010," because "she called for the repeal of 'don't ask/don't tell,' supported same-sex marriage and raised AIDS awareness."

Never imagining the power of the mob could reach the crescendo it has in modern America, Thomas Jefferson wrote in 1774, "Let those flatter, who fear: it is not an American art."[8] By Thomas Jefferson's lights, sixteen-year-old Canadian singer Justin Bieber is more of an American than native-born suck-up Lady Gaga.

When Bieber failed to pay obeisance to the mob's position on premarital sex and abortion in a *Rolling Stone* magazine interview, he was roundly denounced as a jerk. Bieber told the interviewer he believed "you should just wait" until you're in love to have sex. But most risky for his singing career, he said, "I really don't believe in abortion," because "it's like killing a baby."

Bieber was promptly ridiculed by the coven on *The View*.[9] MSNBC's Beltway blog bravely derided Bieber in an anonymous item intended to teach Justin "about keeping your mouth shut with reporters." It wittily said, "Dear Biebs: You are simply adorable when talking about girls and music, but talking politics with *Rolling Stone* is not a wise move. We know you're just a 16-year-old Canadian, but that's all the more reason you shouldn't be pontificating about American politics, abortion and rape."[10]

And there went Bieber's chance of ever being named the "most socially conscious celebrity."

Liberals speak with the fatuous lunacy of people in the old Soviet Union, passing out awards to one another for imaginary heroism and denouncing others for class crimes. Honesty is irrelevant—it would never occur to them as an issue. While Trey Parker and Matt Stone, creators of *South Park* and *Team America: World Police,* are mocking Scientologists, Barbra Streisand, and Militant Islam, actors think they're speaking truth to power by opposing a proposition that banned gay marriage while living in 90 percent gay Hollywood.

Someone needs to sit down with Hollywood and explain to it what "courage" is. It is not, for example, going on CNN and ridiculing

Christians. It is not going on the Bill Maher show and being outspokenly pro-abortion. The first tip-off should be the standing ovation. *Uh oh, I thought what I was saying was courageous, but the audience is applauding, so it must agree with me.*

Liberal logic is exactly backwards. They think: *How do I know Lebron James just made a great shot? Answer: Because the cheerleaders cheered him.* They have no capacity to reason in the absence of thunderous applause or booing from the bleachers indicating what they should think.

It is so embedded in celebrities' DNA to think whatever they do is courageous that they begin with the conclusion and reason backwards: *Okay what that singer just said was courageous. Now how do we get there? Oh, I know! It upset people in the red states!* Meanwhile, all traditional signs point to it being ass-kissy.

The mob's craving for conformity is common to all primitive beings, Le Bon says. Look at how liberals dress alike,[11] mimic their professors, use the same leaden platitudes, and laugh on cue at prominent conservatives' names—and ask yourself if these are swashbuckling rebels.

People desperate for a badge of identity are highly susceptible to groupthink. Most people, Le Bon says, "especially among the masses, do not possess clear and reasoned ideas on any subject whatever outside their own specialty."[12] Thus, they need someone to serve as their guide. In a crowd, "the foolish, ignorant, and envious persons are freed from the sense of their insignificance and powerlessness."[13] But the mere fact that a person is part of a crowd means "his intellectual standard is immediately and considerably lowered."[14]

Jon Stewart transmits the party line to idiots, who sit in the audience of *The Daily Show* and maniacally applaud everything he says. They don't get all the jokes, but they know who they're supposed to hate. For some people, nothing is more important than to think of themselves as smart and hip, way better than other people. The very act of applauding a joke—instead of laughing at it—serves no function apart from associating oneself with the crowd. Laughter is involuntary, like a sneeze. By contrast, applauding a joke is a public gesture intended to announce, *I'm with him!*—rather like a "Heil Hitler" salute.

To truly witness the horrible spectacle of a man desperately in need of the crowd's approval, we turn to financial reporter Jim Cramer.

Cramer got in trouble with the mob when he criticized the angel Obama on March 3, 2009, calling Obama's agenda "radical" and saying "this is the most, greatest wealth destruction I've seen by a president." *The Daily Show*'s Jon Stewart—remembering that his role as a comedian required him to do something important—began repeating the White House line on Cramer, denouncing him for faulty financial predictions he made on CNBC.

At that point, Cramer had to choose: Make a Damascus Road conversion like Dennis Miller, Bernie Goldberg, and Brit Hume or go the whimpering sycophantic route of Chris Matthews.

The day he was to appear on Stewart's *Daily Show,* Cramer did a round of appearances on NBC programs to prepare for his monumental suck-up that night. On the *Martha Stewart Show* he droned on about his tremendous support for Obama, "I happen to support his agenda. . . . I'm a lifelong Democrat. There isn't a part of his agenda I don't support."

He called Stewart his "idol" and said, "This is killing me. My kids only know I have a show because Jon Stewart is skewering me. 'Dad's got a show! Holy Cow!' No he's the best there is." The boundless sycophancy continued as they made a banana cream pie: "How bad is it going to be? . . . Is he going to kill me? . . . Well, it's his home turf so I will pay homage. . . . Can I tell him that you said it was okay that I was on?"

Finally, for the cherry on top, Cramer said, "The reason why it's been so hard for me, the attacks, is that early on I patterned my show off of his."[15]

Cramer's actual appearance on Stewart's show was even more humiliating. The opening exchange got the ball rolling:

*Stewart:* How the hell did we end up here, Mr. Cramer? What happened?

*Cramer:* I don't know. I don't know. Big fan of the show. Who's never said that?

The key to understanding liberals is that "It is the need not of liberty, but of servitude that is always predominant in the soul of crowds."[16] It's striking how people in thrall to groupthink will, as Le Bon says, obey their designated leaders "much more docilely than they have obeyed any government."[17]

As Stewart relentlessly badgered and insulted him, Cramer rolled on his back, bleating, "I got a lot of things wrong. . . . I don't think anyone should be spared in this environment. . . . I try really hard to make as many good calls as I can. . . . You had a great piece about short selling earlier. . . . Absolutely we could do better. Absolutely. . . . I should do a better job at it. . . . I'm trying. I'm trying. Am I succeeding? I'm trying. . . . How about if I try it? Try doing that. I'll try that. . . . I'm sorry. You're absolutely right. . . . Look, I have called for star chambers— I want kangaroo courts for these guys. . . . Okay. All right. You're right. I don't want to personalize it. . . . True. True. I think, as a network, we produce a lot of interviews where I think that we have been—there have been people who have not told the truth. Should we have been constantly pointing out the mistakes that were made? Absolutely. I truly wish we had done more. . . . I wish I had done a better job. . . ."[18]

The next day, Cramer failed to show up for his scheduled appearance on MSNBC's *Morning Joe,* presumably because he was still showering off the humiliation. The herd was ecstatic—they had forced a loudmouthed liberal to issue obsequious, abject apologies for deviating from the party line on Obama. James Fallows exclaimed in the *Atlantic,* "Jon Stewart has become Edward R. Murrow" and compared Stewart's idiotic grandstanding to David Frost interviewing Richard Nixon.[19]

What was the point of Stewart's holier-than-thou showboating? Cramer and others on CNBC made lots of bad calls. So what? Some of their calls were accurate and some were not. Showing video of the specific bad calls to prove an analyst sucks is like showing video of Alex Rodriguez striking out a dozen times to prove he's a lousy baseball player.

It was just the ritualistic bloodletting to show that you must never diverge from liberal groupthink, rather like the ceremonial execution of the admiral in Voltaire's *Candide* for the minor offense of failing to engage a French fleet at a closer distance. His merciless execution was necessary, Candide is told, "to encourage the others."[20]

Wanting the good opinion of Jon Stewart, two months after Stewart had gone on CNN's *Crossfire* back in 2004, and attacked the show for "hurting America," then–network president Jon Klein announced that he was canceling *Crossfire* and cutting all ties to co-host Tucker Carlson. Klein explained that his decision to dump Carlson was inspired by Stewart's *Crossfire* appearance. "I agree wholeheartedly with Jon Stewart's overall premise," he said.[21] Carlson's co-host, Paul Begala, was presumably as guilty of "hurting America" as Carlson, inasmuch as he was one-half of the same debate show. But Begala was a liberal, so he was off the hook. The problem, evidently, had less to do with the debate format than the participation of a conservative.

Sarah Palin is catnip for very insecure people trying to make their bones with liberal elites. If your politics are sincerely Hollywood liberal, this is a very good time to be an American. You can make a lot of money sneering at Sarah Palin.

No one is more desperate for acceptance by liberal intellectuals than ex–morning show hosts whose idea of a major "get" is the co-inventor of the Snuggie. You don't win any points at the *New York Review of Books* by dropping names like "Katie Couric" or "Charlie Gibson" around the editorial offices. But in 2008, Couric and Gibson finally had a chance to establish their heavy-duty intellectual bona fides by kicking Palin's butt in an interview. Obviously, this was important to both of them.

It's interesting that even when driven by a penny-ante intellectual mob, behavior activated by groupthink seems to show some of the earmarks of actual possession. The famous Catholic exorcist Malachi Martin reports that those in the grip of possession always speak as if they are talking to someone else in the room. "She was speaking for the benefit of someone else's ear," he said of one woman before an exorcism, "repeating what somebody else was telling her."[22] (Obviously, I'm not saying Couric is possessed by the devil—even Lucifer couldn't sit through the *CBS Evening News with Katie Couric*.)

The tone of both of their interviews with Palin was: You're not as smart as we are. This, from people whose fame was based on showcasing winning recipes and hair care products. Thus, Gibson interviewed Marsha Brooks as she prepared a prizewinning apple pie. (*Gibson: "Now one of the things Marsha did, just as soon as she found out you'd won, you took the pies down to your local firehouse."*)[23] And Couric investigated the claims of a "Twist-a-Braid" infomercial (*Couric: Well, nobody has hair like this chick, that's for sure.*)[24] Having your intelligence questioned by Katie Couric must be like having Michael Moore say to you, "Have you put on a few pounds?"

Consider Couric's question about what Palin reads. The question wasn't terribly interesting. It's the sort of thing that gets posted on Facebook, not asked of vice presidential candidates. But the point wasn't to interview Palin, it was to nurture Couric's own self-esteem. In addition to national and political news, Palin probably read a lot of Alaska newspapers, hunting news, *Guns & Ammo* magazine, and religious publications and she correctly surmised that such literary preferences wouldn't help her with Couric's audience, so she avoided answering the question.

There is hardly a person in public life who wouldn't be embarrassed by that question. Why wasn't Obama asked what he reads? How about Joe Biden? There is no question but that Palin reads more widely than Patty Murray or Barbara Boxer—and has better reading comprehension. But a Democrat would never have been asked the question. Its only purpose was to make Palin look stupid, coming from someone who is herself barely hanging by a thread intellectually.

What Palin reads had nothing to do with any campaign issues. As the most knowledgeable governor in the country on energy, Palin had boatloads to say about the nation's energy policy, but she was never asked about that. The last thing the media were going to do was raise an issue that would help the Republicans.

Gibson's question to Palin about "the Bush doctrine" was similarly asinine. He chose a deliberately arcane way to ask a simple question in order to make himself look brilliant. The subject matter wasn't obscure, but Gibson's label was inscrutable.

No one talked about "the Bush doctrine" the way they talked about, for example, "WMDs" or "preemptive war." It simply didn't come up in conversation. Charles Krauthammer couldn't have answered that question—because no one knew what "the Bush doctrine" was. Even the *Washington Post* ran an article with various foreign policy experts scratching their heads about what Gibson meant.[25]

If Gibson really wanted to know Palin's position on Iraq, why didn't he just ask, "Do you think it was legitimate to invade Iraq?" No, he couldn't do that: It wouldn't have been a calculated attempt to trip her up. Both Couric's and Gibson's interviews had little to do with Palin. The ex–morning show hosts were aggressively pursuing their own agendas to win acceptance from their betters.

It was just like the time the no-name radio host in Boston decided to show he was a badass by giving presidential candidate George W. Bush a pop quiz on the names of various obscure world leaders during the 2000 campaign. He was a star for a week . . . and then was never heard from again. But for a brief shining moment this punk was part of the herd! The joy!

Sarah Palin was ideal for the middlebrow obsessions of people on the left. Professional atheist Sam Harris complained in *Newsweek* that Palin "didn't have a passport until last year."[26] Huffington Post editor Roy Sekoff—who went to a single mediocre college—sneered about "the six colleges that she attended."[27] Keith Olbermann thinks he's gotten a great dig in at Palin when he compulsively suggests a dinner with her would involve "a nice glass of Pinot Grigio or Mountain Dew."[28]

This is *Real Housewives* snobbery—white trash acting as if they're jetsetters. Maybe it's true that red-staters don't travel as much as blue-staters do. At least we manage not to spoil our ballots as often as Democratic voters do. One also can't help noticing that red-staters aren't terrified of literacy tests, as the Democrats are.

Screenwriter Aaron Sorkin (musical theater major, Syracuse University) cannot write a script without a moment when some character asks, "Why are people resented because they are more intelligent?" Sorkin's *West Wing* president, Josiah Bartlet, was forced to play down his brilliance, until finally one of his advisers tells him, "I'm telling you, be the smartest kid in your class. Be the reason why your father hated you. Make this an election about smart and stupid, about engaged and not, qualified and not."

As Sorkin explained his motive for that scintillating speech, "It was frustrating watching Gore try so hard not to appear smart in the debates—why not just say, 'Here's my f—ing résumé, what do you got?' "[29]

What we "got," evidently, is better word comprehension than Sorkin.

Two years earlier, the *Washington Post* had reported that, after Gore got into Harvard, helped by his prominent senator father (unlike George W. Bush, who got into Yale when his father was an obscure congressman), he ranked in the bottom fifth of the class for his first two years. In his sophomore year, "Gore's grades were lower than any semester recorded on Bush's transcript from Yale."[30] Gore went on to Divinity School, where he failed five of eight classes before dropping out. As Gore was failing out of Divinity School, Bush was earning his MBA from Harvard. Maybe that's why Gore didn't want to bring up the subject of educational achievement by saying, "Here's my f—ing résumé, what do you got?"

No matter what their own credentials, liberals are always dying to blurt out, "I'm smarter than you!" Normal people aren't driven by what other people think of them. They don't spend every waking moment thinking, "How do I get this person to acknowledge my intellectual gifts?" Normal people, thankfully, are not liberals.

The media so lost their composure with Sarah Palin that they slipped and gave away their contempt for people who live in places they would never visit and know nothing about. They simply forgot themselves. Noticeably, no Democratic politicians ever attacked Palin the way the media did. Politicians are well aware that there are a lot more people in the country like Sarah Palin than there are like Frank Rich.

Naturally, the people most ostentatiously bothered by Sarah Palin's purported idiocy were the most aggressive social climbers. Their pinup is Keith Olbermann, who was practicing radio at age six, while other boys were learning how to throw things and prevent girls from beating them up. Keith neurotically cites his nonexistent "Ivy League education" while ridiculing others for their stupidity.

When he was still employed at MSNBC, Keith had a four-page typewritten sheet taped to the outside of his office door titled "People Who Watch This Show," followed by a list of low-level celebrities. He is the sort of person who would write Mensa to argue that he should be admitted (and misspell "Mensa"). Now his fans are lost, adrift, unsure whom they're supposed to hate in order to impress *Rolling Stone* magazine.

Appealing to the herd is irresistible to the alternative prom crowd on MSNBC. These are people who have been awkward throughout their entire lives. They laugh a little too hard at jokes that aren't funny, and get too excited at minor flubs by their enemies. Usually, the socially mal-adroit don't hurt anyone and, with luck, will eventually find someone who appreciates their license plate collections.

No one enjoys picking on dorks. But the nightly smirkathons on MSNBC canceled out the usual solicitude. Things change when the lonely nerds decide they will lash out at the world from their sets at MSNBC.

As the famous psychiatrist M. Scott Peck says, "We are impressed not only by the innocence but also by the cruelty of children. An adult who delights in picking the wings off flies is correctly deemed sadistic and suspected to be evil. A child of four who does this may be admonished but is considered merely curious; the same action from a child of twelve is cause for worry."[31]

Sure that someday he would be quoted like Oscar Wilde, in 2009, Olbermann manfully ripped into twenty-year-old Miss USA runner-up Carrie Prejean, night after night, giggling mercilessly with the *Village Voice*'s Michael Musto in their gay coffee klatch about how stupid Prejean was.

> *Musto:* This is the kind of girl who sits on the TV and watches the sofa. She thinks the innuendo is an Italian suppository. . . .
>
> *Olbermann:* The moral in this is, what, never cross a beauty pageant official who knows you've had implants?
>
> *Musto:* Yes, exactly, that's it. This has escalated to a public shaving. . . . They also paid for Carrie to cut off her penis, and sand her Adam's Apple, and a get head-to-toe waxing. . . . Now he's a babe who needs a brain implant. Maybe they could inject some fat from her butt? Oh, they have?
>
> *Olbermann:* I didn't like her earrings.[32]

That's not Oscar Wilde: That's what gets your face smashed in and your lunch money taken away in high school. But Keith thought he had achieved such comedy gold that he replayed that segment on four other shows.[33]

I guarantee that Carrie Prejean is no dumber than Cindy Crawford, Stephanie Seymour, Christy Turlington, Linda Evangelista, Claudia

Schiffer, or Naomi Campbell, who are treated like a virtual Bloomsbury group by the elites. This is not a criticism, just a suggestion to cut the crap with conservative Christians like Prejean.

Liberals are people whose entire lives are consumed with following the crowd. Otherwise, how will they get a reputation for speaking truth to power?

Ever since David Letterman has become a tired old hack, watched by people about to collect Social Security, he has specialized in cheap applause. In June 2009, Letterman told this knee-slapper about Sarah Palin going to a Yankees game with her daughter: "There was one awkward moment during the seventh-inning stretch: her daughter was knocked up by Alex Rodriguez."

Except Bristol, the Palin daughter who got pregnant out of wedlock, wasn't at the game. Fourteen-year-old Willow was. And Rodriguez hasn't gotten anyone pregnant out of wedlock. The only way the joke works is if you're willing to accept that being a compulsive womanizer is close enough to getting girls pregnant and Willow Palin is close enough to Bristol Palin.

But Letterman was bullying the daughter of a hated Republican, so the audience knew it was supposed to laugh at the lame joke. The *New York Times* "ethicist" couldn't even acknowledge it lacked the basic elements of a joke, explaining that even though Willow isn't Bristol, and dating women isn't impregnating them, "a joke is a form of fiction, the punch line a contrivance: the bartender was not actually talking to the duck. A premise, too, can be invented: a man with a duck did not really walk into a bar."[34]

Yes, but if the talking duck runs into Alex Rodriguez and Willow Palin in the bar, Willow can't suddenly become Bristol and Rodriguez can't become John Edwards.

*How about a joke about Obama getting smashed?* Did I miss something—is he a drinker? *No, it's just funny that he's drunk.* But he isn't known for being a drunk.

*Wouldn't it be hilarious if Obama were cleaning a gun and it went off and hit Michelle in the shoulder?* But that didn't happen.

*What if Harry Reid was in a hotel room with Nancy Pelosi? Then we could go to town!* Yes, the only problem is: It didn't happen.

*How about a joke about Amy Fisher being at Yankee Stadium with Palin?* But she wasn't there. Neither was Bristol Palin.

This isn't a question of whose ox is gored. A joke is supposed to start with actual events and then veer into fiction for the punch line. Here's Jay Leno's joke on Palin's pregnant daughter: "Governor Palin announced over the weekend that her seventeen-year-old unmarried daughter is five months pregnant. And you thought John Edwards was in trouble before!"[35] That makes sense because Palin's seventeen-year-old daughter had gotten pregnant out of wedlock and Edwards, unlike A-Rod, had impregnated his mistress.

If art is going to confuse anyone, by rights it should confuse stupid people.* But the only people who could possibly find Letterman's Palin joke funny were idiots who don't know Bristol Palin had a child out of wedlock and who don't know that A-Rod hasn't gotten any of his girlfriends pregnant. Stupid people get to laugh and smart people can't because they're wondering, "Wait—was Bristol at the Yankees game? Did A-Rod get someone pregnant? Did I miss a news story?"

Letterman's writers have gone from Olympian in the early days, to imitators in the middle years, to finger-in-the-wind hacks who want to go home early in the later years. But as long as they attack mob-approved targets, everyone pretends not to notice.

Indeed, like the high school bullies studied by researchers at University of California at Davis, some liberals were psychologically compelled to describe Letterman's provably unfunny joke as hilarious out of a desperate quest for popularity.

Pleading over the airwaves for Letterman to have him on, Dick Cavett—inventor of the "name drop"—called the lame joke "witty" and "wonderful" and said he would do the joke himself if he had one as good "as delivered by Letterman's writers." Being his own Boswell, Cavett then repeated the jokes "most people remember" from his own column on Palin. (Illustrating why he's not in the top status group, Dick Cavett said, "I thought that referring to Sarah's slutty stewardess looks probably was over the line," adding, "I think he should apologize for that. Not to her, but to the stewardesses." Ba-da-bump!)[36]

---

*Anonymous.

Air America's Sam Seder proclaimed Letterman's bomb of a joke—
"in the final analysis"—"a funny joke." He boasted that jokes about
Palin were "like T-ball . . . it's not even softball. I mean, she just literally
holds it out there." (Literally!) And yet, he was unable to come up with
any jokes himself, easy as it was—literally.[37]

How about a Top Ten list for Dave's "*Late Show* interns I would
have knocked up if they weren't on the pill because no woman could
stand having a child who looks like me"? Just a few months after making
nonsensical jokes about Palin's daughter getting "knocked up," it came
out that Letterman had been carrying on with interns and other *Late
Show* female employees for years, despite having a wife—who had also
worked for him—and child on the side. The only way Dave can get a
woman to sleep with him is by preying on women underneath him pro-
fessionally, who want to move up.

A certain kind of idiot thinks he's made a great intellectual point
by saying, "Follow the money." Every bush-league Marxist assumes the
only reason anyone ever does anything is for money. But as we have
seen, lots of people also behave certain ways to be megalomaniacal and
suck up to the *New York Times.*

Once you have a certain amount of money, all kinds of things become more important to you than the next dollar—being thought of as
a sensitive, cool, deeply caring person, for example. People will spend a
lot of money to hang out with actresses. They will never spend so much
that they become part of the middle class themselves, mind you. But the
very rich have a long way to go before facing that calamity.

It's a simple equation: Do you, fabulously rich person, want to be
hated like Republicans Richard Mellon Scaife and David and Charles
Koch—or do you want to be widely admired as a great philanthropist
and lover of mankind like Warren Buffett and Bill Gates?

As Eugene Lyons described the posh opinion in favor of the Soviet
Union in the thirties, "Marx and martinis, bridge and dialectics, social
consciousness and social climbing were all mixed up on the banks of
luxurious private swimming pools."[38]

Poseurs are everywhere—Wall Street Marxists, the chubby college
coed wailing about global warming, the MSNBC host posting on his
door a list of semifamous people who watch his show, other MSNBC

hosts holding nightly smirkathons in order to bond with their insecure viewers, and professors defending morons with ed school degrees while denouncing actually educated conservative speakers in the name of freedom of speech. All this is the result of groupthink.

Mobs "stand in need of ready-made opinions on all subjects," Le Bon says, and the "popularity of these opinions is independent of the measure of truth or error they contain." The power of prestige "entirely paralyses our critical faculty, and fills our souls with astonishment and respect."[39] The weak-minded just go with the crowd, ridicule the designated scapegoats, and then pass out awards to one another for their courage.

The same mob mentality that leads otherwise law-abiding people to hurl rocks at cops also leads otherwise intelligent people to refuse to believe anything they haven't heard on NPR. To improve their social standing with the crowd, people will passionately assert whatever the official groupthink position is. Power today comes not from the guillotine, but from self-regard.

# FIFTEEN

# INHERITORS OF THE FRENCH REVOLUTION: LIBERALS ♥ MOBS

emocrats are heirs to the French Revolution, the uprising of a mob. Conservatives are heirs to the American Revolution and the harmonious order of a republic. (Even the flakiest, most out-of-step, financially irresponsible founding father, Thomas Jefferson, was an apparent God-believer, immediately taking him out of the running as a modern Democrat.)

That's why liberals avoid mentioning the French Revolution, except to absurdly claim that it was in the great tradition of the American Revolution—everyone move along now, there's nothing to see here.

Every single American knows about the Third Reich, a more recent and more efficient barbarism than the French Revolution. But Hitler got his playbook from Robespierre, as did all the great liberal "reformers" of the twentieth century, from Lenin to Hugo Chávez. It was the Rousseauian idea of a few select individuals exercising the "general will" that gave the world the gulag, the concentration camp, the killing fields, the reeducation camps, and corpse upon corpse, without end.

And yet for all it is studied, the French Revolution might as well be a history of the Maori settlements of New Zealand.

Cornell University doesn't have a single course on the French Revolution in the 2010–11 academic year. It has fifteen on Asia, including "Pop Culture in China" and "East Asian Martial Arts." Isn't the French Revolution at least as important as "A Social History of Food and Eating" or "Women and Black Nationalism in the United States"?[1] The French Revolution was the precursor to Women and Black Nationalism in the United States! But liberals don't want anyone to make that connection, so we never hear about the French Revolution, except in chirpy op-eds on Bastille Day claiming the French Revolution was the spitting image of the American Revolution.

With dozens of course offerings, UCLA's history department doesn't have a single course on the French Revolution, or even a course that would seem to cover Western Europe during that period. There are courses on European history in the fifteenth and nineteenth centuries, as well as from 1450 to 1660. And there's a Western Civilization class covering the period up to 1715. But if you want to know what was happening outside of the United States circa 1750 to 1800, you're limited to Latin America or Africa. The UCLA history department doesn't seem to be short on teaching staff: It offers classes on American Indian Peoples, Philippine History, History of Chicano Peoples, and Armenian History.[2] But no history of the French Revolution.

Even at America's premier university, Harvard, the history department offers only one course on the French Revolution. There are three classes on Germany, two on Vietnam—and seven history courses on "women" or "gender," including "Women Acting Globally" and "Gender, Migration and Globalization in 20th Century U.S. History."[3]

It would be as if the nation's math departments decided algebra was superfluous knowledge. The French Revolution is not only a gripping story, full of warnings for any civilized society, but remains the template for every bloody totalitarian dictatorship to this day. France was one of the most advanced, sophisticated, important nations in the world in the eighteenth century. And then the rabble destroyed it. Isn't that an interesting story?

In the blink of an eye, a great civilization was reduced to rubble, its most valuable citizens dead or living elsewhere. In the course of France's short revolution, 600,000 French citizens were killed and another 145,000 fled the country.[4] That's in a country with between 24 and 26 million people, about the current population of Texas. In terms of population loss, that would be the equivalent of the United States having a 9/11 attack every day for seven years.

In the American Revolution, fewer than 10,000 died in battle and another 10,000 died of disease or exposure during the war. And our king was fighting back! France's king capitulated immediately, but the revolutionaries proceeded to liquidate more than half a million of their fellow citizens anyway, in what the revolutionary leaders themselves called the "Terror." Tories fled America during our Revolution, but no one tried to massacre their remaining relatives.

How did the nation of Voltaire, Descartes, Pascal, and Molière transform itself into a bloody saturnalia overnight? This is a question liberals don't want us to think about.

The inheritors of the French revolutionary tradition always adhere to the same basic program. Psychopaths from Lenin, Stalin, and Mao Zedong to Kim Il Sung, Pol Pot, and Fidel Castro have used the rabble to grab power, with essentially the same justification, the same objectives, and the same bloody results.

All these monsters were praised in the pages of the *New York Times* and enthusiastically supported by the Democratic Party.

Stalin's crimes were lied about in the famous reportage of the *Times*'s Walter Duranty, who won a Pulitzer Prize for calling the forced starvation of an estimated 15 million Ukrainians a false rumor.[5]

In 2003, the Pulitzer Prize board came under pressure from Ukrainians—those Stalin hadn't killed—to revoke the prize based on Duranty's having covered up genocide. That's a rare transgression even among *Times* reporters.

In response, the *New York Times* hired a Columbia University history professor, Mark von Hagen, to review Duranty's articles and recommend whether the *Times* should return the prize. Von Hagen, an expert on early-twentieth-century Russian history, reviewed most of Duranty's articles from 1931 and produced an eight-page report.

He concluded that Duranty had uncritically parroted "the Soviet self-justification for its cruel and wasteful regime"; that his objective had been to goad the United States into establishing formal relations with the USSR; that he had a lover working for the Soviet secret police; that he inflated Stalin's accomplishments while hiding mass murder; and that he gave his imprimatur to a "dull and largely uncritical recitation of Soviet sources." Von Hagen concluded, naturally, that the prize should be rescinded, saying, unironically, "They should take it away for the greater honor and glory of the *New York Times.*"

The *Times* came back and asked Von Hagen if he thought the prize should be returned, taking into account only those articles for which the Pulitzer had been awarded. Von Hagen said yes, the prize should be returned on the basis of those articles alone.

Arthur Sulzberger Jr., publisher of the *Times,* then wrote to the Pulitzer board that he had decided to keep the award. To return it, he said, would be the same as the "Stalinist practice to airbrush purged figures out of official records and histories." *Times* executive editor Bill Keller agreed with the nincompoop's rationale, saying, "The notion of airbrushing history kind of gives me the creeps."[6]

Von Hagen replied incredulously in a letter to the editor, "Airbrushing was intended to suppress the truth about what was happening under Stalin. The aim of revoking Walter Duranty's prize is the opposite: to bring greater awareness of the potential long-term damage that his reporting did for our understanding of the Soviet Union."[7] The *Times* held Von Hagen's letter for two weeks before publishing it.

Twenty years after one *Times* reporter was covering up the Ukrainian famine, another *Times* reporter was writing mash notes to Fidel Castro in his Cuba reportage. Herbert Matthews, who, like Duranty, moved to communist whitewashing after serving in the *Times*'s Paris bureau, described Castro as "the rebel leader of Cuba's youth."

In an interminable front-page article after his first date with Castro, Matthews claimed that "thousands of men and women are heart and soul with Fidel Castro and the new deal for which they think he stands." He blithely assured the *Times*'s readers that Fidel's plan—the "new deal"—was "democratic and therefore anti-Communist." Indeed, "Senor Castro," in Matthews's hilarious locution, spoke with "extraordinary eloquence" about his "strong ideas of liberty, democracy, social justice, the need to restore the Constitution, to hold elections." Castro assured Matthews that "you can be sure we have no animosity toward the United States and the American people."[8] And you can take that to the banco.

After Castro seized power, canceled elections, and began confiscating private property, *National Review* ran a cartoon parody of a *Times* "Help Wanted" ad, with Fidel joyfully announcing, "I got my job from the *New York Times!*"

Liberals helped Mao get his job not only from the pages of the *New York Times* but from inside the Democratic administrations of Franklin D. Roosevelt and Harry Truman.

*New York Times* reporter Brooks Atkinson wrote glowing reports about Mao, describing the Chinese Communist Party, which would go on to murder 78 million people, as an "agrarian or peasant democracy." He reported that Mao was not a communist but simply objected to China's "lack of democracy." Calling the communist city of Yan'an "a Chinese Wonderland City," he raved about how the soldiers provided for themselves "without imposing any burden on the people."[9]

By contrast, Atkinson said our ally, the anti-communist Chiang Kai-shek, operated "a moribund, corrupt regime that is more concerned with maintaining its political supremacy than driving the Japanese out of China."[10]

Meanwhile, Soviet agents working for the Roosevelt and Truman administrations (Harry Dexter White, Solomon Adler, and Lauchlin Currie), as well as Soviet sympathizer John Stewart Service, conspired to send damaging information back to Washington about Chiang Kai-shek. Most damagingly, they blocked a crucial gold shipment to Chiang's Nationalist government as it was being besieged by Mao's communists.

American liberals were hysterically opposed to war with Germany—as long as Stalin was allied with Hitler. Only when Germany attacked Mother Russia were these stone-cold pacifists seized with war fever.

Back in the halcyon fifties, Democrats were merely obtuse about communist dictatorships. For example, Truman's secretary of state Dean Acheson casually announced at the National Press Club in January 1950 that America would not defend South Korea—leading, like night into day, to a Soviet-backed invasion from the North five months later.[11] But by 1970, Robert Scheer—later a Democratic candidate for Congress and a longtime *Los Angeles Times* columnist—would return from a fact-finding mission to North Korea proclaiming he had seen the future that works.[12]

Key Obama advisers Bernardine Dohrn and William Ayers, frequent *New York Times* contributor Todd Gitlin, and future Democratic office-holder Tom Hayden openly supported a communist takeover of Southeast Asia. They were given warm audiences with Cambodian and Vietnamese communists in Cuba—as well as with Democrats in Congress.

By the early seventies, the whole Democratic Party was getting mouthier about defending communist mobs around the globe. For years, liberal Democrats in Congress had been trying to amend spending bills with resolutions that would cut off all aid to the anti-communist governments of Cambodia and Vietnam. This wasn't about ending the war: Nixon had negotiated a cease-fire in 1973, and there hadn't been an American soldier in Vietnam for two years. Our allies in South Vietnam and Cambodia only needed material support to hold off the communist onslaught.

But when massive Democratic majorities swept Congress after Nixon's resignation in August 1974, there was nothing Republicans could do to prevent them from betraying our allies and handing Southeast Asia over to totalitarian monsters. The Democrats' very first act in the new 1975 Congress was to cut off all aid to Vietnam and Cambodia, guaranteeing a communist sweep of Southeast Asia.[13]

Republicans frantically warned that cutting off aid would lead to wholesale slaughter, but Democrats turned a blind eye, refusing to send even ammunition to the besieged Cambodians and South Vietnamese. Senator John Kerry (D-MA) dismissed Republican arguments as "anti-communist hysteria." Congressman Tom Downey (D-NY) said, "The administration has warned that if we leave there will be a bloodbath. But to warn of a new bloodbath is no justification for extending the current bloodbath." Then-congressman Christopher Dodd (D-CT) said the "greatest gift our country can give to the Cambodian people is peace, not guns. And the best way to accomplish that goal is by ending military aid now."

This would be like suggesting that the best way to help a woman being raped is to give her a little privacy.

The Democrats' foreign policy bigwig, Anthony Lake, wrote a

column in the *Washington Post* urging American support for the Khmer Rouge, which he touted as more "nationalist" than "communist."[14] Admired for his sage advice, Lake later served in both the Carter and Clinton administrations.

Backed by the Soviets, the North Vietnamese launched a major offensive, in violation of the 1973 Paris Peace accords. Without the material support promised by the United States under the accords, South Vietnam's brave army couldn't match the Soviet-backed North Vietnamese. But the Democrats respected the peace accords as much as the Vietcong did—so communist hordes swept through South Vietnam.

Weeks before the North Vietnamese had completely vanquished the South—whereupon they executed tens of thousands of South Vietnamese—a pro-Vietcong propaganda film, *Hearts and Minds,* won best feature documentary at the Oscars. At the ceremony, the producers, Peter Davis and Bert Schneider, praised the coming "liberati[on]" and read a letter of thanks from the Vietcong to "our friends in America." For this, they received a standing ovation. (Bob Hope immediately drafted a disclaimer on behalf of the Academy that was then read by Frank Sinatra, over the strenuous objection of Shirley MacLaine.)[15]

When the Democrats cut off aid to the Cambodian government, Pol Pot's Khmer Rouge constituted less than one percent of the population. By September of 1975, they had triumphed and the wanton slaughter had begun.[16] In the next two years, communists in Vietnam and Cambodia would kill about 2.7 million Southeast Asians—far more than had died throughout the entire fifteen years of the Vietnam War. With the advantage of Pol Pot's having studied in Paris, his slaughter was the more prodigious: He murdered an estimated 1.7 Cambodians—nearly a quarter of the population.[17]

Years later—after even the *New York Times* had acknowledged the carnage—liberal icon Noam Chomsky was still defending the Khmer Rouge, maintaining that Pol Pot had murdered just a "few thousand" Cambodians,[18] and noting its "constructive achievements for much of the population."[19] The skulls tell a different story.

It's not just communists whom liberals admire; they defend all mobs. Princeton professor Richard Falk cheered the downfall of the shah of Iran, writing in the *New York Times* in February 1979 that the Ayatollah Khomeini had been "defamed," and mocking claims that he would "turn the clock back 1,300 years, with virulent anti-Semitism, and with a new political disorder, 'theocratic fascism,' about to be set loose on the world." To the contrary, Falk said, Khomeini would "provide us with a desperately needed model of humane governance for a third-world country."[20]

These days, Falk, who is still at Princeton, is a prominent 9/11 truther and a UN "Rapporteur" on "human rights in the Palestinian territories occupied since 1967." So he wasn't just naive back in 1979— he's still defending Khomeinist proxies.

Amazingly, just a few years before Ronald Reagan achieved the final victory over Soviet communism, "Conscience of the Senate" Teddy Kennedy was sending secret messages to Soviet leader Yuri Andropov complaining about Reagan. Kennedy said how "very impressed" he was with Andropov, while decrying "Reagan's belligerence." The communist bootlicker asked for pointers on responding to Reagan's "propaganda," particularly any tips on Reagan's vulnerabilities. Most perplexing for the Soviets must have been Kennedy's suggestion that Andropov embark on an American media tour to counter Reagan, with Kennedy proposing interviews with Walter Cronkite or Barbara Walters.[21]

American liberals not only defend each successive iteration of the French Revolution around the globe, they try to imitate it at home. No matter how many carcasses pile up, liberals simply cannot shake their belief that government is the key to improving the human condition.

It's striking how uniform the playbook is. Totalitarians use mobs to seize power, impose their theories on the populace for the good of humanity, and then set about exterminating a lot of that humanity. Each new set of reformers never notices that the last mob claiming to be fighting for "the people" ended up killing the people.

Or perhaps they notice, but it doesn't bother them because they view humans as nothing but raw material for their schemes. The chilling phrase "You can't make an omelet without breaking eggs" is attributed to both Lenin and Robespierre *(On ne fait pas d'omelette sans casser des oeufs)*. Rousseau's successors discern no spark of divinity in humans; they believe man achieves moral stature only through the government.

A mob can't be fired up by promises of gradual, incremental change based on individual rights and voluntary transactions. There must be promises of grand social transformation overnight. It's the serpent's lie from the Garden of Eden: "Your eyes will be opened, and you will be like God" (Genesis 3:1–6).

No matter how mad the plan is—Fraternité, the "New Soviet Man," the Master Race, the Great Leap Forward, the Cultural Revolution, Building a New Society, ObamaCare—a mob will believe it. Time and again, the world has to relearn Michael Oakeshott's rule: "The conjunction of ruling and dreaming generates tyranny."

One of the main theoreticians of the French Revolution was Saint-Just. His utopian plan was that men should be only soldiers or farmers. Children would be taken from their parents at a young age and turned into "an army of robots," as historian Erik Durschmied says. Women were irrelevant to Saint-Just's plan.[22]

Saint-Just, Robespierre, Desmoulins, and the rest had their disagreements, but they couldn't have cared less what the French people wanted. This tiny group of fanatics would impose its program on the entire country. As with Obama and his national health care, they would suppress freedom to enact the "general will."

Hitler did everything in the name of the mob he dubbed "Das Volk." In *Mein Kampf,* he declared "war against the order of things which exist, against the structure of the world which presently exists."[23] He denounced both Bolshevism and Christianity as Jewish conspiracies.

As is common to mob movements, the Nazis' new order would require elimination of the Christian Church—messianic government doesn't like competition. As Joseph Goebbels explained: "The insanity of the Christian doctrine of redemption really doesn't fit at all into our time."[24] Sounding remarkably like the French revolutionaries, the Nazis demanded that priests and ministers swear loyalty to the state and its Fuhrer. In 1935, Heinrich Himmler prohibited SS officers from being members of religious organizations or even participating in services, in or out of uniform.

Reminiscent of France's "Cult of Reason," the Nazis planned to replace Christianity with the "Reich Church," based on a 30-point plan drawn up by Nazi leader Alfred Rosenberg. Crosses were to be stripped from churches, cathedrals, and chapels and replaced by the swastika. Bibles, crucifixes, and saints would be forbidden from the altars, which would instead display a copy of *Mein Kampf* and a sword.[25] (If they had thought of it, they might have put Christ in a jar of urine.)

A century earlier, Heinrich Heine had observed that Christianity had only "mitigated that brutal German love of war," not extinguished it. But should the cross be destroyed, he said, the "insane Berserk rage of which Nordic bards have spoken and sung so often, will once more burst into flame." And when it did, "A play will be performed in Germany which will make the French Revolution look like an innocent idyll."[26]

Again in Russia, we find a tiny group of zealots—calling themselves "the majority" (Bolsheviks)—who planned to control everything from a central authority. Lenin wrote most of the "scientific" program for a dictatorship of the proletariat in Russia, which was then debated and modified by other communist leaders. Socialism had to be imposed from above, by educated elites. There would be no from-the-bottom-up modifications. And so a small group of men spent their time banging out grand theories for how to control every aspect of a gigantic nation, down to setting prices for 24 million different goods.[27]

In Cambodia, the communist Khmer Rouge's first order of business was to empty the cities for the new back-to-nature agricultural plan. The millions of Cambodians who lived in cities—about half the population—were given 24 hours to leave their homes. Within a week the cities were emptied. Then the planners congratulated themselves on having solved "the ancient antagonism between urban and rural areas." As in France, it was a new world—it was "Year Zero."

Next, the Cambodian planners turned to the destruction of religion, commerce, education, and parental authority. Young people were taken from their parents to be raised in communes. Money was abolished in a week. As with the ludicrous French calendar, workers were allowed one day off every ten days. Religion was inconsistent with the program, so nearly half of all Catholics were exterminated and the cathedral in Phnom Penh reduced to rubble.[28] Buddhist monks were slaughtered and their temples destroyed.

The details of totalitarian regimes may vary, but the inspiration is always the same Rousseauian fantasy: A select group of elites with absolutely no grasp of human nature will figure out the program, inflexibly impose it on the people, and thereby regenerate mankind. You will note the similarities in all these totalitarian plans to many of the Democrats' schemes.

Finley Peter Dunne described a fanatic as "a man that does what he thinks the Lord would do if He knew the facts of the case." Inasmuch as liberals don't believe in God, it's a one-step process: "What would I do?" What they would do is use the power of the state to revoke nature, tradition, the market, the existence of two sexes, and popular opinion—all of which liberals disdain. They can't leave anything alone, except sodomy. It's just a good thing we have no idea what they were doing in Gomorrah or liberals would be pushing that on us too.

# SIXTEEN

# THE TOTALITARIAN INSTINCT AND SEXUAL PERVERSITY OF LIBERALS

n Hillary Clinton's famed "politics of meaning" speech during her husband's first year as president, she said we must "remold society by redefining what it means to be a human being in the twentieth century."[1] A decade later, at a campaign event in California, Hillary vowed to raise taxes, saying, "We're going to take things away from you on behalf of the common good."[2]

More disturbing—if that is possible—Obama has repeatedly appealed for votes by saying that the difference between the parties is that Democrats "believe that I am my brother's keeper."[3] If he were our brother, that would be a lovely sentiment. But he's our president, the commander in chief, the nation's chief law enforcement officer—which makes the statement terrifying.

Unlike the leaders of the French Revolution, America's founding fathers did not presume that elected officials would embody the "general will." Indeed, the framers did not imagine there was such a thing as the "general will." Having some grasp of human nature, they knew there would always be many competing factions. Interestingly, Alexander Hamilton chided Lafayette at the outset of the French Revolution for "the reveries of your Philosophic politicians," saying they were aiming "at more refinement than suits either with human nature or the composition of your nation."[4]

Instead of expecting government officials to express the "general will," our Constitution spreads opposing interests across separate governing bodies in a sort of organizational jujitsu, and provides explicit protections for individual rights. "Even the bill of rights," as Professor Jeremy Rabkin says, "sticks for the most part to affirming the continued force of traditional legal safeguards of individual rights, saying nothing about citizenship, sovereignty, or the general will."[5]

Liberals are constantly pushing for the Rousseauian approach to governance in defiance of our nation's history and Constitution. They not only believe there is a "general will," they are sure their policies express it. Instead of allowing ordinary people to have more control over their lives, Democrats produce inflexible, universal plans, sublimely confident of their ability to build a perfect system. They get angry when people say, "I don't think your plan will work in this part of the country." All plans, all rules, all regulations must be universal.

It's an obsession with the Democrats to nationalize everything: health care, welfare, the speed limit, abortion, the drinking age—so there's no escape. Like all totalitarians, the Democrats' position is: *We thought up something that we know will work better than anything anyone else has done for the last 30,000 years. We don't know why no one else has thought of it. We must be smarter.*

This is why the history of liberalism consists of replacing things that work with things that sounded good on paper.

When the Democrats were pushing national health care, Americans kept saying, "Do we really have to junk our entire health care system?" But Democrats explained they had figured everything out and would prefer if there wasn't a lot of "discussion" to keep interrupting their thought process.

Democratic Speaker of the House Nancy Pelosi said, "We have to pass the bill so that you can find out what is in it, away from the fog of the controversy."[6] (And now the Republicans are going to have to repeal it, so we can find out what's not in it.)

Following the mob-rule playbook, Democrats spent decades creating

a synthetic crisis in health care by issuing both federal and state government mandates dictating what insurance companies were required
to cover. Politicians forced insurance companies to pay for everyone's
Viagra, prenatal counseling, shrinks, marital counseling, and drug
rehab—all of which made health insurance ridiculously expensive (especially for those of you who aren't likely to need treatment for a gambling
addiction or self-esteem issues).

The whole idea of insurance is to insure against catastrophes, such as
fires, diseases, accidents, or sudden marriages to a Kardashian daughter.
But because of government intervention, the American consumer had no
choice about whether to pay for everyone else's shrinks and Viagra. In its
infinite wisdom, the government also made it illegal to buy health insurance across state lines to prevent competition. They can't keep Mexicans
out of Laredo, but they can sure keep an Indiana State Farm agent out
of Ohio.

Having wrecked the market for health insurance, liberals demanded
a national health care system to "fix" the very problems their meddling
had created in the first place. As usual, the Democrats' solution to problems created by government intervention was more government intervention. This is like trying to sober up by having another drink—except
at least trying to sober up by drinking more is fun.

And Democrats promised utopia: ObamaCare would provide health
care for 30 million uninsured Americans, everyone else's health care
would improve—and their plan would save money! It was a delicious
all-you-can-eat chocolate cake that actually burned calories!

Only the mob could believe it. When most Americans objected, liberals explained, *We know you don't want it, but my roommate and I are
both Rhodes scholars and we worked it all out on paper. This will turn out
fantastically well!* As was said of Pol Pot, "It seemed that the only thing
needed was sufficient willpower, and heaven would be found on Earth."[7]

Frustrated that, in a democracy, they can't implement their grand
plans to save humanity with the ease of a dictator, liberals demonize
those who stand in their way. That's why Americans who objected to
ObamaCare had to be anathematized for "obstructing" the plan for
health care utopia.

The mob can make a person a pariah in an instant with rumors, outright lies, and the crowd's trademark smirking. They did it to Marie Antoinette. They did it to Joe McCarthy. They did it to Richard Nixon, the shah of Iran, Ronald Reagan, Dick Cheney, Donald Rumsfeld, Halliburton, Margaret Thatcher, Dan Quayle, Bush I, Bush II, "neoconservatives," Sarah Palin, Michele Bachmann, Allen West—the list is endless. It's important to liberals to express contempt for an adversary. Belittling people is pleasurable for them as well as tactically useful.

Instead of "counterrevolutionaries," liberals' opponents are called "haters," "those who seek to divide us," "tea baggers," and "right-wing hate groups." Meanwhile, conservatives call liberals "liberals"—and that makes them testy.

They make wild, lying accusations against conservatives, especially the Tea Partiers—to the point of accusing conservatives of complicity in a liberal lunatic's shooting spree at a Tucson Safeway that left six dead and a dozen wounded.

They terrorize their political opponents by ginning up psychopaths to physically attack conservatives at the Republican National Convention, conservative rallies, Republican luncheons, book signings, speeches—even at the political opponent's home. Then they turn around and claim to be afraid of Tea Partiers.

Violence from the Left is never criticized by allegedly respectable Democrats. Generally, it's not even reported, allowing liberals to go on physically intimidating conservatives without everyone noticing their mob behavior. Just as they forget to mention the entire history of the French Revolution, they forget to report the constant mayhem and tumult being created by liberals.

When liberal activists used fake press credentials to sneak into the 2008 Republican National Convention and disrupt Sarah Palin's speech, only two newspapers in the country bothered to mention it in their pages—the *Idaho Falls Post Register* and *St. Paul Pioneer Press.* The protesters were major Obama fundraisers, Jodie Evans and Medea Benjamin of CodePink—a group whose raison d'être is to assault conservatives.

After illegally sneaking into the convention hall, the protesters waited for Palin—a major party's vice presidential candidate—to begin speaking and then stripped to reveal their costumes, pink dresses with anti-Palin slogans. They unfurled banners denouncing Palin, and began screeching. Although not as scary as a Tea Partier peacefully protesting ObamaCare in a public place, isn't that newsworthy?

When CodePink activists returned to the Convention Hall the next night to heckle John McCain's speech, again, only a handful of newspapers reported this shocking assault on a party's political convention. Earlier in the day, CodePink loons had violently disrupted a pro-life luncheon, storming the stage and ripping the microphone from Phyllis Schlafly's hand.

If a couple of John Birchers had stood up and started shouting during Barack Obama's convention speech, would that have been considered newsworthy?

One of the rabble-rousers, Jodie Evans, not only was a bundler for Obama but also had served in the cabinet of California governor Jerry Brown during his first administration. She ran Brown's 1992 presidential campaign and held fundraisers for him during his 2010 gubernatorial run.

She's also led protests in Santa Monica against the Israeli skin care company Ahava[8] and tried to stage a citizen's arrest of Karl Rove. And yet Evans is as welcome in the Democratic Party as the Koch brothers are in the Republican Party.

Part of what gives mob movements their fury is that they're always claiming to be righting the wrongs of the past—the corrupt royalty and clergy in France, the oppressive tsars in Russia, the hyperinflationary Weimar Republic in Germany, the inept Kuomintang in China. You will find that the most bloodthirsty regimes in history are those claiming to be redressing the wrongs of previous regimes.

In America, it's "discrimination" and "white male patriarchy" that's always being redressed, naturally with even more discrimination. We've gone from Democrats imposing discriminatory laws on blacks in the South to national Democrats imposing federally sanctioned, government-supported race, gender, and disability quotas on the entire country.

Following their totalitarian forebears, liberals went from punishing acts to punishing thoughts and motives in the blink of an eye. In lieu of class crimes and counterrevolutionaries, American liberals have given us "hate crimes," "disparate impact" rules, "sexists," and "bigots." Acts are irrelevant; your motives are on trial. You are presumed guilty and acquittals are rare.

The American Left also shares the French revolutionaries' blind hatred of tradition when it comes to morals and culture. Ironically, liberals are hidebound reactionaries when it comes to recent innovations such as government pensions: It's the thousand-years-old building blocks of civilization they want to shatter. The definition of "family" and "human life" are up for grabs, but the retirement age for Social Security is written in stone tablets.

Liberals never bother to ask whether there might have been a reason for a thousand-years-old convention such as marriage. They don't care. Their approach is to rip out society's foundations without considering whether they serve any purpose. *Why do we need immigration laws? What's with these borders? Why do we have the institution of marriage anyway? What do we need standardized tests for? Why do children have to have a mother and father? Hey, I like Keith Richards—why not make heroin legal? Let's take a sledgehammer to all these load-bearing walls and just see what happens!*

Liberals even manipulate children to falsely accuse their elders, a specialty of all totalitarians. There is something so vile about turning a child against his parents as to be bone-chilling. But for liberals, it's just one more weapon in their quest for power.

Just as Marie Antoinette's son was brainwashed into accusing his mother of incest, a slew of American children in the eighties were manipulated by liberals into accusing completely innocent adults of child molestation. The psychologist Le Bon says the appeal of children's testimony to a mob is that children are easy to manipulate. "It would be better to decide the fate of an accused person by the toss of a coin," he says, "than, as has been so often done, by the evidence of a child."[9]

Dade County, Florida, state attorney Janet Reno made a name for herself as one of the leading witch-hunters in the child-abuse hysteria era. In the similarly ludicrous Fells Acres case, brought by then–district attorney Scott Harshbarger in Middlesex, Massachusetts, Gerald Amirault served eighteen years in prison, and his mother and sister served eight years, for imaginary crimes. Without a shred of physical evidence to support the allegations, children coached by liberal therapists with naked dolls and "let's pretend" games made preposterous claims of rape with butcher knives, naked children tied to trees, and animal sacrifices.

Not one child ever spontaneously claimed to have been abused. Indeed, no allegations of abuse arose until the child therapists showed up. More than a decade after their convictions, when defense lawyers played the tapes showing how child therapists had coaxed accusations from the children, reporters from Miami to Boston gasped, "Oh my God!"[10]

And yet mostly liberal prosecutors put innocent people in jail on the basis of fantastical stories that had been implanted by alleged therapists. It is terrifying that this could have happened in America. This was one of the most egregious mass violations of people's rights in U.S. history. (A decade later, Reno would top it by killing nearly eighty civilians in Waco, Texas.)

Almost all of these cases were brought and defended by liberals—Janet Reno, Scott Harshbarger, and Martha Coakley. The ACLU was too busy forcing a small town in South Dakota to take down a crèche to notice the mass imprisonment of people for crimes that had never happened.

Harshbarger used the case as a launching pad to run for attorney general and then governor of Massachusetts. After losing his gubernatorial bid, he was made president of the liberal group Common Cause, where he lobbied for campaign finance reform. Janet Reno went from imprisoning innocent people in Florida to being appointed attorney general by Bill Clinton (and not imprisoning guilty people).

When similar claims of sexual molestation and ritual satanic abuse at Breezy Point day care center in Bucks County, Pennsylvania, were presented to the Republican district attorney, Alan Rubenstein, he concluded that the charges were utterly baseless. Indeed, after he discovered that the child-abuse "expert" was actually an unemployed plumber, Rubenstein warned him that if he set foot in Bucks County, he'd be arrested for fraud.[11]

This is not the only way liberals have used children for political gain. Liberals specialize in promoting the backstabbing children of prominent conservatives. In 2004, the Democrats featured Ronald Reagan's son, incorrectly known as Ron Reagan Jr., speaking in favor of embryonic stem cell research, a policy that would have been detested by his staunchly pro-life father. There was no reason for anyone to care what "Ron Jr." had to say about stem vegetables, much less stem cells—other than as a postmortem rebuke to his father.

In 2008, Ron triumphantly endorsed Barack Obama. In 2011, he wrote a book absurdly announcing that his father had Alzheimer's as president—a medical diagnosis that was promptly dismissed by Reagan's White House doctors, as well as disproved by his medical records.[12]

Most despicably, while Reagan was still alive, *Playboy* magazine put a full nude torso shot of Patti Reagan on its cover, with only a black man's hands covering her breasts. "Ronald Reagan's Renegade Daughter," the skin magazine proclaimed.

The son of the great Christian theologian Francis Schaeffer attacked his father as a fraud and con man in a book called *Crazy for God: How I Grew Up as One of the Elect, Helped Found the Religious Right, and Lived to Take All (or Almost All) of It Back.* Solely because of who his father was, Schaeffer was given a platform by the Left to launch venomous attacks against the entire evangelical movement. In no time, he was writing for the Huffington Post and appearing on MSNBC'S *Rachel Maddow Show.*

Sadly for liberals, they have been unable to turn any of Sarah Palin's actual children against her and had to settle for risible attacks from the nitwit biological father of Palin's illegitimate grandchild, Levi Johnson.

It isn't random which children turn on their parents. The benefits flow only to those who tattle on conservative parents. Who could write a better "Mommy Dearest" book than Chelsea Clinton? How about Amy Carter? But no conservative publisher would seek out such a book. Conservatives don't use children as weapons against their political opponents.

As with the vile accusations against Marie Antoinette, liberals revel in obscene bacchanals—while hurling accusations of sexual depravity at their enemies. Soviet spy Alger Hiss's partisans started a rumor that his accuser, Whittaker Chambers, had committed incest with his brother who later committed suicide. When told of the disgusting slander, Chambers exclaimed, "What kind of beasts am I dealing with?" Only minds "deformed by something more than malevolence could have excreted it."[13]

The first George Bush was falsely accused of having an affair, John

McCain was falsely accused of having an affair, Sarah Palin was falsely accused of having an affair—and also of not having given birth to Trig—Clarence Thomas was falsely accused of talking dirty to a coworker, and on and on. This, from the party whose motto is "Everybody does it."

During the investigation of Bill Clinton's actual sexual congress with a White House intern and associated felonies, Clinton adviser and *Hustler* magazine magnate Larry Flynt offered a reward for information about sexual affairs of any Republican members of Congress.

After Clinton's impeachment, his partisans sponsored an investigation by writer and fantasist John Connolly into the sex lives of wholly private citizens to punish them for having supported Clinton's impeachment. Commissioned by Tina Brown's Talk Miramax, the book was canceled after it was spectacularly revealed that Connolly had hired a detective to snoop into private individuals' sex lives.[14]

Liberals will even dirty up the founding fathers' sex lives for political gain. They have absurdly accused Abraham Lincoln of being gay based on his sleeping in the same bed with a male friend, as was common in the era before reliable indoor heating.

They have accused Thomas Jefferson of having an affair with his slave Sally Hemings in order to help Bill Clinton in the middle of the Monica Lewinsky scandal. This was in defiance of evidence that overwhelmingly suggests that Hemings's only Jefferson consort was the president's younger brother, Randolf, who frequently socialized with the slaves. (At least they were holding Jefferson clear of being gay.)

Strikingly, with every mob uprising we see the recrudescence of hatred toward religious morality—from the French Revolution to Nazi and communist ideologies to Islamic barbarians and our liberal friends in this country. "History tells us," Le Bon says, "that from the moment when the moral forces on which a civilization rested have lost their strength, its final dissolution is brought about by those unconscious and brutal crowds known, justifiably enough as barbarians."

In his book on the French Revolution, the British historian Simon Schama describes a moral weakening of the entire country that paved the way for the coming massacre. None of the libelous attacks on Marie Antoinette, Schama says, "would have been possible had there not already been a rich and unsavory vein of court pornography to tap."

Although pornography wasn't new, Schama says, "it evolved into a particularly ripe phase during the last years of Louis XV"—on account of the king's openly acknowledged mistress and his private brothel at Versailles.[15] Schama says, "Virtually everything short of outright atheism, tracts preaching regicide and pornography got published" between 1750 and 1763.[16]

It was a small step from there for the porn peddlers to turn on the queen—to make their material politically relevant. In no time, pamphlets attacking the demure Princess Lamballe leeringly alleged that the princess widened Antoinette's labia so that the king's soft penis could enter.[17]

During the revolution, one mob commander of the French Revolution, P. J. Picot-Bellac, went straight to the churches in every town he besieged in order to give mock "sermons" in which he called the Virgin Mary a "whore" and said Jesus had "scored"—using a French vulgarity—with Mary Magdalene.[18]

Compare that with Amanda Marcotte, blogger for the campaign of John Edwards—an apparently serious Democratic presidential candidate. She wrote, "Q: What if Mary had taken Plan B after the Lord filled her with his hot, white, sticky Holy Spirit? A: You'd have to justify your misogyny with another ancient mythology." Another of Marcotte's charming observations was: "[Y]ou motherf**kers who want to ban birth control will never sleep. I will f**k without making children day in and out and you will know it and you won't be able to stop it. Toss and turn, you mean, jealous motherf**kers. I'm not going to be 'punished' with babies."

After writing those gems, Marcotte was hired by Edwards—and not to sweep floors but to write for his blog, based on her earlier oeuvre. Perhaps it is not surprising that such a person as this would find work with a smarmy pro-abortion hustler, who, while he was running for president, cheated on his cancer-stricken wife with a New Age flake, got her pregnant, and then lied about it even after getting caught. Still, Edwards isn't Dennis Department-of-Peace-guided-talking-dolphins Kucinich. He was the Democrats' vice presidential candidate in 2004. Marcotte fits comfortably within the mainstream of the Democratic

Party in America—the party of abortion, adultery, and everything bestial in society.

Key Obama adviser Bernardine Dohrn notoriously sported a button in her younger years that said, "Fellatio Is Fun, Cunnilingus Is Cool." Dohrn, Ayers, and the other former radicals, now university professors and presidential advisers, engaged in bisexual orgies as part of their mission to "smash monogamy," with Ayers having sex with his best male friend.[19]

Liberals promote sexual vulgarity to tear down values that make civilized society possible. Liberal women at American universities protest pro-life speakers by chanting, "I f—k to c—m, not to procreate!" They protest conservative speakers by shouting "Lick my cl—t!" During one act of the charmingly titled play *The Vagina Monologues,* written by silly liberal Eve Ensler, the audience is directed to chant in unison, "C—T! C—T! C—T!"

Liberals don't just hate tradition and morality, they hate God. That's not our country and that's not our revolution.

Leading our revolutionary troops in 1776, General George Washington sent a message to the troops that said, "The blessing and protection of Heaven are at all times necessary, but especially so in times of public distress and danger. The general hopes and trusts that every officer and man will endeavor to live and act as becomes a Christian soldier, defending the dearest rights and liberties of his country."

A few years later, in 1778, Washington directed that church services be conducted for the troops every Sunday at 11 a.m., saying of this directive, "While we are duly performing the duty of good soldiers, we certainly ought not to be inattentive to the higher duties of religion. To the distinguished character of a patriot, it should be our highest glory to add the more distinguished character of a Christian."[20]

Washington's religiosity was utterly typical of our revolutionary forebears. John Adams, second president of the United States and also a signer of the Declaration, wrote to his wife in 1775, "Statesmen may plan and speculate for liberty, but it is Religion and Morality alone which can establish the principles upon which freedom can securely stand. A patriot must be a religious man."[21] One of America's most important founding fathers, Roger Sherman of Connecticut, who signed all three of America's founding documents—the Articles of Confederation, the Declaration of Independence, and the Constitution—wouldn't even travel on Sunday, so dutiful was he about keeping the Sabbath.[22]

Samuel Adams, sometimes called the "Father of the American Revolution," who signed the Declaration of Independence and voted to ratify the U.S. Constitution, said, "I conceive we cannot better express ourselves than by humbly supplicating the Supreme Ruler of the world . . . that the confusions that are and have been among the nations may be overruled by the promoting and speedily bringing in the holy and happy period when the kingdoms of our Lord and Savior Jesus Christ may be everywhere established, and the people willingly bow to the scepter of Him who is the Prince of Peace."[23]

Even the flaky Thomas Jefferson, who was not an orthodox Christian, was a virtual Jerry Falwell compared with today's Democrats. Jefferson said, "Can the liberties of a nation be secure when we have removed their only firm basis, a conviction in the minds of the people that these liberties are of the gift of God?"

The only founding father besides Jefferson with unconventional religious tendencies was Benjamin Franklin. Yet it was Franklin who proposed a prayer at the Continental Convention for the drafters of the Constitution—a motion shot down by the devout Alexander Hamilton on the grounds that a prayer would send a signal that the Convention was in trouble.[24]

Meanwhile, over in France, their revolutionary heroes were torching churches, axing priests, and giving sermons calling the Virgin Mary a whore.

That's the Democrats' revolutionary tradition.

# SEVENTEEN

## LUCIFER:
# THE ULTIMATE MOB BOSS

I n the psychiatrist M. Scott Peck's book *People of the Lie,* he describes evil in the same terms that Le Bon uses to describe mobs, saying it is "a kind of immaturity." Writing about an exorcism he participated in, he says when the possessed was asked if he was multiple demons or just one, Satan—speaking through the possessed—replied, "They all belong to me."[1] God oversees individual souls, but Satan has the mob.

The mob is satanic and Satan can only destroy. In the Bible, Jesus says to the crowd following the devil, rather than God, "You are the children of your father the devil, and you love to do the evil things he does. He was a murderer from the beginning. He has always hated the truth, because there is no truth in him. When he lies, it is consistent with his character; for he is a liar and the father of lies" (John 8:44).

Peck says there is nothing creative in the devil; his only will is to annihilate.[2] Le Bon describes mobs in similar terms, saying that crowds are determined "to utterly destroy society as it now exists, with a view to making it hark back to that primitive communism which was the normal condition of all human groups before the dawn of civilization."[3] Crowds, he says, "are only powerful for destruction."[4]

It's not an accident that Saul Alinsky, forefather to community organizers like Barack Obama and Hillary Clinton, dedicated his book *Rules for Radicals* to "the first radical known to man who rebelled against the establishment and did it so effectively that he at least won his own kingdom—*Lucifer*." (I suppose it could have been worse. He could have dedicated his book to George Soros.)

This is why liberals are shrieking oppositionists, braying, abortion-obsessed feminists, SEIU thugs, Earth Liberation Front loons, Bill Maher audiences, and querulous dissidents from every measure taken in defense of their own country. This is why they mock all that is good—America, religion, patriotism, chivalry, the rule of law, truth, the creation of wealth, life—while hysterically attacking those who oppose them.

The mob will never support defending America, only those who seek to undermine it. The mob will never side with those who seek to protect human life, only those who seek to destroy it. The mob will never support the creation of wealth, only those who seek to punish it. The mob will never defend traditional morality, only those who seek to subvert it. And if you oppose the mob, it will come after you like a pack of ravenous hyenas.

There is no coherence to the Left's positions, except its will to destroy. When Islamic terrorists came along, liberals rushed to their defense, having more warmth of feeling for violent Muslims than, for example, a Methodist women's Bible study. Liberals' Islamic friends practice clitorectomies, honor killings, and dropping walls on gays. (Other than that, they're mostly peaceful.) Is that part of the beautiful mosaic of multiculturalism? Do liberals suppose Osama bin Laden railed, *What I cannot abide is that the United States didn't sign the International Treaty on the Rights of the Child!* . . . *Hey, why can't I get* Two and a Half Men *in my cave?* . . . *WHAT? THE UNITED STATES IS TRYING TO OUTLAW LATE-TERM ABORTION???* *That is the last straw!*

The only common thread is destruction. It's the only move a mob has.

Liberals care less about achieving their vision of a centralized government than they do about destroying their enemies. Night after night, MSNBC hosts will maniacally fixate on some conservative they hate—Bill O'Reilly, Mike Huckabee, Rand Paul, Sarah Palin, David Koch,

Christine O'Donnell, Sharron Angle, Glenn Beck—even beauty pageant winner Carrie Prejean. It's impossible to imagine such obsessive public shamings on Fox News or even CNN. The sneering and snickering at opponents—out of all proportion to any principled disagreement—is a specialty of the Left.

Democrats didn't love Soviet agents as much as they detested "red-baiters" like Joe McCarthy. They didn't like Clinton as much as they hated Ken Starr, Linda Tripp, and the rest of the "vast right-wing conspiracy." They didn't even admire Saddam Hussein as much as they despised Dick Cheney. Some liberals still trundle off to the National Archives every Saturday to listen to the Nixon tapes so they can hate him even more. Please—it's 2011.

Conservatives aren't wild about their opponents, but only because of ideological disagreements. Conservatives didn't want ObamaCare; they aren't hoping Obama will slip on a banana peel so they can laugh at him. Ask yourself if liberals wish for that with Sarah Palin and you will see the difference in the right and left in America.

Conservatives wanted to liberate Iraq—and if liberals like Joe Lieberman and Alan Dershowitz did, too, we were happy to have them. Conservatives want a free market without burdensome government red tape—and if George McGovern agrees, we're happy to have him. Conservatives believe in protecting unborn humans—and if Nat Hentoff, Christopher Hitchens, and Jack Nicholson agree, we're happy to have them.

Liberals get excited about conservative defectors only when they're dishing dirt on Sarah Palin's e-mail account[5] or about George W. Bush's secret hatred of Christians.[6]

Ron Paul, Bob Novak, and Pat Buchanan all agreed with the Left on foreign policy, but liberals still shunned them. It's not agreement with liberals on a particular issue that wins their phony "respect," it's attacking other conservatives. This is the basis of the expression "Strange New Respect," which is what liberals accord those conservatives who so crave liberal approval, they will gratuitously attack fellow conservatives. It is the slutty girl's path to popularity. Senator John McCain won "Strange New Respect" from the Left when in 2000—for no reason—he attacked Jerry Falwell and Pat Robertson as "agents of intolerance" who "shame our faith, our party and our country."[7]

Liberals loathe conservative women beyond reason, perceiving them as the natural keepers of religious faith and morality. Republicans dislike Harry Reid about the same as they dislike Nancy Pelosi, and they dislike Hillary about the same as Bill. (And, of course, conservatives wouldn't physically attack any of them.) But Democrats reserve unfathomable venom, often coupled with physical violence, for conservative women— Sarah Palin, Michele Bachmann, Phyllis Schlafly, Condoleezza Rice, Christine O'Donnell, and Nikki Haley.

House Republicans voted to block federal funding of abortions in the 2012 budget and the *New York Times* responded with an angry editorial titled "The War on Women."[8] But when a Palin-obsessed liberal journalist rented the house right next to Sarah Palin's home for more convenient stalking, liberals couldn't understand the fuss.

The Left's constant prattle about the "right-wing hate machine" is not merely a tactical device to make conservatives look bad. It reveals leftist thinking: They can't imagine an opposition that isn't a "hate machine" because that's their view of politics—one hate machine against the other. Historians say that Stalin was paranoid. But perhaps he wasn't paranoid as much as he was projecting: He simply assumed that everyone was in a conspiracy to provoke chaos and violent subversion—just as his Bolsheviks were. Like liberals, he couldn't conceive of an organized political group that made appeals to logic and argument.

Politics for liberals is: Our mass against their mass. Except conservatives don't have a mass; liberals do. (But enough about Michael Moore.)

This is why conservatives and all law-abiding Americans have been under nonstop attack from liberal mobs since the founding of this nation. But lately, instead of recognizing mobs as a threat to the nation to be thwarted, conservatives have been bowing and scraping and apologizing to the barbarians.

Despite endless, epic mob violence from the left, lily-livered Republicans can't stop appeasing liberals. When Democrats slandered anti-ObamaCare protesters by falsely claiming that some of them had shouted the N-word at black members of Congress, then–House minority leader John Boehner immediately went on NBC's *Meet the Press* and said "there were some isolated incidents on the Hill yesterday that were reprehensible."[9]

After the continuous stream of hoax racism charges over the past few decades—from Tawana Brawley to the Duke lacrosse players—Republicans might consider waiting twenty-four hours before leaping to the conclusion that such accusations are always true.

When the two Obama supporters sneaked into the Republican Convention and began screeching in the middle of Palin's speech, convention security guards did nothing. Two lunatics were approaching a major party's vice presidential candidate, but the male guards stood frozen, whispering into their walkie-talkies, as if they were Louis XVI, paralyzed with fright. The crazed women were able to walk toward the stage in the middle of a nationally televised, $100 million, years-in-the-making convention.

The protesters must have been as stunned as Palin that security let them carry on so long. But the convention's sergeant at arms later bragged that the protesters didn't actually make it *onto* the stage. "That's why you hire good people," convention chairman Mike Duncan said.[10] This is a bit like the head of security at Ford's Theatre boasting, *Mrs. Lincoln didn't get a scratch on her!* The deranged Obama supporters weren't charged with so much as a misdemeanor. Instead, they were firmly asked not to do it again. (That's why you hire good people.) Guess what they did again the next night during John McCain's speech?

Next time, Republicans: Hire Rand Paul supporter Tim Proffit to do convention security. (Or let Sarah bring her hunting rifle.)

In 2010, when Proffit stepped in to protect Republican Senate candidate Rand Paul from an attack by a vile creature with a criminal record, liberals screamed bloody murder and conservatives prostrated themselves. Paul was arriving at a candidates' debate when he was attacked through his car window by left-wing agitator Lauren Valle. A professional rabble-rouser and lawbreaker, Valle ran at Paul's car and shoved a large cardboard sign through the window, hitting him in the face. Try doing that to a Democratic Senate candidate and see what happens.

After her second run at Paul, Valle threw herself on the ground and Proffit roughly stepped on her shoulder to hold her there. He was instantly accused of "stomping" on Valle's "head" throughout the media, despite the videotape showing no such thing. Nonetheless, the Paul campaign fired him and banned him from attending future events.

Republican Fayette County prosecutor Ray Larson's office brought charges against Proffit—not Valle—for assault.

And then conservatives all congratulated themselves for "policing their own."

Who's going to police liberals? The attorney general of the United States won't prosecute armed thugs standing outside a polling place threatening voters, but Proffit faces criminal charges for assault.

Liberals who do not want to be manhandled by conservatives must do the following: Don't physically attack a Republican. Conservatives who want to avoid being manhandled by liberals must do . . . what? Not give a speech at your party's convention? Never roll your car window down in the presence of liberals? Not attend your own candidates' debate? Never give a speech on a college campus? Not attend the Bridgehampton arts fair?

Compare Proffit's nonexistent "head-stomping" with what a liberal protester did to a New York City cop at the 2004 Republican National Convention. Officer William Sample was knocked down by the crowd and then beaten and stomped on so badly by a liberal that he lost consciousness and had to be carried from the scene by other officers. He was hospitalized for a serious head injury.[11]

Too bad Proffit wasn't there.

Google the names "William Sample" and "Lauren Valle" to see which incident was deemed the greater threat to the body politic. The alleged assault on Valle was discussed on CBS's *Early Show,* the *CBS Evening News,* NBC, CNN, Fox News, and every five minutes on MSNBC. The vicious beating of police officer William Sample—whose head actually was stomped on—wasn't mentioned by a single TV network.

Conservatives never make a fuss about such things. In the bizarro world of modern America, right-wingers are hawks when it comes to the nation's foreign enemies, but doves when it comes to anarchists at home.

The conservative ObamaCare protester who had his finger bitten off by a Moveon.org liberal, Bill Rice, told Neil Cavuto he wouldn't press charges. "No, sir, I don't wish to sue anybody," he said, "I'm not a litigious person."[12] (Of course, he wouldn't be able to point out his attacker, anyway.)

That's a good conservative instinct when your McDonald's coffee is too hot. But when you've been physically attacked by a liberal because of your politics, you're putting all conservatives in danger by ruling out a criminal prosecution. Having your finger chomped on by a liberal is not a slip-and-fall case. Our founding fathers set up a constitutional republic with a powerful judicial branch precisely in order to protect individual rights—such as the right not to have body parts bitten off by liberals. You won't become John Edwards if you press charges. (Unless, during his final summation to the jury, your lawyer channels the final thoughts of your severed finger.)

Say, did Tim Proffit sever any of Lauren Valle's appendages?

Unless conservatives stop capitulating and start defending the nation from liberal ferocity, it will never end. Faced with a mob, a physical attack is not your personal business—it's a battle for the country. As Nixon said of the student riots in the sixties, "This is the way civilizations die." He cited Sinclair Lewis, saying, "None of us has a right to suppose that it cannot happen here."

The slippery slope is always real with a mob because mobs are completely irrational and emotional. Arrest, press charges, call out the police, the National Guard, and the military. Hire Tim Proffit. To appease a mob is to play Russian roulette with civilization.

For those who will look, this is the lesson of history. Although it is accepted wisdom that the Allies were too harsh on Germany after World War I, leading to World War II, in fact, the truth is the opposite. We didn't crush Germany sufficiently the first time. Consequently, in 1919, a lot of Germans accepted the claim that they had not really been defeated but had just been "stabbed in the back" by civilians. No one said that in 1946; Germany's defeat was monolithic.

The belief that Germany had been treated unfairly after World War I was concocted by documented crackpot John Maynard Keynes in his 1920 book *The Economic Consequences of the Peace*.[13] When the Nazis came to power and war broke out, Keynes's insane thesis was immediately enshrined as a form of religion among foreign policy experts. *You see! If only we had appeased the Teutonic brutes and rebuilt their cities, this never would have happened!*

The stabbed-in-the-back theory was easy to implant because when

World War I ended, there were no foreign troops on German soil. Having no firsthand experience of the devastation of war, Germans weren't particularly averse to it. (In that sense, they were like modern liberals who have no idea what it's like to be physically attacked, and are therefore not particularly exercised when it happens to conservatives.)

A contrary theory was tried on the Germans in World War II, when the Allies announced that they would accept nothing but "unconditional surrender" from the Axis powers. By the time Germany surrendered, Allied troops had seized control of every part of the country.

This time, they got the message. Germany has been as peaceful as a lamb since then—other than during World Cup soccer season. It's always a liberating moment when you realize some timeworn shibboleth was just a cockamamie liberal idea that's been repeated so often even you believed it.

Japanese kamikazes were pretty fanatical, too. Who would have imagined the architects of the Pearl Harbor attack were governable? Two well-placed nuclear bombs put an end to the legendary Japanese belligerence.

Similarly, Russian tsars are criticized for overreacting to peaceful protests in 1905 by firing on the crowd—which historians claim led immediately to the revolution of 1910 (leaving the question of how "immediate" it was with a five-year time lapse). Another view is that the tsars shut down the mobs quite effectively in 1905 but compromised with the mobs when they rose again in 1910, and that it was the appeasement the second time around—not what had happened five years earlier—that was ineffective.

By the time Nixon became president of the United States, it was almost too late for this country. But the mob knew Nixon wouldn't tolerate riots. Even after the butterfingered Weathermen blew up some of their own, they kept setting bombs. That didn't stop them. But the shooting at Kent State shut down campus riots pretty quickly.

The same was true for New York City when Rudy Giuliani was elected mayor. In a city that had been a criminal bacchanal, he enforced a "zero tolerance" policy toward crime, arresting every turnstile jumper—to the evident displeasure of the *New York Times*. Within a few years, the "ungovernable city" was the safest big city in the country and property values went through the roof.

Napoleon said that if only King Louis XVI had shown any force against the revolutionaries, "victory would have been his."[14] Would you worry more about someone who hates your guts, or someone who hates your guts and has just had the crap beaten out of him? With liberals, as with Muslim terrorists, it's more important that they fear you than they like you.

It is the rare individual who does not succumb to horrendous physical pain. Unfortunately, benign and advanced civilizations generally lack the will to apply it.

Tranquil, law-based societies are the most vulnerable to attack because those with an interest in defending it are calmly following the law. They don't like disorder even in defense of order. But as Evelyn Waugh said, barbarism "is never finally defeated." And if our present society falls, he warned, "we shall see not merely the dissolution of a few joint-stock corporations, but of the spiritual and material achievements of our history."[15]

Republicans are the party of peaceful order; Democrats are the party of noisy, violent mobs. Republicans would do well to remember that George Washington sent troops to crush the Whiskey Rebellion. Abraham Lincoln used the U.S. military to squash racist—and Democrat-led—riots in New York City. This nation's heroes knew what Louis XVI did not: A mob cannot be calmly reasoned with; it can only be smashed.

When faced with a mob, civilized society's motto should be: Overreact!

# APPENDIX

*Prosecutor Elizabeth Lederer (Q):* Where did you go?

*McCray (A):* We went to Central Park.

*Q:* Where did you go in Central Park?

*A:* We went, um, we went to 110th Street.

*Q:* And what did you do when you got to 110th Street?

*A:* We got to 110th Street, we went up the hill in Central Park, you know? We was on the road.

*Q:* What happened next?

*A:* We was walking, then we seen a bum.

*Q:* You saw a bum?

*A:* Yeah.

*Q:* What did you do when you saw the bum?

*A:* We let him pass by, and then this kid with three gold caps grabbed him, threw him on the ground.

*Q:* How did he grab him?

*A:* By the, by the shirt.

*Q:* He grabbed him and threw him on the ground?

*A:* Yes.

*Q:* And what did everybody else do?

*A:* Everybody started kicking him and hitting him.

*Q:* Did you start kicking him and hitting him?

*A:* I hit him.

*Q:* Where?

*A:* In the chest.

*Q:* With your hand?

*A:* My hand.

*Q:* So you hit him with your hand in the chest. Was he already on the ground when you hit him?

*A:* I hit him like once, twice.

*Q:* What happened when you got to the tennis court?

*A:* We was at the tennis court and then we seen this lady, jogging lady, she had on blue shorts and a white shirt, she was jogging and everything, we was gonna let her go but then we just grabbed her.

*Q:* Where did you wait?

*A:* Behind the trees, on the grass, a couple of us.

*Q:* Right next to the path around the reservoir?

*A:* Yes.

*Q:* And everybody sort of hid?

*A:* Yeah.

*Q:* What happened as she came closer?

*A:* That's when we all charged her.

*Q:* Did you charge her?

*A:* Yes.

*Q:* What happened when you charged her?

*A:* We charged her, we got her on the ground, everybody started hitting her and stuff, she was on the ground, everybody stompin' and everything. Then we got each, I grabbed one arm, some other kid grabbed one arm and we grabbed her legs and stuff. Then we all took turns getting on her, getting on top of her.

*Q:* Did you hit her?

*A:* Yes, kicked her.

*Q:* Where did you kick her?

*A:* I don't know, just kicked her, I felt it, just kicked her, it was like a whole bunch of us.

*Q:* Who else kicked her?

*A:* Um, um, Kevin [Richardson, another defendant], um, all of us.

*Q:* That tall thin black guy I was asking you about, did you see him hit her in the ribs?

*A:* I heard it. I heard it.

*Q:* What did you hear?

*A:* It sounded like when you get hit in your chest. Sounded like that.

*Q:* Was she screaming, is that how you could tell she was being hit?

*A:* She wasn't screaming. She was hurt, though. She wasn't screaming.

*Q:* How could you tell she was hurt?

*A:* 'Cause she was lying there.

*Q:* First you knocked her down, then you started hitting. Did anybody have a weapon?

*A:* Yeah, a black pipe [indicates it was more than a foot long].

*Q:* A little less than two feet?

*A:* About two feet, I guess.

*Q:* And was it a stick or a pipe?

*A:* A pipe.

*Q:* Who had that pipe?

*A:* At first, I don't really know but I think the tall black kid had the pipe. I don't know.

*Q:* Did you see what he did with the pipe?

*A:* No, I just heard it. He got off of her and she got hit again with the pipe in the head, then . . .

*Q:* Was she standing up?

*A:* No, she was on the ground and then we left.

*Q:* Well, let's go back for a second, when she was on the ground and you said that you kicked her. Were other people also kicking and hitting her?

*A:* Yes.

*Q:* How many times did you kick her?

*A:* I kicked her like twice.

*Q:* When you were kicking her, were other people kicking and hitting her?

*A:* Um-hum.

*Q:* Was that before or after she was hit with the pipe?

*A:* Before.

*Q:* Was she still moving at that point?

*A:* She was just turning her head, stuff like that, she was moving.

*Q:* How many times was she hit with the pipe?

*A:* Twice, in the side and in the head.

*Q:* You heard her?

*A:* I heard her get hit in the ribs.

*Q:* Did you see her get hit in the head?

*A:* I heard it, not only, I seen it.

*Q:* Who did it?

*A:* The tall, black kid.

*Q:* After she was hit in the head with the pipe, did somebody take her clothes off?

*A:* Yeah.

*Q:* Who took her clothes off?

*A:* One of us, not one of us, I let her arms go?

*Q:* Were you holding her arms?

*A:* Yeah.

*Q:* Were you holding them over her head or to the side?

*A:* I had her like this.

*Q:* Was she trying to pull her hand away?

*A:* Um-hum.

*Q:* Was somebody holding her other hand? Who?

*A:* This kid, Puerto Rican kid.

*Q:* Was somebody holding her feet?

*A:* Yeah.

*Q:* Who?

*A:* I don't know.

*Q:* Did somebody take her clothes off?

*A:* Yes.

*Q:* What was she wearing?

*A:* I think a white T-shirt, something like that.

*Q:* Who took off her shirt?

*A:* The tall black kid.

*Q:* Who took off her pants?

*A:* I think it was him.

*Q:* Did somebody have sex with her?

*A:* Yeah.

*Q:* Did a lot of people have sex with her?

*A:* Yeah.

*Q:* Who was the first person to get on top of her?

*A:* The tall black guy.

*Q:* Did he take his pants off or just open his fly? What did he do?

*A:* He didn't take down his pants.

*Q:* By this point, though, she wasn't dressed anymore, right? Her pants were off?

*A:* Yeah.

*Q:* Did you touch her breasts?

*A:* No.

*Q:* Did somebody else get on top of her then?

*A:* He grabbed one of her arms, this other kid got on top of her.

*Q:* Who was that?

*A:* This Puerto Rican guy.

*Q:* Did you have your fly open?

*A:* Yeah, but my penis wasn't in her.

*Q:* What happened?

*A:* I just like, my penis wasn't in her. I didn't do nothing to her.

*Q:* When you got on top of her, you got on top of her so you could have sex with her, right?

*A:* Not really, I was just doing it so everybody, so . . . I didn't do anything.

*Q:* You said you were doing it so everybody what?

*A:* Everybody would just like, would know I did it.

*Q:* When you got on top of her, you had your penis out of your pants?

*A:* Yes.

*Q:* And it was between her legs?

*A:* No.

*Q:* It was against her?

*A:* Yeah.

*Q:* Did you rub against her?

*A:* Yeah.

*Q:* Did you have an erection?

*A:* No.

*Q:* How long did you do that for?

*A:* I don't know, a couple of minutes.

*Q:* What happened after Kevin was done?

*A:* Then we left her then, then this guy hit her in the head. Then we left.

*Q:* Who hit her?

*A:* I don't know. I just, the pipe, I think the tall skinny kid.

*Q:* After you were all done, somebody still hit her in the head?

*A:* Yeah.

*Q:* She wasn't moving anymore by this time, was she?

*A:* No.

*Q:* What did you do then?

*A:* We all left.

*Q:* Where did you go?

*A:* We was walking down, down to the reservoir and then we seen a jogger.

*Q:* Who was that?

*A:* He had on a green army jacket, some pants and he had on a Walkman.

*Q:* And he was running?

*A:* Um-hum.

*Q:* What happened when you saw him?

*A:* We was gonna let him go 'cause we thought he was a cop, he was jogging kind of slow. We was gonna let him go.

*Q:* Did you catch him?

*A:* Yeah.

*Q:* When you saw him, what happened?

*A:* We thought it was a police officer, so we were gonna let him go, he said something smart.

*Q:* You said you were going to let him go, did somebody grab him first?

*A:* Nah, we was gonna let him pass by and he said something smart.

*Q:* What did he say?

*A:* I don't know. I know he said something smart, though.

*Q:* When he said whatever he said, what did it mean to you?

*A:* He was acting like he was bad.

*Q:* So that pissed you off?

*A:* No.

*Q:* Somebody else?

*A:* Yeah, and then when we let him go and he said something.

*Q:* OK, so he goes by and he says something to try and sound bad, what did you guys do then?

*A:* We came, and this kid with a pullover, goose-down jacket, he grabbed him and threw him down, and that's when we all started charging him.

*Q:* What were you all doing to him?

*A:* Kicking, punching him.

*Q:* Did you kick him?

*A:* Yes.

*Q:* Did anybody have a weapon?

*A:* That pipe.

*Q:* The tall black guy, did he hit him with the pipe?

*A:* Yeah, we didn't hit him in the head.

*Q:* Where did he hit him?

*A:* The back and the legs and then, like, it kinda slipped out, right? And I hit him in the leg, and I think somebody was hitting him with a piece of wood over the head, 'cause it hit Steve in the leg, and he got hurt.

*Q:* Where did it hit him in the leg?

*A:* I don't know, like down here, like on the shin or something.

*Q:* And what did you do when you got home?

*A:* I told my mother we was playing tag and that's why I was so dirty.

*Q:* When you guys went into the park, what were you going into the park for?

*A:* Just to have fun.

*Q:* Did you have a good time?

*A:* Nah, not when we was getting chased.

*Q:* Before you got chased?

*A:* Not when we was hitting that man, and everything wasn't fun then.*

---

*"Emily Sachar Jogger Jury Sees a Confession," *Newsday* (New York), July 19, 1990.

# NOTES

## ONE. THE LIBERAL MOB

1. Erik Durschmied, *The Blood of Revolution: From the Reign of Terror to the Rise of Khomeini* (Arcade Publishing, 2002), 30.
2. George Monbiot, "Why the Police Provoke Crowds," *The Guardian* (London), June 20, 1996.
3. "Hay Festival: George Monbiot Calls for Citizen's Arrest of John Bolton," *Guardian Unlimited*, May 25, 2008.
4. Gustave Le Bon, *The Crowd: A Study of the Popular Mind* (Dover, 2002) (1895), 69.
5. Ibid., 74.
6. Ibid., 77–78.
7. Ibid., 21–22.
8. *Live With Cenk Uygur*, MSNBC, February 22, 2011.
9. *Live With Cenk Uygur*, MSNBC, February 23, 2011.
10. See, e.g., Baird Helgeson, "In Pension and Benefits, Wisconsin Tops Minnesota," *Minneapolis Star Tribune*, February 24, 2011.
11. See, e.g., Jake Tapper, "Obama Says Republicans Cannot Have the Keys Back to the Car: 'No! You Can't Drive,'" ABC News's *Political Punch*, May 13, 2010.
12. Kenneth P. Vogel, "Wall Street Invested Heavily in Obama," Politico, January 20, 2009.
13. Barack Obama (D): "Top Contributors," OpenSecrets.org, available at http://www.opensecrets.org/pres08/contrib.php?cycle=2008&cid 00009638.
14. Carl Hulse, "The Blackout: Legislation," *New York Times*, August 16, 2003.
15. Paul Krugman, "Clueless in Crawford," *New York Times*, August 13, 2002.
16. Paul Krugman, "The Ascent of E-Man R.I.P.: The Man in the Gray Flannel Suit," *Fortune*, May 24, 1999, available at http://money.cnn.com/magazines/fortune/fortune_archive/1999/05/24/260257/index.htm ("the company's pride and joy is a room filled with hundreds of casually dressed men and women staring at computer screens and barking into telephones, where cubic feet and megawatts are traded and packaged as if they were financial derivatives").

17. Le Bon, 30–31.

18. Ibid., 26.

19. Ibid., 26.

20. Al Gore, *Earth in the Balance: Ecology and the Human Spirit* (paperback) (Rodale Books, 2006), 325–26. ("[I]t ought to be possible to establish a coordinated global program to accomplish the strategic goal of completely eliminating the internal combustion engine over, say, a twenty-five-year period.")

21. See generally, Michael Fumento, "Why the Media Miss the Stem-Cell Story," *Citizen Magazine,* May 2005, available at http://www.fumento.com/biotech/stem-cell-story.html.

22. Matthew 27; Luke 23.

## TWO. AMERICAN IDOLS: THE MOB'S COMPULSION TO CREATE MESSIAHS

1. Gustave Le Bon, *The Crowd: A Study of the Popular Mind* (Dover, 2002) (1895), 38.

2. Ibid., 21–22.

3. Ibid., 30–31.

4. Ibid., 30.

5. Lance Morrow, "Why Is This Man So Popular?," *Time,* July 7, 1986 (quoted in Brent Baker, Tim Graham, Rich Noyes, and Jessica Anderson, "Ronald Reagan: The 40th President and the Press: The Record," Media Research Center, June 14, 2004, available at http://www.mediaresearch.org/specialreports/2004/report0604_p1.asp).

6. Eleanor Clift on *The McLaughlin Group,* July 12, 1992; on *Inside Politics,* CNN, July 10, 1992; and on *The McLaughlin Group,* July 4, 1992 (quoted in "*Newsweek* Removes Noted Clinton Sycophant from the White House Beat," MediaWatch, Media Research Center, October 1994).

7. "Gregory Craig Urges Country to Move Beyond Juanita Broaddrick Allegation," *Larry King Live,* CNN, March 10, 1999.

8. Jonathan Alter, "President Best Friend," *Newsweek,* November 16, 1992.

9. Howard Fineman, "The New Age President," *Newsweek,* January 25, 1993.

10. "Media's Friends of Bill," Notable Quotables, Media Research Center, August 3, 1992 (quoting Peter Jennings during ABC convention coverage, July 15, 1992).

11. "*Time* Swoons Over the Sexy President," Notable Quotables, Media Research Center, November 23, 1992, available at http://www.mrc.org/notablequotables/1992/nq19921123.asp.

12. Judith Warner, "Sometimes a President Is Just a President," *New York Times,* Opinionator blog, February 5, 2009.

13. Media Research Center, The Best Notable Quotables of 2008 (quoting Cowan's article for "The Peacock," an NBC advertising supplement included in the March 23–29 edition of the *American Profile* magazine newspaper insert), available at http://www.mrc.org/notablequotables/bestof/2008/welcome.asp.

14. Senator Barack Obama discusses country's economic problems, upcoming election, etc., *Today Show*, NBC, October 20, 2008.
15. "Campaign 2008 Review: Barack Obama's Media Groupies," Media Research Center, November 3, 2008.
16. Joe Klein, "Why Barack Obama Could Be the Next President," *Time*, October 2, 2006.
17. Notable Quotables, Media Research Center, November 3, 2008 (quoting MSNBC's Chris Matthews talking about Democratic candidate Barack Obama and his wife on the *Tonight Show*, NBC, January 16, 2008).
18. "Campaign 2008 Review: Barack Obama's Media Groupies" (quoting ABC's David Wright report on the January 28, 2008, *World News* program).
19. *Good Morning America*, ABC, November 24. 2008.
20. Nancy Gibbs, "How Obama Rewrote the Book," *Time*, November 5, 2008.
21. "Time Swoons Over the Sexy President."
22. Joe Klein, "On the Road Again," *Newsweek*, August 17, 1992.
23. Phil McCombs, "The President's Beachhead: A Vacationing Clinton Finds Waves of Support in Ritzy California Enclave," *Washington Post*, March 30, 1994.
24. Terry Moran, "The Next Big Thing; Senator Barack Obama's Star Power," *Nightline*, ABC, November 6, 2006.
25. "Large Crowd Gathers to Hear Obama Speak in Germany," *NBC Nightly News*, July 24, 2008.
26. Jennifer Senior, "The Benjamin Button Election," *New York*, November 8, 2010.
27. Jon Meacham, "Rocking the Vote, in the 1820s and Now," *New York Times*, October 21, 2010.
28. The "I Pledge" video, available at http://www.youtube.com/watch?v=FRrdmZwdW-c.
29. Michael Whack, "The 'BAM' . . . The Obama Handshake!," Organizing for America Community Blogs, January 12, 2008, available at http://my.barackobama.com/page/community/post/michaelwhack/CVBJ, cited in Jason Mattera, *Obama Zombie: How the Liberal Machine Brainwashed My Generation* (Threshold Editions, 2010), xvi.
30. Ameena Schelling, "Reserved Passion: Kagan '81," *The Daily Princetonian*, May 3, 2010.
31. Brent Bozell, "Smearing Republican Women," Newsbusters.org, June 15, 2010.
32. Mary Jordan and Kevin Sullivan, "Rocking the Planet," *Washington Post*, December 12, 2007.
33. Tim Graham, "Margaret's Flagrant Foul," *National Review* Online, November 25, 2000.
34. Martha Sherrill, "Hillary Clinton's Inner Politics," *Washington Post*, May 6, 1993.
35. The Best Notable Quotables of 1999, Media Research Center (quoting *Time*'s Lance Morrow in a July 12 "Viewpoint" piece).

36. Bill Peterson, "The Word According to Human Events; Reagan: 'I'm Still Reading You Guys, But I'm Enjoying It Less,'" *Washington Post,* March 14, 1982.

37. Michael Calderone, White House spokesman, praises MSNBC hosts after Obama's Fox swipe, Yahoo News, September 28, 2010 (quoting White House spokesman Bill Burton, who was quoting the president), available at http://news.yahoo.com/s/yblog_upshot/20100928/cm_yblog_upshot/white-house-spox-praises-msnbc-hosts-after-fox-swipe.

38. Ira R. Allen, "Poll Says Reagan No Longer Most Admired Conservative," United Press International, September 22, 1981.

39. Dan Murphy, "New Poll Finds Obama Has Already Rebuilt America's Global Brand," *Christian Science Monitor,* October 6, 2009.

40. "Barack Obama and the Dalai Lama Sit on Top of World Leaders Barometer," Business Wire, April 27, 2010.

41. "Obama Is World's Sexiest Politician," *Daily Record,* January 2, 2009.

42. Jeffrey M. Jones, "Clinton Edges Out Palin as Most Admired Woman; Obama Easily Wins Most Admired Man Title," Gallup Poll News Service, December 30, 2009.

43. "Pitt Tops 'Celeb Dads Most Women Want to See in Their Undies' List," *Hindustan Times,* June 16, 2009.

44. Michael Leahy and Juliet Eilperin, "Obama and Oil Drilling: How Politics Spilled into Policy," *Washington Post,* October 12, 2010.

45. Le Bon, 38.

46. Jonathan Alter, "The Two Mr. Clintons," *Newsweek,* August 24, 1998.

47. Geraldo Rivera, *Rivera Live,* NBC, March 8, 1999.

48. Ginger Thompson, "The Public; Cry of Halt, Unheard, Is Getting Louder," *New York Times,* January 25, 1999.

49. Le Bon, 22.

50. Matthew Saltmarsh, "Soros to Get a Day in Court over Insider Trading Case," *New York Times,* September 16, 2010.

51. Interview, George Soros, *60 Minutes,* CBS, December 20, 1998, available at http://www.sorosmonitor.com/absolutenm/templates/news.aspx?articleid=33&zoneid=1.

> *Kroft:* My understanding is that you went out with this protector of yours who swore that you were his adopted godson.
>
> *Mr. Soros:* Yes. Yes.
>
> *Kroft:* Went out, in fact, and helped in the confiscation of property from the Jews.
>
> *Mr. Soros:* Yes. That's right. Yes.
>
> *Kroft:* I mean, that's—that sounds like an experience that would send lots of people to the psychiatric couch for many, many years. Was it difficult?
>
> *Mr. Soros:* Not—not at all. Not at all. Maybe as a child you don't—you

don't see the connection. But it was—it created no—no problem at all.

*Kroft:* No feeling of guilt?

*Mr. Soros:* No.

52. Jack Shafer, "Screw You, Mr. President," Slate, March 12, 2003 (quoting Thomas's remarks to John Bogert in a January 19, 2003, article in the *Daily Breeze,* Torrance, CA).

53. The Best Notable Quotables of 2006, Media Research Center (quoting Harry Belafonte, at a televised rally with Venezuelan president Hugo Chávez), available at http://www.mrc.org/MainSearch/search.html.

54. Joe Klein, "Blessed Are the Poor—They Don't Get Tax Cuts," *Time,* June 2, 2003.

55. William Raspberry, "A Reckless Blast That Hits the Target," *Columbus Ledger-Enquirer,* June 29, 2004.

56. "Inside Washington," WJLA-TV, November 6, 2005.

57. House Committee on Foreign Affairs, Joint Hearing Before the Subcommittee on International Organizations, Human Rights, and Oversight and the Subcommittee on Europe (110th Congress, 1st Sess.), April 17, 2007 (testimony of Michael F. Scheuer, former chief, Bin Laden Unit, Central Intelligence Agency).

58. Joe Hagan, "Dan Rather to Bush: 'Answer the Questions,'" *New York Observer,* September 20, 2004.

59. Video at Andrew Breitbart, Feelin' the Healin': Young Jeezy, Jay-Z Perform "My President Is Black," Remix on Inauguration Eve, BigHollywood. com, January 21, 2009, available at http://bighollywood.breitbart.com/ abreitbart/2009/01/21/feelin-the-healin-young-jeezy-jay-z-perform-"my-president-is-black"-remix-on-inauguration-eve/; see also Mattera, xvii.

60. Lynn Sweet, "Dems Seek Strategy Against 'Birthers,'" *Chicago Sun-Times,* August 5, 2009.

61. Quest for Camelot, *The Hotline,* January 14, 2010.

62. "Jimmy Carter Speaks Out Against Anti-Obama Racism," *NBC Nightly News,* September 15, 2009.

63. Video: "Are We Running Out of Oil?," *The Nation,* January 5, 2011, available at http://www.thenation.com/video/157441/are-we-running-out-oil.

64. The Best Notable Quotables of 1998, Media Research Center, available at http://www.mrc.org/notablequotables/bestof/1998/best1-3.asp.

65. Lonnae O'Neal Parker, *I'm Every Woman: Remixed Stories of Marriage, Motherhood, and Work* (Amistad, 2005), 105.

66. *Inside Washington,* NPR, July 8, 1995, available at http://www.mediaresearch .org/notablequotables/dishonor1999/welcomeaward6.asp.

67. See, e.g., "Empty Promise," *New York Post,* June 1, 2008; "A Celebrity Exodus over Bush Win: Now That's Entertainment," *Chicago Tribune,* December 6, 2000.

68. See, e.g., Matthew L. Wald, "T.W.A. Crash Investigators Ridicule a Missile Theory and Pin Hopes on Research," *New York Times,* March 14, 1997; George Johnson, "Pierre, Is That a Masonic Flag on the Moon?," *New York Times,* November 24, 1996.

69. George Rush and Joanna Molloy, "Monica Rules Out Prez Reunion," *Daily News* (New York), January 13, 2000.

70. Todd S. Purdum, "G.O.P. Candidates Taking Streisand Shots," *New York Times,* October 17, 2002.

71. Remarks by President Barack Obama at a Democratic National Committee (DNC) Fundraiser Dinner (as Released by the White House), Federal News Service, October 20, 2009.

72. Foreign Policy Implications of U.S. Efforts to Address the International Financial Crisis (111th Congress, 1st Sess.) (2009) (Hearing of the Terrorism, Nonproliferation and Trade Subcommittee of the House Foreign Affairs Committee), Federal News Service, June 10, 2009.

73. Bill O'Reilly, "Talking Points Memo and Top Story," Fox News, February 26, 2009.

## THREE. CONTRADICTIONS: YOU CAN LEAD A MOB TO WATER, BUT YOU CAN'T MAKE IT THINK

1. Gustave Le Bon, *The Crowd: A Study of the Popular Mind* (Dover, 2002)(1895), 30–31.

2. "No Prison for Libby," *American Morning,* CNN, July 3, 2007. (Senator Hillary Clinton: "And what we saw today was elevating cronyism over the rule of law.")

3. Matthew Saltmarsh, "Soros to Get a Day in Court over Insider Trading Case," *New York Times,* September 16, 2010.

4. "Al Gore's Personal Energy Use Is His Own 'Inconvenient Truth,'" Tennessee Center for Policy Research, February 25, 2007, available at http://www .tennesseepolicy.org/tag/al-gore/.

5. Keith Olbermann, *Countdown,* MSNBC, October 23, 2006.

6. "Keeping Emotions Under Control at Jogger Trial," *New York Times,* July 2, 1990.

7. Dennis Duggan, "The Cool, Meticulous Prosecutor," *Newsday* (New York), July 3, 1990.

8. Chapin Wright, "Tawana Brawley Greets 2 Defendants," *Newsday* (New York), July 31, 1990.

9. "Trial Sets Alight a Bonfire of Profanities," *Courier-Mail,* August 1, 1990; Richard Bernstein, "The Arts Catch Up with a Society in Disarray," *New York Times,* September 2, 1990.

10. Emily Sachar, "Split Verdicts at 2nd Central Park Trial," *Newsday* (New York), December 12, 1990.

11. "Keeping Emotions Under Control at Jogger Trial."

12. John Kifner, "Tension in Brooklyn; Blacks March by Hasidim Through a Corridor of Blue," *New York Times*, August 25, 1991.

13. David Herszenhorn, "Alan Grayson, the Liberals' Problem Child," *New York Times*, October 31, 2009.

14. "Investigating the President: Ken Starr Fights Back," *Larry King Live*, CNN, June 16, 1998.

15. James Carville on the investigating of the president, *Larry King Live*, CNN, February 23, 1998.

16. Pete Yost, "Prosecutors Strike Back at White House," Associated Press, *The Star-Ledger* (Newark, NJ), February 25, 1998.

17. David Tell, Editorial: "Sid Vicious," *The Weekly Standard*, May 11, 1998.

18. Talk of the Nation: "Where Do We Go Next?," NPR, May 11, 2009.

19. "A Conversation with Larry Summers," *The Charlie Rose Show*, August 21, 2007.

20. Keith Olbermann, *Countdown*, MSNBC, April 4, 2007.

21. Bill Maher (guest host), "Scandal and Politics," *Larry King Live*, CNN, January 13, 2006.

22. Talk of the Nation: "The Making of a Successful Justice," NPR, November 3, 2005.

23. "Flip-Flopping in Politics," Weekend Edition, Sunday National Public Radio (NPR), August 8, 2004.

24. Jim Lehrer, "Terrorism on Trial," *The NewsHour with Jim Lehrer*, PBS, May 29, 2001.

25. "Will Edwards Be Kerry's Running Mate?," *Capital Gang*, CNN, February 28, 2004.

26. Peter Schweizer, *Architects of Ruin: How Big Government Liberals Wrecked the Global Economy—and How They Will Do It Again if No One Stops Them* (HarperCollins, 2009), 111–18.

27. Chris Matthews, *Hardball*, MSNBC, April 16, 2010.

28. Keith Olbermann, *Countdown*, MSNBC, March 31, 2010.

29. Interview with Representative Barney Frank, *The Rachel Maddow Show*, MSNBC, June 25, 2010.

30. Interview with Elizabeth Warren, *The Rachel Maddow Show*, MSNBC, September 14, 2009.

31. George Stephanopoulos, "Sunday Headliner: John Edwards," *This Week*, ABC, June 15, 2008 (affair first reported by the *National Enquirer* in October 2007; "Edwards Admits Affair, but Denies Paternity of Child," August 8, 2008; "Edwards Admits Paternity of Love Child," August 14, 2009).

32. Video and transcript at Noel Sheppard, "Bob Schieffer: I Didn't Ask Holder About Black Panther Case Because I Just Didn't Know About It," Newsbusters, July 18, 2010, available at http://newsbusters.org/blogs/noel-sheppard/2010/07/18/bob-schieffer-i-didnt-ask-holder-about-black-panther-case-because-i-just-didnt-know-about-it#ixzz1CZmMlEuV.

33. Madison Gray, "The L.A. Riots: 15 Years After Rodney King: Reginald Denny," *Time*, 2007, available at http://205.188.238.181/time/specials/2007/la_riot/article/0,28804,1614117_1614084_1614511,00.html.

34. Seth Mydans, "Jury Acquits 2 on Most Charges in Beatings in Los Angeles Riots," *New York Times*, October 19, 1993.

35. See, e.g., Jay Nordlinger, "Shrill Waters," *National Review*, January 25, 1999.

36. Greg Miller and Josh Meyer, "Interrogation Memos Opened," *Chicago Tribune*, April 17, 2009.

37. Stephen Holden, "At Human Rights Film Festival, Horror and Hope," *New York Times*, June 8, 2006.

38. A. O. Scott, "Taking a Long, Bumpy Ride to Systematic Brutality," *New York Times*, January 18, 2008.

39. Editorial: "Justice 5, Brutality 4," *New York Times*, June 13, 2008.

40. "Trucker Beaten in Riot Is Hospitalized Again," Associated Press, *New York Times*, June 18, 1992.

41. "5th Man Held in Los Angeles in Beating of a Truck Driver," *New York Times*, June 20, 1992.

42. "60 Arrested in Disturbance at Site of Los Angeles Riots," *New York Times*, December 15, 1992.

43. Bob Herbert, "That Weird Day," *New York Times*, July 21, 1993.

44. Bob Herbert, "Madness and Shame," *New York Times*, July 22, 2008.

45. Jon Ward, "Obama Releases Memos Detailing Interrogations," *Washington Times*, April 17, 2009.

46. "Has L.A. Healed Since the Riots?," *Daily News* (Los Angeles), April 27, 1997.

47. Stephen Phillips, "Gloves Off for 'Thinking Man's Michael Moore,'" *New York Times* Higher Education Supplement, August 13, 2004.

48. Liane Hansen, National Public Radio Weekend Edition, November 14, 2004.

49. Wayne Parry, "NJ Muslims, Libertarians Glad to See Ashcroft Go," Associated Press, November 10, 2004.

50. Jeff Jacoby, "We Owe Ashcroft Thanks," *Boston Globe*, November 18, 2004.

51. Ibid.

52. Ibid.

53. "50 Years of Covering War, Looking for Peace and Honoring Law," *New York Times*, December 16, 2001.

54. Le Bon, 10–11.

55. Ibid., 30–31.

56. Ibid., 30–31.

## FOUR. CRACKPOT CONSPIRACY THEORIES — OR, AS LIBERALS CALL THEM, "THEORIES"

1. Gustave Le Bon, *The Crowd: A Study of the Popular Mind* (Dover, 2002) (1895), 15.

2. *The Ed Show*, MSNBC, January 10, 2011.

3. John McCormack, "We Report, We Get Pushed," *The Weekly Standard*,

January 12, 2010, video available at http://www.weeklystandard.com/blogs/video-someone-coakley-campaign-pushes-me-metal-railing.

4. Keith Olbermann, *Countdown,* MSNBC, October 26, 2010.

5. Le Bon, 22.

6. "Writer's Room Is Searched," *New York Times,* November 27, 1997.

7. Alex Koppelman, "Did Anyone Really Yell 'Kill Him'?: The Secret Service Says Allegations That Attendees at Two of Sarah Palin's Rallies Called for the Death of Barack Obama Are Unfounded," Salon.com, October 16, 2008.

8. Le Bon, 15.

9. Robert M. Andrews, "Federal Officials Discount Plastic Handgun Threat," Associated Press, March 4, 1986; Robert M. Andrews, "Legislators Plead for Ban on Plastic Handguns," Associated Press, May 15, 1986.

10. Ike Flores, "All-Plastic Weapon May Transform Industry; Critics Fear Undetectability," Associated Press, May 26, 1987.

11. Andrews.

12. Bud Newman, "Reagan Not Ready to Back Plastic Handgun Ban," United Press International, May 20, 1987.

13. Keith Olbermann, *Countdown,* MSNBC, August 3, 2007.

14. "NTSB: Design Flaw Led to Minnesota Bridge Collapse," CNN, November 14, 2008, available at http://articles.cnn.com/2008-11-14/us/bridge.collapse_1_gusset-plates-bridge-collapse-bridge-designs?_s=PM:US.

15. Joe Klein, "Nevermind," *Time,* December 17, 2007.

16. Bill Press, "World War III on Hold," *Contra Costa Times* (California), December 31, 2007.

17. Keith Olbermann, *Countdown,* MSNBC, December 5, 2007.

18. Keith Olbermann, *Countdown,* MSNBC, December 6, 2007.

19. Keith Olbermann, *Countdown,* MSNBC, December 5, 2007.

20. Keith Olbermann, *Countdown,* MSNBC, December 6, 2007.

21. Keith Olbermann, *Countdown,* MSNBC, December 7, 2007.

22. Nazila Fathi, "Iranian Leader Calls Report of U.S. Confession 'Mistake,'" *New York Times,* December 6, 2007.

23. Keith Olbermann, *Countdown,* MSNBC, December 5, 2007.

24. Valerie Lincy and Gary Milhollin, "In Iran We Trust?," *New York Times,* December 6, 2007.

25. Alberto Hurtado, "Sullivan Thinks Southerners Are Murdering Ignoramuses," *Southern Appeal,* September 26, 2009, available at http://www.southernappeal.org/index.php/archives/12675.

26. Lachlan Markay, "Contrary to Leftist Accusations, Census Worker's Death Ruled Suicide," Newsbusters, November 24, 2009, available at http://newsbusters.org/blogs/lachlan-markay/2009/11/24/contrary-leftist-accusations-census-workers-death-ruled-suicide#ixzz13LMizxOp.

27. Ibid.

28. Anderson Cooper, *360 Degrees,* CNN, September 25, 2009.

29. See, e.g., *The Ed Show,* MSNBC, September 28, 2009.

30. *The Rachel Maddow Show,* MSNBC, September 23, 2009.

31. *The Rachel Maddow Show,* MSNBC, September 25, 2009.

32. Ibid.

33. *The Rachel Maddow Show,* MSNBC, November 24, 2009 (Howard Dean guest-hosting).

34. *The Rachel Maddow Show,* MSNBC, February 17, 2011.

35. "Rachel Maddow Says Wisconsin Is on Track to Have a Budget Surplus This Year," *Wisconsin Journal-Sentinel,* February 18, 2011, available at http://www.politifact.com/wisconsin/statements/2011/feb/18/rachel-maddow/rachel-maddow-says-wisconsin-track-have-budget-sur/.

36. Stuart Taylor Jr., "In Duke Case, a Rogues' Gallery," *The National Journal,* May 20, 2006.

37. See, e.g., Stuart Taylor Jr., "An Outrageous Rush to Judgment," *The National Journal,* April 29, 2006; Taylor, "In Duke Case, a Rogues' Gallery."

38. Melissa Harris Lacewell, "Catching Up on the Top Stories of Spring! 1. Duke Rape Case," Bloggin' In, July 1, 2006 available at http://web.archive.org/web/20060721165301/melissaharrislacewell.com/blog.htm.

39. "Report of the Lacrosse Ad Hoc Review Committee," Duke News & Communications, May 1, 2006, available at http://www.dukenews.duke.edu/mmedia/pdf/lacrossereport.pdf.

40. Monica Lewis, "Support for Accused Duke Rapists by Women's Lacrosse Team Rankles Many," BlackAmericaWeb.com, June 3, 2006.

41. See, e.g., Gary D. LaFree, "Male Power and Female Victimization: Toward a Theory of Interracial Rape," *American Journal of Sociology,* Vol. 88, No. 2 (September 1982) (Throughout the 1970s, black-on-white rape was at least ten times more common that white-on-black rape); William Wilbanks, "Frequency and Nature of Interracial Crimes," submitted for publication to the *Justice Professional* (November 7, 1990). Data derived from Department of Justice, Criminal Victimization in the United States, 1987, p. 53 (in 1988 there were 9,406 cases of black-on-white rape and fewer than ten cases of white-on-black rape); Department of Justice, Criminal Victimization in the United States, 1997 Statistical Tables, Table 42, available at http://bjs.ojp.usdoj.gov/content/pub/pdf/cvus97.pdf; Department of Justice, Criminal Victimization in the United States, 2005 Statistical Tables, Table 42, available at http://bjs.ojp.usdoj.gov/content/pub/pdf/cvus05.pdf; Department of Justice, Criminal Victimization in the United States, 2006 Statistical Tables, Table 42, available at http://bjs.ojp.usdoj.gov/content/pub/pdf/cvus0602.pdf. See also, Andrew Hacker, *Two Nations: Black and White, Separate, Hostile, Unequal* (Paperback) (Ballantine Books 1995) at 192 (noting that black men commit rape at five to six times the rate of white men and choose white women as their victims approximately 30 percent of the time).

42. *Hardball,* MSNBC, March 29, 2010.

43. *Countdown,* MSNBC, August 18, 2009.

44. Eugene Robinson, "Duke Scandal Raises Many Questions," *Charleston Gazette* (West Virginia), April 26, 2006.

45. Le Bon, 35–36.

46. Maureen Dowd, "The Unfair Game," *New York Times,* October 12, 2010.

47. Le Bon, 35–36.

48. In the February 12, 2002, memo, Plame writes "it seems that Niger has signed a contract with Iraq to sell them uranium," and then says our embassy disputes that. She goes on to say:

> *So where do I fit in? As you may recall, [redacted] of CP/[office 2] recently approached my husband to possibly use his contacts in Niger to investigate [a separate Niger matter]. After many fits and starts, [redacted] finally advised that the station wished to pursue this with liaison. My husband is willing to help, if it makes sense, but no problem if not. End of story.*
>
> *Now, with this report, it is clear that the IC is still wondering what is going on . . . my husband has good relations with both the PM and the former minister of mines, not to mention lots of French contacts, both of whom could possibly shed light on this sort of activity. To be frank with you, I was somewhat embarrassed by the agency's sloppy work last go-round, and I am hesitant to suggest anything again. However, [my husband] may be in a position to assist. Therefore, request your thoughts on what, if anything, to pursue here. Thank you for your time on this.*

See Byron York, "Did Valerie Plame Wilson Tell the Truth?," *National Review,* May 25, 2007.

49. Patrick E. Tyler, "Standoff in the Gulf," *New York Times,* December 18, 1990.

50. Neil A. Lewis, "First Source of C.I.A. Leak Admits Role, Lawyer Says," *New York Times,* August 30, 2006.

51. Georges Sada, *Saddam's Secrets: How an Iraqi General Defied & Survived Saddam Hussein* (Integrity Publishers, 2006).

52. See, e.g., Andrew McCarthy, "Iraq & al Qaeda: The 9/11 Commission Raises More Questions Than It Answers," *National Review,* June 17, 2004.

53. Le Bon, 32.

## FIVE. I'LL SEE YOUR BIRTH CERTIFICATE CONSPIRACY THEORY AND RAISE YOU ONE OCTOBER SURPRISE

1. John Avlon, "The 'Birthers' Began on the Left," The Daily Beast, February 8, 2010.

2. Jaymes Song, "Hawaii Again Declares Obama Birth Certificate Real," Associated Press, July 28, 2009.

3. "Obama Tells Ohio Plumber He Favors 'Spreading Wealth' to Poor," *The Frontrunner,* October 15, 2008.

4. Gabriel Winant, "The Birthers in Congress," Salon, July 28, 2009, available at http://www.salon.com/news/feature/2009/07/28/birther_enablers.

5. Sheryl Gay Stolberg and James Dao, "Congress Ratifies Bush Victory After a Rare Challenge," *New York Times,* January 7, 2005.
6. Byron York, "Democrats and the *Fahrenheit 9/11* Trap: Do They Endorse Michael Moore's Kookiness?," *National Review,* June 24, 2004, available at http://old.nationalreview.com/york/york200406240908.asp.
7. Dana Milbank, "Democrats Play House to Rally Against the War," *Washington Post,* June 17, 2005.
8. See Federal Judicial Center, http://www.fjc.gov/history/home.nsf/page/topics_ji_bdy:

   *Harry E. Claiborne, U.S. District Court for the District of Nevada*
   Impeached by the U.S. House of Representatives, July 22, 1986, on charges of income tax evasion and of remaining on the bench following criminal conviction; convicted by the U.S. Senate and removed from office, October 9, 1986.

   *Alcee L. Hastings, U.S. District Court for the Southern District of Florida*
   Impeached by the U.S. House of Representatives, August 3, 1988, on charges of perjury and conspiring to solicit a bribe; convicted by the U.S. Senate and removed from office, October 20, 1989.

   *Walter L. Nixon, U.S. District Court for the Southern District of Mississippi*
   Impeached by the U.S. House of Representatives, May 10, 1989, on charges of perjury before a federal grand jury; convicted by the U.S. Senate and removed from office, November 3, 1989.

9. Steve Weinberg, "The October Surprise: Enter the Press," *Columbia Journalism Review,* March/April, 1992.
10. Flora Lewis, "The Wiles of Teheran," *New York Times,* August 3, 1987.
11. Gary Sick, "The Election Story of the Decade," *New York Times,* April 15, 1991.
12. Marilyn Milloy and Gaylord Shaw, "Carter Urges Probe of Hostage Story," *Newsday* (New York), April 26, 1991.
13. Frank Snepp, "Brenneke Exposed," *Village Voice,* September 10, 1991.
14. Michael Tackett, "With a Uniform and a Line, Gunther Russbacher Eased His Way into the Confidence of Military and Law Enforcement Officials," *Chicago Tribune,* March 17, 1992.
15. Robert G. Kaiser, "Circus: From 'Nightline' to Obscurity the Washington Way," *Washington Post,* June 24, 1984.
16. Steve Emerson and Jesse Furman, "The Conspiracy That Wasn't," *New Republic,* November 18, 1991.
17. Judith Cummings, "Friends Say Feminist Heroine Is Sincere if Eccentric," *New York Times,* August 30, 1983.
18. Marilyn Milloy and Gaylord Shaw, "Carter Urges Probe of Hostage Story," *Newsday* (New York), April 26, 1991.
19. All this is available on the Internet! http://www.whatreallyhappened.com/RANCHO/POLITICS/MENA/the_oral_deposition_of_richard_j._brenneke_6-21-91.html.

20. *Nightline,* ABC, June 20, 1991.
21. Jim Drinkard, "House Approves Probe of Alleged 1980 Hostage Deal," Associated Press, February 5, 1992.
22. Text of KGB Letter on Senator Ted Kennedy, Freerepublic.com (citing Kengor at p. 317).
23. Steve Emerson and Jesse Furman, "The Conspiracy That Wasn't," *New Republic,* November 18, 1991.
24. John Barry, "Making of a Myth," *Newsweek,* November 11, 1991.
25. Steven Emerson, "Gary Sick's Bald-Faced Lies," *The American Spectator,* March 1993.
26. Committee on Foreign Relations 1992, 115 (cited in Daniel Pipes, "Remember Ronald Reagan's October Surprise? It Never Happened," History News Network, March 29, 2004, available at http://hnn.us/articles/4249.html).
27. Daniel Pipes, *Conspiracy Theories in American History: An Encyclopedia,* 2003, available at http://www.danielpipes.org/article/1654 (citing Committee of the Whole House on the State of the Union 53).
28. Gary Sick, "Last Word on the October Surprise?," *New York Times,* January 24, 1993.
29. Daniel Pipes, "Gary Sick's Same Old Song," *Wall Street Journal,* May 2, 1991: "But Mr. Sick seems to have forgotten his own thinking. Here is a statement he made, quoted by the *Rocky Mountain News* on Oct. 30, 1988—at the very peak of the 1988 presidential campaign—in which he discussed the possibility of a hostage deal: " 'At first I dismissed this, but not any more. I'm convinced on the basis of what I heard that there were some meetings in Paris. I know that the Iranians changed their policy at that time.' Just over a month before that, on Aug. 26, 1988, Mr. Sick told the *New York Daily News* in a telephone interview: 'There is something here. I just don't know how much.' "
30. Kenneth R. Timmerman, "October Surprise, Part 3: Clinton Sought Dirt on W's Dad," World Net Daily, September 27, 2000, available at http://www.wnd.com/?pageId=6748.
31. Le Bon, 14.

## SIX. THE FRENCH REVOLUTION: WHEN LIBERALS ATTACK

1. Gustave Le Bon, *The Crowd: A Study of the Popular Mind* (Dover, 2002) (1895), 22.
2. Christopher Hibbert, *The Days of the French Revolution* (Harper Perennial 1999), 65–82.
3. Alexander Hamilton, *Writings* (Library of America, 2001) (letter dated October 6, 1789), 521.
4. Stefan Zweig, *Marie Antoinette: The Portrait of an Average Woman* (Grove Press, 2002), 60–61.
5. Ibid., 73.
6. Le Bon, 38.
7. See, e.g., Zweig, 29.

8. Zweig, 105.
9. Ibid., 114.
10. Ibid., 62.
11. Ibid., 289.
12. "At length I recollected the thoughtless saying of a great princess, who, on being informed that the country people had no bread, replied, 'Then let them eat pastry!' " Jean Jacques Rousseau, *The Confessions of Jean Jacques Rousseau* (paperback) (Nabu Press, 2010), 220.
13. Zweig, 259–60.
14. Hibbert, 100.
15. Hibbert, 101.
16. Kennedy, 194.
17. See, e.g., T. Jeremy Gunn, "Religious Freedom and Laicite: A Comparison of the United States and France," *Brigham Young University Law Review,* January 1, 2004.
18. Michael L. Kennedy, *The Jacobin Clubs in the French Revolution, 1793–1795* (Berghahn Books, 2000), 164–66.
19. Erik Durschmied, *The Blood of Revolution: From the Reign of Terror to the Rise of Khomeini* (Arcade Publishing 2002), 21.
20. Ibid., 21.
21. Ibid., 22.
22. Ibid., 25–27.
23. Hibbert, 161.
24. Henry Goudemetz, *Historical Epochs of the French Revolution* (Hard Press, 2006) [No page numbers] available at http://www.scribd.com/doc/2379520/Historical-Epochs-of-the-French-RevolutionWith-The-Judgment-And-Execution-Of-Louis-XVI-King-Of-FranceAnd-A-List-Of-The-Members-Of-The-National-Con#outer_page_124.
25. Ibid.
26. See, e.g., Gunn.
27. Durschmied, 30.
28. Hibbert, 170.
29. See, e.g., Hibbert, 170–71; Durschmied, 30.
30. Durschmied, 30.
31. Goudemetz.
32. G. Lenôtre, *The Tribunal of the Terror: A Study of Paris in 1793–1795* (Paperback) (University of Michigan Library, 1909), 37, available at http://www.ebooksread.com/authors-eng/g-lenotre/the-tribunal-of-the-terror-a-study-of-paris-in-1793-1795-ala/page-4-the-tribunal-of-the-terror-a-study-of-paris-in-1793-1795-ala.shtml.
33. Hibbert, 171.
34. Lenôtre, 35–37; Hibbert, 175.
35. G. Lenôtre, 35–37; Hibbert, 174.
36. Lewis Goldsmith Stewarton, *The Female Revolutionary Plutarch, Containing*

*Biographical, Historical and Revolutionary Sketches, Characters and Anecdotes* (J. & W. Smith, 1808), at 225, available at http://books.google.com/books?id= 95bzlnsVu7cC&pg=PA224&lpg=PA224&dq=goddess+of+reason+Momoro& source=bl&ots=n-ZhPxWwN8&sig=8xsgafh5pvoWvHCBCj92DtMg0_g&hl= en&ei=5wwkTcX6GsWblgewk9nZCw&sa=X&oi=book_result&ct=result& resnum=1&ved=0CBMQ6AEwAA#v=onepage&qomoro&f=false.

37. Charles Buke Yonge, *The Life of Marie Antoinette, Queen of France* (Duke, Project Gutenberg, 2004), available at http://infomotions.com/etexts/ gutenberg/dirs/1/0/5/5/10555/10555.htm.
38. Hibbert, 175.
39. See, e.g., Durschmied, 31; Hibbert, 175–76.
40. Goudemetz.
41. Ibid., 227. See also Stewarton (Stewarton and Goldsmith say the heads were presented at the Jacobin Club).
42. Goudemetz.
43. Kennedy, 169.
44. Durschmied, 37.
45. Maximilien Marie Isidore Robespierre, "Against Granting the King a Trial," *Bartleby's The World's Famous Orations, Continental Europe (380–1906)*, available at http://www.bartleby.com/268/7/23.html.
46. See Shaun Bishop, "Academic Senate Opposes War," *The Daily Bruin*, April 14, 2003, available at http://www.dailybruin.com/index.php/article/ 2003/04/academic-senate-opposes-war.
47. Durschmied, 38.
48. Hibbert, 184.
49. Ibid., 184–85.
50. Ibid., 185.
51. Durschmied, 38.
52. Ibid., 36, 38, n. 19.
53. Hibbert, 186.
54. Ibid., 186–87.
55. E. L. Higgins, ed., *The French Revolution as Told by Contemporaries* (Houghton Mifflin, 1966), 272–73. See also, http://www.historyguide.org/intellect/louis _trial.html. There are various basically similar versions of the king's brief speech. See also Hibbert, 188 ("I forgive those who are guilty of my death and I pray God that the blood which you are about to shed may never be required of France").
56. Durschmied, 41, 43.
57. Hibbert, 224.
58. Kennedy, 193.

## SEVEN. THE FRENCH REVOLUTION PART DEUX: COME FOR THE BEHEADINGS, STAY FOR THE RAPES!

1. Erik Durschmied, *The Blood of Revolution: From the Reign of Terror to the Rise of Khomeini* (Arcade Publishing, 2002), 44–45.

2. Ibid., 46.
3. Lewis Goldsmith Stewarton, *The Female Revolutionary Plutarch, Containing Biographical, Historical and Revolutionary Sketches, Characters and Anecdotes* (J. & W. Smith, 1808), 238, available at http://books.google.com/books?id= 95bzlnsVu7cC&pg=PA224&lpg=PA224&dq=goddess+of+reason+Momoro& source=bl&ots=n-ZhPxWwN8&sig=8xsgafh5pvoWvHCBCj92DtMg0_g&hl= en&ei=5wwkTcX6GsWblgewk9nZCw&sa=X&oi=book_result&ct=result& resnum=1&ved=0CBMQ6AEwAA#v=onepage&qomoro&f=false.
4. Michael L. Kennedy, *The Jacobin Clubs in the French Revolution* (1793–1795) (Berghahn, 2000).
5. Ibid., 176.
6. Ibid., 166.
7. T. Jeremy Gunn, "Religious Freedom and Laicite: A Comparison of the United States and France," *Brigham Young University Law Review,* January 1, 2004.
8. Ibid.
9. Janet T. Marquardt, *From Martyr to Monument: The Abbey of Cluny as Cultural Patrimony* (Cambridge Scholars Publishing, 2008), 14.
10. Gunn.
11. Kennedy, 176.
12. Ibid., 176.
13. Ibid., 166–67.
14. Ibid., 176.
15. Ibid., 165.
16. Ibid., 162.
17. Ibid., 154.
18. Schom, 253.
19. See, e.g., Kennedy, 153–54.
20. Stewarton, 236.
21. Henry Goudemetz, *Historical Epochs of the French Revolution* (Hard Press, 2006) [No page numbers] available at http://www.scribd.com/doc/2379520/ Historical-Epochs-of-the-French-RevolutionWith-The-Judgment-And -Execution-Of-Louis-XVI-King-Of-FranceAnd-A-List-Of-The-Members-Of -The-National-Con#outer_page_124.
22. Schom, 253–54.
23. Ibid., 253.
24. Kennedy, 154.
25. Ibid., 155.
26. Kennedy, 189–90.
27. See, e.g., Stewarton, 240–42; Michael Burleigh, *Earthly Powers: The Clash of Religion and Politics in Europe, from the French Revolution to the Great War* (HarperCollins, 2006), 79; Gunn; Kennedy, 177.
28. Stewarton, 243; Goudemetz.

29. Stewarton, 244.

30. Kennedy, 192.

31. Ibid., 167, 168.

32. Ibid., 169.

33. Ibid., 169.

34. Goudemetz.

35. See Charles Duke Yonge, *The Life of Marie Antoinette, Queen of France* (Duke, Project Gutenberg, 2004), available at http://infomotions.com/etexts/gutenberg/dirs/1/0/5/5/10555/10555.htm; Hibbert, 222.

36. Yonge.

37. *Trial of Marie Antoinette, late Queen of France* (compiled from a manuscript sent from Paris, and from the journals of the Moniteur) (Logographic Press 1794), passim, 52.

38. Thomas Carlyle, *The French Revolution* (Modern Library, 2002), 669.

39. Carlyle, 669.

40. *Trial of Marie Antoinette,* 30.

41. Ibid., 30–31.

42. Ibid., 32.

43. Carlyle, 669 (citing Vilate, *Causes secretes de la Révolution de Thermidor*) (Paris, 1825), 179.

44. Antonia Fraser, *Marie Antoinette* (Anchor Books, 2001), 431–32.

45. Le Bon, 15.

46. Yonge.

47. See, e.g., Stefan Zweig, *Marie Antoinette: The Portrait of an Average Woman* (New York: Grove Press, 2002), 450–51.

48. See, e.g., Zweig, 451.

49. See Christopher Hibbert, *The Days of the French Revolution* (Harper Perennial, 1999), 236; Pamela Grant, *Marie Antoinette Story,* ParisMarais.com, available at http://www.parismarais.com/marie-antoinette-story.htm.

50. Hibbert, 225.

51. William Ayers, *Fugitive Days: Memoirs of an Anti-War Activist* (Boston: Beacon Press, 2009), 130.

52. Durschmied, 53.

53. Hibbert, 225–27.

54. Durschmied, 53.

55. Goudemetz.

56. Andres, 229.

57. See Andres, 168, 229.

58. See Hibbert, 243–45.

59. Ibid., 245–46.

60. Ibid., 246.

61. Ibid., 248.

62. Durschmied, 58–59.

63. Hibbert, 261.
64. Durschmied, 64.

### EIGHT. THE AMERICAN REVOLUTION: HOW TO THROW A REVOLUTION WITHOUT LOSING YOUR HEAD

1. Editorial: "The Powerful Idea of Human Rights," *New York Times,* December 8, 1999.
2. Editorial: "French Pique," *New York Times,* July 1, 2000.
3. Ralph C. Hancock, "Two Revolutions and the Problem of Modern Prudence," in Ralph C. Hancock and L. Gary Lambert, *The Legacy of the French Revolution* (Rowman & Littlefield Publishers, 1996), 272.
4. Joseph J. Ellis, *His Excellency: George Washington* (Vintage, 1st Vintage edition, November 8, 2005), 61.
5. David Hackett Fischer, *Paul Revere's Ride* (Oxford University Press, 1994), 25–26.
6. Letter of John Adams to General James Warren, dated December 17, 1773, available at http://query.nytimes.com/mem/archive-free/pdf?res=F60E13F63D 5D1A7493C3AB1789D95F458784F9.
7. Fischer, 23.
8. David McCullough, *John Adams* (New York: Simon & Schuster, 2001), 66–68.
9. Jill Lepore, "Tea and Sympathy: Who Owns the American Revolution?," *The New Yorker,* May 3, 2010.
10. Howard Zinn, *A People's History of the United States* (Harper Perennial Modern Classics, 2010), 66.
11. Fischer, 237.
12. Ibid., 93–97.
13. Ibid., 99–103.
14. Henry Wadsworth Longfellow, "Paul Revere's Ride" (1861).
15. Fischer, 139.
16. Ibid., 109.
17. Ibid., 129.
18. Ibid., 131.
19. Ibid., 131.
20. Ibid., 134.
21. Ibid., 136.
22. See Fischer generally.
23. Ibid., 243–44.
24. Ibid., 254.
25. Ibid., 204–5.
26. Ibid., 110.
27. M. Stanton Evans, "Faith of Our Fathers," *The American Spectator,* February 2007.
28. See, e.g., David Limbaugh, "Liberal Paranoia About Christian

Conservatives," Townhall, available at http://townhall.com/columnists/
DavidLimbaugh/2010/02/26/liberal_paranoia_about_christian_conservatives/
page/2.

29. Letter from John Adams to Benjamin Rush, from Quincy, Massachusetts,
    dated December 21, 1809, available at http://www.wallbuilders.com/
    LIBissuesArticles.asp?id=8755#FN1.

30. Terence Marshall, "Human Rights and Constitutional Government: A Franco-
    American Dialogue at the Time of the Revolution," in *The Legacy of the French
    Revolution* (Hancock, ed., Rowman & Littlefield, 1996), 164, n. 62. (citing
    Rousseau . . . ).

31. See, e.g., Limbaugh.

32. Alexander Hamilton, James Madison, and John Jay, *The Federalist Papers*
    (Penguin Classics, 1987), No. 10, 124–25.

33. Edmund Burke, *Reflections on the Revolution in France,* edited by Conor Cruise
    O'Brien (Penguin Classics, 1976), 13.

34. Goudemetz.

35. Madison, Hamilton, and John Jay, 64–65.

36. Ibid., 42.

37. Ibid., 43–44.

38. Ibid., 45.

39. Ibid., No. 55, at 336.

40. Ibid., No. 51, 320.

41. Ibid., No. 10, 123.

42. Leslie M. Harris, *In the Shadow of Slavery: African Americans in New York City,
    1626–1863* (University of Chicago Press, 2003), excerpt available at http://
    www.press.uchicago.edu/Misc/Chicago/317749.html.

43. See, generally, Juan Williams, *Eyes on the Prize: America's Civil Rights Years,
    1954–1965* (Penguin Books, 1987), 178–94.

44. David Garrow, *Bearing the Cross* (Perennial Classics, 2004), 251, 264.

45. Williams, 190.

46. Taylor Branch, *Parting the Waters: America in the King Years 1954–63* (Simon
    & Schuster, 1988), 217.

47. Ibid., 190.

## NINE. THE SIXTIES: THE MOB GOES TO COLLEGE

1. Nathan Glazer, " 'Student Power' in Berkeley," reprinted in Daniel Bell and
   Irving Kristol, eds., *Confrontation: The Student Rebellion and the Universities*
   (Basic Books, 1968), 5–6.

2. "Occupied Berkeley," *Time,* May 30, 1969.

3. Quoted in Jack Newfield, "Setting Matters Straight at Columbia," *New York,*
   November 25, 1968.

4. Glazer, 47.

5. Ibid., 51.

6. Thai Jones, *A Radical Line: From the Labor Movement to the Weather Underground, One Family's Century of Conscience* (New York: Free Press, 2004), 163.
7. Biographies, *The National Journal,* November 8, 2008.
8. Glazer, 57.
9. Ibid., 52, 57.
10. James Rosen, "New Light Shed on Kent State Killings," *Washington Times,* May 4, 2010.
11. Erik Durschmied, *The Blood of Revolution: From the Reign of Terror to the Rise of Khomeini* (Arcade Publishing, 2002), 25.
12. Susan Braudy, *Family Circle: The Boudins and the Aristocracy of the Left* (Knopf, 2003), 107, 135.
13. Ibid., 105.
14. Ibid., 223.
15. Ibid., 280.
16. Ibid., 192.
17. Ibid., 188.
18. Michael W. Flamm, "Law and Order at Large: The New York Civilian Review Board Referendum of 1966 and the Crisis of Liberalism," *The Historian,* March 22, 2002 (citing Associated Press Release, December 13, 1968, "Memos to DJ Officials from AG, 1968–69 [1]," Papers of Ramsey Clark, Box 109, LBJ Library. See also Lionel H. Mitchell [a black conservative], "When Law and Order Fail," *National Review,* July 30, 1968, 741–42).
19. Braudy, 195.
20. Ibid., 208.
21. Ibid., 212.
22. Ibid., 206.
23. Ibid., 249.
24. Ibid., 277.
25. Ibid., 265–66.
26. Ibid., 267.
27. Ibid., 424, n. 272.
28. Ibid., 267.
29. Ibid., 305.
30. See, e.g., Steve Lieberman, "Ex-Police Chief Reflects on Career," *The Journal News* (Westchester County, NY), June 6, 2004.
31. Gustave Le Bon, *The Crowd: A Study of the Popular Mind* (Dover, 2002) (1895), 22.
32. Mel Gussow, "The House on West 11th Street," *New York Times,* March 5, 2000.
33. Ibid.
34. Braudy, 328.
35. Ibid., 380.
36. Ibid., 161.

37. Elizabeth Kolbert, "The Prisoner," *The New Yorker,* July 16, 2001. ("Dohrn teaches law at Northwestern University and is, at fifty-nine, still notably glamorous.")

38. Braudy, 369–70.

39. Kolbert.

40. Ibid.

41. Braudy, 316.

42. Ibid., 210.

43. Noel Sheppard, "Axelrod Joke: Obamas Considered Naming Dog Miss California," Newsbusters, May 16, 2009.

44. William Ayers, *Fugitive Days: A Memoir* (Boston: Beacon Press, 2001), passim.

45. Paul Mulshine, "The Founder of Kwanzaa Has a Lot of Explaining to Do," *Star-Ledger* (Newark, NJ), December 20, 1998 (quoting the *Los Angeles Times*).

46. California State University at Long Beach, Faculty, Black Studies Department, Ron Karenga, available at http://www.csulb.edu/colleges/cla/departments/ africanastudies/people/mkarenga.htm.

47. David Hilliard, *This Side of Glory: The Autobiography of David Hilliard and the Story of the Black Panther Party* (Lawrence Hill Books, 2001), 264–65.

48. David Hilliard, Biography and Booking Information, SpeakOut!, available at http://www.speakoutnow.org/userdata_display.php?modin=50&uid=64.

49. Kolbert.

50. Edmund Burke, *Reflections on the Revolution in France* (Dover, 2006) (first published in 1790), 80–81.

51. "Like the Plague, the Sixties Will Always Be with Us," *The American Spectator,* July 1997 (quoting *Reassessing the Sixties: Debating the Political and Cultural Legacy* (ed. Stephen Macedo) [Norton, 1997]).

## TEN. CIVIL RIGHTS AND THE MOB: GEORGE WALLACE, BULL CONNOR, ORVAL FAUBUS, AND OTHER DEMOCRATS

1. *"Our Country: The Shaping of America from Roosevelt to Reagan:* Interview with Michael Barone," CSPAN Booknotes, 1990, available at http://www .booknotes.org/Watch/11988-1/Michael+Barone.aspx.

2. See Jack Kelly, "Time to Tell the Truth: The Great Movement of Blacks to the Democratic Party Took Place for Economic Reasons, Not Because of Civil Rights," *Jewish World Review,* December 20, 2002.

3. See, e.g., Robert A. Caro, *The Years of Lyndon Johnson,* vol. 3: *Master of the Senate* (Vintage, 2003) (2002).

4. Ibid., 905.

5. Ibid., 907.

6. Damon W. Root, "When Bigots Become Reformers: The Progressive Era's Shameful Record on Race," *Reason,* May 2006.

7. Lawrence Jacob Friedman, *White Savage: Racial Fantasies in the Postbellum South* (Prentice Hall, 1970), 156.

8. R. W. Apple Jr., "G.O.P. Tries Hard to Win Black Votes, but Recent History Works Against It," *New York Times,* September 19, 1996.

9. Ibid.

10. Jack White, "Lott, Reagan and Republican Racism," *Time,* December 14, 2002.

11. "Was It Ever Going to Be Easy?," a *Newsweek* forum, *Newsweek,* May 5, 2008.

12. Taylor Branch, *Parting the Waters: America in the King Years, 1954–63* (Simon & Schuster, 1988), 360.

13. Henry A. Rhodes, "An Analysis of the Civil Rights Act of 1964: A Legislated Response to Racial Discrimination in the U.S.," Yale–New Haven Teachers Institute, 1982, available at http://www.yale.edu/ynhti/curriculum/units/1982/3/82.03.04.x.html.

14. Caro, xv.

15. Ibid., 858.

16. Ibid., 946.

17. Senate Roll Call Vote #284 *HR. 8601. PASSAGE OF AMENDED BILL.* 86th Congress (Apr. 8, 1960), available at http://www.govtrack.us/congress/vote.xpd?vote=s1960-284.

18. See Senate Roll Call Vote #284 *HR. 8601. PASSAGE OF AMENDED BILL.* 86th Congress (Apr. 8, 1960), available at http://www.govtrack.us/congress/vote.xpd?vote=s1960-284; House Roll Call Vote #106, *HR 8601. CIVIL RIGHTS ACT OF 1960. APPROVAL BY THE HOUSE OF THE SENATE'S AMENDMENTS.* 86th Congress (Apr. 21, 1960), available at http://www.govtrack.us/congress/vote.xpd?vote=h1960-106

19. House Roll Call Vote #106, *HR 8601. CIVIL RIGHTS ACT OF 1960. APPROVAL BY THE HOUSE OF THE SENATE'S AMENDMENTS.* 86th Congress (Apr. 21, 1960), available at http://www.govtrack.us/congress/vote.xpd?vote=h1960-106.

20. Root.

21. Thomas Sowell, *Black Rednecks and White Racists* (Encounter Books, 2005), 241.

22. Bart Barnes, "Barry Goldwater, GOP Hero Dies," *Washington Post,* May 30, 1998.

23. Ibid.

24. Thomas Sowell, "Government's Role in Racial Bias," *St. Louis Post-Dispatch* (Missouri), August 11, 1995.

25. Quotes from *Real Time with Bill Maher,* The Real Bill Maher blog, Nov 5, 2010, available at http://therealbillmaher.blogspot.com/2010/11/quotes-from-real-time-with-bill-maher.html.

26. Sarah Woolfolk Wiggins, *Civil War to Civil Rights, Alabama 1860–1960: An Anthology from The Alabama Review* (University of Alabama Press, 1987) (describing Gayle as a "Machine stalwart," meaning the machine of Democrat Williams Adam Gunter), 465.

27. Noel Sheppard, "Bill Maher Calls Sarah Palin a Dumb [Vagina]," Newsbusters, March 19, 2011, available at http://newsbusters.org/blogs/noel-sheppard/ 2011/03/19/bill-maher-calls-sarah-palin-dumb-vagina#ixzz1H7VwHm5Z.

28. Barone, *Our Country* (Free Press, 1992), 449.

29. Patrick J. Buchanan, "The Neocons and Nixon's Southern Strategy," *The American Conservative,* December 30, 2002.

30. Conrad Black, *The Invincible Quest: The Life of Richard Milhous Nixon* (McClelland & Stewart, 2007), 647.

31. Ibid., 650.

32. Dean J. Kotlowski, "Richard Nixon and the Origins of Affirmative Action," *The Historian,* March 22, 1998.

33. Taylor, 365–69.

34. Ibid., 368.

35. Ibid., 366.

36. Associated Press, "Reagan's Margin Is 16,876,932 Votes," *New York Times,* December 22, 1984.

37. "Orval Faubus Is Dead at 84; Governor Made History in '57 Crisis," *Arkansas Democrat-Gazette* (Little Rock), December 15, 1994.

38. *Booknotes with Brian Lamb: No Surprises: Two Decades of Clinton Watching,* by Paul Greenberg, July 7, 1996.

39. Chris Matthews, *Hardball,* MSNBC, March 29, 2010.

40. Mark Leibovich, "The Aria of Chris Matthews," *New York Times,* April 13, 2008.

41. Keith Olbermann, *Countdown,* MSNBC, January 27, 2010.

42. Gustave Le Bon, *The Crowd: A Study of the Popular Mind* (Dover, 2002) (1895), 32.

43. *The Rachel Maddow Show,* MSNBC, September 21, 2009.

44. See Statemaster, Vermont, at http://www.statemaster.com/state/VT-vermont.

45. Mary Vespa, "Tom Wicker and Pam Hill: a Mixed-Media Marriage Changes Their Luck," *People,* April 28, 1975.

46. Philip Weiss, "Fishing with Howell," *New York Magazine,* May 8, 2006.

47. Tracy Jordan, "Guardian Angels Visit Poconos," *The Morning Call,* August 14, 2006, at http://www.guardianangels.org/pdf/1529.pdf.

48. Le Bon, 33–34.

49. Paul Johnson, *Modern Times: The World from the Twenties to the Nineties* (Harper Perennial, 1992), 117.

### ELEVEN. TIMOTHY McVEIGH IS NOW A TEA PARTIER

1. John Elvin, "Washington in Brief," *Insight,* May 29, 1995.

2. See, e.g., James King, "Jared Loughner, Alleged Shooter in Gabrielle Giffords Attack, Described by Classmate as 'Left-Wing Pothead,'" January 8, 2011, available at http://blogs.phoenixnewtimes.com/valleyfever/2011/01/jared _loughner_alleged_shooter.php.

3. Paul Krugman, "Climate of Hate," *New York Times,* January 9, 2011.

4. *The O'Reilly Factor,* November 4, 2010.
5. Dana Milbank, "Stop, You're Killing Me," *Washington Post,* November 10, 2010.
6. CNN Reliable Sources, November 14, 2010.
7. Keith Olbermann, *Countdown,* MSNBC, October 15, 2010.
8. *The Rachel Maddow Show,* MSNBC, November 24, 2009 (Howard Dean guest-hosting) (announcing "Fed" murder was actually a suicide); *The Rachel Maddow Show,* MSNBC, October 20, 2010 (admitting that Stockman received no "advance notice" of the Oklahoma City bombing) (The congressman, Representative Steve Stockman of Texas, had merely been faxed a note by a civic-minded individual about an hour after the bombing, telling him what was happening at the scene of the crime. See Jack Coleman, "Rachel Maddow at Most Shameless: Claims GOP Congressman 'Received Advance Notice' of Oklahoma City Bombing," Newsbusters, October 19, 2010, available at http://www.newsbusters.org/blogs/jack-coleman/2010/10/19/rachel-maddow-most-shameless-claims-gop-congressman-received-advance-n#ixzz1FLTR46E6.)
9. *Today,* NBC, October 25, 2010.
10. Larissa MacFarquhar, "The Deflationist: How Paul Krugman Found Politics," *The New Yorker,* March 1, 2010.
11. Mark Hemmingway, "Dem Congressman Who Called for GOP Gov. to Be Put Against a Wall and Shot Now Pleads for Civility," *Washington Examiner,* January 11, 2011, available at http://washingtonexaminer.com/blogs/beltway-confidential/2011/01/dem-congressman-who-called-gop-gov-be-put-against-wall-and-shot-n?page=1&sms_ss=digg&at_xt=4d2ced89b6b1c52a%2C0.
12. Video available at http://www.thedailyshow.com/watch/wed-september-29-2010/indecision-2010---taliban-dan---boo-gate.
13. "Burning Effigies in Virginia Have Been Canceled," The Pajama Pundit, November 17, 2009, available at http://www.thepajamapundit.com/2009/11/burning-effigies-in-virginia-have-been.html.
14. "Rep. Kratovil hung in effigy by health care protester UPDATE," Politico, July 28, 2009.
15. Anthony Man, "Congresswoman's Initials on Target at Gun Range Prompts Republican Activist's Resignation," *Sun Sentinel,* October 23, 2009, available at http://weblogs.sun-sentinel.com/news/politics/broward/blog/2009/10/download_file.html.
16. Sean Hannity, interview with Sarah Palin, Fox News Network, January 17, 2011.
17. *The Ed Show,* MSNBC, January 10, 2011.
18. Sarah Wheaton, "A Tucson Victim Is Arrested at a TV Forum," *New York Times,* January 15, 2011.
19. Jeff Poor, "Prostitute-Patronizing Democratic Wisconsin State Rep. to Female GOP Colleague: 'You are f*cking dead,'" *The Daily Caller,* February 28, 2011.
20. Le Bon, 10–11.

21. Lydia Saad, "In 2010, Conservatives Still Outnumber Moderates, Liberals," June 25, 2010, available at http://www.gallup.com/poll/141032/2010 -conservatives-outnumber-moderates-liberals.aspx.

## TWELVE. IMAGINARY VIOLENCE FROM THE RIGHT VS. ACTUAL VIOLENCE FROM THE LEFT

1. Toni Locy, "Tourist Tells How Shooter Was Tackled," *Washington Post,* March 23, 1995.
2. See, e.g., Members of the U.S. Congress Who Have Died of Other Than Natural Causes While in Office, CRS Report for Congress, Updated March 13, 2002, available at http://www.scribd.com/doc/46521198/CRS-Congress-Deaths. (One congressman, Democrat John McPherson Pinckney, was killed in Hempstead, Texas, trying to break up a fight.)
3. Southern Poverty Law Center, Intelligence Report: Eco-Violence: The Record, Fall 2002, available at http://www.splcenter.org/get-informed/ intelligence-report/browse-all-issues/2002/fall/from-push-to-shove/ eco-violence-the-rec.
4. Michael Petrocelli, "Head of Radical Environmentalist Group Stays Silent at Hearing on Ecoterrorism," *Houston Chronicle,* February 13, 2002.
5. *Rita Cosby Live,* MSNBC, March 28, 2006.
6. "Activists Protest Outside AIG Execs' Homes," *USA Today,* March 23, 2009.
7. Barbara Hollingsworth, "Group Targets Speaker Boehner's (Small-h) House," *Washington Examiner,* February 17, 2011, available at http:// washingtonexaminer.com/blogs/beltway-confidential/2011/02/ group-targets-speaker-boehner-s-small-h-house#ixzz1Fne1xpKS.
8. Mark Hemmingway, "Unions Protest Wal-Mart by Distributing Flyer of Developer's Home Address with Crosshairs," *Washington Examiner,* January 19, 2011, available at http://washingtonexaminer.com/blogs/beltway-confidential/ 2011/01/unions-protest-wal-mart-distributing-flyer-developers-home-address #ixzz1FngxWmRE.
9. Nina Easton, "What's Really Behind SEIU's Bank of America Protests?," *CNN Money,* May 19, 2010, available at http://money.cnn.com/2010/05/19/news/ companies/SEIU_Bank_of_America_protest.fortune/.
10. Monica Davey and Steven Greenhouse, "Angry Demonstrations in Wisconsin as Cuts Loom," *New York Times,* February 16, 2011, available at http://www .nytimes.com/2011/02/17/us/17wisconsin.html?_r=2.
11. Easton.
12. "Man Convicted of Trespassing During Reagan Speech," Associated Press, June 13, 1986.
13. "Judge Hears Protesters' Injunction Request," Associated Press, July 9, 1987.
14. "Toxic Texan and Grim Reaper Brought to Book," *Morning Star* (London), July 20, 2001.
15. Louise Hogan, "Citizen's Arrest Warrant Drawn for Bush," Press Association, June 25, 2004.

16. Tobi Cohen, "Down in the Anti-Bush League," *Ottawa Sun,* December 1, 2004.

17. Bryan Curtis, "Another Peaceful Protest March," Slate, August 31, 2004.

18. "Army Veterans Lead Washington Protest," *Morning Star* (London), March 20, 2008.

19. "Pandora," *The Independent* (London), June 2, 2008.

20. "Parisians Protest Bush's Visit," *The Washington Report on Middle East Affairs,* August 2008.

21. The Canadian Press, "Bush Speaks in Calgary; Politics Police Keep Protesters Outside," *Telegraph-Journal* (New Brunswick), March 18, 2009; leftdog [*sic*], "Attempt at a 'Citizen's Arrest' of Bush Gets Protester Arrested," *Buckdog,* March 17, 2009.

22. "Hay Festival: George Monbiot Calls for Citizen's Arrest of John Bolton," *Guardian Unlimited,* May 25, 2008.

23. Jason Hancock, "Protesters Await Rove's Return to Iowa," *Iowa Independent,* July 24, 2008; Michael Gillespie, "Four Anti-Rove Activists Arrested in Iowa," *The Washington Report on Middle East Affairs,* September 2008 / October 2008.

24. Rebecca Mead, "Downtown's Daughter," *The New Yorker,* November 15, 2010.

25. Letter: "Summit Protesters Deserved a Laurel," *Toronto Star,* June 25, 1988.

26. George Monbiot, "Wanted: Tony Blair for War Crimes," *The Guardian* (London), January 26, 2010.

27. See, e.g., James Queally and Eric Durkin, "Former Mayor Rudy Giuliani Is a Loon and He Is Out to Get Me, Says Hamptons Hothead John McCluskey," *Daily News* (New York), May 24, 2009; Taylor Vecsey and Ginger Adams Otis, "Rudy Giuliani Stands Up to Crazed Attacker on Hamptons Stroll," May 23, 2009.

28. "Rudy Giuliani's Bridgehampton Heckler Speaks Out," Gawker, May 24, 2009, available at http://gawker.com/5268106/ rudy-giulianis-bridgehampton-heckler-speaks-out.

29. Lynn Sweet, "Dems Seek Strategy Against 'Birthers,'" *Chicago Sun-Times,* August 5, 2009.

30. *The Situation Room,* CNN, August 5, 2009.

31. "Wash. Rep. Baird Apologizes for Town-Hall Remarks," Associated Press, August 12, 2009.

32. "Health Care Bill Opponents Pleased by Democratic Anger at Town Hall Meeting Protests," *The White House Bulletin,* August 5, 2009.

33. Chris Matthews, Interview with Barbara Boxer, *Hardball,* MSNBC, August 4, 2009.

34. William McGurn, "Harry Reid's 'Evil' Moment," *Wall Street Journal,* August 18, 2009.

35. Police Report available here: http://www.docstoc.com/docs/15739780/ GLADNEY-PART-21; see also Mychal Massie, "It's Not a Hate Crime If . . . ," WorldNetDaily, December 1, 2009; "Police Report of SEIU Thug Attack on Kenneth Gladney," *The Foxhole,* November 19, 2009 (quoting police

report no longer available on the web), available at http://sfcmac.wordpress
.com/2009/11/19/police-report-on-seiu-thug-attack-on-kenneth-gladney/.

36. Neil Cavuto, "Democrats Plan to Push Healthcare Reform Through," Fox
News, September 3, 2009 (interview with Bill Rice); Doug Mainwaring,
"Defined by Principle, Not Just Protest," *Washington Times,* May 3, 2010.

37. *Hardball,* MSNBC, January 11, 2011.

38. Keith Olbermann, *Countdown,* MSNBC, June 10, 2009.

39. *The Rachel Maddow Show,* MSNBC, June 11, 2009.

40. Ed Schultz, *The Ed Show,* MSNBC, June 11, 2009.

41. Kathy Shaidle, "Holocaust Museum Shooter von Brunn a 9/11 'Truther'
Who Hated 'Neo-Cons,' Bush, McCain," *Examiner,* June 10, 2009, available
at http://www.examiner.com/conservative-politics-in-national/holocaust
-museum-shooter-von-brunn-a-9-11-truther-who-hated-neo-cons-bush
-mccain.

42. CNN's Erickson: I'll "[p]ull out my wife's shotgun" if they try to arrest me for
not filling out the American Community Survey, Media Matters for America,
April 1, 2010.

43. Noel, Sheppard, "Bill Maher Wishes Glenn Beck Had Been Killed at
Pentagon," Newsbusters, March 6, 2010, available at http://www.newsbusters
.org/blogs/noel-sheppard/2010/03/06/bill-maher-wishes-glenn-beck-had-been
-killed-pentagon-thursday#ixzz1DJnxVWjZ.

44. Ray Rivera, "104 Are Arrested in Connection with Crips-Bloods Alliance,"
*New York Times,* April 16, 2010.

45. Evan Thomas, "Al Qaeda in America," *Newsweek,* June 23, 2003.

46. Tom Troy, "Most Indicted Members of Militia Group Are Voters," *Toledo
Blade,* April 1, 2010.

47. Juan Williams, *Eyes on the Prize: America's Civil Rights Years, 1954–1965*
(Penguin Books, 1987), 102.

48. See, e.g., Steve Gilbert, "Quotes Not Appearing in Sheehan's Book," Sweetness
& Light, November 19, 2005, available at http://sweetness-light.com/archive/
some-cindy-sheehan-quotes.

49. "New York Dames Come to Blows over Bush Stickers," Agence France-
Presse—English, October 5, 2004.

50. Thai Jones, *A Radical Line: From the Labor Movement to the Weather
Underground, One Family's Century of Conscience* (Free Press, 2004), 163.

51. Bob Greene, *Homecoming: When the Soldiers Returned from Vietnam* (G. P.
Putnam's Sons, 1989).

52. Tom Hayden, "Dissent Must Come Alive in New York," *Newsday* (New York),
August 20, 2004.

53. Eliana Johnson, "At Columbia, Students Attack Minuteman Founder,"
October 5, 2006.

54. Aaron Smith, "Search On for Officer's Attacker," *New York Sun,* September 1,
2004; Lindsay Faber, "Papers: Convention Kicker Confessed," *Newsday* (New
York), September 30, 2004.

## THIRTEEN. RAPED TWICE: LIBERALS AND THE CENTRAL PARK RAPE

1. *Rita Cosby Live,* MSNBC, March 28, 2006.
2. Le Bon, 13.
3. See generally Jeremy Rabkin, "Revolutionary Visions in Legal Imagery: Constitutional Contrasts Between France and America," in *The Legacy of the French Revolution* (Hancock, ed., Rowman & Littlefield, 1996).
4. See, e.g., Julia Preston, "Prosecutor Seeks to End Time Limit in Rape Cases," *New York Times,* April 29, 2005.
5. Michael F. Armstrong, Stephen L. Hammerman, Jules Martin, Report for New York Police Department on Matias Reyes and April 19, 1989, 2.
6. Ibid., 33–34.
7. Chris Smith, "Central Park Revisited," *New York* [no date], available at http://nymag.com/nymetro/news/crimelaw/features/n_7836/.
8. Ronald Sullivan, "Defendant Told of Jogger Rape, Detective Says," *New York Times,* November 28, 1990.
9. Mitch Gelman, "Wily Cop Dug into Large Bag of Tricks," *Newsday* (New York), July 25, 1990.
10. Mike Wallace, "Yusef Salaam, Accused of 1989 Central Park Jogger Rape," *60 Minutes,* CBS, March 15, 1992.
11. Armstrong, Hammerman, and Martin, 33 (citing notes from Detective August Jonza).
12. Ibid., 35.
13. Emily Sachar, "Jogger Jury Sees a Confession," *Newsday* (New York), July 19, 1990.
14. Ronald Sullivan, "Confessions Lawyers Couldn't Undo," *New York Times,* August 20, 1990.
15. Armstrong, Hammerman, and Martin, 33.
16. Ryan Affirmation in Response to Motion to Vacate Judgment of Conviction, People v. Wise, fn ** at 12. Both accounts noted that Jackson had spontaneously told the police this when they were not even interviewing her, but her brother.
17. See, e.g., Samuel Maull, "DNA Expert: No Semen Links to Defendants," Associated Press, July 14, 1990.
18. Bruce Buursma, "Genetic 'Fingerprints' Next Crime-Fighting Tool," *Chicago Tribune,* April 30, 1989.
19. Harold M. Schmeck Jr., "DNA Findings Are Disputed by Scientists," *New York Times,* May 25, 1989.
20. Shirley E. Perlman, "DNA Test Ordered of Serial Rapist," *Newsday* (New York), May 10, 1989.
21. Richard Saltus, "Court Use of DNA 'Fingerprinting' Challenged," *Boston Globe,* May 23, 1989.
22. Schmeck.

23. Daniel Wise, "Central Park Jogger Trial: Ups and Downs for Defense," *New York Law Journal,* July 23, 1990.
24. Sachar.
25. Sullivan, "Defendant Told of Jogger Rape, Detective Says."
26. Associated Press, "Witness Tries to Link Jogger's Hair to Suspect," *Record* (Bergen County, NJ), November 15, 1990.
27. Ryan, 26–27.
28. Ibid., 27.
29. Ibid., 45.
30. Ibid., 46.
31. Ibid., 45–46.
32. Ibid., 24.
33. Armstrong, Hammerman, and Martin, 33.
34. Peck, *People of the Lie,* 218.

## FOURTEEN. STATUS ANXIETY: PLEASE LIKE ME!

1. "Study: Popular Kids—But Not the Most Popular—More Likely to Torment Peers; Popularity Increases Aggression Except for Those at Top of Social Hierarchy," *The American Sociological Review,* February 8, 2011.
2. Tara Parker-Pope, "Web of Popularity, Achieved by Bullying," *New York Times,* February 14, 2011.
3. Eugene Lyons, *Red Decade* (Arlington House, 1941), 101.
4. Gustave Le Bon, *The Crowd: A Study of the Popular Mind* (Dover, 2002) (1895), 79.
5. Ibid., 79.
6. Allison Stewart, "Getting Gaga," *Washington Post,* February 20, 2011.
7. "Red Hot," *Chicago Tribune,* December 28, 2010.
8. Thomas Jefferson, Summary View of the Rights of British America (1774).
9. Shari Weiss, "Justin Bieber's Abortion Comments in *Rolling Stone* Slammed on 'The View,'" *Daily News,* February 18, 2011, available at http://www.nydailynews.com/gossip/2011/02/18/2011-02-18_justin_biebers_abortion_comments_in_rolling_stone_slammed_by_the_view_cohosts.html#ixzz1EYMRB6B8
10. BLTWY, "When Celebs Talk Politics, Odd Things Happen," MSNBC.com, available at http://bltwy.msnbc.msn.com/politics/when-celebs-talk-politics-bad-things-happen-9526.gallery.
11. A former riot policeman says protesters everywhere even dress the same. The riot uniform consists of: "military fatigues (rather ironic since they detest the military and war), bandanas (sometimes over their faces), chains, boots, stocking caps, and gloves. Some have mops of longish hair or dreadlocks." In their nonconformity, he said, "they assume a look that conforms to half the people at any protest in the country." Loren W. Christensen, *Riot: A Behind-the-Barricades Tour of Mobs, Riot Cops and the Chaos of Crowd Violence* (Paladin Press, 2008), 48.

12. Le Bon, 74.
13. Ibid., 22.
14. Ibid., 24.
15. Jim Cramer, "Jon Stewart Is My Idol," *New York Examiner,* March 12, 2009, available at http://www.examiner.com/x-668-TV-Examiner-y2009m3d12 -Jim-Cramer-Jon-Stewart-is-my-idol.
16. Le Bon, 75.
17. Ibid., 74–75.
18. Transcript of *Daily Show* interview between Jon Stewart and Jim Cramer, *Vancouver Sun,* March 13, 2009.
19. James Fallows, "It's True: Jon Stewart Has Become Edward R. Murrow," *The Atlantic,* March 13, 2009.
20. Voltaire, *Candide* (CreateSpace, February 6, 2010), 96.
21. Bill Carter, "CNN Will Cancel 'Crossfire' and Cut Ties to Commentator," *New York Times,* January 6, 2005.
22. Malachi Martin, *Hostage to the Devil* (HarperOne, 1992) (first published 1976), 57.
23. *Good Morning America,* ABC, November 8, 2001.
24. "Twist-a-Braid Infomercial Gets Put to the Test," *Today,* NBC, February 27, 2002.
25. Michael Abramowitz, "Many Versions of 'Bush Doctrine,' " *Washington Post,* September 13, 2008.
26. Sam Harris, "When Atheists Attack," *Newsweek,* September 20, 2008.
27. *The Joy Behar Show,* Headline News, January 13, 2010.
28. Keith Olbermann, *Countdown,* MSNBC, August 6, 2010.
29. Larry Elder, "Bush Dumb, Gore Bright?," World Net Daily, March 6, 2002.
30. David Maraniss, Ellen Nakashima, "Gore's Grades Belie Image of Studiousness; His School Transcripts Are a Lot Like Bush's," *Washington Post,* March 19, 2000.
31. M. Scott Peck, *People of the Lie: The Hope for Healing Human Evil* (Touchstone, 1983), 222.
32. Keith Olbermann, *Countdown,* MSNBC, April 30, 2009.
33. *Countdown* episodes: September 1, 2009, December 22, 2009, December 28, 2009, December 30, 2009.
34. Randy Cohen, "The Ethics of Letterman's Palin Joke," *New York Times,* June 22, 2009.
35. Sheila Marikar, "Comics Crack Wise on Palin's Pregnant Daughter," abcnews .go.com, September 4, 2008.
36. David Asman, *American Nightly Scoreboard,* Fox Business Channel, June 11, 2009.
37. "Letterman vs. Palin; Spies Hiding Among Us?," CNN, June 11, 2009.
38. Lyons, 185.
39. Le Bon, 82–83

## FIFTEEN. INHERITORS OF THE FRENCH REVOLUTION: LIBERALS ♥ MOBS

1. Cornell University Arts and Sciences: History Department Course and Time Roster Fall 2010, available at http://registrar.sas.cornell.edu/courses/roster/FA10/HIST/.

2. Department of History, UCLA, available at http://www.history.ucla.edu/academics/courses.

3. Harvard History and Undergraduate Courses, available at http://isites.harvard.edu/icb/icb.do?keyword=historyba&tabgroupid=icb.tabgroup106325.

4. Alan Schom, *Napoleon Bonaparte* (HarperCollins, 1997), 253.

5. See, generally, S. J. Taylor, *Stalin's Apologist, Walter Duranty: The New York Times's Man in Moscow* (New York: Oxford University Press, 1990).

6. Jacques Steinberg, "Times Should Lose Pulitzer from 30's, Consultant Says," *New York Times,* October 23, 2003.

7. Mark Von Hagen, "Walter Duranty's Pulitzer," *New York Times,* November 13, 2003.

8. Herbert L. Matthews, "Cuban Rebel Is Visited in Hideout," *New York Times,* February 24, 1957, available at http://www.nytimes.com/packages/html/books/matthews/matthews022457.pdf.

9. Jay Taylor, *The Generalissimo: Chiang Kai-shek and the Struggle for Modern China* (Belknap Press, 2009), 274.

10. Ibid., 295.

11. Stanlet Kober, "The Debate over No First Use," *Foreign Affairs,* Summer 1982; see also Walter Issacson and Evan Thomas, *The Wise Men: Six Friends and the World They Made* (New York: Simon & Schuster, 1997), 477.

12. Peter Collier and David Horowitz, *Destructive Generation: Second Thoughts About the '60s* (New York: Free Press); first edition (August 12, 1996), 292.

13. See James Webb, "Sleeping with the Enemy," *The American Enterprise,* May/June 1997.

14. Phil Brennan, "Possible Homeland Intelligence Chief Has Strong Clintonista Ties," NewsMax.com, October 9, 2002, available at http://www.newsmax.com/archives/articles/2002/10/7/164844.shtml.

15. Raymond Strait, *Bob Hope: A Tribute* (Pinnacle, 2003), 426–27.

16. Stéphane Courtois, et al., *The Black Book of Communism* (Mark Kramer, ed. and Jonathan Murphy, trans., Harvard University Press, 1999), 632.

17. Estimates of the dead range from 1.2 million (U.S.) to 3 million (People's Republic of Kampuchea), with Amnesty International putting the figure at 1.4 million and the Yale Genocide Project at 1.7 million. Stephane Courtois, et al., *The Black Book of Communism,* 607.

18. See, generally, Collier and Horowitz; Stephane Courtois, et al., *The Black Book of Communism: Crimes, Terror, Repression* (translated by Kramer and Murphy) (Cambridge: Harvard University Press 1999); Webb, available at http://archive

.frontpagemag.com/readArticle.aspx?ARTID=18440; David Horowitz, "Pol Pot," Discover the Networks: A Guide to the Political Left, available at http://www.discoverthenetworks.org/individualProfile.asp?indid=1998.

19. Noam Chomsky and Edward S. Herman, *The Political Economy of Human Rights*, Vol. 2: *After the Cataclysm: Postwar Indochina and the Reconstruction of Imperialist Ideology*, 1979, xii-xiii.

20. Richard Falk, "Trusting Khomeini," *New York Times*, February 16, 1979.

21. "Big Dupes at Big Peace: Ted Kennedy—Part 2," Big Peace, October 10, 2010 (Interview with Paul Kengor about his book, *Dupes: How America's Adversaries Have Manipulated Progressives for a Century* [Intercollegiate Studies Institute, 2010], which reprints the KGB memo discussing Kennedy's letter), available at http://bigpeace.com/stzu/2010/10/10/big-dupes-at-big-peace-ted -kennedy-part-2/; Text of KGB Letter on Senator Ted Kennedy, Freerepublic .com (citing Kengor at page 317), available at http://www.freerepublic.com/ focus/f-news/1760564/posts.

22. Erik Durschmied, *The Blood of Revolution: From the Reign of Terror to the Rise of Khomeini* (Arcade Publishing, 2002), 36.

23. *Mein Kampf*, Worldview and Organization chapter; see generally Henry Ashby Turner, *German Big Business and the Rise of Hitler* (Oxford University Press, 1985); George Victor, *Hitler: The Pathology of Evil* (Potomac Books, 1999).

24. Eric Metaxas, *Bonhoeffer: Pastor, Martyr, Prophet, Spy* (Thomas Nelson, 2010), 166.

25. Ibid., 170–71.

26. Quoted in Metaxas, 163–64.

27. Thomas Sowell, *Intellectuals and Society* (Basic Books, 2010), 25.

28. Courtois et al., 593–94.

## SIXTEEN. THE TOTALITARIAN INSTINCT AND SEXUAL PERVERSITY OF LIBERALS

1. Hillary Rodham Clinton, *Living History* (Simon & Schuster, 2003), 161.

2. Beth Fouhy, "San Francisco Rolls Out Red Carpet for the Clintons," Associated Press, June 28, 2004.

3. The White House Office of the Press Secretary, Remarks by the President and the Vice President at a DNC "Moving America Forward" Rally in Philadelphia, October 10, 2010.

4. Alexander Hamilton: Writings (Library of America, 2001) (letter dated October 6, 1789), 521.

5. Jeremy Rabkin, "Revolutionary Visions in Legal Imagery: Constitutional Contrasts between France and America," in *The Legacy of the French Revolution* (Hancock, ed., Rowman & Littlefield, 1996), 227.

6. Pelosi: Remarks at the 2010 Legislative Conference for National Association of Counties, Congressional Documents and Publications, March 9, 2010.

7. Courtois, *The Black Book of Communism: Crimes, Terror, Repression* (translated by Kramer & Murphy), (Harvard University Press, 1999), 577.

8. See "Pretty Upset," *Santa Monica Daily Press,* July 29, 2009, available at http://www.smdp.com/Gallery-1852.113116-2614.113116_PRETTY_UPSET.html.

9. Gustave Le Bon, *The Crowd: A Study of the Popular Mind* (Dover, 2002) (1895), 19.

10. Rabinowitz, "Through the Darkness," available at http://www.lukeford.net/Dennis/p48.html.

11. Dorothy Rabinowitz, "Justice and the Prosecutor," *Wall Street Journal,* March 21, 1997, available at http://nsulaw.nova.edu/faculty/documents/P%20-%2012%20-%20Buck's%20County%20-%20March%2021,%201997.pdf; "Republican Rubenstein Wins in Bucks County on Both Tickets," *Morning Call* (Allentown, PA), May 31, 1997.

12. Paul Bedard, "Reagan Son Claims Dad Had Alzheimer's as President," *U.S. News & World Report,* January 14, 2011.

13. Whittaker Chambers, *Witness* (Regnery Publishing, 1987), 733.

14. "*New York Observer* Writer John Connolly's Upcoming Book on Clinton Critics' and Impeachment Lawyers' Sex Lives and Business Dealings," *Rivera Live,* CNBC News, June 7, 2000.

15. Simon Schama, *Citizens: A Chronicle of the French Revolution* (Vintage, 1990), 210.

16. Ibid., 99.

17. Christopher Hibbert, *The Days of the French Revolution* (New York: Harper Perennial, 1999), 22.

18. Michael L. Kennedy, *The Jacobin Clubs in the French Revolution 1793–1795* (Berghahn Books, 2000), 157.

19. William Ayers, *Fugitive Days: Memoirs of an Anti-War Activist* (Beacon Press, 2009), 147.

20. M. Stanton Evans, "Faith of Our Fathers," *The American Spectator,* February 2007.

21. Ibid.

22. Ibid.

23. Samuel Adams, *The Writings of Samuel Adams,* edited by Harry Alonzo Cushing (G. P. Putnam's Sons, 1908), vol. 4, 407 (quoting Massachusetts Governor Samuel Adams, Fast Day Proclamation, March 20, 1797).

24. Evans.

## SEVENTEEN. LUCIFER: THE ULTIMATE MOB BOSS

1. M. Scott Peck, *People of the Lie: The Hope for Healing Human Evil* (Touchstone, 1983), 202.

2. Ibid., 204.

3. Gustave Le Bon, *The Crowd: A Study of the Popular Mind* (Dover, 2002) (1895), xi.

4. Ibid., xiii.

5. See, e.g., "Sean Cockerham Bailey book: Manuscript about Palin leaked," *Anchorage Daily News,* February 18, 2011.

6. David Kuo, *Tempting Faith: An Inside Story of Political Seduction* (Free Press, 2006).

7. "Sen. John McCain Attacks Pat Robertson, Jerry Falwell, Republican Establishment as Harming GOP Ideals," CNN Transcripts, February 28, 2000, available at http://transcripts.cnn.com/TRANSCRIPTS/0002/28/se.01.html.

8. Editorial: "The War on Women," *New York Times,* February 26, 2011.

9. David Gregory, *Meet the Press,* NBC, March 21, 2010.

10. John O'Connor, "McMaster's 'Black Hats' Prevail," *The State* (Columbia, SC), September 5, 2008.

11. Aaron Smith, "Search On for Officer's Attacker," *New York Sun,* September 1, 2004.

12. Neil Cavuto, "Democrats Plan to Push Healthcare Reform Through; Reviewing the Numbers," *Cavuto,* Fox News, September 3, 2009.

13. John Maynard Keynes, *The Economic Consequences of the Peace* (Harcourt, Brace and Howe, 1920).

14. Erik Durschmied, *The Blood of Revolution: From the Reign of Terror to the Rise of Khomeini* (Arcade Publishing, 2002), 28.

15. Evelyn Waugh, "Conservative Manifesto," in *Essays, Article and Reviews of Evelyn Waugh,* edited by Donat Gallagher (Boston: Little, Brown, 1984), 161–62. Quoted in Roger Kimball, *Tenured Radicals: How Politics Has Corrupted Our Higher Education,* 3d ed. (Ivan R. Dee, 2008), 308.

# ACKNOWLEDGMENTS

**E**veryone I've ever met has been forced to read a portion of this book over the past year, and most were surprisingly generous in answering, "This sentence or that?" "This joke or that?" "Is this grammatically correct?" "Am I being unfair?" "Please read this chapter" and so on.

Before getting to everyone I've been tormenting this way, I especially want to thank Jeremy Rabkin, my professor from Cornell, who knows everything about everything, including the French and American Revolutions. Inasmuch as few people seem to know the first thing about the French Revolution, his advice was invaluable, even when he told me to stop comparing MSNBC to the Jacobins.

I also need to single out Marshall Sella for his hours of tireless editing, eventually leading him to scream at me: "DID COMMAS DO SOMETHING TO YOUR FAMILY?"

I also want to thank my extremely clever friends, who have helped not only with enormous portions of this book, but also my columns over the years—Bill Armistead, Hans Bader, Trish Baker, Robert Caplain, Rodney Lee Conover, Miguel Estrada, Sandy Frank, Steve Gilbert, Melanie Graham, James Higgins, Jim Hughes, David Limbaugh, Jay Mann, Gene Meyer, Jim Moody, Ned Rice, and Jon Tukel. You all have busy lives, but you've been great friends and terrific editors and joke-generators for me.

I am honored to say that Juan Williams read a portion of this book at my request and gave me some great ideas and edits. I would especially like to thank NPR for irritating Juan enough that he doesn't even mind that I'm thanking him.

Allan Ryskind and Stan Evans read portions of the book—I'm not telling which portions to protect their reputations—as did law professors Bill Otis and Gary Lawson, who gave me great tips, both legal and libertarian. Eddie Scarry helped find some legislative history for me, and Beda Koorey has provided emergency secretarial services (and hilarious e-mails) over the years.

Thanks to my agent Mel Berger for plowing through the whole first draft—before I even translated it into English! And out of tradition, thanks to my agent for life, Joni Evans.

Finally, humble, amazed, huge, sincerest thanks to my publisher Tina Constable, my editor Sean Desmond, my copy editor Toni Rachiele, my long-suffering footnote editor Stephanie Chan—and everyone at Crown Forum Books, whom I subjected to a special torture by turning my book in three months late. (I had a lot to say!) It's an amazing team that performed miracles to get this book out on time.

# INDEX

## A

ABC, 19, 20, 42, 87, 91, 92, 199, 215

Abortion, 10, 49, 152, 166, 175, 181–182, 194, 199, 202, 206–207, 251, 290

Abrams, Robert, 37

Abt, John, 210

Acciardo, Gilbert, 68–69

Acheson, Dean, 268

ACLU (American Civil Liberties Union), 66, 119, 281

Adams, John, 132–134, 140–142, 147, 285

Adams, Samuel, 133, 135–138, 286

Addington, David, 75

Adler, Solomon, 268

Affirmative action, 177, 185, 186

AFL-CIO, 215

Ahmadinejad, Mahmoud, 29, 63–64, 66, 86–87

al Qaeda, 44, 45, 77

Alinsky, Saul, 288

Alter, Jonathan, 17–18, 28

Altman, Robert, 33

American Civil War, 148, 149, 175

American Revolution, 99–100, 111, 129–146, 148, 225, 264–266

Amirault, Gerald, 244, 280

Andropov, Yuri, 271

Angle, Sharron, 27, 289

Animal Liberation Front, 211

Anorexia, deaths from, 58, 60

Anti-war protests, 157, 194, 196, 213

Apple, R. W., 176–177

Armitage, Richard L., 75, 76

Articles of Confederation, 146, 147, 286

Ashcroft, John, 45–48

Askin, Frank, 45

Associated Press, 24, 25, 92, 187, 199

Atkinson, Brooks, 268

Atlanta Olympic park bombing, 47

Atta, Mohammed, 76

*Audacity of Hope, The* (Obama), 26

Avlon, John, 79

Axelrod, David, 168

Ayers, William, 125, 160, 164, 168–169, 171, 269, 285

## B

Bachmann, Michele, 67, 172, 204, 278, 290

Baez, Joan, 158

Baird, Brian, 216

Baird, Zoë, 102

Baldwin, Alec, 33

Barbour, Haley, 19

Barone, Michael, 173–174

Bastille, storming of, 100–102, 131, 132, 140, 144

Baucus, Max, 83

Bay of Pigs, 17

Beatles, the, 19–20

Beck, Glenn, 200, 220, 289
Beckel, Bob, 198
Begala, Paul, 255
Belafonte, Harry, 29
Benjamin, Medea, 278
Berkeley "Free Speech" movement, 158
Bernanke, Ben, 34
Biaggi, Mario, 60
Biden, Joe, 10, 66, 214
Bieber, Justin, 26, 32, 251
Bill of Rights of 1791, 129, 276
bin Laden, Osama, 43, 45, 77
*Birth of a Nation* (movie), 175
Bishop, Amy, 219
Black, Hugo, 56
Black Liberation Army, 165, 171
Black Panthers, 162, 170, 174, 188, 196
Black Power movement, 152
Blair, Jayson, 193
Blair, Tony, 6, 103, 215
Blankfein, Lloyd, 43
Bloomingdale, Stephanie, 9
Blumenthal, Sidney, 40
Blunt, Roy, 191–192
Boehner, John, 290
Bolshevism, 129, 273, 290
Bolton, John, 6, 64, 214, 215
Bond, Julian, 184
Booth, John Wilkes, 209
Boston Massacre, 133–134
Boston Tea Party, 56, 132–134
Boudin, Jean, 161–163
Boudin, Kathy, 161–168
Boudin, Leonard, 161, 163–166
Boudin, Michael, 161
Bourne, Russell, 134
Boxer, Barbara, 22, 82, 216, 256
Bozell, Brent, 197
Braudy, Susan, 161–162, 164–165
Brawley, Tawana, 37, 59, 82, 291
Breitbart, Andrew, 52
Brenneke, Richard, 88–90
Briscoe, Michael, 241

Brissot, Jacques Pierre, 126
Broadrick, Juanita, 214
Brown, Jerry, 279
Brown, Scott, 30, 32–33
Brown, Tina, 283
Brown, Waverly, 165, 167
Brown, Willie, 59
*Brown v. Board of Education* (1954), 177, 186
Brownell, Herbert, 178
Bryant, Anita, 212
Buchanan, Pat, 289
Buckley, William F., 7, 25, 34, 212
Buffett, Warren, 36, 262
Bullying, 249–250
Burke, Edmund, 133, 144, 172
Burns, Ken, 23
Burr, Aaron, 131, 132
Bush, Barbara, 22
Bush, George H. W., 7, 22, 33, 89, 91–93, 278, 282
Bush, George W., 11, 12, 16, 20, 28–33, 59, 62, 63–64, 66, 70, 76–78, 82–84, 91, 152, 193, 201, 213–214, 218, 222, 257, 258, 278, 289
Byrd, Robert "Sheets," 174

**C**

Cambodia, 269–270, 273
Camelot cult, 17
Campbell, John, 81
Carlson, Margaret, 22, 28, 41
Carlson, Tucker, 255
Carlyle, Thomas, 122
Caro, Robert A., 174, 178
Carter, Amy, 282
Carter, Billy, 85
Carter, Jimmy, 31, 84–87, 92, 93, 187, 189
Carter, Ruth, 85
Carville, James, 39, 215
Casey, Robert, Sr., 182

Casey, William, 89–90, 94
Castro, Fidel, 134, 142, 161, 165, 266, 267–268
Cato, Gavin, 38, 39
Cavett, Dick, 261
Cavuto, Neil, 217, 292
Cazotte, Jacques, 111
CBS, 30, 42, 60, 81, 292
Census, 66–67
Center for Civil Discourse, 39, 40
Central Park jogger rape case, 37, 39, 226–243, 297–303
Cermak, Anton, 209
Chambers, Whittaker, 282
Chappaquiddick, 35, 80
Chávez, Hugo, 29, 83, 264
Cheney, Dick, 6, 11, 39, 61, 63–65, 76, 278, 289
Child-abuse cases, 46, 48, 280–281
Chomsky, Noam, 31, 270
Church and state, separation of, 56, 57
Churchill, Winston, 40
CIA (Central Intelligence Agency), 65, 75, 76
Citizen's arrests, 213–215, 279
Civil rights, 150–152, 173–193
Civil Rights Act of 1866, 175
Civil Rights Act of 1957, 178–180, 182
Civil Rights Act of 1960, 179, 180
Civil Rights Act of 1964, 35, 174, 178–181
Clark, George A., 210
Clark, Wesley, 83
Cleaver, Emanuel, 204
Clift, Eleanor, 17
Clinton, Bill, 16–18, 20, 22, 25, 27, 28, 30, 36, 39–40, 49, 59, 64, 76, 77, 80, 90, 103, 171, 174, 188, 189, 193, 197, 213, 214, 240, 283, 290
Clinton, Chelsea, 193, 282
Clinton, Hillary, 16, 22, 26–28, 36, 192–193, 275, 288, 290

CNN, 30, 37, 52, 67, 201, 215–216, 251, 254–255, 289, 292
Coakley, Martha, 53–54, 281
CodePink, 194, 278–279
Coleman, James, 72
Columbia University, 86–87, 159
Common Sense (Paine), 139
Concord, Battle of, 138–139
Congressional midterm elections (2010), 31, 182
Connerly, Ward, 32
Connolly, Gerald, 34
Connolly, John, 283
Connor, Theophilus Eugene "Bull," 150–151, 174
Conspiracy theories, 79–94
Constitution of the United States, 56–57, 129, 134, 135, 146–148, 175, 179, 221, 225, 276, 286
Conyers, John, 82
Coolidge, Calvin, 16–17
Coons, Chris, 57–58
Coplon, Judith, 161
Couric, Katie, 255–257
Cowan, Lee, 18
Cramer, Jim, 252–254
Cronkite, Walter, 202, 271
Crowd, The: A Study of the Popular Mind (Le Bon), 5–6
Crown Heights, Brooklyn, 38, 47
Currie, Lauchlin, 268
Czolgosz, Leon, 209

**D**

Daily Kos, 55, 64
Dalai Lama, 26
Daschle, Tom, 83, 102
Davis, Angela, 170
Davis, Peter, 270
Dawes, William, 136, 137
De Antonio, Emile, 164, 165
Dean, Howard, 45, 69, 84
Death penalty, 49, 112

Debs, Eugene, 188
Declaration of Independence, 55, 56, 131–132, 134, 135, 140–141, 143, 221, 286
Declaration of the Rights of Man and of the Citizen of 1789, 100, 116, 129, 130, 142–145
DeLay, Tom, 11, 237
Dellums, Ron, 65
*Demons, The* (Dostoyevsky), 172
Denny, Reginald, 43–45
Dershowitz, Alan, 40, 289
Desmoulins, Camille, 126–127, 272
Diana, Princess of Wales, 91
Diebold Corporation, 59
Dimon, Jaime, 43
DNA evidence, 233–235, 238
Dodd, Christopher, 42, 43, 269
Dohrn, Bernardine, 125, 140, 162–164, 168, 169, 269, 285
Dole, Bob, 34
Dostoyevsky, Fyodor, 172
Douglas, William, 225
Dowd, Maureen, 74, 75, 212
Downey, Tom, 269
Draft Riots of 1863, 148–149, 295
*Dreams from My Father* (Obama), 25–26
Dukakis, Michael, 91
Duke University lacrosse players rape case, 59, 71–74, 82, 153, 212, 224–225, 244, 291
Dunne, Finley Peter, 274
Duran, Francisco Martin, 208
Duranty, Walter, 266–267
Durbin, Dick, 30
Durschmied, Erik, 4, 106, 272

**E**

Earth First!, 194, 196
Earth Liberation Front, 211, 288
Eckford, Elizabeth, 221, 223
*Economic Consequences of the Peace, The* (Keynes), 293

Economic crisis, 9–11, 14, 42, 43
Edwards, Elizabeth, 41, 284
Edwards, John, 40–42, 45, 59, 80, 225, 260, 261, 284, 293
Edwards, Jonathan, 131
Eisenhower, Dwight D., 18, 177–179, 182, 186
Ellsberg, Daniel, 161
Elrod, Richard, 163
Emancipation Proclamation, 148
Emanuel, Rahm, 10
Emerson, Ralph Waldo, 40–41
Emerson, Steve, 92
Emerson, William, 139
Energy issues, 49
English Bill of Rights of 1689, 129
Enron, 11, 12
Ensler, Eve, 285
Environmentalists, 211
Erickson, Erick, 219–220
Ervin, Sam, 174, 178, 179, 223
Establishment Clause of First Amendment, 57
Evans, Jodie, 278, 279
Evers, Charles, 194
Evers, Medgar, 194
Evolution, 49

**F**

*Fahrenheit 911* (movie), 82, 83
Falk, Richard, 270–271
Fallows, James, 254
Falwell, Jerry, 25, 289
Fannie Mae, 10, 42
Farrakhan, Louis, 29
Faubus, Orval, 150, 178, 187–188, 192, 221, 223
al-Fayed, Mohamed, 91
FBI (Federal Bureau of Investigation), 68, 72, 164
*Federalist Papers, The* (Hamilton, Madison, and Jay), 135, 143, 146–147, 148

Feinstein, Dianne, 22
Fells Acres case, 280–281
Fernsler, Terry, 213
Fifteenth Amendment, 175
Fineman, Howard, 18, 64
First Amendment, 57
Fischer, David Hackett, 137
Fitzgerald, Scott, 212
Flowers, Gennifer, 80
Flynt, Larry, 283
Fonda, Jane, 157
Ford, Gerald, 210
Fouché, Joseph, 117–119, 127
Fourteenth Amendment, 175, 179
Fox News, 61, 67, 79, 195, 198,
    200–201, 217, 289, 292
Frank, Barney, 40, 42, 43
Franklin, Benjamin, 133, 286
Freddie Mac, 10
French Revolution, 4, 99–132, 134,
    136, 139–146, 148, 157, 172,
    225, 264–266, 283–284, 286
Friedman, Milton, 130, 212
Frist, Bill, 34
Fromme, Lynette "Squeaky," 196, 210
Fuhrman, Mark, 172
Fukino, Chiyome, 80
Fulbright, J. William, 174
Fuller, J. Eric, 205


**G**

Gaga, Lady, 250–251
Gage, Thomas, 136
Gainor, Dan, 205
Galligan, Thomas B., 235
Gandhi, Mahatma, 152
Garfield, James, 209
Garofalo, Janeane, 29, 190, 197
Gaston, A. G., 151
Gates, Bill, 36, 262
Gay rights, 5, 49, 251
Gayle, William A. "Tacky," 182
Geithner, Timothy, 102

George III, 140, 141, 143
Gephardt, Dick, 29
Geragos, Mark, 40
Gibbs, Nancy, 19
Gibbs, Robert, 216
Gibson, Charlie, 51, 255–257
Giffords, Gabrielle, 197, 204
Gilbert, David, 164, 165
Gilchrist, Jim, 222
Ginsburg, Douglas, 36
Gitlin, Todd, 269
Giuliani, Rudy, 215, 294
Gladney, Kenneth, 216
Glass, Carter, 180
Glazer, Nathan, 158
Global warming, 5, 13, 49, 58–59,
    80, 214
Glock gun, 60, 61
Glover, Danny, 166
*Godless: The Church of Liberalism*
    (Coulter), 77
Goebbels, Joseph, 272
Gold, Ted, 163
Goldman, Emma, 209
Goldman, Ron, 235
Goldwater, Barry, 7, 34, 62, 180–181,
    189
González, Elián, 48
Gore, Al, 9, 13, 22, 29, 33, 36, 38, 59,
    174, 193, 214, 257–258
Gore, Al, Sr., 174, 258
Grant, Ulysses S., 175
Grayson, Alan, 39, 53, 203–205
Great Society, 183
Greenberg, Paul, 188
Greene, Bob, 222
Groupthink, 249–263
Guantánamo Bay, 43, 44
*Guardian,* 5, 214–215
Guevara, Che, 134
Guiteau, Charles J., 209
Gumbel, Bryant, 197
Gussow, Mel, 166
Gwinnett, Button, 132

## H

Haley, Harold, 170
Haley, Nikki, 290
Hamilton, Alexander, 102–103, 132, 140, 147, 275–276, 286
Hamilton, Lee, 90, 93
Hampton, Fred, 162
Hancock, John, 135–138, 141
Hancock, Roger, 130–131
Harkin, Tom, 83
Harris, Katherine, 172
Harris, Leslie M., 149
Harris, Sam, 257
Harris-Lacewell, Melissa, 71–73
Harshbarger, Scott, 280, 281
Hayden, Tom, 157, 222, 269
Health care, 5, 13, 30–31, 34, 51, 52, 216, 217, 276–277, 289, 290, 292
*Hearts and Minds* (movie), 270
Hébert, Jacques, 121–123, 125
Heine, Heinrich, 273
Helms, Jesse, 33
Hemings, Sally, 283
Henry, Patrick, 131, 135
Hentoff, Nat, 289
Herbert, Bob, 44
Hill, Anita, 87
Hilliard, David, 170
Himmler, Heinrich, 272
Hinckley, John, 67
Hinds, James M., 210
Hintz, Gordon, 205
Hiss, Alger, 80, 161, 282
Hitchens, Christopher, 86, 89, 103, 129, 289
Hitler, Adolf, 5, 27, 32, 94, 184, 264, 268, 272
Hoffman, Dustin, 166
Holder, Eric, 42
Hollings, Ernest, 83, 174
Holocaust Museum, Washington, D.C., 217–218
Holtzman, Liz, 16, 22
Honegger, Barbara, 88–89

Hoover, Herbert, 209
Hope, Bob, 21, 270
Horner, Chris, 204
Horowitz, David, 212
Hoyer, Steny, 216
Huckabee, Mike, 288
Hughes, Howard, 89
*Human Events,* 23, 79
Humphrey, Hubert, 183
Humphries, Trent, 205
Hunter, Rielle, 41, 42, 59, 80, 284
Hussein, Saddam, 49, 76, 289
Hutaree, 219–221

## I

Ickes, Harold, 40
Idolization of politicians, 16–23, 26–27
Ifill, Gwen, 55
Intelligence, 64–66, 76
Interrogation techniques, 43–45
Iran, Shah of, 84, 85, 271, 278
Iranian hostage crisis, 85–89, 91–93
Iranian nuclear weapons program, 63–66, 70
Iraq War, 62, 74, 112

## J

Jackson, Andrew, 20–21, 198, 208
Jackson, George, 170
Jackson, Hugh, 26
Jackson, Jesse, 152, 217
Jackson, Melody, 233
Jamal, Mumia Abu, 58
Jay, John, 147
Jefferson, Thomas, 57, 132, 135, 142, 146, 251, 264, 283, 286
Jeffreys, Alec, 234
Jennings, Peter, 18
Jesus, 14–15, 19, 20
Jewell, Richard, 47
Jim Crow laws, 175, 181
Johnson, George M., 178

Johnson, Levi, 282
Johnson, Lyndon B., 17, 84, 174, 178,
    179, 181–185, 206
Johnson, Paul, 194
Johnson, Sonia, 213
Jones, Jim, 59, 152, 196, 210
Jones, Paula, 40, 80

**K**

Kaczynski, Ted, 197
Kagan, Elena, 21–22
Kanjorski, Paul, 202
Karenga, Ron, 169
Keller, Bill, 267
Kennedy, Edward M., 10, 19, 27, 32,
    35, 92, 271
Kennedy, Jackie, 19
Kennedy, John F., 16, 17, 19, 20, 25,
    27, 28, 181–183, 185–186, 206,
    209–210
Kennedy, Robert F., 17, 210
Kent State University, 46, 160–161,
    164, 294
Kerry, John, 40, 59, 269
Keynes, John Maynard, 293
Khadafy, Moammar, 27, 60
Khmer Rouge, 270, 273
Khomeini, Ayatollah Ruhollah, 4,
    85–88, 91, 271
Killefer, Nancy, 102
Kilmeade, Brian, 201
Kim Il Sung, 93, 266
King, Coretta Scott, 185, 186
King, Martin Luther, Jr., 17, 150–152,
    183, 185–186
King, Martin Luther, Sr., 186
King, Rodney, 4, 44, 47
Klein, Joe, 19, 20, 29, 63, 255
Klobuchar, Amy, 62, 63
Klonsky, Mike, 170
Koch brothers, 262, 279, 288
Kofinas, Chris, 41
Koplewicz, Harold, 20

Koppel, Ted, 40, 92
Koresh, David, 46
Kramnick, Isaac, 146
Kratovil, Frank, 203
Krause, Allison, 160
Kristol, Bill, 212
Krugman, Paul, 11, 12, 45, 130,
    200–202, 204
Ku Klux Klan, 4, 150, 151, 175, 176,
    190, 193, 194, 195, 196
Kuby, Ron, 193
Kucinich, Dennis, 81, 284
Kurtz, Howard, 201
Kutcher, Ashton, 21
Kyoto treaty, 152

**L**

LaBianca, Leno, 162
LaBianca, Rosemary, 162
Lacayo, Richard, 197
Lackawanna Six, 221
Lafayette, Marquis de, 144–145,
    275–276
Lake, Anthony, 269–270
Lamballe, Princess, 110–111, 121, 284
Lang, Robert, 70
Lapham, Lewis, 197
LaPierre, Wayne, 197
LaRouche, Lyndon, 84, 86, 87
Lauer, Matt, 18
Lawrence, Richard, 208
Le Bon, Gustave, 5–8, 12, 13, 16, 27,
    29, 34, 35, 48, 51, 54, 58, 74, 78,
    95, 99, 103, 123, 165, 191, 194,
    205, 225, 250, 252, 253, 263, 280,
    283, 287
Leahy, Pat, 6
Lederer, Elizabeth, 228, 297–303
LeMay, Curtis, 189
Lemon, Don, 52
Lenin, V. I., 264, 266, 271, 273
Leno, Jay, 261
Letterman, David, 260–262

Levin, Brian, 67
Lewinsky, Monica, 64, 80, 283
LeWinter, Oswald, 91
Lewis, Anthony, 45
Lewis, Flora, 86
Lewis, John, 52
Lewis, Sinclair, 293
Libby, Scooter, 36, 75, 172
Libya, 27, 115
Liddy, G. Gordon, 212
Lieberman, Joe, 103, 289
Limbaugh, Rush, 54
Lincoln, Abraham, 132, 149, 150, 175, 209, 283, 295
Lincy, Valerie, 65
Lindsay, John, 16
Lipset, Seymour Martin, 159
Lipton, Eric, 199
Litjens, Michelle, 205
Locke, John, 130
Long, Huey, 152, 210
Longfellow, Henry Wadsworth, 136
Lopez, Steven, 230, 240
*Los Angeles Times,* 25, 45, 269
Lott, Trent, 192
Loughner, Jared, 36, 39, 53, 167, 197–200, 205
Louis XIV, 160–161
Louis XVI, 100, 103, 105–108, 111–114, 121, 160, 284, 295
Louis XVII, 121–124, 280
Lyons, Eugene, 250, 262

**M**

MacLaine, Shirley, 270
MacNelly, Jeff, 86
Maddow, Rachel, 42, 45, 59, 62, 63, 64, 68–71, 73, 191, 200, 202, 218
Madison, James, 143, 147, 148
Madonna, 22
Magna Carta, 129, 140
Magnuson, Warren, 174

Maher, Bill, 182, 199, 220
Mahoney, Charles, 178
Malveaux, Suzanne, 215
Mansfield, Harvey, 172, 210
Mansfield, Mike, 174
Manson, Charles, 162, 168, 171, 211
Mao Zedong, 4, 129, 130, 266, 268
Marat, Jean-Paul, 108
Marcotte, Amanda, 284
Marie Antoinette, 100, 102–106, 110, 111, 121–125, 277–278, 280, 282–284
Marshall, Burke, 151
Marshall, Thurgood, 130, 150–152, 186
Marx, Karl, 148
Mattera, Jason, 21
Matthews, Chris, 18, 19, 42, 75, 82, 190–191, 198, 204, 216, 217
Matthews, Herbert, 266–267
McAuliffe, Terry, 82, 83
McCain, John, 33, 54–55, 103, 218, 279, 282, 289, 291
McCarthy, Joseph, 45, 164, 174, 178, 278, 289
McCaskill, Claire, 102
McCluskey, John, 215
McCombs, Phil, 20
McConaughey, Matthew, 26
McCormack, John, 53
McCormack, Martha, 53–54
McCowan, Elston, 216
McCray, Antron, 227–233, 235–237, 239–241, 243, 244, 297–303
McDermott, Jim, 83
McGovern, George, 179, 184, 188, 289
McGuire, Philip C., 60
McKenna, Thomas, 230
McKinley, William, 208, 209
McVeigh, Timothy, 28, 45, 196–198, 200, 217, 221, 226
Meacham, Jon, 20–21
*Mein Kampf* (Hitler), 272, 273

Mendel, Ellen, 28
Menendez, Alicia, 34
Milbank, Dana, 200–201, 204
Milhollin, Gary, 65
Miller, Jeffrey, 160
Minutemen, 135–136, 139
Mississippi River bridge collapse, 61–63, 70
Mitchell, Andrea, 18–19
Mitchell, John, 184, 185
Molens, Perry, 216
Monbiot, George, 5–6
Mondale, Walter, 85, 91, 187
Moore, Michael, 40, 49, 59, 82–84, 176, 209, 214, 215, 256
Moore, Sara Jane, 210
Moran, Terry, 20
Morgenthau, Robert, 229, 238
Morrow, Fredrick, 178
Morrow, Lance, 17, 22
Morse, Wayne, 174
Moulitsas, Markos, 55
Moveon.org, 174, 195, 292
Mrazek, Robert, 60
MSNBC, 4, 9, 19, 21, 23, 30, 32–33, 37, 39, 41–43, 45, 53–55, 61–63, 67–71, 73, 75, 77–78, 82, 190, 192, 198, 200–201, 215, 217–219, 221, 224, 258–259, 262, 282, 288–289, 292
Murray, James, 174
Murray, Patty, 40, 256
Mussolini, Benito, 5
Musto, Michael, 259

**N**

NAACP, 181, 183, 194
Napoleon, 120, 127, 130, 146, 295
Nathanson, Bernard, 175
*Nation, The,* 45, 86, 87
*National Journal,* 24, 71
*National Review,* 79, 268
National Rifle Association, 61, 197

Nazi Germany, 129, 264, 272–273, 293–294
NBC, 18, 20, 292
Nelson, Bill, 83
Nelson, Lemrick, Jr., 47
Neufeld, Peter, 234
*New Republic,* 40, 92
*New York* magazine, 67, 229
*New York Times,* 7, 11, 18, 24, 28, 37, 38, 44, 45, 60, 65, 67, 74–76, 81, 85–88, 91–94, 129, 130, 165, 166, 176, 187, 192, 193, 199–200, 202, 217, 219, 233, 234, 245, 250, 266–268, 270, 271, 290, 294
*New Yorker,* 134, 167, 168, 202
*Newsweek,* 17–20, 28, 29, 54, 64, 67, 92, 177, 221, 257
Newton, Huey, 158
Nicholson, Jack, 289
NIE (National Intelligence Estimate), 63–65
Nietzsche, Friedrich, 15
9/11 terrorist attack, 48, 62, 65, 76–78, 83, 84, 91
Nixon, Richard M., 22, 170, 176–178, 182–187, 189, 206, 209, 243, 269, 278, 289, 293, 294
Novak, Bob, 184, 289
NPR, 30, 33, 37, 40, 84, 134
Nuclear power, 49, 70
Nuclear weapons, 63–66

**O**

Oakeshott, Michael, 272
Obama, Barack, 10–11, 13, 16, 18–21, 25–28, 30–31, 34, 43, 54–55, 59, 81, 103, 130, 152, 163, 170, 190, 193, 198, 212, 219, 253, 272, 275, 288, 289
Obama, Michelle, 18, 103
Obama birthplace issue, 58, 71, 76, 79–84, 94

ObamaCare, 5, 30–31, 51, 52, 216, 217, 277, 289, 290, 292
October Surprise conspiracy theory, 84–95
O'Donnell, Christine, 27, 56, 57–58, 289
O'Donnell, Rosie, 84
O'Grady, Edward, 165, 167
Oil, 11–13
Oklahoma City bombing, 39, 196–197, 202, 226
Olbermann, Keith, 32–33, 36, 40–42, 45, 54–55, 62–65, 68, 73, 77–78, 177, 200, 201, 215, 217–218, 257–259, 262
O'Mahoney, Joseph, 174
Onaka, Alvin, 80
O'Reilly, Bill, 34, 200–201, 288
Oswald, Lee Harvey, 33, 209–210

**P**

Paige, Peter, 165
Paine, Thomas, 108, 112–114, 135, 139, 140, 145–146
Palin, Bristol, 260–261
Palin, Sarah, 39, 51, 54–56, 58, 121, 163, 168, 172, 182, 197, 198, 204–206, 255–258, 260–262, 278, 282–283, 288–291
Palin, Trig, 58, 283
Palin, Willow, 260
Parker, Caitie, 199
Parker, Lonnae O'Neal, 32
Parker, Trey, 251
Parks, Rosa, 182
Paul, Rand, 27, 53, 211, 288, 291
Paul, Ron, 289
Pawlenty, Tim, 62
PBS (Public Broadcasting System), 55, 87, 91, 134
Pearl, Daniel, 201
Peck, M. Scott, 244, 259, 287

Pelosi, Nancy, 11, 30–31, 126, 216, 276, 290
Penn, Sean, 209
People's Temple, 152, 196, 210
Percy, Lord Hugh, 135, 139
Perriello, Tom, 203
Petraco, Nicholas, 237
Phelps, Fred, 219
Philadelphia Plan, 185
Pickering, Charles, 193–194
Pitt, Brad, 26
Pitt, William, 121
Plame, Valerie, 49, 74–77
*Planned Parenthood v. Casey* (1992), 206
Plastic handguns, 59, 60–61
*Playboy* magazine, 86, 282
*Plessy v. Ferguson* (1896), 175
Pochoda, Dan, 166
Pol Pot, 129, 266, 270, 277
Polis, Jared Schultz, 160
Political violence, 208–223, 278–279, 291–292
Pontius Pilate, 14–15
Port Huron Statement, 157
Posey, Bill, 81–82, 84
Potter, Charles, 179
Powell, Adam Clayton, Jr., 177
Prejean, Carrie, 168, 172, 259–260, 289
Prescott, Samuel, 137
Presidential Daily Briefing of August 6, 2001, 77–78
Presidential elections
  1864, 150
  1952, 177
  1956, 177
  1960, 185–186
  1964, 7, 176, 189
  1968, 176, 183, 189
  1972, 176, 184, 187, 189
  1976, 187
  1980, 84–86, 89, 91, 187

1984, 187
1992, 7, 33, 91–92
2000, 33, 83
2004, 59, 82, 83–84
2008, 33, 54–55, 59, 79, 80
Press, Bill, 63, 219
Priest, Dana, 30
Proffit, Tim, 53, 291–292, 293

**Q**

Quayle, Dan, 104, 172, 278
Quinn, Sally, 17

**R**

Rabkin, Jeremy, 276
Race riots, 4, 157
*Rachel Maddow Show,* 42, 68–71, 73,
    210, 282
Raines, Howell, 193
Rajendran, Manju, 224
Rangel, Charles, 83, 102
Raskin, Eleanor, 160, 170, 222
Raspberry, William, 29
Rather, Dan, 30, 59, 81, 91
Reagan, Patti, 282
Reagan, Ron, Jr., 281–282
Reagan, Ronald, 16, 17, 21, 23–25,
    62, 67, 84–88, 91–93, 130, 158,
    175, 187, 213, 214, 271, 278,
    281–282
Reconstruction Act of 1867, 175
Rector, James, 158
Reid, Harry, 31, 216, 290
Reno, Janet, 45–48, 280, 281
Revere, Paul, 133, 135–138, 139, 140
Reyes, Martias, 227–228, 230,
    237–239, 241–243
Rice, Bill, 217, 292
Rice, Condoleezza, 211, 290
Rich, Frank, 67, 88, 258
Rich, Marc, 36

Richardson, Bill, 190
Richardson, Kevin, 227–231, 233,
    235–237, 239–241, 243
Richardson, Scovel, 178
Rivera, Geraldo, 28
Robbins, Terry, 160
Roberts, John, 22
Robertson, Pat, 289
Robespierre, Maximilien de, 100, 105,
    108, 112, 115, 123, 126–128,
    142, 153, 223, 225, 245, 264,
    271, 272
Robinson, Eugene, 73, 221
Robohm, Peggy Adler, 90
Rockefeller, Winthrop, 187–188
Rodriguez, Alex, 260
*Roe v. Wade* (1973), 181, 206, 207
Romero, Anthony, 45
Roosevelt, Franklin D., 16, 17, 28,
    49, 86, 209, 268
Roosevelt, Theodore, 208
Rose, Charlie, 40
Rosen, James, 160
Rosen, Jeffrey, 40
Rosenbaum, Yankel, 38, 47
Rosenberg, Alfred, 273
Rosenberg, Ethel, 58, 80, 209
Rosenberg, Julius, 58, 80, 209
Rosenberg, Susan, 171
Rousseau, Jean-Jacques, 32, 104, 108,
    114, 116, 130, 142, 148, 150,
    225
Rove, Karl, 49, 75, 78, 172, 214, 279
Rubenstein, Alan, 281
Rudd, Mark, 170
Rumsfeld, Donald, 278
Russbacher, Gunther, 88
Russbacher, Raye, 88
Russell, Cheryl, 18
Russell, Richard, 174
Russian revolution, 4, 294
Ryan, Leo, 210
Ryskind, Allan, 23

**S**

Sada, Georges, 76
Saint-Just, Louis de, 115, 125, 127, 272
Salaam, Yusef, 227–231, 233, 235–237, 239–241, 243
Salinger, Pierre, 33
Salon, 55, 81
Sample, William, 292
Sanford, Mark, 41
Santana, Raymond, 227–231, 233, 235–237, 239–241, 243
Sarandon, Susan, 33, 134
Savage, Charlie, 199
Scaife, Richard Mellon, 262
Scalia, Antonin, 59
Schaeffer, Francis, 282
Schama, Simon, 283–284
Scheck, Barry C., 234, 244
Scheer, Robert, 268–269
Scheuer, Sandra, 160
Schieffer, Bob, 42
Schlafly, Phyllis, 212, 223, 279, 290
Schneider, Bert, 270
School prayer, 188
Schorr, Daniel, 40
Schrank, John, 208
Schroeder, William Knox, 160
Schultz, Debbie Wasserman, 203
Schultz, Ed, 39, 67–68, 218, 219
Schumer, Chuck, 30, 60, 197
Schwarzenegger, Arnold, 27
Scientific progress, 12–13
Scott, Rick, 202
SDS (Students for a Democratic Society), 125, 140, 152, 157, 160, 162, 194, 196
Secret Service, 55, 89
Segregation, 175–177, 181, 182, 184, 186–188
SEIU (Service Employees International Union), 53, 212, 216, 217
Sekoff, Roy, 257
Seligman, Reade, 71

Service, John Stewart, 268
Sexual accusations, 282–285
Shane, Scott, 199
Shapiro, Walter, 18, 19
Sharpton, Al, 36–39, 82, 150
Shays, Daniel, 146
Shays' Rebellion, 129, 146, 148
Sheehan, Cindy, 222
Sheehan, Mike, 229–230
Sheen, Charlie, 202
Sherman, Roger, 286
Sherrill, Martha, 22
Shultz, George P., 185
Sick, Gary, 86–87, 91–94
*Silent Scream* (movie), 175
Simpson, Nicole Brown, 235
Simpson, O.J., 17, 42, 59, 82, 234, 235
Sinatra, Frank, 21, 270
Sirhan, Sirhan, 210
Slaughter, Louise, 62, 63
Slavery, 175, 283
Slogans, 6–7
Smerconish, Michael, 217
Smith, Will, 26
Snepp, Frank, 87–88, 90, 92
Snowden, Grant, 46
Sorkin, Aaron, 257
Soros, George, 29, 36, 288
Sowell, Thomas, 180, 181
Sparkman, Bill, 66–69
Sparkman, John, 177
Stabenow, Debbie, 83
Stack, Joseph, 218–219
Stalin, Josef, 31, 266–267, 268, 290
Starr, Ken, 28, 39–40, 93, 172, 289
Status anxiety, 249–263
Steele, Michael, 83
Steele, Shelby, 32
Stem cell research, 13, 281–282
Stephanopoulos, George, 19, 42
Stevenson, Adlai, 177
Stewart, Jon, 252–255
Stewart, Marvin, 222

Stone, I. F., 80, 166
Stone, Matt, 251
Streisand, Barbra, 33
Student protests, 157–161, 188, 293, 294
Sullivan, Andrew, 67
Sulzberger, Arthur, Jr., 267
Supreme Court of the United States, 118, 175, 177, 183, 186, 207
Sweetness & Light, 79
Symbionese Liberation Army, 188

**T**

Talk radio, 10, 28, 39, 67, 197, 198
Tate, Sharon, 171
Taylor, Stuart, 71
Tea Party movement, 6, 30, 31, 50, 53, 55–56, 73, 81, 132, 134, 183, 190, 195, 197, 198, 215–217, 221, 278
Thatcher, Margaret, 213, 214, 278
Thirteenth Amendment, 175
Thomas, Clarence, 32, 36, 87, 172, 283
Thomas, Evan, 221
Thomas, Helen, 29, 40
Thomas, Norman, 188
Three Mile Island, 46
Thurman, Uma, 22
Thurmond, Strom, 174, 177, 192
Tiller, George, 202, 206
Time, 17–19, 22, 63, 177, 197
Totalitarian regimes, 265–274, 279
Totenberg, Nina, 30, 33
Tripp, Linda, 172, 289
Truman, Harry, 178, 181, 268
Tucson, Arizona shootings, 36–38, 53, 62, 197–200, 205, 278

**U**

Unger, Craig, 85–86
United Press International, 23, 24

**V**

Valle, Lauren, 53–54, 291–292, 293
Van Zandt, Clint, 67–68
vanden Heuvel, Katrina, 9
Vanity Fair, 29, 33
Vedder, Eddie, 33
Venona Papers, 80, 166
Vietnam War, 17, 152, 164, 206, 269, 270
Village Voice, 87, 90, 92
Vincent, Billie H., 60
Von Brunn, James, 218
Von Hagen, Mark, 266–267

**W**

Waco, Texas, 46, 48, 281
Waldman, Stephen, 131
Walker, Edwin A., 209
Walker, Scott, 9, 70, 212
Walker, Wyatt, 151
Wallace, George, 150, 174, 177, 183, 188, 189
Walters, Barbara, 271
Ward, Jacob J., 221
Warner, Judith, 18
Warren, Elizabeth, 42
Warren, Joseph, 136
Washington, Booker T., 176
Washington, George, 105, 133, 145, 285, 295
Washington Post, 17, 20, 22–26, 29, 30, 32, 37, 181, 200, 217, 221, 250–251, 256, 270
Watergate, 65, 179
Waters, Maxine, 3, 43–45
Waugh, Evelyn, 295
Weathermen, 54, 152, 160–172, 174, 188, 194, 196, 211, 222, 294
Webster, Dan, 203
Weiss, Carl, 210
West, Allen, 278
West, Kanye, 20
Westboro church, 219

Whack, Michael, 21
Wharton, Clifton R., 178
Whiskey Rebellion, 295
White, Betty, 138
White, Harry Dexter, 268
White, Jack, 177
Wicker, Tom, 192, 193
WikiLeaks, 49
Wilkens, J. Ernest, 178
Williams, Armstrong, 32
Williams, Brian, 20
Williams, Damian, 43, 45
Williams, Juan, 221
Williams, Ronald, 243
Wilson, James, 140
Wilson, Joseph, 74–76
Wilson, Owen, 44
Wilson, Representative Joe, 212
Wilson, Woodrow, 175–176, 223
Winter, Thomas, 23

Wisconsin budget crisis, 70, 194
Wise, Kharey, 227–231, 233, 235–237, 239–241, 243
Wofford, Harris, 185
Wolcott, James, 29
Wolffe, Richard, 54, 64
Wolfowitz, Paul, 222
Wright, David, 19
Wright, Jeremiah, 31

**Y**

Young, Andrew, 59

**Z**

Zangara, Giuseppe, 209
Zinn, Howard, 134–135
Zubaydah, Abu, 43–45
Zweig, Stefan, 104